Culture and Social Change

Transforming Society Through the Power of Ideas

A volume in
Advances in Culture Psychology

Series Editor:
Jaan Valsiner, *University Worcester*

Advances in Culture Psychology

Jaan Valsiner, Series Editor

Challenges and Strategies for Studying Human Development in Cultural Contexts (2005)
edited by Cynthia Lightfoot, Maria Lyra, and Jean Valsiner

Becoming Other: From Social Interaction to Self-Reflection (2006)
edited by Alex Gillespie

Transitions: Symbolic Resources in Development (2006)
edited by Tania Zittoun

Trust and Distruct: Sociocultural Perspectives (2007)
edited by Ivana Markova and Alex Gillespie

Semiotic Rotations: Modes of Meanings in Cultural Worlds (2007)
edited by SunHee Kim Gertz, Jaan Valsiner, and Jean-Paul Breaux

Otherness in Question: Development of the Self (2007)
edited by Livia Mathias Simão and Jaan Valsiner

Discovering Cultural Psychology: A Profile and Selected Readings of Ernest E. Boesch (2007)
by Walter J. Lonner and Susanna Hayes

Innovating Genesis: Microgenesis and the Constructive Mind in Action (2008)
edited by Emily Abbey and Rainer Diriwächter

Relating to Environments: A New Look at Umwelt (2009)
edited by Rosemarie Sokol Chang

Rethinking Language, Mind, and World Dialogically (2009)
by Per Linell

Living in Poverty: Developmental Poetics of Cultural Realities (2010)
edited by Ana Cecília S. Bastos and Elaine P. Rabinovich

Methodological Thinking in Psychology: 60 Years Gone Astray? (2010)
edited by Aaro Toomela and Jaan Valsiner

Apprentice in a Changing Trade (2011)
edited by Jean-François Perret, Anne-Nelly Perret-Clermont, Danièle Golay Schilter, Claude Kaiser, and Luc-Olivier Pochon

Constructing Patriotism: Teaching History and Memories in Global Worlds (2012)
by Mario Carretero

Cultural Dynamics of Women's Lives (2012)
edited by Ana Cecília S. Bastos, Kristiina Uriko, and Jaan Valsiner

Cultural Psychology and Psychoanalysis (2012)
edited by Sergio Salvatore and Tania Zittoun

Researcher Race: Social Constructions in the Research Process (2012)
by Lauren Mizock and Debra Harkins

Culture and Social Change: Transforming Society through the Power of Ideas (2012)
edited by Brady Wagoner, Eric Jensen, and Julian A. Oldmeadow

Culture and Social Change

Transforming Society Through the Power of Ideas

edited by

Brady Wagoner
Aalborg University

Eric Jensen
University of Warwick

and

Julian A. Oldmeadow
University of York

IAP

Information Age Publishing, Inc.
Charlotte, North Carolina • www.infoagepub.com

Library of Congress Cataloging-in-Publication Data

Culture and social change : transforming society through the power of ideas / edited by Brady Wagoner, Eric Jensen, and Julian A. Oldmeadow.
p. cm. -- (Advances in culture psychology)
Includes bibliographical references.
ISBN 978-1-61735-757-2 (pbk.) -- ISBN 978-1-61735-758-9 (hc) -- ISBN 978-1-61735-759-6 (ebook) 1. Culture--Psychological aspects. 2. Social change.
I. Wagoner, Brady, 1980- II. Jensen, Eric. III. Oldmeadow, Julian A.
HM621.C8577 2012
303.4--dc23

2011052476

Book cover photo taken by Brady Wagoner in downtown Cairo just off Tahrir Square, shortly after violent clashes between police and protesters.

Printed in the United States of America

CONTENTS

SERIES EDITOR'S PREFACE

Semiotic Freedom For The Social Sciences: Inquiry in a New Key

Jaan Valsiner

Psychology has been in a conceptual limbo over the last century. As an aspiring science it has found its comfort in dependence on social norms that streamline its methodology to resemble that of "the *real* sciences", and on theories that are accepted as finished and immutable conglomerates of thoughts. Thus, much of psychological discourse has been devoted to issues of *following* key thinkers of the past—Jean Piaget, Lev Vygotsky, B. F. Skinner, to mention a few—rather than *transcending* their legacies in new directions. Following in science indicates an inferiority complex. This collective inferiority complex leads to a kind of supremacist self-identity in a discipline that has historically been caught between *Geisteswissenschaften* and *Naturwissenschaften* (Valsiner, 2012)—emulating the latter while being of the former. Such ambivalence has granted the discipline extensive productivity—without intensive breakthroughs in the understanding of the *psyche*.

Cultural psychology—the new perspective that has emerged since the 1990s—promises a correction – as it builds its knowledge in dialogue with sociology, anthropology, language sciences, and history. Yet it is far from clear what forms such correction can take at the intersection of theory and empirical research. To remain viable epistemologically, cultural psychology needs to re-think the basic canons of methodology. The reader of this

Culture and Social Change: Transforming Society Through the Power of Ideas, pp. vii–xiv

book—*Culture and Social Change: Transforming Society Through the Power of Ideas*—can discover a number of leads in the direction of how psychology as science can innovate itself by taking culture—a vague and undefinable notion as it may seem—seriously. The book continues the stream of inquiries into complex cultural issues that operate through the human minds—"otherness" (Simão & Valsiner, 2007), dialogicality (Linell, 2009), focus on ruptures (Zittoun, 2006) or on the subconscious (Salvatore & Zittoun, 2011). Relevant phenomena—women who bear children (Bastos, Uriko, & Valsiner, 2012) people in poverty (Bastos & Rabinovich, 2009), or men under apprenticeship (Perret & Perret-Clermont, 2011) abound in human lives—ready for cultural psychology to study. Human beings create humor (Jensen, 2012b) under adverse societal circumstances. They are able to laugh and make merry while their political freedom is curbed and they are under indefinite surveillance.

All this gives us a picture filled with unity of opposites within the same whole—human ways of living. Yet psychological science—despite all its efforts on "measurement" of almost anything one's mind can invent (Toomela & Valsiner, 2010)—has no adequate understanding of such heterogeneous and complex phenomena. They are simultaneously social and personal, are built on the history of human life courses—and face indeterminate futures. The contributors to *Culture and Social Change* address the complexity of social and personal phenomena with their youthful energy and readiness to search for new ways of doing science—at the intersection of psychology and sociology. Taken together, the contributions to this book constitute a move towards a new form of social psychology that emerges from the classic traditions of Frederic Bartlett, Lev Vygotsky, Serge Moscovici, and Pierre Bourdieu but that cannot be reduced to them. What is new is a social psychology of *processes of construction*—of the culturally organized mind in a constantly changing society.

In the present book the reader can find a number of constructive elaborations of topics that are usually assumed to be taken as givens. Readiness to open "black boxes" in our standard discourses in sociology and psychology leads to possible extensions—which still need to be nurtured.

ELABORATION 1: RESEARCH AS DRAMATIZATION

Social psychology is capable of escaping—from the monastic laboratory rooms into the middle of crowds in public places (Chapter 2, this volume; Drury, Reicher, & Stott, 2012) as well to the enacted prison contexts for the benefit of BBC (Chapter 4, this volume; Haslam & Reicher, 2012). Turning psychology's methods from looking at action outcomes to that of processes—which are necessarily constructive as Frederic

Bartlett understood in the first half of twentieth century (Chapter 9, this volume; Wagoner, 2012)—guarantees that the research act itself is that of a ritual performance unfolding in time. The intricate coordination of group identities of persons-in-roles under conditions of possibility of social change that the ESIM (elaborated social identity model—see Chapter 2, this volume) explicates may be the core for understanding public events that change the world. Tahrir Square—rather than the Hyde Park corner—is a living laboratory that repeatedly tests ESIM in deeply meaningful moments in the lives of a society and of the swarming of people whom we so easily call "the crowd." The unity of desires of large numbers of persons take collective forms that can be understood through the meanings involved in such action. The "crowd" makes collective meanings—it is here where traditional psychology of Le Bon from the nineteen century meets the basic theoretical ideas of twenty-first century cultural psychology.

In the context of any society, an effort to study a psychological or social phenomenon amounts to a *research act* (analogically to *tourist act*—Gillespie, 2006). It is a dramatized social event in amidst any others—ranging from asking college students to put pencil marks onto rating scales in a laboratory, to creation of social contexts of a prison, a zoo, a brothel, a market, or on a couch in the apartment of a gentleman from Vienna. The researcher is a theater director who sets up the stage—yet who appears on that stage, as the acting cast is ambiguous in the social sciences. If it were a theatrical performance in its narrow sense—the "research participants" should be actors who perform for a real or imaginary audience. Yet in the research contexts of the social sciences the focus is on "ordinary persons"—that is, the members of the audience of an actual theatre performance. The research-as-theatre metaphor brings to our focus the issue that the research act is accomplished by way of coercing (on their "free will," of course!) persons ready for improvisation on the theater stage to perform to the audience—that consists of the researcher. The audience turns into actors and the theatre director into the audience—this is a carnevalesque move that indeed may be fit the social realities worldwide, so that non-Westerners can believe in it (Chapter 5, this volume; Moghaddam, Warren, & Vance-Cheng, 2012). The role of the researcher in the dramatized research act can fluctuate—it can move from that of a beggar (when contacting relevant—or randomly sampled—research participants) to that of a dictator (when deciding to eliminate the "outlayers" who mess up a nice Gaussian distribution of the data, in the statistical analysis). In any case, the researcher is not a boring tax collector who just serves the interest of the government!

ELABORATION 2. SCIENTIFIC KNOWLEDGE—SIEVED THROUGH SOCIAL AND POLITICAL ACTIONS

Knowledge is not an entity—but a constantly negotiated understanding of the world that is collectively negotiated and considerate of ideological positions. Eric Jensen (Chapter 10, this volume; Jensen, 2012a) analyzes the social functions of scientific controversies when moved from the seclusion of the discursive arena of the scientists into the public domain. The "dependent independence" of science in relation with society is of course blatantly visible in the public negotiation of what sciences do, and how they are expected to do whatever they do. Sciences' autonomy is always relative to the borders of their social nonautonomy. The borders are attacked—through the organizational role of the media—and defended. Public controversies overturn the existing symbolic order in the sciences—leading to opening of new alleys and closing others. The notion of "scientific consensus" is of value as social capital for public discourses—while the actual processes of science are ambivalent about it (Chapter 11, this volume; Holliman, 2012). Such public reference to "scientific consensus" is a mechanism of social guidance of both science and its applications. It leads to exaggerated myth-making of the power of science—at times encoded even on postage stamps (see Figure 10.1). It can also bring mythologizing of "the other"—the "immoral" or "the unfortunate"—for the purposes of social sciences so that a crucial feature of the interfaces between the person and society may be overlooked (Chapter 3, this volume; Cornish, 2012, for analysis). Dragging scientific controversies into the public domain—or forcing public disputes to be "enriched" by "the contribution" from the (selected) science creates an arena for boundary negotiations of sciences' autonomy. As a consequence, what becomes constructed as "scientific knowledge" in a given discipline is a result of a social filtering process. Psychology's knowledge base provides many examples—the survival of theoretically empty concepts (e.g., "intelligence") that—being "measurable" through "standardized methods"—remain socially engrained in what is presented as science—at least in textbooks.

ELABORATION 3. *TRANSFORMATIONS* OF SOCIAL CAPITAL THROUGH HUMAN MINDS IN ACTIONS

The *habitus* of the social sciences at the turn of the twenty-first century includes the use of the notion of *social capital* in various versions. The focus on that concept can take different forms—such capital can be seen as a solid given (in analogy with a pot filled with gold coins, or in the recently shattered belief in the ever-increasing property value of American homes), or as an ephemeral entity (such as stock values) that can increase or decrease as a result of some social transaction. What needs to be investigated is how the reality of social capital manifests itself in the collective actions of communities. As Mendoza (Chapter 14, this volume; Mendoza, 2012) points out the states of social capital are set by community organization. Using the social history of Bolivia as the empirical model—which is most appropriated given the political push for community participation—we can discover forms of social capital transformation (using the metaphors of *bonding*, *stretching*, *linking*, and *bridging*—see Figure 15.1.). All that can be studied if a collective—be it called *community*—is taken as a unit for sociocultural analysis. That community can develop—gain a voice of its own (Chapter 15, this volume; Sammut, Andreouli, & Sartawi, 2012)—and reposition itself in the wider social field. Of course it is the macroscale sociopolitical factors that canalize the possibilities of such movements within the field. Ryabchuk (Chapter 16, this volume; Ryabchuk, 2012) provides illuminating evidence of various forms of social transformations of the field in the post-Soviet Ukraine.

ELABORATION 4. CULTURAL TRANSMISSION AS CONSTRUCTION OF RELATIVE NOVELTY

The reader will discover the dialogue between *diffusion* of culture and its *construction* in this book. These are not necessarily opposite notions—they are better treated as processes that feed forward into each other. The cultural world is built on the construction of phenomena that are similar to previously encountered ones—but not the same (Sovran, 1992). Yet such similarity has made it possible to gloss over the small innovations constantly being produced by persons in joint action contexts, and treat these as if they are the same. The unidirectional culture transmission—diffusion—model follows the latter. The bidirectional model—emphasizing the joint feed-forward inputs in creating innovations—includes the unidirectional model as its null case. The Bartlettian universe—based on the inquiry into the reconstruction of myth stories at times when all cultural texts were orally transmitted—is that of *diffusion* ***through*** *reconstruction* (see Chapter 9, this volume; Wagoner, 2012a). Such transmission includes triggering counteraction (or resistance—see Chapter 12, this volume; Jensen, 2012b—also "resistance or protest *habitus*"—Chapter 17, this volume; Raudsepp, 2012). Culture becomes reconstructed through such—explicit or implicit—resistances. The Bartlettian reconstructive focus needs to be supplemented with the notion of tension between suggestions and countersuggestions (Wagoner, 2012b).

ELABORATION 5. CATALYTIC—RATHER THAN CAUSAL—NATURE OF SOCIAL CHANGE

Psychology at large has been suffering from the consensual importation of the notion of linearity into its explanatory models. The result has been over half-a-century of "normal science" (Toomela & Valsiner, 2010) that fills the pages of peer-reviewed empirical journals and produces extensive social capital to the authors. Yet the linearity of the human mind is a questionable assumption—from the times of Georg Wilhelm Hegel in the early nineteeth century philosophy to the biochemistry of Hans Krebs in the 1930s-40s. Biological systems are characterized by cyclical—rather than linear—organizational forms. In the case of such forms, the traditional focus of explaining the phenomena through the actions of a sum of causal agents (the analysis of variance model) is axiomatically untenable. The alternative—introduction of the notion of catalysis into the social sciences (Valsiner & Cabell, 2011)—is realistic. In fact, it would have been available for the social sciences ever since late 1830s if the consensus in these fields had considered chemistry—rather than physics—as their potential models from the side of "the sciences." At times a consensus within a discipline about what other discipline to emulate leads to long delays in the move of simple ideas across disciplinary boundaries. In the present book, the catalytic notions of new technologies that make new relations of society and persons possible are entertained—yet not fully spelled out.

Of course all these themes are only beginnings for further search for solutions to unsolved basic problems. The readers are invited to join in—to develop further the embryonic ideas that may indicate the semiotic liberation of psychological research from the confines of heightened normativity of the existing dogmas (see Abbey & Surgan, 2011). The drama of making sense of complex psychological ideas continues—and cultural psychology takes the lead.

Jaan Valsiner, Chapel Hill, NC
July, 2011

REFERENCES

Abbey, E. A., & Surgan, S. (Eds.) (2011). *Emerging methods in psychology*. New Brunswick, NJ: Transaction.

Bastos, A. C., & Rabinovich, E. (Eds.). (2009). *Living in poverty: Developmental poetics of cultural realities*. Charlotte, NC: Information Age.

Bastos, A. C., Uriko, K., & Valsiner, J. (Eds.). (2011). *Cultural Dynamics Of Women's Lives*. Charlotte, NC: Information Age.

Cornish, F. (2012). Collectives may protest, but how do authorities respond? In B. Wagoner, E. Jensen, & J. Oldmeadow (Eds.), *Culture and social change: Transforming society through the power of ideas*. Charlotte, NC: Information Age.

Drury, J., Reicher, S., & Stott, C. (2012). The psychology of collective action: Crowds and change. In B. Wagoner, E. Jensen, & J. Oldmeadow (Eds.), *Culture and social change: Transforming society through the power of ideas*. Charlotte, NC: Information Age.

Gillespie, A. (2006). *Becoming other: From social interaction to self-reflection*. Greenwich, CT: Information Age.

Haslam, A., & Reicher, S. (2012). Change we can believe in: The role of social identity, cognitive alternatives and leadership in group mobilization and transformation. In B. Wagoner, E. Jensen, & J. Oldmeadow (Eds.), *Culture and social change: Transforming society through the power of ideas*. Charlotte, NC: Information Age.

Holliman, R. (2012). The struggle for scientific consensus: Communicating climate science around COP-15. In B. Wagoner, E. Jensen, & J. Oldmeadow (Eds.), *Culture and social change: Transforming society through the power of ideas*. Charlotte, N.C.: Information Age.

Jensen, E. (2012a). Scientific Controversies and the Struggle for Symbolic Power. In B. Wagoner, E. Jensen, & J. Oldmeadow (Eds.), *Culture and social change: Transforming society through the power of ideas*. Charlotte, NC: Information Age.

Jensen, E. (2012b). Mediating social change in authoritarian and democratic states: Irony, hybridity and corporate censorship. In B. Wagoner, E. Jensen, & J. Oldmeadow (Eds.), *Culture and social change: Transforming society through the power of ideas*. Charlotte, NC: Information Age.

Linell, P. (2009). *Rethinking language, mind, and world dialogically*. Charlotte, NC: Information Age.

Mendoza, M. (2012). Assessing social change through social capital: Local leadership and social-political change in Bolivia. In B. Wagoner, E. Jensen, & J. Oldmeadow (Eds.), *Culture and social change: Transforming society through the power of ideas*. Charlotte, NC: Information Age.

Moghaddam, F., Warren, Z., & Vance-Cheng, R. (2012). Change non-westerners can believe in. In B. Wagoner, E. Jensen, & J. Oldmeadow (Eds.), *Culture and social change: Transforming society through the power of ideas*. Charlotte, NC: Information Age.

Perret, J. -F., & Perret-Clermont, A. -N. (2011). *Apprentice in a changing trade*. Charlotte, NC: Information Age.

Raudsepp, M. (2012). Dependent independence: A mechanism for conciliating determinism and freedom. In B. Wagoner, E. Jensen, & J. Oldmeadow (Eds.), *Culture and social change: Transforming society through the power of ideas*. Charlotte, NC: Information Age.

Ryabchuk, A. (2012). Changing fields, changing habitus: The field of public service in post-Soviet Ukraine. In B. Wagoner, E. Jensen, & J. Oldmeadow (Eds.), *Culture and social change: Transforming society through the power of ideas*. Charlotte, NC: Information Age.

Salvatore, S., & Zittoun, T. (Eds.). (2011). *Cultural psychology and psychoanalysis: Pathways to synthesis*. Charlotte, NC: Information Age.

Sammut, G., Andreouli, E., & Sartawi, M. (2012). Social influence and social change: States and strategies of social capital. In B. Wagoner, E. Jensen, & J. Oldmeadow (Eds.), *Culture and social change: Transforming society through the power of ideas*. Charlotte, NC: Information Age.

Simão, L. M., & Valsiner, J. (Eds.). (2007). *Otherness in question*. Charlotte, NC: Information Age.

Sovran, T. (1992). Between similarity and sameness. *Journal of Pragmatics, 18*, 4, 329-344.

Toomela, A., & Valsiner, J. (Eds.). (2010) *Methodological thinking in psychology: 60 years gone astray?* Charlotte, NC: Information Age.

Valsiner, J. (2012). *A guided science: History of psychology in the mirror of its making*. New Brunswick, NJ: Transaction.

Valsiner, J., & Cabell, K. R. (2011). Self-making through synthesis. In H. Hermans & T. Gieser (Eds.), *Handbook of Dialogical Self.* Cambridge, England: Cambridge University Press.

Wagoner, B. (2012a). The meeting of ideas: Diffusion, dialogical interaction and social change. In B. Wagoner, E. Jensen, & J. Oldmeadow (Eds.), *Culture and social change: Transforming society through the power of ideas*. Charlotte, NC: Information Age.

Wagoner, B. (2012b). Culture in constructive remembering. In J. Valsiner (eds.), *The Oxford Handbook of Culture and Psychology*. Oxford, Englamd: Oxford University Press.

Zittoun, T. (2006). *Transitions: Symbolic resources in development*. Greenwich, CT: Information Age.

CHAPTER 1

INTRODUCTION

Changing Times, Changing Science

Brady Wagoner, Eric Jensen, and Julian A. Oldmeadow

Social change can be dangerous, particularly for those who hold positions of power. In 2011 masses rose up throughout the Middle East demanding democratic reforms and the resignation of their ineffectual and self-serving political leaders. Tunisia and Egypt ousted their presidents and began the bumpy road of political transition; rebels in Libya struggled in a bloody civil war for over 6 months before defeating government forces; and protesters in Syria, Yemen, and Bahrain held increasingly tense and fatal demonstrations in their major cities. For many people in all these countries, a historical turning point has been reached: they have been inspired by the idea that change can happen, that a new and better society is possible and worth struggling for. These events have even become a symbol for others around the world that took to the streets in 2011 to demonstrate against their governments' policies (e.g., in Spain, Greece, Chile, Malawi, United States). Such is the power of ideas.

The dramatic events of 2011 in the Middle East and around the world pose a major challenge for the present book. Are the social sciences up to the task of effectively analyzing the complex processes involved in such examples of social change? And even more, can they help to facilitate positive change? Whether the present book is successful in this question we

Culture and Social Change: Transforming Society Through the Power of Ideas, pp. 1–15

will leave to the reader to decide. However, many of the social and cultural processes important to the recent revolutions are addressed in this volume, such as: The social and psychological dynamics of protest; the importance of language and communication in mobilizing people; the significance of mass media in this process; the role of leadership in coordinating social action; and the character of obstacles encountered before and after the occurrence of dramatic social changes.

The aim of this book is to develop an interdisciplinary dialogue on the topic of culture and social change, identifying key cultural processes that propel, slow-down and retract social change. Researchers from social and cultural psychology, sociology, communications, art, anthropology, and political science have contributed their expertise to this end. These different approaches were put into dialogue through commentary chapters to foster a genuine meeting of different theoretical and methodological approaches with the aim of generating new ideas for the study of social change. Before getting into the substance of this book, let us briefly define what we mean by the terms "culture" and "social change" and how we see them as being related, so as to more precisely articulate this book's focus.

SOCIAL CHANGE AS A CULTURAL PROCESS

By "social change" we wish to focus on collective, symbolic, meaningful and substantial processes of change affecting one or more society. Our particular interest is in processes that transform society through new ideas (e.g., Protestantism, women's suffrage, the green movement, nationalisms, gay pride, etc.) and the cultural resources (e.g., technology, symbols, gatherings, and practices) through which those ideas shape and change society. Moreover, we do not consider social change good or bad in itself, nor do we consider change in a certain direction to be inevitable (whether it be towards democracy, socialism, scientific enlightenment, etc.). Instead, we view social change as historically, culturally, and socially contingent. Our task is one of exploring how change comes about as well as some of its after effects. Investigating this process requires attending to BOTH social structure AND agency. As such, this book aims to advance theories and methods that bridge this divide in the study of social change.

The question of agency also bears directly on our understanding of "culture," The word 'culture' is one of the most complicated in the English language. It shares a root with "colony," "cult" and "cultivated," and the meaning of "culture" has ranged from "inhabit, cultivate, protect" to "[to] honour with worship" (Williams, 1983, p. 87). In contemporary public and scientific discourse, culture is often taken to refer to a bounded group of people that somehow "belong together" by sharing a certain language, religion or geographical location (see Valsiner, 2007, p. 25ff). Thus, "Welsh" is a culture because its people share language, music and customs and have lived together on the British Isles over many years. This conceptualization, however, encounters problems when we begin to attend to culture's complex heterogeneity, hierarchical structure, and dynamism. Could one, for example, delineate *the* Indian culture given the 1612 languages spoken there, 675 precolonial small kingdoms and complex mixture of different religions (p. 25ff)? Moreover, given that each Indian appropriates different aspects of culture, some of which come from outside India, where should we locate culture? Does culture belong to the person or is it an objective entity that exists separately from them? Our view is that culture is neither or both.

An alternative way of conceptualizing culture is as a *resource* intentionally used by individuals and groups in relating to the environment in which they live (Valsiner, 2007). This conceptualization of culture is consistent with hermeneutic approaches, such as Weber's view of culture as a device to solve problems of meaning. There are different possibilities for creating a typology of resources. Zittoun (2006) distinguishes four kinds of resources based on their *content*:

1. *Social resources* are a person's social support and interpersonal relationships ("social capital" theories have perhaps done the most to develop this idea—see Mendoza, this volume; and Sammut & Sartawi, this volume).
2. *Material resources* are financial means, material tools, and physical possessions, such as clothing and food. This kind of resource points to the importance of the role played by new technology as well as economic development in social change (see Moghaddam, Warren, & Rhea Vance-Cheng, this volume).
3. A person can mobilize forms of *knowledge and experience as a resource*. The use of social, cognitive and technical knowledge as well as particular skills and strategies are all examples. For instance, young people's skills using online social networking sites (e.g., Facebook) played a key role in the recent Middle Eastern revolutions—it was at this time that the Internet experienced the largest shut down in its history. In Chapter 12, Haslam and Reicher demonstrate how the skill of leadership is used to promote social change in their mock prison experiment.
4. *Cultural resources* are meaning-making devices, such as shared values, beliefs, customs, social representations and cultural practices. In one sense, all resources could be said to be 'cultural'; this type of

resource is focused on ideational content. Still, it is the most general and diverse of the resource types and can be found in all chapters of this volume.

It is also possible to distinguish resources based on their *use* (see Gillespie & Zittoun, 2010). One could, for example, use a resource in a socially novel or conventional way. The metaphor of resource tends to focus us on the creative and free aspects of culture, which are forces for social change; however, the same forces also operate to constrain action at the next moment. We must simultaneously understand how culture both enables *and* constrains action, as both resource and impediment. Thus, change and stability need to be conceptualized together as both tendencies that are always at work in social life. Bauman (2000) aptly describes this paradox:

> "Culture" is as much about inventing as it is about preserving; about discontinuity as much as about continuity; about novelty as much as about tradition; about routine as much as pattern-breaking; about norm-following as much as about the transcendence of norm; about the unique as much as about the regular; about change as much as about monotony of reproduction; about the unexpected as much as about the predictable. (p. xiv)

In Bourdieu's theory of practice, for example, the metaphor of resource plays an important though circumscribed role as a form of *capital* used by social actors competing within a social *field*, which operates as a constraint, but one that simultaneously gives meaning to one's action. His notion of *field* draws on a number of metaphorical sources, including that of a game or battle *field* where social actors compete over different forms of capital. Entering such fields (constraint) entails tacit acceptance of the resources valued within those domains of practice. Arguably, such acceptance helps to make the game of life feel like it is worth playing; otherwise, there would be nothing to strive for in one's professional life. Yet, it is fair play to renegotiate "the rules of the game" (constraints) and thereby affect change in the game itself.

Cultural psychology has also dealt with the duality of culture as both resource and constraint. To do this, a distinction is made between "personal" and "collective" culture (Valsiner, 2000). "Collective culture" describes the external public forms of culture, which constitute a collective, such as rules, symbols, artifacts and other products created by human beings. These forms are "internalized" by individuals, integrating collective culture into themselves, transforming collective culture into personal culture (e.g., one's favorite book or the narrative one tells about their life). In so doing, individuals actively "cultivate" (or "culture") themselves through the publicly available cultural forms. This is a creative and transformative process. Innovations made by the individual can then feed back into culture "out there" becoming possible objects for others to use as resources. Most of the time, the majority resists radical innovations but with persistence, consistency and flexibility individuals can at times get their ideas accepted into the normative framework (Moscovici, 1990; see also Kashima, Bratanova, & Peters, this volume; Wagoner, this volume).

While individual agency is critical, we must not equate collective culture with restraint and construe change as an individual creative process. Change is a *social* process and is very often *enabled* by collective culture. There are many examples, some discussed in the following chapters, where new technologies or scientific discoveries enable cultural development and change. The most successful ideas and technologies are those that not only solve the problem for which they were designed but also fertilize and enable the development of new cultural forms that make use of them, as the Internet and mobile phones have done. Publicly available cultural resources can enable change and renewal. Thus social change is not necessarily born of a conflict between culture and the individual, nor is change necessarily the enemy of culture. On the contrary, culture is renewed in endless change.

CHANGING SOCIAL SCIENCE

The social sciences were born of changes in society beginning in the late eighteenth century. Hobsbawm (1962/2007) has called this period the "Age of Revolution," which encompasses both the spread of industrial capitalism and political revolutions. Both the industrial and political revolutions were forged out of the enlightenment ideas of rationality, freedom and progress. The social sciences both reflected these social changes and emerged as frameworks to understand them. Evolutionary models of society gained wide circulation (Darwin's theory of the evolution of species was simply an instance within this broader *Zeitgeist*). Theorists spun many tales of progress from "tradition" to "enlightenment" (Kant), "primitive" to "advanced" culture (Tylor), "theology" to "positive science" (Comte), and more generally constraint to freedom. In these accounts, culture (understood as tradition) was usually something that needed to be overcome.

Classical sociological theorists, most notably Marx, have been criticized for giving short shrift to the primary role of culture within their models of society, with Marx treating culture as largely epiphenomenal (Thompson, 1990). However, each of the three "fathers" of sociology (i.e., Marx, Weber, and Durkheim) makes a contribution to the study of culture along side their theories of social change. One of Emile Durkheim's most direct engagements with culture is his theory of the societal development from "mechanical" to "organic" solidarity. By this he means that societies held together by shared beliefs and similarities of practices and productive activity (mechanical solidarity) must eventually develop increasingly differentiated roles as they modernize. The cohesion of differentiated societies is based on interdependence between specialized members of society. Max Weber, in his most famous work *The Protestant Ethic and the Spirit of Capitalism*, develops the insight that cultural phenomena such as the Calvinist predestination doctrine (that holds that everyone's fate as "saved" and "damned" is determined by God before birth) can have unexpected and unintended social and economic consequences. Karl Marx identifies the economic and productive systems as the primary engines of societal development, but also acknowledges a role for culture. He views culture as the means by which the economic system of capitalism is maintained as apparently normal, necessary and legitimate, despite endemic exploitation and alienation of workers.

In contrast to sociologists, psychologists have been much more ambivalent about studying culture and change. The "social" branch of psychology in the nineteenth and early twentieth century (e.g., *Völkerpsykologie*) made a study of social changes and the concomitant changes in mentality an important topic for the discipline, which would compliment the investigation of individual psychological processes. However, individualistic approaches to social psychology have dominated since the Second World War (see Farr, 1996; Greenwood, 2004) and as a result the issues of both culture and social change have been sidelined. Since this time differences in social contexts have been seen by most psychologists as incidental to how the mind works, which they believe requires studying the deep central processing level of the mind, rather than the shallow level of culture (Shweder, 1991). As a result, psychologists have generally focused their efforts on explaining negative behaviors (e.g., prejudice, oppression, aggression, rape, etc.) as being somehow a *natural* part of human psychology, rather than asking how social conditions might be changed to foster different behavior. In this way, most contemporary psychology tends to affirm the *status quo* by naturalizing it rather than offering solutions to overcome it (see Haslam & Reicher, this volume).

Furthermore, psychologists in the twentieth century have tended to court the role of servicing large-scale social institutions, such as education and the army, by developing various psychometric tests and other technologies for rationalizing these institutions (Danziger, 1990). Thus, psychologists have generally put themselves in with those who hold positions of power. There are important examples of psychologists who developed approaches that challenged existing power relations. For instance, Kurt Lewin established the *Society for the Psychological Study of Social Issues*

(SPSSI) to direct psychologists' efforts at transforming social conditions. However, more powerful social groups, such as the U.S. government, targeted the group: academics were fired, funding was pulled and the group took on the added meaning of "communist" in the era of McCarthy. The group has since been reformed in the American Psychological Association but its methods and scope are much more constricted than in Lewin's vision.

The present book focuses on some of the *emancipatory* dimensions of social science, which have often been sidelined by positivist approaches. It asks how changing social conditions can lead to new forms of behavior. This is a question that can be seen across social science disciplines, though it is perhaps most thematized in sociology and cultural psychology. The chapters of this book grapple with many specific examples of social change as a cultural process with the help of general theoretical models and new methodological strategies. The book's strategy is to promote innovations in theory and methods through a careful study of particular single cases (Moghaddam, this volume; Wagoner, this volume).

PREVIEW OF THE BOOK

The book is divided into three Parts each focusing on a different aspect of social change. Part I: Collective Action in Context, explores how social groups mobilize themselves to effect change. Here the reader will find discussions about crowds, inter-group dynamics, agency, leadership and drama in social change. Part II: Communicating Change, highlights the role of various communication processes in canalizing social change, such as the use of figurative language in political speeches, the spread of ideas through society and the role of mass media. Part III: Societies in Transition, focuses on cases studies within different societies (i.e., Saudi Arabia, United States, Bolivia, Ukraine, and Estonia) to further develop theoretical and methodological tools to describe and explain large-scale social change. As already stated, all three parts are composed of target chapters with linked commentaries, whose purpose is to expand on ideas found in the target chapter. The commentaries further develop ideas of their target chapters; however, they can also fruitfully be read independently of them.

Part I: Collective Action in Context

Drury, Reicher, and Scott begin Part I by exploring the social and psychological processes involved in crowd action. Their starting point is the observation that crowd events both develop out of culturally and historically given norms and values of crowd participants, and at the same time can be psychologically and socially transformative, that is they can change the very culture from which they took their meaning. The authors review the development of theories of crowd psychology, which have attempted with varying degrees of success to capture these features of determination and transformation. Most of these theories founder on an inadequate conceptualization of self. As such, Drury et al. describe the elaborated social identity model (ESIM) of crowd action developed from social identity theory. The authors suggest that the ESIM has at its core a concept of self adequate to explaining the dynamics of both cultural reproduction and change in crowd events.

Cornish extends Drury et al.'s theoretical framework by arguing that greater research attention needs to be paid to the behavior of the authorities who are the targets of collective protest. Drawing on George Herbert Mead's concept of the social act, she argues that our conceptualization of collective protest needs to (a) attend to the behavior of authorities as much as the behavior of the crowd, (b) analyze the behavior of each party as a response to the behavior of the other, unfolding in time, and (c) interpret the behavior of each party as a self-conscious, strategic response, crafted to achieve desired results. This position is illustrated by drawing on case studies of the efforts of sex workers' organizations to influence the behavior of police and politicians, and studies of successful social movements' strategies for being heard by politicians with the power to effect change. Both cases show grassroots groups strategically and self-consciously positioning themselves to influence the powerful, either by offering them concrete favors, or by defining their cause in such a way as to attract public (and thereby political) support. From this perspective, to fully understand dynamics of protest and social change, we need to expand the social psychological gaze, to the discomfort of the authorities, whose acts play a powerful role in enabling or preventing change.

Following up the discussion of the previous two chapters, Haslam and Reicher set out to explore the genesis of social movements and their strategies to effect social change. They critique most of social psychology for naturalizing the status quo rather than addressing questions of change and asking how social psychology might make social change possible rather than unimaginable. To do this, they develop the notion of "cognitive alternatives," which people use to imagine a different social reality and mobilize individuals to achieve it. "Cognitive alternatives" are generated in the tensions between dominant and subordinate groups as well as leaders and followers (similar to Mead's theory of the social act—see Cornish, 2012). Their theory of cognitive alternatives is illustrated in action through the BBC prison study, where participants are assigned to prisoner and guard roles within a mock prison. Unlike Zimbardo's famous mock prison study, they manipulate key variables in the situation by, for example, closing movement between the groups and introducing personalities with strong leadership skills. Partly as a result of this, their study ends with radical social changes being introduced, which was very different from the outcome of Zimbardo's Stanford Prison study.

In Chapter 5, Moghaddam, Warren, and Vance-Cheng follow up Haslam and Reicher's argument that change is complex and that it remains in many respects an enigma for psychology. They point out that the standard 1-hour psychology laboratory experiment and the traditional causal model are not suitable for studying complex change processes, such as those associated with national development in low-income societies. The argue that a major engine of global change is technology, but that art also plays an important role, in part through influencing identities and identifications. In this vein, they see Reicher and Haslam's (Chapter 4, this volume) BBC Prison Study as a form of experimental theater, which has made a valuable contribution by demonstrating that the dramaturgical approach has great potential for studying and influencing social change.

Part II: Communicating Change

Part II focuses on the processes of communication that stimulate and channel social change. In Chapter 6, Ritchie argues metaphors, stories, and humor are as important as "content" when studying language, and that the perceptual, imaginative, emotional and relational nuances of language use can reveal as much about the role of communication in social change as the propositional aspects. Furthermore, he argues that change at the "micro" level of interpersonal relationships is often as important as change at the "macro" level of national politics. Using examples from actual discourse, including political speeches, a controversy over a comedian's insensitive remark, and an informal conversation among a group of neighbors, he shows how the *non*propositional (emotional and imaginative) basis for dealing with change is constructed, not through arguments, facts, and reasoning but through metaphors, stories and, often, humor. Understanding the discursive processes at each level and their relationship to the problems and opportunities associated with social change requires attention, not merely to the propositional content of language, but also to the imagined or simulated experience of perceptions and emotions associated with the metaphors, stories, word-play and teasing.

Cornejo broadens Ritchie's thesis by providing a philosophical framework to better understand the primacy of propositional language in modern psychology. He argues that the distinction between literal and figurative language relies on an outdated epistemology in which words hold meanings rather than being catalysts that stimulate subjective acts of understanding. Instead of treating words as if they carried some transcendental meaning, social scientists should study them in their concrete use in communicative action. From the perspective of situated language use, metaphor becomes a dynamic means of seeing the world in new ways, and as such it provides a fertile mechanism for promoting social change.

Kashima, Bratanova, and Peters also address communication as a socially situated act in Chapter 8. They outline a theory of cultural dynamics based on what they call "neodiffusionism," a metatheory of culture in which culture is construed as a collection of nongenetically transmitted information that is shared within a population across generations. According to their model, situated activities shared with others are central to the process of cultural transmission among individuals. Depending on the nature of joint activities that people engage in, they transmit culturally conservative information (e.g., information consistent with culturally shared stereotypes) or innovative information (e.g., information inconsistent with culturally shared stereotypes), which constitutes enabling conditions for cultural maintenance and change, respectively. They outline two general clusters of joint activities in contemporary society: the microprivate sphere involving close and significant others connected by strong ties, and the macropublic sphere involving acquaintances or other members of a broader community connected by weak ties (while also suggesting an intermediate cluster of work-activities). In the macropublic sphere, culturally conservative information is more likely to be transmitted; in the microprivate sphere, both culturally conservative and innovative information has a chance of transmission. This distribution of joint activities in a society is itself a sociocultural system, which makes it possible to balance the dual needs for stability and change of culture.

In his commentary, Wagoner (Chapter 10, this volume) extends Kashima et al.'s (this volume) ideas to develop a more constructive, social and dialogical theory of communication and social change. He begins by reexamining early diffusionist theories, especially those put forward by Frederic Bartlett, extracting three key methodological principles: (1) the conceptualization of stability and change as dialectically interdependent concepts, (2) the recognition that cultural transmission also involves creative transformation of the transmitted idea, and (3) the need to study social groups in their complex particularity and generality. Moscovici's study of how the idea of psychoanalysis entered the French public sphere in the 1950s is then used as a case study to illustrate and advance diffusionist ideas in the context of cultural transmission in contemporary society. In Moscovici's framework "diffusion" is only one of three "communication genres" used to transmit new ideas. The others— "propagation' and 'propaganda"—set up "semantic barriers" to the free discussion of new ideas and thus limit their group's social creativity. The chapter concludes by situating ideas within a dialogical interaction, whereby they are intersubjective perspectives on the world that position us vis-à-vis others. Wagoner argues that it is only when the above factors are taken into account that we can fully understand the multitude of ways an idea can be held, shared and acted upon for the purposes of social change.

The struggle over the communication of controversial ideas is further theorized in Chapter 10. Jensen begins with the premise that new scientific ideas routinely take on symbolic and even metaphorical meanings, especially when they are communicated to publics outside of a specialist scientific subfield. Scientific institutions and individual scientists routinely intervene in the process of connecting particular symbols or metaphors to their more technical referents within scientific practice. In scientific controversies, there is a struggle over the symbolic representation of new scientific developments, which can determine public attitudes on topics such as nuclear power, human cloning and genetically modified crops (Jensen & Wagoner, 2009). Jensen argues that scientific controversies can undermine the normal social order favoring experts, institutions, and corporate interests in communication about scientific issues in the public sphere. Contrary to the negative view of such controversies as irrational and destabilizing, Jensen contends that they promote the development of democratic social change precisely because they occasion disorderly displays of disagreement about underlying cultural values.

Holliman (Chapter 10, this volume) elaborates Jensen's account in his commentary chapter by bringing to light the implications of the mirror image of scientific controversy, namely scientific consensus. He reviews the social aspects of the struggles for scientific consensus and how it can be communicated and debated in the digital age. Specifically, he explores the role of professional and social media in representing anthropogenic climate change around the United Nations Copenhagen Summit (also known as COP-15). Two examples are analyzed in detail: the publication of e-mails from the Climatic Research Unit at the University of East Anglia (also known as "climategate"); and the rate of decline of the Himalayan glaciers from the fourth assessment report (AR4) of the Intergovernmental Panel on Climate Change (IPCC). He argues that attempts to promote, maintain, destabilize, and repair the scientific consensus of anthropogenic climate change may have profound implications for science communication. Digital media have extended the ways that scientific information can be circulated and discussed in the public sphere, making it easier for actors to challenge a scientific consensus. Communication around COP-15 may indirectly influence the ways that scientific knowledge is produced, verified, and archived, and what information and data are required to be circulated in the public sphere when a peer reviewed paper is published. Within this wider context calls for social change in how we respond to a changing climate may be more effectively sought via the rhetoric of precaution.

Part III: Societies in Transition

Part III of the book addresses the ways in which ideas with the potential to promote large-scale transitions in society are forestalled or enabled. In Chapter 12, Jensen considers the largely conservative role of mass media in the reproduction of the existing social order in cultures around world. In Western democratic societies, a pluralistic public sphere, and a critical press are viewed as vital institutions for the maintenance of free speech and debate. However, there are always institutional and systemic forces that resist the transformative potential of free speech behind the scenes by curtailing the scope of mass media discourse. Authoritarian regimes supplement their control over mass media with overt repression and censorship of potentially subversive political speech. Yet, Jensen argues that presumed differences between democratic and authoritarian systems when it comes to quashing dissident political speech are greatly exaggerated. In the interests of maintaining the ideological and material status quo, attempts to transform society through the power of new or challenging ideas are routinely subjected to harsh reprisals under both systems of government. In Western democracies, reprisals target dissidents' economic, symbolic or political standing, and media corporations are a primary if unofficial instrument of censorship and social control. In authoritarian societies such as China or Saudi Arabia, government bureaucrats screen mass media and web-based content, with the threat of coercion looming over media producers and Internet users alike. Jensen draws upon two case studies to argue that under both authoritarian and democratic regimes humor is an effective means of introducing ideas that challenge the existing social order. At the same time, stepping outside the cloak of humor escalates the risk of reprisals under both systems.

The role of humor and irony in efforts to circumvent censorship and promote progressive societal transitions is further explicated in Sayles' commentary (Chapter 13, this volume). Sayles highlights the role of humor in artists' attempts to foster social change, while acknowledging that in the broader society humor is often employed to maintain existing modes of thought through ridicule of new or unorthodox ideas. To investigate the subversive potential of humorous art, Sayles considers several cases of contemporary artists' work designed to undermine, for example, conservative gender norms and heteronormativity. Sayles concludes that humor has the potential to circumvent social systems of control, thereby allowing artists and other change agents to challenge existing modes of thought and introduce radical new visions of social reality.

An enduring theoretical challenge for social scientists has been the identification of the key factors behind large and complex processes of social change. In Chapter 14, Mendoza focuses on a particular factor, leadership, which he conceptualizes as a process of "stretching social capital"—in other words, how leaders "stretch" their communities' norms and values towards the achievement of social and/or political goals. In order to illustrate these theoretical propositions, Mendoza uses empirical evidence from an emblematic process of institutional reform in the developing world: *Popular Participation* in Bolivia. He argues that the decentralization reforms adopted in this country for over 15 years were more than just administrative readjustments; instead the new institutional design fostered a larger process of social change. This change, however, would not have been possible without the commitment of a myriad of local leaders—representing all sorts of formal and informal institutions—that managed to harmonize local social and political demands with the larger national reformist agenda of the Bolivian state. Moreover, this grassroots leadership, such as that of indigenous groups and women organizations, has penetrated enclaves of political power that were restricted to them in the past, demonstrating the strength of social change observable in this Andean nation.

In their commentary Chapter 15, Sammut and Sartawi explore the different conceptualizations of social capital in recent years and analytically distinguish between *states* and *strategies* of social capital. They argue that "bonding" and "bridging" social capital are states of social groups that reflect their states of internal cohesion and external ties, respectively. On the other hand, "linking" and "stretching" social capital are strategies that social groups employ to further their levels of social capital, through political affiliation in the former and representation in the latter. The authors argue that Mendoza's (Chapter 14) notion of "stretching social capital" is a form of minority influence that enables a community to sit at the negotiation table with dominant groups and to seek to further the aims of the minority group. While negotiation can succeed or fail, they argue that representation in itself yields dividends in social capital through instituting a subordinate community's project.

Ryabchuk continues the discussion of group strategies for negotiating social change in Chapter 16. She uses the Pierre Bourdieu's theoretical framework to investigate how public sector works in Ukraine adapt within their increasingly privatized professional field. Her respondents manifested a "positional suffering": on the one hand they defined themselves through a "heroic image" of servicing the public good and criticized the 'new middle class' as just caring about money. On the other hand, they expressed superiority vis-à-vis the working class and justified taking extra money for public services. Thus, they draw on both the old soviet and new neoliberal discourses to negotiate their position in the changing professional field of public sector working. Ryabchuk suggests that the *habitus* (i.e., dispositions) of public sector workers has only partially adapted itself to the transformed structural conditions of postcommunist Ukraine.

In Chapter 17, Raudsepp expands on Ryachuk's approach and develops an integrative framework for discussing previous chapters. She discusses Bourdieu's theory, social representations theory and semiotic cultural psychology vis-à-vis one another. With the help of the last in the list, she advances the concept of "semiotic freedom," whereby social agents can distance themselves from the here-and-now and develop new directions to action. In combining the three theories, she points to new ways of looking at the interaction between objective and subjective aspects of social change. Two empirical illustrations from Estonia are given for understanding the experience of social change in post-Soviet societies: First, she looks at autobiographies and interviews with people who have lived through various political regimes and transitional periods. Second, she explores the structural suffering of Russians living in Estonia.

CONCLUSION

The concluding chapter of the book aims to bring the preceding discussions together within a general model of social change. This integrative and multidisciplinary theoretical model defines social change as a continuous, long-term, contingent and culturally bound process. Four "aspects" or "processes" of social change are identified and described, which encompass the diverse cases examined in this volume. First, *communication processes* are implicated when social actors and institutions engage in a struggle over ideas and normative conclusions. Through these communication processes, new ascendant ideas are articulated and related norms are identified. The ascendance (or not) of such ideas is shaped by many factors explored in this volume such as access to mass media. Second, *implementation processes* appear at the interface between ascendant ideas and routine social and professional practices. The process of embedding a new norm in people's daily practices can be fraught with resistance and renegotiation. Third, *public engagement processes* govern the translation of now amended social and professional practices into public-facing behaviors, which must contend with the preexisting ideas, norms and economic interests of affected publics and stakeholders. Fourth, deliberative processes gather up and articulate flaws and inconsistencies in the new norm or idea that has by this point been implemented. These inconsistencies and flaws detected along the pathway to public-facing delivery then underpin a return to communication processes to work out new ascendant ideas that can accommodate the experiences from implementation and public engagement processes.

REFERENCES

Bauman, Z. (2000). *Culture as Praxis*. London: SAGE.

Cornish, F. (2012). Collectives may protest, but how do authorities respond? In B. Wagoner, E. Jensen and J. Oldmeadow (Eds.), *Culture and social change: Transforming society through the power of ideas*. Charlotte, NC: Information Age.

Danziger, K. (1990). *Constructing the subject: Historical origins of psychological research*. Cambridge, England: Cambridge University Press.

Farr, R. (1996). *The roots of modern social psychology*. Oxford, England: Blackwell.

Gillespie, A., & Zittoun, T. (2010). Using resources: Conceptualising the mediation and reflective use of tools and signs. *Culture & Psychology, 16*, 37-62.

Greenwood, J. (2004). *Disappearance of the social in American social psychology*. Cambridge, England: Cambridge University Press.

Hobsbawm, E. (2007). *The Age of Revolution: 1789-1848*. London: Abacus. (Original work published 1962)

Jensen, E., & Wagoner, B. (2009). A cyclical model of social change. *Culture & Psychology, 15*(2), 217-228.

Moscovici, S. (1990). Towards a theory of conversion behavior. *Advances in experimental social psychology, 13*, 209-239.

Sammut, G., Andreouli, E., & Sartawi, M. (2012). Social Influence and Social Change: States and Strategies of Social Capital. In B. Wagoner, E. Jensen, & J. Oldmeadow (Eds.), *Culture and social change: Transforming society through the power of ideas*. Charlotte, NC: Information Age.

Shweder, R. (1992). *Thinking through culture: Expeditions in cultural psychology*. Chicago, IL: Chicago University Press.

Thompson, J. B. (1990). *Ideology and modern culture: critical social theory in the era of mass communication*. Palo Alto, CA: Stanford University Press.

Valsiner, J. (2007). *Culture in minds and societies*. New Delhi, India: SAGE.

Williams, R. (1983). *Keywords*. New York, NY: Oxford University Press.

Zittoun, T. (2006a). *Transitions: Symbolic resources in development*. Greenwich, CT: Information Age.

Zittoun, T. (2006b). Dynamics of interiority: ruptures and transitions in the self development. In L. Simao & J. Valsiner (Eds.), *Otherness in question: development of the self* (pp. 187-214). Charlotte, NC: Information Age.

PART I

COLLECTIVE ACTION IN CONTEXT

CHAPTER 2

THE PSYCHOLOGY OF COLLECTIVE ACTION

Crowds and Change

John Drury, Stephen D. Reicher, and Clifford Stott

Crowd events are sites of both social determination and social-psychological change. On the one hand, the form of crowd behavior is a function of the culturally and historically given norms and values of crowd participants. On the other hand, crowd events can be psychologically and socially transformative: they can change the very culture from which they took their meaning. In this chapter we argue that most models of crowd behavior deny and hence are incapable of explaining either social determination or change. We describe the elaborated social identity model (ESIM) of crowd action, which we suggest has at its core a concept of self or identity adequate to explaining the dynamics of cultural reproduction and change in crowd events.

THE OBJECT OF INVESTIGATION

For some of the most useful accounts of crowd events, and to get a sense of what sort of features an adequate theory of crowd behavior needs to

Culture and Social Change: Transforming Society Through the Power of Ideas, pp. 19–38

explain, there are few better sources than the work of historians such as E. P. Thompson, Eric Hobsbawm, and George Rudé. They argued for a "cultural" and "bottom-up" approach to historiography, which meant the study of the everyday lives of "ordinary" people. Interestingly, "ordinary" people were often found to be involved in acts of collective refusal and resistance. A close examination of the nature of these collective events points to the need for a certain kind of psychological theory.

For example, the food riots that Thompson (1971) studied might be thought of simply as "instinctual" explosions, expressing a basic need. They would therefore be uncontrolled, visceral; surely people just get hungry and desperate, and seize what grain or bread that they can from the stores?

Thompson (1971) analyzed around 700 food riots that occurred in England between 1750 and 1820. He shows, first, that they did not happen at times of greatest dearth but characteristically when grain supplies were increasing. Indeed, he suggests that the meaning and social context of the events seemed to be more important in explaining what people did than do references to absolute poverty or "basic needs." Thus the food riots were generally initiated by specific events, notably the transport of grain out of the locality, reflecting the development of market principles in the wider economy.

Second, the "riots" were far from primitive: grain was seized, sold at a popular price, the money and often the grain sacks were handed back to the merchants. The acts of the crowd were restrained, selective, disciplined and patterned rather than being out of control.

Third, then, Thompson (1971) shows that this pattern of behavior was based on the clash between a "moral economy"—a traditional view of rights and obligations based on the locality where there was a requirement to meet local needs when resources were available—and an emerging free market system where goods are taken to wherever they can command the best price. These two conceptions of legitimacy came into conflict at the point where grain was transported. With the notion of the moral economy—a system of culturally shared social beliefs about proper practice—Thompson suggests an answer to the question of how is it that, in riots and other such "novel" crowd events, hundreds if not thousands of people are able to act as one.

Thus historians like Thompson (1971) suggest how crowd events are socially determined. Behavior is a cultural product. But part of the interest in the events he describes lies in their association with change. The foot rioters, Luddites, swing rioters, and others became radicalized—adopted direct action—in their attempts to hold on to the old way of life in the face of the development of capitalism. Similarly, the French revolutionary crowds studied by Rudé (1981) were those who brought about the end of the old order.

There is a general point here, which is that while by no means all crowds are forces for social change, social change commonly seems to involve crowd events (Ackerman & Kruegler, 1994). In particular, because combination (whether in organized form, as in trades unions, or in more ad hoc form, as in street protests) gives power to those who are otherwise powerless, the kind of change that entails a challenge to the status quo involves popular collective action. This is why, not only is the tradition of cultural history, exemplified by the work of Thompson (1971), replete with examples of crowd action, but any attempt at a "people's history" inevitably takes the form of a history of collective action. "People" enter history in the form of a mass, acting on the world, often in opposition to the forces of established power (see, e.g., Zinn, 1996). Further, not only change to institutions but certain changes *within* institutions can often be traced back to collective action. Now, Black studies, feminist studies, Marxism, and environmental studies are established academic disciplines—but this only came about after Black, feminist, socialist, and environmentalist struggles on the streets and on the campuses in the 1960s and '70s. As Eyerman and Jamison (1991) put it, collective action can have effects on (what counts as) knowledge.

More than this, however, there is a link between crowd events that impinge upon the social world and *psychological* change. We have already mentioned the radicalization described by Thompson (1971). But scattered across the literatures of various disciplines are accounts that illustrate very vividly how participation in crowds and other forms of collective action can engender experiences of psychological change, both for the individual participant and for the collective as a whole (e.g., Britt & Heise, 2000; Kelly, 1993; McAdam, 1989):

> Hand in hand, for nine miles we formed a living chain to lock in the horrors or war.... How strong I felt when I joined my voice to the waves of voices shouting Freedom.... Confidence and strength were growing. While the police stood in groups waiting for orders, women all around me were laughing! ... Women were feeding each other, hugging each other, crying in each other's arms, strengthening each other with word and with song. (Greenham Common anti-nuclear camp participant, 1980s, as cited in Harford & Hopkins, 1984, pp. 92-93)

> When I look at myself now, I just can't believe I'm the same person. I've grown so big with the knowledge I've got from it. I've never been so motivated to get on with things before. Now there's nothing I can't do, I don't think. Absolutely nothing! (1984-85 miners' strike participant, as cited in Salt & Layzell, 1985, p. 9)

These then are some of the features of crowd behavior[1] as a phenomenon against which we can measure psychological theories of the crowd. In particular: does the theory explain social and cultural determination—the socially-shaped features of common behavior in a novel event, and the links between the behaviors and their social and historical context? And can the theory say anything about the relationship between collective action and social and psychological transformation? As we shall see, for most of the history of crowd psychology, theory has not been adequate to these tasks.

FROM "CROWD SCIENCE" TO CIVIL RIGHTS

The crowd first became an object of scientific investigation at the end of the nineteenth century. It was particularly in France, where the bourgeois revolution was most bloody and where its working class supporters threatened to extend it to the abolition of class society itself, where crowd science first emerged in a systematic form (Barrows, 1981; Nye, 1975; Reicher & Potter, 1985; Stott & Drury, in press).

The first debates, however, were legalistic. A debate around criminal responsibility arose from the problem of whether the behavior exhibited by people in crowds was due to the qualities of the individuals involved or was instead explicable in terms of something about the crowd itself, which made otherwise law-abiding individuals act in uncharacteristic ways. A number of theorists suggested that there was something new and terrible about collectivity, which explained the striking discontinuity between individual and crowd behavior. However, only one of these theorists is well-remembered today: Gustave Le Bon.

Le Bon's (1895/1968) answer to these questions was in terms of "transformation":

> by the mere fact that he forms part of an organized crowd, a man descends several rungs in the ladder of civilization. Isolated, he may be a cultivated individual; in a crowd, he is a barbarian—that is, a creature acting by instinct. He possesses the spontaneity, the violence, the ferocity, and also the enthusiasm and heroism of primitive beings, whom he further tends to resemble by the facility with which he allows himself to be impressed by words and images … and to commit acts contrary to his most obvious interests and his best-known habits. An individual in a crowd is a grain of sand amid other grains of sand, which the wind stirs up at will. (pp. 32-33)

"Submerged" in the crowd, the individual personality disappears, to be replaced by the "racial unconscious." Ideas and sentiments spread easily through the 'suggestible' crowd in a process of 'contagion'. This, Le Bon

(1895/1968) argued, explained why people behave so uncharacteristically in crowds. Yet, because such a transformation was meaningless—a reversion to a set of "racial" instincts—then it left no trace. Just as the crowd had no ideas of its own, only had power for destruction and could not itself transform culture or society in a positive way,[2] so the individual gained no insights and was not permanently transformed by his "unconscious" experience in the crowd.

By the 1920s, the argument of Le Bon (1895/1968) that crowd psychology was qualitatively distinct from individual psychology came under sustained attack. The developing behaviorist *Zeitgeist* involved scepticism towards such nebulous entities as Le Bon's "mental unity." Instead, the "crowd" was understood as a nominal fiction and its behavior explicable simply in terms of that of the individuals making up that crowd. Allport (1924) was the champion of this individualist, and supposedly more scientific, approach to the crowd. Unlike Le Bon, he drew upon laboratory experimental evidence. He shared with Le Bon the assumption that what needed to be explained was the irrational, mindless violence that inevitably seemed to accompany collectivity. Where he differed was in explaining this mass irrationality simply in terms of the stimulation or "social facilitation" in the crowd causing the individual's underlying biological reflexes to overcome learned, civilized responses. For Allport, then, the difference between individual and group was quantitative rather than qualitative.

Allport's (1924) is sometimes described as a "convergence" model (e.g., Turner & Killian, 1972). Convergence means the coming together of people of similar psychological constitution. Some convergence theories stress that the types of people who get together to take part in riots are those who are most socially marginalized and least socialized (see Fogelson, 1971; and McPhail, 1971, for useful critiques). Like Allport, these "riff raff" theories explain crowd events through reference to the given preexisting attributes of *individuals*—their (similar) education or attitudes, for example. What people do in a crowd, according to all these accounts, is merely to express or act out preexisting characteristics. This adds to Le Bon an attempt at an explanation for why people come together in the first place: it is due to the coincidence of preexisting interests or natures. But this kind of assumption loses perhaps the only valuable aspect of his account: the recognition (albeit in distorted form) of psychological transformation in crowd events. These are theories of psychological accentuation, where "change" in the crowd is a matter of degree, not of quality.

The concept of "de-individuation" (Diener, 1980; Prentice-Dunn & Rogers, 1989) was an attempt to render key features of Le Bon's account into a modern, scientific form, and has become one of the most widely cited effects of group membership. Shorn of references to the "racial unconscious" or "law of mental unity," Le Bon's account of submergence (loss of self) leading to antinormative and disinhibited behavior was studied in the form of laboratory analogues of crowds, which attempted to determine the effects of key variables—such as anonymity, group presence and decreased self-awareness. The most well-known research examples in this tradition appeared to show that, when made anonymous (and supposedly "de-individuated") people were more likely to exhibit antinormative behavior (e.g., administer electric shocks) than otherwise (Zimbardo, 1970).

While the methodology was that of modern social psychology, the conceptual framework of the various versions of de-individuation theory takes us no further forward than that provided by Le Bon (see Postmes & Spears, 1992; and Reicher, Spears, & Postmes, 1995). In fact, de-individuation is a step backwards from the Gestalt-influenced, interactionist models, which developed at the same time and which suggested that the presence of a group leads to more not less conformity to group norms (Asch, 1952).

To understand the limitations common to Le Bon, Allport and de-individuation theory, we need to briefly revisit what we know about crowd events.

In the first place, it is clear that their default assumption of crowd violence or "antinormative" behavior is simply wrong. Most crowds are not violent.

Second, even when crowd behavior is violent, it displays a clear ideological pattern distinct to each crowd and event. The targets of the food rioters were different to those of the *sans culottes*, which in turn were different to those of the Gordon rioters, and so on. The "irrationalist" tradition offers explanations for the spontaneous collectivity in crowds—the fact of hundreds of people acting as one without plan, conspiracy or formal direction. But concepts such as "contagion" and "social facilitation" say nothing about the cultural *content* and hence *limits* of that collectively shared behavior.

Third, this neglect of specific cultural content and limits is achieved by abstracting instances of crowd behavior from their historical and social context. Instead of understanding the ("violent") crowd behaviors observed (typically through partial, secondary sources) as part of an ongoing relationship with another, more powerful group (such as the police or army) they reify such behaviors into a universal feature of "the crowd."

In short, then, because these theories separate the crowd from its social context they cannot explain the social determination of crowd behavior. And because they see crowd behavior as meaningless, they cannot provide an account of social-psychological transformation in crowd events either—beyond suggesting that such "transformations" are themselves meaningless and hence short-lived.

Psychology's interest in crowd behavior has waxed and waned in line with the extent to which crowd events are prominent and defined as a "social problem." Hence academic interest in the crowd was renewed in the 1960s when collective action again seemed to pose a threat to the existing order—in the form of the civil rights movement, anti-Vietnam protests, and, in particular, the U.S. urban riots. The early theorists of the crowd were essentially on the outside looking in at alien behavior. But the theorists of the 1960s were often involved in some of the events themselves—such as the Vietnam protests on college campuses. At the very least, they were interested in participants' own accounts and reasons, and not just their behaviors. They suggested that what happened in crowd events, even the most violent ones, might be explicable in terms of the same concepts that explained other areas of social life.

One of the first attempts to suggest a continuity between everyday social behavior and crowd events was Turner and Killian's (1972) emergent norm theory (ENT). Turner and Killian looked to the small group tradition in social psychology, as represented in the work of Sherif (1936/1965), which pointed to the way norms developed through interaction amongst people. Based on these ideas, they suggested that crowd behavior should be understood as rule-governed rather than "instinctual" and atavistic.

A different reaction against the irrationalist account of Le Bon was the argument that collective behavior was in fact highly rational. Thus the *game-theory* approaches of Berk (1974) and Brown (1965), which were based on economic models of decision making, explained the behavior of a looting rioter, for example, in terms of a calculus of gains versus losses. This approach, like Allport's (1924), could be classified as *individualist*, because its focus is on within-individual processes rather than groups and collective processes. The "social" aspects of Berk's (1974) fine-grained analysis of a student protest event, for example, are all borrowed from ENT.

The emphasis in ENT on *norms* serves to stress the socially determined nature of crowd behavior. For the first time, then, here was an explanation for the limits of crowd behavior—norms defining what was (in)appropriate—*and* an implication that crowd events were transformative in a meaningful way. ENT suggested that in novel situations, such as riots or disasters, people look for the appropriate way to behave. Through a gradual process of communication ("keynoting" by influential individuals, rumor as sense-making, and "milling"), the new norm emerges.

Empirically, the reliance on the ideas of Sherif (1936/1965), according to which face-to-face interaction was necessary for a shared product, presented a potential problem, however. It suggested that norms take time to develop (from a period of supposed "normlessness"), when in fact studies of riots show that people can switch from one shared behavior to another in rapid succession, and without necessarily having to debate the issue (Reicher, 1984b).

Thus while these later models take us beyond the limits of irrationalist theories of crowd behavior, there is further yet to go. In particular, we suggest that the key concepts of "rationality" and "norms" are more fully explicated if subsumed under that of social identity. That is, a social identity determines what counts as "rational" and "normative"; and transformation in social identity means transformation of "rationalities" and "norms." These arguments are developed in turn in the next sections.

THE SOCIAL IDENTITY MODEL OF THE LIMITS OF CROWD BEHAVIOR

The social identity model of crowd behavior (SIM; Reicher, 1982, 1984b, 1987) developed out of the wider social identity approach (Tajfel & Turner, 1979). The social identity approach had already been applied to, and provided a nonreductionist, nonpathologizing account of a range of collective phenomena, including different forms of intergroup conflict. Through its development into self-categorization theory (Turner, Hogg, Oakes, Reicher, & Wetherell, 1987), the social identity approach provided a set of principles to explain how it was that people could see themselves and act as a group in the first place—including in situations where the 'group' was dispersed across time and space. Reicher's SIM was an application of these principles to the specificities of crowd behavior.

The best empirical illustration of the SIM is perhaps Reicher's (1984b, 1987) study of the St. Pauls riot. While the proximal cause of the riot was a police raid on a community café, the distal relationship of ongoing antagonism from the police to St. Pauls, a predominantly Black district of Bristol, was also key to the understanding of what took place. Reicher's interview and archive study showed that the identity of "members of the St Pauls community" was defined in terms of locality, "freedom" and the antagonistic relationship with police. These features made sense of the distinctive pattern of the riot, which was one of the first of a wave of urban riots affecting U.K. cities in the 1980s.

First, then, the limits to the crowd's behavior were clearly in line with the definition of the identity: the targets of attack were the police and certain kinds of property. Banks, the benefits (social security) office, the rent office, and the post office were singled out at agents of the community's continued powerlessness, whereas local shops and homes were actively protected from rogue elements. Second, there were clear limits to who got involved; only those who shared the identity were influenced by other crowd participants. Relatedly, the most influential people were those who were seen to best embody the crowd identity—in this context, older Rastafarians. Finally, there were geographical limits on the rioting, which remained within the St. Pauls district.

Reicher's SIM suggests that commonality in crowd behavior, rather than being due to contagion or social facilitation, is due to participants sharing a common social identity. This common identity specifies what counts as normative conduct. However, crowd events such as riots are novel situations where it is not always clear what is normative. In such cases, the SIM suggests that participants look to prototypical in-group members to define appropriate behaviors. Unlike the "classic" crowd theories, which tended to presume that collectivity was associated with uncontrolled violence (due to a regression to instinctive drives or a pre-existing "racial unconscious"), the SIM explicitly acknowledges variety by suggesting that different identities have different norms, logics or "rationalities"—some peaceful, some conflictual—and that, even where crowds are conflictual, the targets will be only those specified by the particular social identity of the crowd.

The St. Pauls study, along with Reicher's (1984a, 1987) experimental research on anonymity in groups, was a powerful riposte to the "irrationalist" tradition, from Le Bon to de-individuation. But the study and the SIM itself left a number of unanswered questions and hence possible explanatory problems. The emphasis on social identity as the determinant of collective behavior potentially led to a rather unidimensional reading of the nature of crowd conflict: conflict was "read off" from the St. Pauls social identity, as if the participants were already "violent"; this left unexplained how such conflict first emerged and escalated over time during the riot. Without further specification, the model risked being read, like Allport's (1924) account, as seeing conflict as a product of fixed and pregiven identities that were simply acted out. How could transformation in the crowd be grasped—yet without falling back into something like the LeBonian account in which the peaceful, rational individual is "transformed" by the (malign) influence of the crowd?

The analysis of the St. Pauls riot was like a snap-shot, examining the nature of the crowd targets, without examining in detail how conflict actually developed over time out of relations with the police, and without including the perspective of the police as a possible contribution to the events. Subsequent studies of crowd events by Reicher and colleagues therefore began to address these absences.

THE ELABORATED SOCIAL IDENTITY MODEL OF CROWD DYNAMICS

Interview, archive, and observational studies by Reicher and Stott identified a common pattern across a variety of crowd events, including a student protest (Reicher, 1996b), the 1990 London "poll tax riot" (Stott & Reicher, 1998a), and cases of football crowd "disorder" (Stott & Reicher, 1998b). At the beginning of the events, the crowd was relatively heterogenous. The majority defined themselves as "moderates" and as different from a minority who were intent on conflict. However crowd members were perceived as a homogenous threat by the authorities (notably the police) and treated as such—that is denied the ability to express themselves in the way they saw as legitimate. This then led to a radicalization, or change in identity, among moderate crowd members who then joined with the minority of "radicals" in challenging the police.

Since this escalation of conflict involved a change of social relations between crowd and authorities and a change of identity among crowd members, it raised a broader question about psychological and social change: how is it that people who enter a crowd event with one sense of identity emerge from it with a different identity? The SIM was elaborated in order to address this issue. Just as the SIM had offered a psychology adequate to E. P. Thompson's (1971) argument that crowd participants are cultural (rather than simply biological) beings, so the elaborated social identity model (ESIM) offers a psychology of how cultural understandings change and develop through crowd action.

The ESIM can be broken down into three parts: (a) an account of the dynamics that produce new identities; (b) a reformulation of the key concepts necessary to grasp identity change; and (c) a specification of the types of psychological change that can occur in and through crowd participation. We describe each of these in turn.

First then, the *dynamics* are the processes whereby police perceptions of the homogeneity of the crowd, and police practices which impose a *common fate* on all crowd members, result in a self-fulfilling prophecy. There are two conditions necessary for this to occur (see Drury & Reicher, 2009): (1) *an asymmetry of categorical representations* between crowd participants and an out-group such as the police; and (2) an *asymmetry of power*, such that the (police) out-group is initially able to impose its definition of legitimate practice on the in-group of crowd participants.

For example, during the poll tax riot, while crowd members understood their own behavior in sitting down in the road as "legal and legitimate traditional protest," police defined it as a "threat to public order"; where police understood their own action as a defensive response to a situation of growing threat from the crowd, the crowd understood the police action as unprovoked and "heavy handed." Moreover, these police perceptions mattered, for the police had the means—the technology, organization and strength in numbers—to act upon them: through forming cordons, coordinating baton charges and otherwise determining the physical movement and experience of the crowd.

In such a situation, the crowd as a whole will unite around a sense of opposition to the police and the authorities they are seen to be protecting. In other words, the initially heterogeneous crowd becomes more homogenous. Moreover, to the extent that police action is seen as not only indiscriminate but also illegitimate (e.g., "heavy-handed" and denying the right to protest), there will be behavioral changes—most notably, a willingness to enter into conflict with the police. In addition, the emergence of an inclusive self-categorization (as "oppositional") within the crowd leads to feelings of consensus and hence to expectations of mutual support; this in turn empowers crowd members to express their opposition and to take on the police. By the same token, oppositional elements are now influential within the crowd when before they were seen as deviant.

These then are the processes of change. But in examining these processes, we are obliged to reconsider two of our key *concepts*. Thus, ESIM involves a reconceptualization of both "context" and "social identity" and, crucially, of the relationship between them. Theorists in the social identity tradition have tended to treat context as a given and hence as an objective determinant of social identity (Reicher, 1996a). However if context is prior and separate to identity in this way, it is hard to see how identity can change through action in context. For ESIM, then, the two are interdependent moments in a single historical process. That is, "social identity" is conceptualized as the way in which people understand how they are positioned relative to others, along with the forms of action which flow from that position. "Context" is conceptualized as those social practices that enable or constrain these actions. The key point is that, in crowds, the understandings of one group inform the actions that constrain the other. That is, identity in effect constitutes context and vice versa.

This argument is again illustrated in our studies of the 1990 London poll tax riot (Stott & Drury, 1999, 2000; Stott & Reicher, 1998a). Here, the context for protesters was the actions of the police—who formed cordons, initiated baton charges and so on. But such actions were at the same time the expression of the police's understanding of their relationship to the protesters—as a threatening, dangerous, hostile crowd.

In summary, if social identity is a representation of one's position in a set of categorical social relations, along with the possible and proper actions that flow from that position, then identities change through crowd action if and when acting in terms of a given understanding of one's social position/social relations leads to one being placed in a different social position/social relations. This dislocation can occur because of the interactive nature of crowd events, and the fact that the action of one party may be interpreted by the other party in ways that are at odds with their own intentions—thus leading to unintended consequences and unanticipated social relations.

Third and finally, then, the ESIM suggests that different *types* of identity change in collective action can flow from this process of repositioning: change in the *content* of identity ("who I am"), in the social *boundaries* of the self (who is now "one of us," and who is now therefore excluded from the in-group), in what becomes possible (i.e., one's sense of *power* in relation to otherwise powerful others), and in what is *legitimate* (both in terms of what kinds of actions are now normative and what is defined as the aim of those actions). These types of change are interlinked and in many cases mutually implicative. They can be illustrated through our longitudinal study of an antiroads protest (Drury & Reicher, 2000, 2005; Drury, Reicher, & Stott, 2003).

The study was an ethnographic investigation of the nature of and change in identities among protesters in the campaign against the building of the M11 Link Road in London, 1993-4. The M11 link road was planned as a 3.5-mile-long stretch of dual carriageway through the London districts of Wanstead, Leytonstone, and Leyton. It was a flagship for the government's national road-building programme of the time.

At first, those who opposed the construction when it began in Wanstead in September 1993 were mainly "activists" who had come from outside the area. They tried to climb on diggers and into trees. They were confronted by security guards who attempted to remove them. Occasionally, the police were involved and campaigners were arrested for minor public order offences. A turning point came in early November. The contractors moved onto Wanstead's George Green and cordoned off a section, including a symbolically important chestnut tree, with eight feet high fencing. A few days later, a crowd overwhelmed the police and security guards. In a spirit of collective celebration, they broke down all the fence panels one by one, with police and security looking on helplessly. A number of them climbed into the tree and occupied the land. However, on December 7 the police and bailiffs returned in large numbers. Despite the presence of some 200 protestors, the police evicted people from the land and the tree in a conflictual day-long operation. The contractors then resumed work on the George Green site. All through the following year, direct actions were mounted against the construction of the road. The contractors, security guards and police confronted them until protestors had been evicted from every tree and every house on the route of the proposed road.

Many of the most striking changes in participants' self-conceptions were centred around the early events—the taking and loss of the Green, which involved unexpected conflict with the police for those inexperienced in protests.

First, then, there was change in the *content* of the social identity—the definition of who "we" are. This was particularly evident at the protest to prevent the tree and the Green from being evicted. While many protesters entered the event considering themselves liberal *individuals*, they were treated collectively as an illegitimate *group*. The police, based on both past experience of the protest, and general conceptions of how crowds behave and should be treated, acted on *all* protesters—both direct activists and those locals who saw themselves as liberal individuals—as one. Moreover this indiscriminate action was experienced by protesters as illegitimate—or, in their words, "heavy-handed," violent, and brutal. A number of anecdotes were mobilized about incidents which served as emblems of the actions of the behavior of the police as a category: an elderly man who had his glasses broken, a women dragged through broken glass.

The context within which many people had come to the event had clearly changed—but inadvertently, through the protesters' own actions. By banding together (for "peaceful, legitimate protest") they were seen as a threat to "public order" by the police, who acted upon this perception. In this changed context, where the behavior of the police was the backdrop to their own self-understanding, the identities of many of the participants also changed. Being treated as oppositional, they then came to see themselves as oppositional; for, far from facilitating their "democratic rights" the police were perceived as obstructing them. Thus many participants were radicalized, politicized. The only people who were not so radicalized were those who already had a critical view of the police and were not surprised by their actions (Drury & Reicher, 2000).[3]

The change in identity definition for many protesters at the eviction of the tree had profound consequences for who they counted as "one of us." In the first place, any division between the "radical" direct activists and the "respectable" locals dissolved. All were now the same group—both in the eyes of outsiders and in their own eyes. In the second place, this widening of identity boundaries extended in both space and time as protesters drew parallels with other groups and struggles. Thus, as protestors radicalized and came to see themselves as "oppositional," so they also saw themselves as one with other oppositional groups world-wide (such as the Nigerian Ogoni tribe then protesting against the Shell oil company) and even those who had fought against "injustice" in the past (such as the British miners during the strike of 1984-5). The "locals," the direct activists and these other groups in other times and places were, in effect, through their identical relations with the police and the state, essentially the "same" people. Third, however, the radicalization of the self meant a distancing from those other local people who rejected themselves from the direct action (Drury et al., 2003). Instead of "one of us," those passive locals who shunned the campaign became "other," or, in the words of one local-turned-activist, "like zombies."

This extension of the group boundaries meant in turn a sense of *empowerment*. While the immediate experience of the loss of the tree and the Green was one of grief and defeat, in the longer term there was a greater sense of connectedness with the nationwide antiroads movement, the world-wide environmental movement, and all the forces fighting injustice across history. The inclusive (indiscriminate) action of the police, which was seen as "political" and hence illegitimate was at the core of the process whereby this change came about. If everyone was a (potential) target, everyone had a common enemy; they were "all in it together" and hence many more people could be called upon for support for action against the illegitimate other. Put differently, as protestors saw themselves as being part of a wider, more homogenous and hence stronger movement, so they had greater expectations that others would be able and willing to support them in in-group-normative activities. This in turn was experienced as encouraging, positive, and even joyful (Drury et al., 2003; Drury & Reicher, 2005). This shift in the nature of targets and aims then takes us to the fourth type of change.

Finally, then, the change in-group relations—in identities and in the perception of the "other"—changed not only what protestors felt able to do but also what they felt was *proper* to do. Once they came to see themselves as operating in a world where the authorities repress rather than enable protest, challenging the authorities and the ways in which they were seen to destroy the environment for profit became an end in itself. Protesters moved from saving particular pieces of land to exposing the illegitimacy of the Department for Transport. Thus, following the eviction of the tree, participants no longer expected to be able to save land from the developers, but defended it in a public show of defiance to expose the lengths to which the authorities would go to impose an unpopular policy. To this extent they succeeded—a mass occupation of a block of houses in the route of the road met with over 400 riot police and bailiffs, and dramatic images of roof-top struggles with pacifist protesters were spread all over the national newspapers the next day. In short then, change encompassed the legitimate *aims and purposes* of being part of the protest.

As indicated in the first part of this chapter, psychological change in and through crowd events is important socially as well as subjectively. If experiences in collective action can feed into what people do in the future, including participation in further collective action and at a higher level of abstraction (e.g., the "right to protest" in general rather than protest over a "single issue"), then this can on occasions lead to change at a societal level.[4]

The poll tax riot was a crucial historical moment in what became an historic U-turn for the then Conservative government who, in the face of such unforeseen and generalized public opposition, was forced to abandon their plans for the tax and put something less controversial (the "council tax") in its place. Those empowered by the riot and by similar "disorderly" antipoll tax protests across the country felt empowered not to pay the tax—they now felt they had popular support for such refusal. With the campaign of mass non-payment on top of the threat of "public disorder" the tax became unworkable and any semblance of legitimacy it ever had disappeared.

The No M11 protesters did not stop the M11 link road from being built, but they did inspire the escalation of a nationwide militant anti-roads movement. Two years later, the government slashed spending on the ambitious national roads program, in effect conceding defeat in the face of "public opinion." What had happened in effect was that the protesters had, through their public profile, transformed the issue of road-building from what had previously been seen as no more than a "technical" issue, and one in which argument ended with the public enquiry, into a *'political'* one, in which controversy and conflict could involve the wider public rather than just a few experts. The social and political landscape of road-building in the U.K. had been transformed.

Here then, we see that social identity can be the hinge between psychological and the social level narratives of change (see Ritchie, this volume, for a discussion of narratives of change). To the extent that more people are psychologically transformed so that they feel more able to act over more or broader issues, then we begin to see particular crowd events as part of social movements, which change societal ideas and institutions, and hence deeper social change itself becomes a possibility.

CONCLUSION

Our argument for the relation between crowds and change can be summarized as follows: people's sense of their social position (social identity) changes to the extent that, in acting on their identity (participating in a crowd event), they are repositioned as a consequence of the understandings and reactions of an out-group (treated as oppositional by the police); this repositioning leads both to a new sense of identity and new forms of action (oppositional conflict).

It should be clear that this is not a claim that all crowds involve psychological change—just as we would not claim that all crowds are involved in social change; some represent forces of reaction and social stability (Drury, 2002). However, what we are arguing is that any psychological theory of the crowd needs to be able to be adequate to the evidence—however rare—of the transformative potential of crowd events.

Conceptually, at the heart of the discussion over whether (and how) crowd events are sites of both social determination and transformation are arguments about the nature of the self or identity. For Le Bon (1895/1968) and de-individuation, the self is just the personal self, and is either present (for the lone individual) or, in the crowd, entirely absent (hence the absence of self-control). For Allport (1924), the basic features of the personal self are merely accentuated in the crowd. By contrast, the social identity approach understands the self as variable, multiple, active and collective (as well as personal), reflecting our variable, multiple, active and collective (as well as personal) relations with others. Our everyday sense of stability and continuity reflects not only our ongoing memory of ourselves but also stabilities in our everyday social environment. Social instability or change, on the other hand, is associated with crowd events and collective action. Our experiences in crowds that "turn the world upside down," whether they do so intentionally or otherwise, can serve to transform our sense of self fundamentally.

We have argued elsewhere that the crowd is a privileged arena to study some of the core ideas in social psychology, including social identity, group norms, social influence, stereotypes, and so on (Drury & Reicher, 2000; Reicher, 1996a, 1996b). In everyday life, understandings are routinized and consensual between groups, making it easy to see them as properties of the groups themselves—as "*things*"—rather than as contingent, interactive relationships. However, in crowd events, when understandings and power are asymmetrical,

> all fixed, fast-frozen relations, with their train of ancient and venerable prejudices and opinions, are swept away, all new ones become antiquated before they can ossify. All that is solid melts into air, all that is holy is profaned, and man is at last compelled to face with sober senses, his real conditions of life, and his relations with his kind. (Marx & Engels, 1848/1976, p. 487)

This contingency and lack of fixedness makes crowd events ideal for studying social identity as a dynamic *process*, changing over time in relation to context and in turn changing that context. In short, it means that the crowd is an ideal location to study the relation between psychological and social change.

NOTES

1. "Crowd behavior" or "collective action?" In the past, psychologists referred to crowd events—along with panics, audience behavior, crazes, mass hysteria and social movements—as ""collective behavior." By contrast, the term *collective action* is used in contemporary social psychology to refer to a vari-

ety of organized or structured phenomena—including membership of trade unions, participation in women's support networks, and even petitioning and voting behavior (e.g., Louis, 2009). The term *collective action* is being used in this chapter to refer specifically to *crowd events*—that is, relatively "unorganized" face-to-face encounters of large numbers of people. The decision to use the terms *crowd behavior* and *collective action* interchangeably, and the rejection of the term *collective behavior*, reflects a particular theoretical perspective within which the notion of the collective as less rational than the individual is rejected in favour of one which finds meaning and purpose in crowd events (see Reicher, 1987).

2. While the default behaviors of the crowd reflected the primitive impulses of the "racial unconscious" and hence were "conservative," Le Bon also argued that the malleability of the crowd meant that its energy could be harnessed to various political projects by a skilled demagogue. Both Hitler and Mussolini are said to have drawn upon Le Bon's recommendations on the rhetorical skills required in the direction of crowds to particular political ends—though in practice the specific cultural contents and referents of their speeches were at least as important as such devices as the recommended 'repetition' and 'simplicity' in delivery (Reicher, 1996c).
3. The study of protest crowds is replete with examples of radicalization, as we indicated at the beginning of the chapter. However, the logic of the ESIM and the social identity approach in general also shows how there can be self-transformation in the other direction, away from opposition. Thus in their study of Euro2004 football crowd (non)-violence, Stott, Adang, Livingstone, and Schreiber (2007) showed that where power is exercized with legitimacy, a crowd can develop more positive views of the police and unite around a norm of suppressing the "hooligan" minority.
4. And clearly, the dynamics involved are broader than violent conflict (the M11 protesters saw themselves as engaged in "nonviolent direct action").

REFERENCES

Ackerman, P., & Kruegler, C. (1994). *Strategic nonviolent conflict: The dynamics of people power in the twentieth century.* Westport, CT: Praeger.

Allport, F. H. (1924). *Social psychology.* Boston, MA: Houghton-Mifflin.

Asch, S. E. (1952). *Social psychology.* Princeton, NJ: Prentice-Hall.

Barrows, S. (1981). *Distorting mirrors: Visions of the crowd in late nineteenth-century France.* New Haven, CT: Yale University Press.

Berk, R. (1974). A gaming approach to crowd behaviour. *American Sociological Review, 39*, 355-373.

Britt, L., & Heise, D. (2000). From shame to pride in identity politics. In S. Stryker, T. J. Owens, & R. W. White (Eds.), *Self, identity and social movements* (pp. 252-268). Minneapolis, MN: University of Minnesota Press.

Brown, R. (1965). *Social psychology.* New York, NY: The Free Press.

Diener, E. (1980). Deindividuation: The absence of self-awareness and self-regulation in group members. In P. B. Paulus (Ed.), *Psychology of group influence* (pp. 209-242). Hillsdale, NJ: Lawrence Erlbaum.

Drury, J. (2002). "When the mobs are looking for witches to burn, nobody's safe": Talking about the reactionary crowd. *Discourse & Society, 13*, 41-73.

Drury J., & Reicher S. (2000) Collective action and psychological change: The emergence of new social identities. *British Journal of Social Psychology, 39*, 579-604.

Drury, J., & Reicher, S. (2005). Explaining enduring empowerment: A comparative study of collective action and psychological outcomes. *European Journal of Social Psychology, 35*, 35-48.

Drury, J., & Reicher, S. (2009). Collective psychological empowerment as a model of social change: Researching crowds and power. *Journal of Social Issues, 65*, 707-725.

Drury, J., Reicher, S., & Stott, C. (2003). Transforming the boundaries of collective identity: From the "local" anti-road campaign to "global" resistance? *Social Movement Studies, 2*, 191-212.

Eyerman, R., & Jamison, A. (1991). *Social movements: A cognitive approach.* Cambridge, MA: Polity.

Fogelson, R. M. (1971). *Violence as protest: A study of riots and ghettos.* New York, NY: Anchor.

Harford, B., & Hopkins, S. (Eds.). (1984). *Greenham Common: Women at the wire.* London: The Women's Press.

Kelly, C. (1993). Group identification, intergroup perceptions and collective action. In W. Stroebe & M. Hewstone (Eds.), *European Review of Social Psychology, 4*, 59-83.

Le Bon, G. (1968). *The crowd: A study of the popular mind* (Original work published 1895). Dunwoody, GA: Norman S. Berg.

Louis, W. (2009). Collective action and then what? *Journal of Social Issues*, 65, 727-748.

Marx, K., & Engels, F. (1976). Manifesto of the Communist Party. In *Collected Works. Volume 6.* London: Lawrence & Wishart. (Original work published 1848.)

McAdam, D. (1989). The biographical consequences of activism. *American Sociological Review, 54*, 744-760.

McPhail, C. (1971). Civil disorder participation. *American Sociological Review, 38*, 1058-1073.

Nye, R. A. (1975). *The origin of crowd psychology: Gustave Le Bon and the crisis of mass democracy in the third republic.* London: SAGE.

Postmes, T., & Spears, R. (1998). De-individuation and anti-normative behaviour: A meta-analysis. *Psychological Bulletin, 123*, 238-259.

Prentice-Dunn, S., & Rogers, R. W. (1989). Deindividuation and the self-regulation of behavior. In P. B. Paulus (Ed.), *Psychology of group influence* (2nd ed., pp.87-109). Hillsdale, NJ: Erlbaum.

Reicher, S. D. (1982). The determination of collective behaviour. In H. Tajfel (Ed.), *Social identity and intergroup relations* (pp. 41-83). Cambridge, England: Cambridge University Press.

Reicher, S. D. (1984a). Social influence in the crowd: Attitudinal and behavioural effects of de-individuation in conditions of high and low group salience. *British Journal of Social Psychology, 23*, 341-350.

Reicher, S. D. (1984b). The St Pauls "riot": An explanation of the limits of crowd action in terms of a social identity model. *European Journal of Social Psychology, 14,* 1-21.

Reicher, S. D. (1987). Crowd behaviour as social action. In J. C. Turner, M. A. Hogg, P. J. Oakes, S. D. Reicher & M. S. Wetherell (Ed.), *Rediscovering the social group: A self-categorization theory* (pp. 171-202). Oxford, England: Blackwell.

Reicher, S. (1996a). Social identity and social change: Rethinking the context of social psychology. In W. P. Robinson (Ed.), *Social groups and identities: Developing the legacy of Henri Tajfel* (pp. 317-336). London: Butterworth.

Reicher, S. (1996b). "The Battle of Westminster": Developing the social identity model of crowd behaviour in order to explain the initiation and development of collective conflict. *European Journal of Social Psychology, 26,* 115-34.

Reicher, S. (1996c). *The Crowd* century: Reconciling practical success with theoretical failure. *British Journal of Social Psychology, 35,* 535-553.

Reicher, S., & Potter, J. (1985). Psychological theory as intergroup perspective: A comparative analysis of "scientific" and "lay" accounts of crowd events. *Human Relations, 38,* 167-189.

Reicher, S., Spears, R., & Postmes, T. (1995). A social identity model of deindividuation phenomena. In W. Stroebe & M. Hewstone (Eds.), *European Review of Social Psychology, 6,* 161-198.

Rudé, G. (1981). *The crowd in history: A study of popular disturbances in France and England, 1730-1848.* London: Lawrence & Wishart.

Salt, C., & Layzell, J. (1985). *Here we go! Women's memories of the 1984/85 miners' strike.* London: Co-operative Retail Services.

Sherif, M. (1936/1965). *The psychology of social norms.* New York, NY: Octagon Books. (Original work published 1936)

Stott, C., Adang, O., Livingstone, A., & Schreiber, M. (2007). Variability in the collective behaviour of England fans at Euro2004: "Hooliganism," public order policing and social change. *European Journal of Social Psychology, 37,* 75-100.

Stott, C., & Drury, J. (1999). The intergroup dynamics of empowerment: A social identity model. In P. Bagguley & J. Hearn (Eds.), *Transforming politics: Power and resistance* (pp. 32-45). London: Macmillan.

Stott, C., & Drury, J. (2000). Crowds, context and identity: Dynamic categorization processes in the "poll tax riot." *Human Relations, 53,* 247-273.

Stott, C., & Drury, J. (in press). A picture of the pathology of the mass: Exploring the politics and ideology of "classic" crowd psychology. In A. A. Romero (Ed.), *Archaeology for the masses: Theoretical and methodological approaches to a neglected identity category.*

Stott, C., & Reicher, S. (1998a). Crowd action as inter-group process: Introducing the police perspective. *European Journal of Social Psychology, 28,* 509-529.

Stott, C., & Reicher, S. (1998b). How conflict escalates: The inter-group dynamics of collective football crowd "violence." *Sociology, 32,* 353-77.

Tajfel, H., & Turner, J.C. (1979). An integrative theory of intergroup conflict. In W. G. Austin & S. Worchel (Eds.), *The social psychology of intergroup relations* (pp. 33-47). Monterey, CA: Brooks/Cole.

Thompson, E. P. (1971). The moral economy of the English crowd in the eighteenth century. *Past & Present, 50*, 76-136.

Turner, J. C., Hogg, M. A., Oakes, P. J., Reicher, S. D., & Wetherell, M. S., (1987). *Rediscovering the social group: A self-categorization theory.* Oxford, England: Blackwell.

Turner, R. H., & Killian, L. M. (1972). *Collective behaviour* (2nd ed.). Englewood Cliffs, NJ: Prentice-Hall.

Zimbardo, P. G. (1970). The human choice: Individuation, reason and order versus de-individuation, impulse and chaos. In W. J. Arnold & D. Levine (Eds.), *Nebraska symposium on motivation 1969* (pp. 237-307). Lincoln, NE: University of Nebraska.

Zinn, H. (1996). *A people's history of the United States: 1492 to present.* London: Longman.

CHAPTER 3

COLLECTIVES MAY PROTEST, BUT HOW DO AUTHORITIES RESPOND?

Flora Cornish

By what means does collective action lead to social change? How does a group of people become a sufficiently powerful force to persuade those in authority to make changes to laws, policies or regulations? The social identity tradition (as elaborated in the chapter by Drury, Reicher, and Stott, this volume) has offered rich and nuanced understandings of the constitution and transformation of crowd behavior and the psychology of crowd members. This commentary seeks to further explore the issues of psychological and social change raised by Drury and colleagues, through the lens of George Herbert Mead's (1925) concept of 'the social act'. Considering protest as a social act, I hope to show, expands the purview of social psychological theorizing about the crowd, to include not only a focus on crowd members, but also on the authorities who are the targets of the crowd's protest, and consequently, on the eventual result of the protest—that is, whether the crowd successfully brings about a social change or not.

Culture and Social Change: Transforming Society Through the Power of Ideas, pp. 39–51

THE SOCIAL ACT OF PROTEST: THE CROWD, AUTHORITIES, AND A CONTENTIOUS ISSUE

A social act is an action that cannot be completed by a single person in isolation, but requires contributions from two (or more) actors in order to be completed (Gillespie, 2005; Mead, 1925). The social act of purchasing, for instance depends upon both a buyer and a seller. One cannot buy without somebody selling, and one cannot sell without somebody buying. The buyer and seller interact in relation to an object, which is the item to be bought/sold. Each has a different perspective and motive regarding that object, but both have a shared interest in the transaction going ahead smoothly. Similarly, a collective protest makes little sense if we consider only the protestors. Protests always target somebody or a group of people. The behavior of those who are targeted by collective action is just as important as the behavior of the protestors. In addition, protests always have an object: they are protests about something.

The social act is a core concept for social psychology, because it gives expression to that elusive *social*—something that cannot be reduced to individuals, or indeed to homogenous groups (Farr, 1996). To understand buyers, we need to understand sellers. To understand protestors, we need to understand authorities. Further, Mead (1925) argued that the social act was the minimum unit of analysis needed to understand consciousness, communication, meaning and social order (Grossen, 2010; Marková, 1987a). From a Meadian perspective, each of these social psychological phenomena depends upon the interactions between self, other, and the shared object of their attention.

The social act is often represented as a triangle linking together self, other and object (Zittoun, Gillespie, Cornish, & Psaltis, 2007). In relation to the phenomenon of collective action, we may represent the social act of protest as a triad of crowd, authorities, and the contentious issue about which they disagree (Figure 3.1). For instance, in the case of the U.K. student demonstrations against increases to university tuition fees, held in late 2010,[1] the social act of protest would comprise the students forming the crowd, the politicians who the students seek to influence, and the contentious issue of tuition fees.

Three theoretical points regarding the social act will prove important to the understanding of the role of crowds in bringing about social change. The first is the importance of considering all three elements of the self-other-object triad, rather than focusing on a single part in isolation, which I have already explained above.

The second point concerns the interdependent and interactive nature of the elements of the social act, which is not well expressed by the snapshot provided by the image of the triangle. We are interested, in this

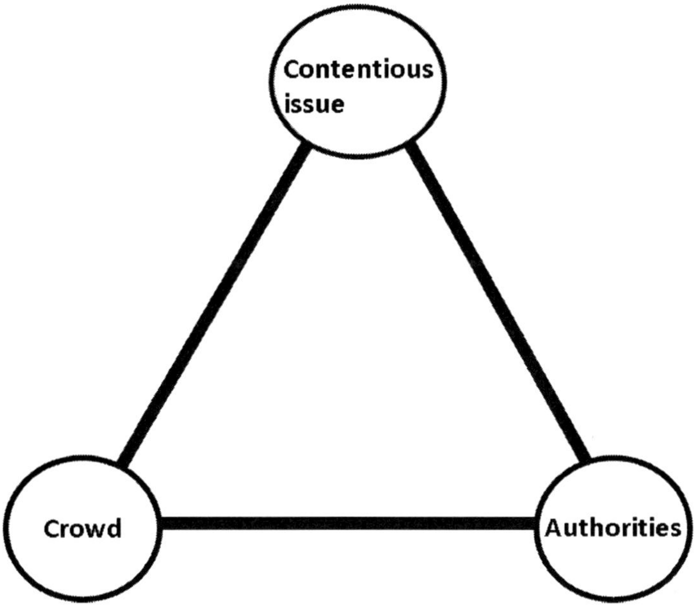

Figure 3.1. The social act of protest.

chapter, in understanding social change. What is the source of change? Why do crowds, authorities, and social issues undergo change? According to a Meadian theorization, the source of change is the interdependence (rather than independence) of each element of the social act. So crowds initiate a protest, not simply because of their own internal dynamics, such as de-individuation, but when the behavior of authorities appears to warrant action. The protest, in turn, changes the authorities, who must respond, perhaps repressing the crowd, or perhaps assenting to a change in laws or other practices. The actions of both crowds and authorities have thereby changed, as has the understanding of the contentious object of the protest. This means that, to understand the process of social change, we need to consider the unfolding of the interaction between crowd and authorities in time. One party acts, this action evokes a new response from the other party, whose response, in turn, calls for a new response from the first actor (Gillespie & Cornish, in press; Marková, 1987b).

Third, the interaction between self and other (or crowd and authorities), in the Meadian conception, is that particularly human form of interaction, complicated by the self-awareness and other-awareness that constitute the reflexivity characteristic of humans. So the responses of crowd and authorities are not simply predictable responses to an objective environment, but responses to the crowd's and the authorities' understandings of themselves and each other. Each is equipped with rich representations of the other party and anticipations of their future actions. In Meadian terms, each *orients* to the other, trying to act in such a way as to elicit a desired response from the other (Gillespie & Cornish, 2010).

To understand the mechanism of social change, then, from this point of view, it is necessary to consider changes to all three elements of the act: changes to the crowd, to the authorities who are the targets of the crowd's action, and to the state of the contentious object of attention. The source of these changes is in the interaction between the two sets of actors and their object, and so attention to their interrelation is important to understand the source of change. That interaction is a conscious, often strategic, mutual orientation between two parties seeking to position themselves, position the other, influence action, preempt a response, persuade, control, and so on.

This position leads to a range of questions that one might ask about the social act of protest, in pursuit of understanding about the means of social change. Focusing on the changes to the two sets of actors in the social act, one can ask: (1) How do crowd members change as a result of the interaction with their opponents and their object? And, (2) How do the targets of a protest change (their attitudes, their behavior) as a result of their being brought into the social act of protest? Focusing on the social change that might result from protest, one might ask: (3) How does a material change to a contentious issue (e.g., a change to a law or a social norm) come about as a result of the attention of crowds and authorities in the course of a protest?

THE ELABORATED SOCIAL IDENTITY MODEL'S CONTRIBUTION TO UNDERSTANDING THE SOCIAL ACT OF PROTEST

The social identity tradition, particularly as represented here in the elaborated social identity model (ESIM), has advanced our understanding of crowd action by making sense of collective action rather than dismissing it as pathological, elucidating the rationality of crowds when considered in their social and political context, and demonstrating the culturally-shaped moral limits to crowd action. Consonant with the theoretical approach of the social act, the ESIM crucially takes a processual approach, looking at how the crowd's and authorities' action *develop over time, through their interaction*. The particular novelty of this model comes from it identifying the sources of the crowd's action, not simply within the psychology of the crowd, but in how the crowd members are constituted by the actions of police or other authorities. Thus, as Drury, Reicher, and Stott show convincingly, the "radicalization" of a crowd can be constituted by police action, which *treats* the crowd as homogenous, or as violent. Police violence or arrests, which appear unjust to crowd members, may themselves constitute the situation as an intergroup, "us versus them" situation, with all the conflictual processes that such situations entail. For instance, the use of masks at protests, hiding protestors' identity, might at first glance suggest de-individuation or even preplanned criminal action for which the protestors seek to avoid being held accountable. However, it is possible to see such mask-wearing as a response to the advent of a policing practice of forthright filming of protestors, irrespective of peaceful, violent, criminal or innocent behavior—making the mask-wearing more comprehensible. Drury and colleagues' theorization makes crowd action understandable, by extending the time horizon under consideration, to look at the sequence of interaction of the two parties, and by considering the action of each party as a response to the other.

Further, the ESIM does not construe the crowd's or authority's actions as a simple expression of some uncontrolled inner instinct, temperament, or attitude—but as a motivated and meaningful communicative action. Protesters may choose to wear masks to preempt what they see as illegitimate and dangerous police surveillance. Police may choose to keep a low profile and portray themselves as enabling legitimate crowd action rather than criminalizing it, again preempting the escalation of conflict and intergroup social dynamics (Stott, Adang, Livingstone, & Schreiber, 2008). And crowd leaders, far from being simple products of existing crowd sentiment, may actively construct a situation as an intergroup one which necessitates violent collective action, or indeed may work hard to construct their protest as a peaceful, legitimate protest, seeking to prevent any opportunity for negative media interpretations or police action arising (Reicher & Hopkins, 2003; Reicher, Haslam, & Hopkins, 2005).

As Drury, Reicher, and Stott state explicitly, however, this theoretical tradition has been brought to bear primarily to understand the psychology and action of *crowd members*, rather than the action of the *authorities* who are the targets of their action, or the overall *social outcome*, in terms of the crowd's success or failure in bringing about the changes that its members seek. In their chapter, Drury and colleagues do make a claim about a social outcome, namely that protests over road-building changed the nature of the debate in the United Kingdom, so that road-building became a contentious, politicized issue, rather than being seen simply as a technical issue. But this social outcome is not the main object of their attention, or the issue to be explained. Returning to the triadic social act suggests that to understand the whole social system of protest and its transformations, we need to understand not only the constitution of crowd action, but also the constitution of the authorities who are the targets of the crowd's action, and changes to the nature of the object about which they disagree (i.e., the resulting social change).

TOWARDS A SOCIAL PSYCHOLOGY OF THE TARGETS OF COLLECTIVE ACTION

In recent work, we have sought to study the "psychology of collective action," in terms of the question of how the audience of collection action is persuaded to change (Campbell, Cornish, Gibbs, & Scott, 2010; Cornish, Shukla & Banerji, 2010). In a parallel step to the ESIM suggestion to study the question of how *crowd* identity and action are constituted by others acting towards them, we focus in this work on the question of how crowd members seek to constitute the actions of the powerful people who are the *targets* of their collective action. This step is intended to highlight two neglected aspects of the question of collective action and change in psychology: firstly, a focus on *concrete social changes*—such as a change to a law, policy, or norm—and how they might result from collective action, and secondly, how crowd members can influence the powerful rather than be the subject of influence themselves.

The starting point for this work is an interest in how health-promoting social changes may be brought about through the collective action of the communities, which are affected by a particular health issue. It is well recognized that the determinants of poor health are not only individual but also social and structural (e.g., lack of access to medicines, clean water or adequate housing), and thus that ordinary people often have little control individually over the sources of their poor health (Marks, 2002). This is not to say that *nobody* has control over important determinants of health, but that some actors—such as politicians, policymakers, and even the media—have more power than others in this context. Hence, our interest in the potential for social movements to influence these more powerful actors to make social changes that will be better for people's health (Cornish et al., 2010; Campbell et al., 2010; see also Speer et al., 2003). The study of social movements which have succeeded in bringing about some of their desired goals offers an opportunity to learn about how crowds concretely bring about change to the actions of the powerful, and consequently, social change.

Communities' Means of Political Influence: Persuading, Protesting and Exchanging Favors

Despite the odds being stacked against them, there are instances in which marginalized and disadvantaged communities succeed in bringing about social change in their interests. In a study of two successful organizations of sex workers (prostitutes) in India, we sought to understand how those organizations had managed to bring about locally significant changes, such as less repressive policing, or better infrastructure provided by the municipal government (Cornish et al., 2010). What sources of influence did these organizations draw upon in order to convince the police to limit violent raids, or to register sex workers' complaints? What sources of influence enabled them to convince politicians that the swampy paths between their houses should be drained and surfaced by the municipality, or that the municipality could donate land for the construction of a clinic? In other words, we considered these improvements as social changes that resulted from the collective's demands, and asked how the actions of the collective brought about changes to the actions of the relevant authorities. To complement earlier work which focused on the "crowd" element of the social act of protest, in terms of how sex workers became constituted as a collectivity, with a shared identity and set of aims (Cornish, 2006; Ghose, Swendeman, & George, 2008), this study focused on the "authorities" element of the social act of protest, and particularly, how the action of collectivities could constitute the authorities' behavior.

From a theoretical point of view, informed by collective action and social movement research, our initial expectations were that collective action in the form of protest would be a core concept. However, what emerged from the analysis was that protest was used only rarely and judiciously. Both organizations were very good at effectively mobilizing large numbers of women to create a noisy public protest at a police station or politicians' office, if they had a complaint to make. They had used protest, for instance, as a response to violent police raids, or failures of government services to provide sex workers with their entitlements, such as free condoms or proper hospital treatment. Two themes seemed to be common to the events which triggered a protest: first, that the "target" of the protest had an interest in a positive public image which would be tarnished by an embarrassing protest, and secondly, that the protestors could stake a legitimate claim that their rights were being unfairly denied. Both themes invoke a third party, beyond the collectives and the authorities. The public nature of protest brings it to an additional audience of media and the wider community, and both instigators and targets of collective action sought to maintain a good reputation in the wider public eye.

Although important, protest was not the predominant form of these organizations' efforts to influence authorities. Protest is a confrontational form of interaction, and the organization's members were keenly aware of the risks of establishing conflictual relationships with powerful others. Hence, they often sought gentler means of influence. We termed these "persuading" and "exchanging favors." By "persuading," we referred to efforts at verbal persuasion, or friendly relationship-building, which came without strings attached such as a threat of a protest, or an offer of something valued. Holding information-giving meetings, or dropping by an office to say "hello," without any immediate particular requests or demands were seen by the organizations as important means of developing a relationship which might later bear more concrete fruit. From a social identity point of view, it might be that, in so doing, the organizations' representatives were building in-group identifications between sex workers and authorities.

"Exchanging favors" is also a cooperative, rather than confrontational, approach. Both organizations had found ingenious ways of positioning themselves so that they had a favor, or an incentive, to offer to their authorities, in implicit exchange for future helpful responses. In one case, reciprocal relationships with the local police station had been built, by the organization providing the police with useful information on local criminal activities, in an implicit exchange for reductions in police violence and harassment. In another, the sex workers' organization offers politicians the role of "Chief Guest" and a slot for speech-making, when they organize public gatherings. The public platform for the politician and apparent endorsement of the sex workers' organization in front of potential voters, are valuable incentives for politicians, encouraging them to retain the organizations' support through providing concrete help, such as improving local infrastructure, or representing sex workers' cause to unhelpful government offices.

The point here is that the sex workers' organizations took carefully calculated decisions about their initiations of interactions with the various authorities, taking into account the projected future response of the authorities, and the impact on their longer-term relationship. They sought actively and strategically to constitute the authorities' responses. In so doing, they considered also the potential responses of the wider community (i.e., a public to which the authorities had to orient), through the question of the perceived legitimacy of their claims and of the authorities' action. Action on the part of authorities, which could clearly be positioned as illegitimate or unjust (such as denial of rights to healthcare), might warrant a public protest, and might be expected to garner public support. More subtle negotiation might be warranted when the issues were less clear, or when the risks were higher. In turn, in choosing a response, the authorities weigh up the public significance of their own action, particularly in terms of what action is likely to be considered legitimate and justifiable. Far from LeBon's (1895) view of a collective "descending" to rely on "primitive," uncultivated instincts, at least some forms of collective action reveal carefully thought out decision making and planning. The act of making choices between these three different forms of political influence illustrates, first, the power of collectives to constitute the responses of authorities, and second, the self-conscious and strategic engagement of the collectives with the interests and perspectives of the authorities. This politicized mutual engagement expresses the complicated intersubjective dynamic of mutual attempts at influence, which animate the social act of protest.

The Power of Ideas: Social Movements' Strategies for Being Heard

The subtitle of this book points to the transformative 'power of ideas' in fostering social change. From a cultural psychological viewpoint, ideas are not immaterial, vague or inconsequential things, but materially constitutive of our psychological and social lives. In the study of sex workers discussed above, the sex workers' persuasive power appeared to be linked closely to the material power that they had, to either mobilize an inconvenient protest, or offer a concrete incentive to the authorities with whom they were negotiating. In a second study, this time of social movements' efforts to get their demands on the agendas of the powerful, it emerged that the social movements cleverly used symbolic power, or the "power of ideas" to position themselves as meriting support and concrete action (Campbell et al., 2010). We analyzed three case studies of social movements, which had achieved successes in their efforts to bring about political or legal changes in the interests of poor communities. Brazil's *Movimento Dos Trabalhadores Rurais Sem Terra* (or Landless Workers' Movement) has mobilized more than 1 million members to demand that idle farmland be redistributed from the rich to the poor, winning 15 million acres, and resettling 250,000 families. *Jan Swasthya Abhiyan*, the Indian wing of the global People's Health Movement has significantly influenced government health policy and practice to be more accountable to poor people. South Africa's Treatment Action Campaign vociferously and successfully campaigned for free universal access to life-saving HIV drugs.

How did these social movements get their agendas heard and acted upon? They successfully mobilized "the power of ideas" to construct their struggle symbolically as one worth supporting, and "the power of association" to create impressive networks that politicians could not risk ignoring. Each social movement created a simple and compelling message, positioned on the "moral high ground," and in line with popular national ideological currents, as well as international discourses. It is difficult to disagree that people suffering from HIV/AIDS should be provided with medicines if those medicines will save their lives, or that public health services ought to be accountable to poor people. The social movements each worked hard to establish the public legitimacy of their causes, by reference to laws (such as the Brazilian constitution's assertion that "land has a social responsibility to be productive") and to national and international currents of opinion (such as the global reemergence of a primary healthcare movement). They took active steps to preempt negative interpretations of their actions, in the case of the Landless Workers' Movement, for example, emphasizing their peaceful activism, or in the case of the Treatment Action Campaign, taking out full-page advertisements in national newspapers to explain the reasons behind its civil disobedience campaign. Thus, these organizations are aware of the potential negative impact of being symbolically constructed as 'troublemakers' and actively work to preempt such impressions, providing, instead, more positive constructions.

The symbolic construction of the social movements and their cause is a key foundation for their ability to attract wide membership and support. Each organization had built impressive networks, both numerically (mobilizing large numbers of grassroots people), and in terms of attracting high-profile and well-connected supporters, who have been able to channel the movements' demands to people in positions of power. Winning widespread popular support meant that it was difficult for politicians to ignore the movements' demands. Drury, Reicher, and Stott have shown that what is deemed "rational" and "normal" is defined, in part, by one's social identity. In a parallel move, these social movements work to define themselves and their norms in such a way that others (including grassroots supporters, politicians, celebrities, etc.) can identify with them. Reicher, Haslam, and Hopkins (2005) have described leaders as "entrepreneurs of identity," who actively constitute particular forms of identity and the viability of their leadership among their followers. In a similarly active process, social movements might be seen as "entrepreneurs of identity," seeking to constitute not only the identities of the social group which they begin by representing, but creating a public identity for themselves which can attract wide identification, drawing in new people, including those with power and influence, who may not have originally identified with the group.

FROM CROWD ACTION TO THE ACTION OF AUTHORITIES

Both the social identity contribution to understanding social change, as elucidated in Drury and colleagues' chapter, and my examples of how organizations and social movements seek to change the actions of the powerful, make the case for the importance of understanding social stasis and social change as dynamic, interactive results of the reflexive mutual orientation of humans and human social groups. Much research on crowd action has assumed that what has to be explained is the violent, "irrational" or "subhuman" nature of people in collectivities. Agreeing with Drury, Reicher and Stott, my examples have suggested that the strategic and self-conscious nature of collective action must also be explained.

Furthermore, I have suggested that, to understand the full social act of protest, we should extend our focus to the actions of authorities and to the resultant social outcome, as much as attending to the actions of the crowd. The nuanced and interactive understanding of crowd behavior put forward in the ESIM tradition has been used to inform policing practices so that they are less likely to elicit violent collective outbursts from the crowd. Police forces may learn from ESIM research that by treating football supporters as legitimate fans rather than as hooligans, treating violence as an unusual individual expression rather than as something characteristic of the crowd as a whole, and by constituting themselves as enablers of legitimate protest, they are less likely to elicit violent collective responses (ESRC, n.d; Reicher, Stott, Drury, Adang, Cronin, & Livingstone, 2007; Stott et al., 2008). Further study of the constitution of authorities' responses might be used to inform collectives with protests to make about how to constitute the behavior of police, politicians, or other authorities, to bring about socially desirable outcomes. A social identity analysis, in this context, could pose useful questions, for example, about how collectivities position themselves to offer identities to politicians that further both groups' agendas (such as "defender of free speech" or "ally of the poor"), or about how people in authority seek to constitute and defend identities which either enable or disable collective action."Studying up," that is, studying those in positions of power and authority is always more difficult for the researcher than studying those of lower status in society (Nader, 1972; Stephens, 2010). Perhaps this is all the more reason to make efforts to do so.

In the examples given above, we have begun to study the constitution of the action of authorities, through considering the strategies used by organizations and social movements to influence relevant authorities. Admittedly, the data in these studies still primarily concern the actions of collectivities, even if it is their action that is designed to influence authorities. The social psychological gaze could be expanded further to better study and understand the social psychological conditions of authorities who are being targeted by collective action, their orientations to anticipated and actual collective action, their decision making and their actions. We could ask questions about the situations, representations, and public identities of those in power, and how those conditions produce responsiveness or unresponsiveness on the part of the powerful to the collectivities who seek to influence them. The position of authorities is not fixed or stable, but often vulnerable. We could ask questions about how authorities' powerful role in relation to a contentious object is established, legitimated, and overturned. Further, we could ask questions about the nature of contentious objects, how different objects allow for different responses, how collectivities and authorities struggle over the definition of a desirable social outcome, and how a change to that contentious object is socially established. In each of these lines of inquiry, it is necessary to consider the actions of collectivities and authorities not as naïve or automatic responses, but as strategic and reflexive responses to each other's past actions, anticipating and constituting future actions. To understand how society is transformed through collective action, then, we cannot limit our attention to any individual element of the triadic social act of protest, but need to consider the interrelations among crowd, authorities and contentious object, in a dynamic relation of mutual orientation and constitution.

NOTE

1. See http://en.wikipedia.org/wiki/2010_UK_student_protests for further information on the student protests.

REFERENCES

Campbell, C., Cornish, F., Gibbs, A., & Scott, K. (2010). Heeding the push from below. *Journal of Health Psychology, 15*(7), 962-971.

Cornish, F. (2006). Challenging the stigma of sex work in India: Material context and symbolic change. *Journal of Community & Applied Social Psychology, 16*(6), 462-471.

Cornish, F., Shukla, A., & Banerji, R. (2010). Persuading, protesting and exchanging favours: Strategies used by Indian sex workers to win local support for their HIV prevention programmes. *AIDS Care, 22,* 1670-1678.

ESRC (n.d). *Controlling without confronting—policing and hooliganism. Impact case study.* Retrieved from http://www.esrc.ac.uk/ESRCInfoCentre/Images/Impact_Case_Study_POLICING_tcm6-34020.pdf

Farr, R. M. (1996). *The roots of modern social psychology, 1872-1954.* Oxford, England: Blackwell.

Ghose, T., Swendeman, D., George, S., & Chowdhury, D. (2008). Mobilizing collective identity to reduce HIV risk among sex workers in Sonagachi, India: The boundaries, consciousness, negotiation framework. *Social Science & Medicine, 67*(2), 311-320.

Gillespie, A. (2005). G. H. Mead: Theorist of the social act. *Journal for the Theory of Social Behaviour, 35*(1), 19-39.

Gillespie, A., & Cornish, F. (2010). Intersubjectivity: Towards a dialogical analysis. *Journal for the Theory of Social Behaviour, 40*(1), 19-46.
Gillespie, A., & Cornish, F. (in press). The Northern Rock bank run: An analysis of communication within a distrust sequence.
Grossen, M. (2010). Interaction analysis and psychology: A dialogical perspective. *Integrative Psychological and Behavioral Science, 44*(1), 1–22.
Le Bon, G. (1895/1968). *The crowd: A study of the popular mind.* Dunwoody, GA: Norman S. Berg.
Marks, D. F. (2002). Freedom, responsibility and power: Contrasting approaches to health psychology. *Journal of Health Psychology, 7*(1), 5-19.
Marková, I. (1987a). *Human awareness: Its social development*. London: Hutchinson.
Marková, I. (1987b). On the interaction of opposites in psychological processes. *Journal for the Theory of Social Behaviour, 17*(3), 279–299.
Mead, G. H. (1925). The genesis of self and social control. *International Journal of Ethics, 35*, 251-277.
Nader, L. (1972). Up the anthropologist: Perspectives gained from studying up. In D. Hymes (Ed.), *Reinventing anthropology* (pp. 284–311). New York, NY: Random House.
Reicher, S., & Hopkins, N. (2003). On the science of the art of leadership. In D. van Knippenberg & M. Hogg (Eds.), *Leadership and power: Identity processes in groups and organizations* (pp. 197-209). London: SAGE.
Reicher, S., Haslam, S. A., & Hopkins, N. (2005). Social identity and the dynamics of leadership: Leaders and followers as collaborative agents in the transformation of social reality. *The Leadership Quarterly, 16*(4), 547-568.
Reicher, S., Stott, C, Drury, J., Adang, O., Cronin, P., & Livingstone, A. (2007). Knowledge based public order policing: Principles and practice. *Policing, 1*, 403-415.
Speer, P. W., Ontkush, M., Schmitt, B., Raman, P., Jackson, C., Rengert, K. M., & Peterson, N. A. (2003). The intentional exercise of power: Community organizing in Camden, New Jersey. *Journal of Community & Applied Social Psychology, 13*(5), 399-408.
Stephens, C. (2010). Privilege and status in an unequal society: Shifting the focus of health promotion research to include the maintenance of advantage. *Journal of Health Psychology, 15*(7), 993-1000.
Stott, C. J., Adang, O. M., Livingstone, A., & Schreiber, M. (2008) Tackling football hooliganism: a quantitative study of public order, policing and crowd psychology. *Psychology, Public Policy and Law, 14,* 115-141.
Zittoun, T., Gillespie, A., Cornish, F., & Psaltis, C. (2007). The metaphor of the triangle in theories of human development. *Human Development, 50*(4), 208-229.

CHAPTER 4

CHANGE WE CAN BELIEVE IN

The Role of Social Identity, Cognitive Alternatives and Leadership in Group Mobilization and Social Transformation

Stephen D. Reicher and S. Alexander Haslam

THE PROBLEM OF SOCIAL CHANGE

The best way to preserve our unequal and unfair world is to declare that it is only natural. Politicians do it. The general public does it. And we do it in our discipline. Indeed much psychology, particularly social psychology, has at its very core a set of assumptions which represent the present as inevitable and hence see change as unimaginable and impossible.

Why do people treat out-groups prejudicially? Because prejudice is a "natural" part of our human make-up (Allport, 1954). Why do people abuse power? Because oppression is the "natural" consequence of giving people powerful roles (Haney, Banks, & Zimbardo, 1973). Why are minorities trodden down by the majority? Because low-status groups tend "naturally" to justify the status quo (Jost & Banaji, 1994). As Moscovici (1976) observed, social psychological theory can be seen to have an inherent *conformity bias*, such that the observed features of the world are seen to be a

Culture and Social Change: Transforming Society Through the Power of Ideas, pp. 53–73

product—and an inevitable consequence—of psychological forces that serve to produce (and reproduce) those features in preference to all others. Such thinking, of course, is not confined to social psychology, but is also widespread in other branches of the discipline: notably clinical, organizational, and evolutionary. Indeed some forms of evolutionary psychology have been likened to an intellectual parlor game in which the academic's role is to explain how maladaptive social behavior, such as rape, might be understood as the expression of an adaptive evolutionary mechanism (e.g., desire to maximize one's reproductive success; see Dupré, 2003). We may not like it but, hey, boys will be boys and what can we do?

As Moscovici (1976) and others (e.g., Turner, 2006) have noted, there are a range of problems with this approach to the subject matter of social psychology. As we have already implied, principal among them is the fact that, by characterizing social problems as the product of natural and ineluctable forces, the possibility of realistically overcoming those problems is ruled out. If prejudice is inevitable, then tolerance is a temporary aberration; if tyranny is a banal product of power, then resistance is futile; if people always justify the status quo, then it will always be reproduced. As Marx (1845) intimated, this way of interpreting the world has blinded philosophers to the task of understanding and explaining how that world might be changed.

Yet for all the pessimism that such messages might promote, a striking feature of the social world is that it does not simply reproduce itself ad infinitum. Rather, as Heraclitus put it 2,500 years ago "change is the only constant" (Frisch, 1949, p. 192). Each age spins an elaborate tale—frequently a tale about human nature—as to why its particular form of society represents the "end of history." But, much like King Canute, none can stop the tides of history rolling in. A short while ago, Stalinism seemed secure in Eastern Europe, and with Nelson Mandela imprisoned on Robben Island, Apartheid seemed impregnable in South Africa. But the wall fell, and Mandela turned his seemingly impregnable prison into the crucible for an alternative regime (Buntman, 2003; Mandela, 1994) and a non-racial regime was born. How was all this possible—and what do can we contribute to explaining the genesis of movements that toppled tyrants?

A key goal of this chapter is to set about answering this question and show how social psychology makes such transformation possible rather than unimaginable (Haslam & Reicher, 2009; Turner, 2005). In doing this, we will draw extensively on some of the key ideas put forward by *social identity theory* (Tajfel & Turner, 1979). In particular, as well as underlining the point that the theory is a theory of change (Reicher, 2004), we will elaborate on one aspect of it which has tended to be underplayed in research to date: the role of *cognitive alternatives* in restructuring people's understanding of the social world and providing a platform for change. Our argument here will be, first, that the term "cognitive alternatives" covers far more ground and incorporates many more elements than is normally acknowledged. It certainly involves imagining an alternative social world—a sense of somewhere different that we want to get to. But it also involves a sense of how we might get there: feelings of collective power and the means to channel that power. Second, we shall argue that the process by which cognitive alternatives come about is more dynamic and nuanced than generally understood. It emerges out of interaction both between the dominant and the subordinate group and also between leaders and followers within the subordinate group. That is, leadership plays a key role in producing cognitive alternatives and hence social change.

Putting these two points together, we argue that change is primarily a process of *mobilizing masses through reimagining their social identity*. That is, it is made possible through interrelated processes whereby leaders collaborate with followers to consider "who we are," to create a vision of "what we might become" and to organize practical action that can turn vision into social reality.

SOCIAL IDENTITY THEORY AND SOCIAL CHANGE

Social identity theory is well known—perhaps *too* well known—for positing that group members wish to have their groups positively evaluated and that, in order to achieve this, they will seek to make themselves better than other groups. This is the process of *social differentiation*.

There is no doubt that this process is part of the theory (Tajfel & Turner, 1979). Serious problems arise, however, if it is taken as the whole of the theory—or at least as the end point of the theory. It leads, for instance, to the conclusion that the theory posits the inevitability of in-group bias (e.g., see Jost & Elsbach, 2001, pp. 182-185). Again, we might regret prejudice and discrimination, but groups will be groups.

There are many reasons why such a conclusion is a misrepresentation of social identity theory (see Reicher, 2004; Reicher, Spears, & Haslam, 2010). But, most importantly, it violates the metatheoretical perspective out of which the theory arose in the first place (see Israel & Tajfel, 1972). Tajfel, along with Moscovici and others, were deeply dissatisfied with a social psychology that divorced psychological processes from social context and proceeded as if we exist and act in a vacuum. His priority was to examine how our psychological nature is given substance by the particular worlds in which we live and to produce models which force the social psychologist to examine (rather than neglect) the nature of the social world in order to understand what people will do in a given time and place (see also Turner, 1999). Indeed, part of the contribution of the social psychologist is to identify what particular features of the social world we should be attending to.

How does this metatheory reflect itself in social identity theory itself? Well, it might be true that people have a general desire for their groups to be positively evaluated. But the sad reality of our world is that many (in fact, most) people are consigned to groups that are negatively evaluated whether in terms of class, race, gender, sexuality, the list is long. So, then, given the desire for positivity, how do people respond to the fact of negativity? How does the process of differentiation affect behavior as a function of social context? When do people use different strategies to address their predicament? Differentiation, then, is the *starting point* for analysis, *not the end point*.

Tajfel and Turner (1979) distinguish between three broad strategies of self-enhancement. The first is an attempt to advance despite one's group membership, to pass into more privileged circles through one's own efforts and by demonstrating superior personal qualities. This is a strategy of individual mobility, which can be contrasted to collective strategies whereby people attempt to improve their lot by acting together with fellow group members. The collective strategies can themselves be split into two. On the one hand, members can seek to find new ways of valuing their social group without challenging the dominant group (social creativity). On the other hand, they can actively challenge the dominance of others and seek to alter social reality (social change).

For social identity theory, which of these strategies is chosen—whether people act individually or collectively, whether they conciliate or challenge—will depend upon the way in which people understand different aspects of social relations in their social world. And what the theory contributes is an analysis of how different dimensions of understanding map on to different strategic choices in order to preserve or challenge the status quo. These dimensions are:

- whether people believe it is possible to pass out of their group and advance despite their group membership (permeability vs. impermeability);
- whether people believe that inequalities between groups are justifiable or not (legitimacy vs. illegitimacy);
- whether people believe that there are viable alternatives to the status quo or not (presence vs. absence of cognitive alternatives).

The latter two factors—which can be glossed as (a) whether things should be changed, and (b) whether things can be changed—together constitute the security of a social system. If the existing system *both* should *and* can be changed (i.e., it is illegitimate and cognitive alternatives exist) it is said to be insecure. But if it *either* should not *or* cannot be changed (i.e., it is either legitimate or cognitive alternatives are absent) then the system is said to be secure.

In the next section we will analyze how social identity theory maps perceptions onto strategies in order to develop a theory of social change. But perhaps we should pause at this point. For there is a danger that we will have seriously overstated the case and seriously misled the reader if we suggest that social identity theory is a fully fledged theory of social change. After all, Tajfel died in 1982, within three years of his first outline of social change issues, and in creating self-categorization theory (Turner, 1982; Turner, Hogg, Oakes, Reicher, & Wetherell, 1987; Turner, Oakes, Haslam, & McGarty, 1994). Turner developed social identity concepts in a somewhat different direction. So while important statements of social identity theory identified some of the key elements that would need to be included in producing an understanding of social change processes, it is clear that much is missing. What are the exact relationships between permeability, legitimacy, cognitive alternatives and security? Should they be seen as independent and part of a linear sequence or might they be interdependent? And where do these perceptions come from? Are they external to and conditions for the change process or do they emerge from the dynamics of the change process itself. It is no criticism of what Tajfel and Turner (1979) achieved to say that these are questions raised by, rather than settled through, their work.

The danger, though, comes again by taking a starting point as an end point. Indeed, if anything, it could be argued that it is more dangerous to think that a social identity theory of social change exists than to believe that social identity theory has nothing to do with social change. In the latter case one can at least try to develop something, whereas in the former one is dissuaded by the belief that the work has already been done. One is then, at best, reduced to a hermeneutic exercise of trying to decipher what Tajfel and Turner really meant in their seminal texts.

Our position, then, is more accurately described by saying that social identity theory is less a theory *of* social change than a theory *oriented to* social change. Our respect for the theory is marked not only by looking backwards to what was written than by looking forward and trying to elaborate the concepts and their inter-relationships—particular those aspects relating to cognitive alternatives. What comes next, then, should not be read as exegesis of preexisting texts but rather as our contribution to a living and ever-developing body of work.

Our arguments will be based on a number of sources, but most directly on the BBC Prison Study (Haslam & Reicher, 2005, 2008-2009; Reicher &

Haslam, 2006a; see also Haslam & Reicher, 2006; Reicher & Haslam, 2006b; see Figure 4.1). Along the lines of earlier large-scale field studies in social psychology (e.g., Festinger, Reicken, & Schacter, 1956; Haney et al. 1973; Sherif, 1956), the study was designed to examine group behavior over an extended period of time (10 days). Like the famous Stanford Prison Experiment (SPE: Haney et al., 1973) we employed a basic paradigm of intergroup inequality whereby participants where randomly divided into prisoners and guards within a simulated prison setting. The guards were given status and resources (e.g., better food, better accommodation, and better clothing) that were denied to prisoners. Unlike the SPE, however, the study was designed as an investigation of social identity theory. Accordingly, we included various interventions that were designed to impact on the variables we have been discussing above: permeability, legitimacy, and cognitive alternatives. In this way, we could examine in detail and at length the unfolding relationship between the perception of social relations in the "prison" and the strategies employed by prisoners to deal with their disadvantage.

STRATEGIES FOR SELF-ENHANCEMENT

Individual Versus Collective Strategies

Perhaps the simplest and most straightforward claim to come out of social identity theory is that, when people believe that individual advancement is possible within a social system (i.e., when it is permeable) then they will employ individual strategies of self-enhancement. But when they believe individual progress to be blocked (impermeable) they will turn to collective strategies as the only way of improving their lot.

One way of restricting collective challenges to the status quo, then, is to promote the perception of mobility. Therein lies the power of large-scale social belief systems such as the "American Dream." Therein lies the power of more situated practices such as tokenism whereby the high profile elevation of one or two members of a subordinate group—a Black person in the Cabinet, a woman in the boardroom—is used to sustain the claim that anyone could get their under their own steam, if they only tried hard enough. Or rather, and more pertinently, resistance is unnecessary because there is nothing to fight against.

The conservative power of tokenism has been empirically demonstrated in a program of experimental research by Wright and colleagues. They show that, even where the likelihood of escaping a low-status group is extremely remote, the slightest sense that such escape is possible serves to dampen the appetite of that group's members for collective conflict with their high-status counterparts. As a stark illustration of this point, in a study where opportunities for members of a disadvantaged group to gain promotion to an advantage group were completely precluded (i.e., 0%), low status group members' support for collective protest was around 7 on a 9-point scale; yet it dropped to less than 5 (i.e., below the scale midpoint) when opportunities for promotion were raised to just 2% (Wright, Taylor, & Moghaddam, 1990; see also Wright & Taylor, 1998). As the researchers conclude, these results show how an apparent opening up of the system can in fact be a means whereby the advantaged group can continue to discriminate with impunity.

The BBC study served to confirm both the general points about permeability and the specific point about tokenism. For, at the start of the study we, in effect, sought to induce permeability perceptions through a tokenistic procedure. Although the allocation of participants as prisoner and guard was actually done randomly, participants were led to believe that they had been selected on the basis of psychometric screening tests they had taken which indicated to us who had the qualities necessary to be an effective guard. This was intended to legitimize the intergroup inequality. However we also told participants that the tests were not perfect. We would therefore be observing their behavior over the first few days and, should anyone show the requisite qualities, there was provision for one (and only one) prisoner to be elevated to guard status. This tokenism induced many of the prisoners to pursue a strategy of individual mobility, striving to improve their circumstances by working hard *as individuals* to win favor with the guards and gain entry into their ranks. This is exemplified by the following exchange between two prisoners in the same cell:

JE_p[1]: Do you want to get promoted?
PP_p: Nah ...
JE_p: Well I do. You guys can do what you like, but I'd like to be a guard because they get all the luxuries and we [do] not.
PP_p: Fair enough.

From this exchange it is clear that not *all* the prisoners sought personal self-advancement within the prison system. Indeed, some (notably PP_p) were implacably opposed to it from Day 1. Nevertheless, the fact that the prisoners found their own personal way of dealing with the situation and acted individually meant that even though the guards were rather diffident about defending it, the system as a whole proved reasonable workable, and certainly there was no orchestrated threat to the status quo.

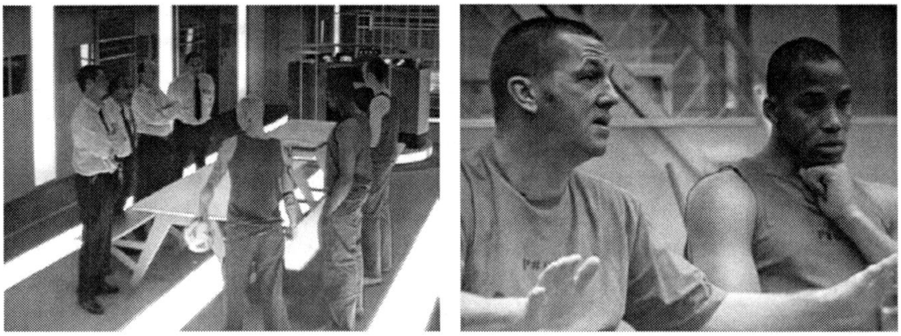

Note: Key catalysts for change in this study were (a) the barring of promotion from prisoner to guard (a manipulation of permeability), and (b) the introduction of a new prisoner with a Trades Union background (a manipulation of cognitive alternatives).

Figure 4.1. Change in the BBC Prison Study (Reicher & Haslam, 2006a; for more information and video clips of key moments visit bbcprisonstudy.org).

On Day 3 of the study, one prisoner was promoted. But at that point, participants were told that there would be no further positions. They were now consigned irrevocably to their groups. The system had become impermeable. And a change of position now meant changing the position of the group as a whole. Within hours—even minutes—the prisoners came together and started planning how they could take on and humiliate the guards. Even if some prisoners had some qualms about what this might do to the guards, their solidarity was not in doubt. Consider the contrast between the interchange reproduced above and that below involving the inmates of the same cell:

> PP_p: Listen, listen mate, you've got to, you've got to start forgetting about other people's feelings and what they're doing because the days when you're sitting here starving hungry and you've got fuck all and you've got nothing mate and you've got a ratty little bed and a stupid little blanket to sit under and they're under there in their duvets, they've got everything they want and they're not giving two fucks about you. So—think on and fuck them.
>
> KM_p I think they do care about us. But guys I'm going to back you all the way. You should no' doubt me.

Clearly, and in line with predictions derived from social identity theory, impermeability produced collectivity. This then leads to the next issue addressed by the theory: what form did that collective action take?

The Conditions for Collective Confrontation

As we have seen, there are two broad ways in which people can act as group members in order to improve the negative evaluation of their group. One, social creativity, is effectively a matter of changing the ways in which people evaluate the existing social reality. Tajfel and Turner (1979) suggest that it can take a number of forms including: (a) finding a new dimension on which to compare in-group and out-group; (b) changing the values assigned to the attributes of the in-group; and (c) engaging in comparisons with different out-groups. The other, social competition, is more a matter of changing social reality itself. This is predominantly a matter of confronting the advantaged group and challenging its power and privilege. For social identity theory, the selection of strategy is a function of perceptions of the security of intergroup relations. Specifically, perceived security (i.e., when relations are seen as legitimate or there are no cognitive alternatives) leads to social creativity, while perceived insecurity (when relations are seen as illegitimate and there are cognitive alternatives) leads to social competition. Rephrased in ordinary language, one can more easily see the logic of this. Thus, if there is either no reason to change the system or no possibility of changing the system, then one will work within it, at most seeking to reevaluate one's position within it. If, on the other hand, there is *both* reason *and* possibility of changing the system, then one will work against it and to supercede it. Both Naomi Ellemers in the Netherlands and Steve Wright in Canada have produced a wealth of laboratory-based evidence to support these ideas (Ellemers, 1993; Wright & Taylor, 1998).

As with permeability, this analysis helps identify the impact of both large-scale belief systems and specific practices on processes of change. There are many belief systems aimed at legitimating and naturalizing inequality such that change becomes unthinkable—what Haslam (2001) calls *supremacist ideologizing*. In particular, psychological models—both lay and academic—have long been used to justify social inequalities as reflecting inherent and hence unchallengeable differences in the nature of people. To take but one of many examples, Leon Kamin provides a classic and coruscating analysis of the science and politics of IQ (Kamin, 1974). Fixed differences in intelligence have been used to legitimate inequalities of almost every sort—in terms of "race," in terms of gender, in terms of class. Famously (or, rather, infamously) Goddard, one of the pioneers of IQ testing, took on those who "in their ultra altruistic and human attitude" think that "great inequalities in social life are wrong and unjust"—the fact, for instance, that some can afford $12 for shoes and others only $3 (Goddard was speaking to an invited audience at Princeton in 1919), that some live in a hovel without carpets and pictures while others reside in artistically decorated homes. But to view this as unjust is fallacious, Goddard asserts, because "it assumes that the one is 'on the same mental level' as the other. They aren't. The poor man didn't have the wit to work well, to save, and doesn't need the fine things to make him happy (all quotes as cited in Kamin, 1974, p. 22).

It is not just that supremacist ideas justify unequal practices, it is also that unequal practices sustain supremacist ideas. The well-dressed and well-versed gent can, by that very token justify his elevated status—and also intimidate the laborer from arguing with him. Taken to the extreme, it is this which led those who ran the Nazi death camps to insist that camp guards look immaculate at all times (Levi, 1958/1987; Rees, 2005). By reinforcing the contrast between guards and inmates, this practice institutionalized the view both that the Nazis were a "master race," that those they were oppressing were inherently and inescapably inferior, and that the prospect of the oppressed overcoming the oppressor was quite unimaginable.

If these illustrations point to the importance of legitimacy and cognitive alternatives in society at large, as well as in experimental studies, they also suggest that these are complex constructs, which may have several aspects to them. This applies particularly to the notion of cognitive alternatives. Thus, on the one hand this may relate to ideologies which suggest that the current state of affairs is the only possible state of affairs. On the other hand it may relate to displays of power which suggest that, even if alternatives are viable in principle, it is impossible to conceive of getting from here to there.

Likewise, the evidence from the BBC prison study both confirmed the importance of perceived security of intergroup relations and also helped us elaborate a number of the ideas—those relating to cognitive alternatives in particular, but also some other aspects of the social identity model of social change. Our education began at the point where the above description ended: just after the promotion, when the prisoners started their plotting.

ELABORATING THE CONCEPT OF COGNITIVE ALTERNATIVES

The Dynamics of Empowerment

The effect of the promotion was not limited to its impact on perceptions of permeability. It also impacted on perceptions of legitimacy and of cognitive alternatives. Recall that we initially legitimated the system by saying that the guards were selected because they had certain qualities such as initiative and drive. Recall also that some of the guards responded to their position with some ambivalence. This made them diffident about exercising their authority. They certainly did not show either drive or initiative. Hence, once people were locked into their groups and irrespective of the qualities they did or did not display, the legitimation for the inequality between groups no longer had any credibility.

What is more, the ambivalence of the guards, combined with the post-promotion unity of the prisoners led the prisoners to perceive that the system was vulnerable, that the guards could be challenged, and that they were incapable of a united response. Hence prisoners both rejected the existing system and felt able to challenge it with impunity. This goes at least some of the way towards answering one of the questions most frequently asked of our study: why was the outcome so different to the Stanford Prison Experiment? For, while we deliberately abstained from intervening in the intergroup dynamics between prisoners and guards, Zimbardo, acting in the role of prison superintendent, acted to ensure that the prisoners had no such sense of agency. In his prestudy briefing to the guards, he told them to instill in the prisoners a sense that:

> You can create in the prisoners feelings of boredom, a sense of fear to some degree, you can create a notion of arbitrariness that their life is totally controlled by us, by the system, you, me—They'll have no freedom of action, they can do nothing, say nothing that we don't permit.... In general what all this leads to is a sense of powerlessness. (Zimbardo, 1989)

When the guards enacted these instructions, the prisoners came to understand that their options were severely constrained, to the point where at one moment "Prisoner #8612 told other prisoners, "You can't leave. You can't quit.'" As Zimbardo (1999-2009) observes, "That sent a chilling message and heightened their sense of really being imprisoned" (p. 22).

Returning to the BBC study, as time went by, the prisoners' sense of agency and of impunity increased through the experience of interactions with the guards. Each challenge revealed the unity of the prisoners and the division amongst guards. Each time the combination of in-group unity and out-group disunity delivered victory to the prisoners. Each successive victory by the prisoners increased their sense of unity and boldness, while it increased the sense of frustration and bitterness amongst the guards. The first major confrontation, for instance, started with one prisoner hurling his food to the ground and complaining that it was inedible. As the guards intervened, his cell mates backed him up by raising more grievances. By contrast, different guards undermined each other by demanding different things of the prisoners. This resulted in the guards backing off and ultimately making multiple concessions. They then retreated to their quarters and bickered over what had been done. One guard complained: "they can see what's happened today, and they can, now they know they can do whatever they want." Another disagreed. "That's wrong," he said. However, the first guard accurately described what was going on in the prisoners' cell at that very moment. The prisoners were, literally, dancing in elation. Each complemented the others for the part they had played in the altercation. "You were flipping quality man" said one. "This is just the start, this is just the start," the other replied.

So, one critical aspect of cognitive alternatives—the sense of power to overcome the present system—developed through the dynamics of the system itself and without the need for any external intervention by us, the experimenters. However, while the prisoners may have developed a sense of their own power, they had no clear idea what to do with it. While they may have felt able to destroy the status quo, they had no sense of what to replace it with. In a sense, toying with the guards and demonstrating their preeminence was enough. What was happening was more a game of cat and mouse than a drive for social change. For that, more was necessary.

Ideology, Practice, and Leadership

Much of what we have just been arguing is encapsulated in the words of Steve Biko (1978/1988), the Black consciousness activist who was murdered by the South African authorities in 1977 for his success in mobilizing against apartheid:

> Black consciousness is in essence the realization by the black man of the need to rally together with his brothers around the cause of their oppression —the blackness of their skin—and to operate as a group in order to rid themselves of the shackles that bind them into perpetual servitude.... It seeks to infuse the black community with a new-found pride in themselves, their efforts, their value systems, their culture, their religion and their outlook to life. The interrelationship between the consciousness of the self and the emancipatory programme is of paramount importance. Blacks no longer seek to reform the system because so doing implies acceptance of the major points around which the system revolves. Blacks are out to completely transform the system. (p. 63)

Thus, the struggle for social change depends upon the development of a collective sense of pride and possibility. People need to start thinking of themselves as group members (as prisoners in the case of our study, as Black people in the case of the antiapartheid struggle) and they need to start thinking of their group as able to determine their own fate. However, Biko's words also add some critical elements that have been missing in our analysis thus far. First of all, in the Black consciousness movement, self-belief is part of a wider ideology. This ideology also specifies what we saw to be missing amongst the prisoners in the BBC study—an idea of the type of society which, with their abilities, group members are seeking to build. Second, these various understandings—of group power and of the "good society"—do not arise spontaneously and from nowhere. They have to be articulated, and the role of leaders (in this case, obviously, Biko himself) in their articulation is quite critical.

It was in order to examine these issues more closely that on day 5 of the BBC Prison Study, after the promotion and the escalation of prisoner-guard conflict, we introduced a new participant (DM) as prisoner. DM had exactly the same briefing as all the others on entering, but given his background as a Trades Union official, we had reason to believe that he would have a clear vision of alternatives to the existing prisoner-guard regime and the skills to implement his vision. Our interest was in how he might advance his vision, whether it would be accepted by others and how it would impact on the overall organization of social relations in the study.

On being shown into his cell, DM had the following exchange with his cell-mates:

DM_p: Has anyone explained why it's an environment like this?
FC_p: It's a prison.
DM_p: Has anyone explained why it's like that though?
FC_p: Because that's part of the experiment, we just ended up in here.
DM_p: Why put up with this?
FC_p: That's a very, very good question. Well, 'cause I signed a form to say I would.
DM_p: No you didn't. I didn't sign a form to say I'd put up with, you know, heat like this. I mean, I signed a form to say I'd participate in an experiment. I didn't sign a form to say I'd put up with this kind of heat.

In analytic terms, what DM was doing here was to question the way in which participants construed their social world and to imply an alternative—a world in which inequality is not taken for granted but rather where rights are assumed. Crucially, in this alternative moral universe, what was reasonable in a prison became unreasonable, indeed illegitimate.

Having begun to raise such doubts with his fellow prisoners, DM then went on to raise them with the guards:

TQ_g: How long are you going to stay in your cell?

DM_p: Until someone says, these are the rules, these are the ones that can be broken, or can be questioned, rather, these are the ones that can't be questioned etc.

TQ_g: OK.

DM_p: When that's completed I'll be more than happy to participate in your work rota.

TQ_g: I'd be more than happy for you to participate in the cleaning right now, and that's a direct order from a Guard. It is taken, it is taken. It can be done. It can be done...

DM_p: I'm sorry, it's not. Because one of the concerns I've got is, that unless I know what the rules are, I don't know if I'm breaking them.

TQ_g: It would be natural for all us to assume that everybody knows, within a prison, there is a certain structure, very loosely, even if you didn't know the specific rules. We can speak broadly, can't we?

DM_p: This isn't a prison.

TQ_g: Why do we have to speak specifically?

DM_p: This isn't a prison.

TQ_g: It is!

DM_p: At the moment, it's not a prison.

TQ_g: It is

....

DM_p: When I've got hold of the rules, then I'll tell you whether or not it's a prison. Do you understand?

Soon, however, DM went further. In private conversation with the guard TQ he explicitly spelt out an alternative to the prison system. He reimagined the setting and the social relations within it using a familiar cultural model: not a prison but an idealized workplace; not division between guards and prisoners but workers unity; not autocracy but workers' rights.

DM_p: If this was a real life situation ...

TQ_g: Yes.

DM_p: ... and you were working in this kind of heat, then you as an employee could well go to the employer and say "The condition is unacceptable, I'm not prepared to work in it". Now let's treat this as a real life situation. You and I – your group and the group I'm in – both have this problem of the heat. And if I've got to sleep in this, there is no way I will. And I, you know, won't bear it. And I think collectively we should do something about it to the people who are running the experiment. Now you know in a normal, day to day, real life situation, that's what would happen.

TQ_g: Well, I am most impressed with your new-found kind of angle on this, which possibly shouldn't come as a surprise to me. But I think that is a very very valid point you are making and I'm going to go along with it completely.

As well as cultivating a new sense of social reality and of social identity that would underpin this new order, DM_p also set about *embedding* this identity in practice. Thus as a first practical step towards participant unity, he mooted the creation of a new negotiating forum which brought guards and prisoners together on an equal footing. This arrangement was accepted by the prisoners as a means of overcoming their disadvantage. No longer were they interested in asserting their power for its own sake and to humiliate the guards. Now they wanted to use their power to achieve social change. Perhaps more surprisingly the new arrangement was also accepted by the guards. Although it involved them surrendering much of their hierarchical advantage, the new system promised to end their constant humiliation and to confirm their position in what promised to be a viable social order.

The importance of the forum, then, was that it gave a tangible form to DM's idea of a new social reality. It was a germ cell of the future social body existing in the present and it helped to create the new social identities that would underpin the future. In sum, the effectiveness of DM's leadership depended upon both its ideological and its practical dimensions. As argued more generally by Haslam, Reicher, and Platow (2011; see also Haslam & Reicher, 2007; Reicher, Haslam, & Hopkins, 2005), vision is necessary but not sufficient for transformational leadership. Leaders must also have the organizational know-how to develop *identity-embedding practices*—those which can channel the energies of the group and thereby transform vision into reality.

The subsequent history of the study only served to confirm the importance of combining ideology and practice. After DM had proposed the negotiating forum, but before it was implemented, we withdrew him from the study. Our interest was precisely in the fate of his alternative vision without him there to bring it into being. The result was stark. The forum never got going because no one really knew how to organize it. Things returned to the status quo ante. Prisoners goaded guards. They undermined them at every turn until the old system simply collapsed. At this point the participants were bemused. They simply did not know how to act. They had no rules, no norms, no structures left to guide them. At this point it is significant that DM's ideas resurfaced as an alternative model. Prisoners and Guards came together and set up what they called "a self-organizing, self-disciplining commune"—a system in which all would be equal. It is also significant that those who proposed and organized the commune were those closest to DM, his erstwhile cell-mates. Yet, deeply as they believed in this new system, the "Communards" did not know how to make it work and how to counter dissent. Towards the end of the study they lost faith in the system and were moving towards acceptance of a rigid hierarchical structure. Twice, then, ideas alone proved insufficient. Twice participants may have subscribed to an egalitarian alternative but twice their inability to embed egalitarian structures led to practical failure and loss of belief.

CONCLUSION

In this chapter we have stressed the importance of a social psychology of social change, we have highlighted the centrality of social change to social identity theorizing, and we have sought to build upon the foundation stones that it provides. We laid stress on the importance of collective action to secure change. We showed how collective action is underpinned by shared social identity. And we demonstrated that such shared identity is facilitated by structural conditions which make changing the position of one's group the only viable way of ameliorating one's position. But our primary focus lies on whether collective action occurs within the system or against the system. More particularly, we have sought to refine the concept of cognitive alternatives—both the nature of the concept itself and the processes through which it is produced. In each domain, our argument can be encompassed in three key points.

In terms of what we mean by the concept, we proposed that 'cognitive alternatives' is something of a misnomer, for it is about far more than simply internalized cognitions. In particular, it encompasses the following three elements:

(a) *A sense of relative power*, such that the in-group is seen as able to impose its will and its preferences over those defending the status quo.
(b) *An ideological vision*, such that group members have in mind what they consider to be a viable alternative to the status quo
(c) *Identity-embedding structures*, which optimize the organization of group members and the channeling of group power in order to turn vision into reality.

In terms of the processes by which the power, vision and structures which constitute cognitive alternatives are brought about, we wish to underscore the following points:

(a) To some extent at least, alternatives are not simply or suddenly imposed from the outside but rather can be an emergent product of the intergroup dynamic itself. Thus, a sense of alternatives gradually develops out of the ways in which dominant groups respond to the challenges of subordinate groups.
(b) The various elements involved in the development of a social change perspective should not be regarded as independent factors linked in a temporal and causal process. Rather the terms might be better understood as interdependent elements of an overall representation such that altering any one will have consequences for the others. Thus, for instance, "legitimacy" and "cognitive alternatives" are intertwined such that, from the perspective of an alternative social system, certain ways of being come to be seen as unacceptable and immoral.
(c) Leadership is a critical element in the development of cognitive alternatives. The leader must attend to all three elements of the construct—unifying group members and organizing structures to channel their social power as well as providing a vision of the future. More generally, leaders, through their ability to mobilize followers, play a key part in producing change.

In sum, our aim has been to work towards a more dynamic, interactive and socially contextualized social identity theory of social change. More basically, though, this paper is also about reminding ourselves that, even if the actuality of change is somewhat rare, the possibility for change is ever-present even in the most unlikely and unequal settings. Even in a prison study. Even in a prison.

This claim is far from uncontroversial. Writing a rejoinder to our focal BBC Prison Study article in the *British Journal of Social Psychology*, Philip Zimbardo (2006) wrote:

> The rather remarkable conclusion of this simulated prison experience is that the prisoners dominated the guards! ... The prisoners soon established the upper hand, working as a team to undermine the guards.... What is the external validity of such events in any real prison anywhere in the known universe? In what kind of prisons are prisoners in charge? How could such an eventuality become manifest? (p. 49)

There is much that might be said in response to this critique (see Haslam & Reicher, 2009). In particular, one might point out that rather than being inimical to resistance, prisons are often located at its very heart (e.g., see Buntman, 2003; McEvoy, 2001). The key point to emphasize here, though, is that Zimbardo sees social change of the form witnessed in our study as utterly inconceivable. From his perspective tyranny and oppression are a "natural" expression of unassailable psychological forces that operate in unequal contexts such as prisons (e.g., see Haney et al., 1973, p. 12).

As we noted at the start of this chapter, such analyses not only overlook the process of change but also render it *unimaginable*. Moreover, through their impact on our culture as a whole (an impact which is particularly clear in the case of Zimbardo's work), it is apparent that such analyses also serve to shape the public imagination—or rather lack of it. And in this way, social psychological theorizing easily comes to buttress the status quo rather than simply explain it. All too easily, then, it can turn from instrument of progress into impediment (Haslam & Reicher, 2006; Reicher, 2004).

The more general point is that, insofar as successful theories of change ipso facto tell people about the possibility of change, then they enter into the very processes they seek to describe. They become a cultural as well as a scientific reality. They are inevitably normative as well as analytic. That goes for social identity theory as much as Zimbardo's role theory. By theorizing the conditions of change, social identity theory helps create the conditions for change. Besides its theoretical merits, the theory has an unashamed normative commitment to challenging inequality and oppression. This is not a weakness, nor is it an epiphenomenon. It is neither secondary nor incidental. It represents a clear response to an unavoidable choice for our discipline: naturalization and reaction or social process and progress. To echo Turner (2006), then, the most pernicious aspect of the Stanford Prison Experiment (and similar studies) has to do with the way that it locks down our theoretical imagination. This limits the horizons not only of academic psychologists but also of those who are disadvantaged by inequality and injustice.

ACKNOWLEDGMENTS

Work on this chapter was supported by the Economic and Social Research Council (RES-062-23-0135).

NOTE

1. The subscripts $_p$ and $_g$ after participants' initials denote their status as prisoner or guard, respectively.

REFERENCES

Allport, G. W. (1954). *The nature of prejudice.* Cambridge, MA: Addison Wesley.

Biko, B. S. (1988). *I write what I like.* London: Penguin. (Original work published 1978)

Buntman, F. L. (2003). *Robben Island and prisoner resistance to Apartheid.* Cambridge, England: Cambridge University Press.

Dupré, J. (2003). *Human nature and the limits of science.* Oxford, England: Oxford University Press.

Ellemers, N. (1993). The influence of socio-structural variables on identity enhancement strategies. *European Review of Social Psychology, 4,* 27-57.

Festinger, L., Riecken, H., & Schachter, S. (1956). *When prophecy fails.* Minneapolis, MN: University of Minnesota Press.

Frisch, H. (1949). *Might and right in antiquity* (C. C. Martindale, trans.) Copenhagen: Gyldendal.

Haney, C., Banks, C., & Zimbardo, P. (1973). A study of prisoners and guards in a simulated prison. *Naval Research Reviews*: September (pp. 1-17). Office of Naval Research: Washington, DC. [Reprinted In E. Aronson (Ed.), *Readings about the social animal* (3rd ed., pp.52-67). San Francisco, CA: W. H. Freeman].

Haslam, S. A. (2001). *Psychology in organizations: The social identity approach.* London: SAGE.

Haslam, S. A., & Reicher, S. D. (2005). The psychology of tyranny. *Scientific American Mind, 16*(3), 44–51.

Haslam, S. A., & Reicher, S. D. (2006). Stressing the group: Social identity and the unfolding dynamics of responses to stress. *Journal of Applied Psychology, 91,* 1037-1052.

Haslam, S. A., & Reicher, S. D. (2007). Identity entrepreneurship and the consequences of identity failure: The dynamics of leadership in the BBC Prison Study. *Social Psychology Quarterly, 70,* 125-147.

Haslam, S. A., & Reicher, S. D. (2008-2009). *Website for the BBC Prison Experiment.* Retrieved from bbcprisonstudy.org

Haslam, S. A., & Reicher, S. D. (2009). *The social psychology of resistance: Prison studies and the case for a more expansive theoretical imagination* (Unpublished manuscript). Universities of Exeter and St. Andrews.

Haslam, S. A., Reicher, S. D., & Platow, M. J. (2011). *The new psychology of leadership: Identity, influence and power.* London and New York: Psychology Press.

Israel, J., & Tajfel, H. (1972). *The context of social psychology: A critical assessment.* Oxford, England: Academic Press.

Jost, J. T., & Banaji, M. R. (1994). The role of stereotyping in system-justification and the production of false consciousness. *British Journal of Social Psychology, 33,* 1-27.

Jost, J. T., & Elsbach, K.D. (2001). How status and power differences erode personal and social identities at work: A system justification critique of organizational applications of social identity theory. In M. A. Hogg & D. J. Terry (Eds.), *Social identity processes in organizational contexts* (pp. 181-196). Philadelphia, PA: Psychology Press.

Kamin, L. J. (1974). *The science and politics of I.Q.* Maryland: Lawrence Erlbaum.

Levi, P. (1987). *If this is a man.* London: Abacus. (Original work published 1958)

McEvoy, K. (2001). *Paramilitary imprisonment in Northern Ireland: Resistance, management, and release.* Clarendon Studies in Criminology.

Mandela, N. (1994). *Long walk to freedom: The autobiography of Nelson Mandela.* London: Abacus.

Marx, K. (1845). Theses on Feuerbach. In K. Marx & J. Engels (Eds.). *Basic writings on politics and philosophy* (pp. 243-245, L. S. Feuer, trans.). Garden City, NY: Doubleday.

Moscovici, S. (1976). *Social influence and social change.* London: Academic Press.

Rees, L. (2005). *Auschwitz: The Nazis and the "Final Solution".* London: BBC Books.

Reicher, S. D. (2004). The context of social identity: Domination, resistance and change. *Political Psychology, 25,* 921-946.

Reicher, S. D., & Haslam, S. A. (2006a). Rethinking the psychology of tyranny: The BBC Prison Experiment. *British Journal of Social Psychology, 45,* 1-40.

Reicher, S. D., & Haslam, S. A. (2006b). On the agency of individuals and groups: Lessons from the BBC Prison Experiment. In T. Postmes & J. Jetten (Eds.), *Individuality and the group: Advances in social identity* (pp. 237–257). London: SAGE.

Reicher, S. D., Haslam, S. A., & Hopkins, N. (2005). Social identity and the dynamics of leadership: Leaders and followers as collaborative agents in the transformation of social reality. *Leadership Quarterly. 16,* 547–568.

Reicher, S. D., Spears, R., & Haslam, S. A. (2010). *The social identity approach in social psychology.* In M. S. Wetherell & C. T. Mohanty (Eds.), *The SAGE Handbook of Identities* (pp. 45-62). London: SAGE.

Sherif, M. (1956). Experiments in group conflict. *Scientific American, 195,* 54-58.

Tajfel, H., & Turner, J. C. (1979). An integrative theory of intergroup conflict. In W. G. Austin & S. Worchel (Eds.), *The social psychology of intergroup relations* (pp. 33-47). Monterey, CA: Brooks/Cole.

Turner, J. C. (1982). Towards a cognitive redefinition of the social group. In H. Tajfel (Ed.), *Social identity and intergroup relations* (pp. 15-40). Cambridge, England: Cambridge University Press.

Turner, J. C. (1999). Some current issues in research on social identity and self-categorization theories. In N. Ellemers, R. Spears, & B. Doosje (Eds.), *Social identity: Context, commitment, content* (pp. 6-34). Oxford, England: Blackwell.

Turner, J. C. (2005). Explaining the nature of power: A three-process theory. *European Journal of Social Psychology, 35,* 1-22.

Turner, J. C. (2006). Tyranny, freedom and social structure: Escaping our theoretical prisons. *British Journal of Social Psychology, 45,* 41–46.

Turner, J. C., Hogg, M. A., Oakes, P. J., Reicher, S. D., & Wetherell, M. S. (1987). *Rediscovering the social group: A self-categorization theory.* Oxford, England: Blackwell.

Turner, J. C., Oakes, P. J., Haslam, S. A., & McGarty, C. A. (1994). Self and collective: Cognition and social context. *Personality and Social Psychology Bulletin, 20,* 454-463.

Wright, S. C., & Taylor, D. M. (1998). Responding to tokenism: Individual action in the face of collective injustice. *European Journal of Social Psychology, 28,* 647-667.

Wright, S. C., Taylor, D. M., & Moghaddam, F. M. (1990). Responding to membership in a disadvantaged group: From acceptance to collective protest. *Journal of Personality and Social Psychology, 58*, 994-1003.

Zimbardo, P. (1989). *Quiet rage: The Stanford Prison Study video*. Stanford CA: Stanford University.

Zimbardo, P. G. (1999-2009). *Website for the Stanford Prison Experiment.* Retrieved from http://www.prisonexperiment.org

CHAPTER 5

CHANGE NON-WESTERNERS CAN BELIEVE IN

Fathali M. Moghaddam, Zach Warren, and Rhea Vance-Cheng

Change is one of the most challenging topics in the social and natural sciences, and one that requires far more attention from a psychological perspective (Moghaddam, 2002). A major reason why change in the social domain is so difficult to explain is its enormous variety and complexity. For example, consider change at three levels: (1) within persons, as when an individual is "moved" by experiencing a form of art; (2) within groups, as when the status hierarchy within a small team or a large organization changes; (3) between groups, as when a low status group mobilizes, takes collective action, and changes its status vis-à-vis a relatively high status group. These three levels by no means exhaust the variety of social change, but indicate its range.

An important domain of change that Reicher and Haslam (this volume) do not touch on, but which concerns most of humanity outside the United Kingdom and other higher income societies, is change associated with national development. A central puzzle is how enormously difficult it is to achieve certain types of change, such as change from dictatorship to democracy. Technology and art play complex roles, transforming human relationships and the nature of communication, but such changes are often impossible to predict. Two of the authors have been directly involved with attempts to nurture more open societies in Iran and

Culture and Social Change: Transforming Society Through the Power of Ideas, pp. 75–95

Afghanistan, and have witnessed the grave difficulty of this enterprise. Even when change does occur, it is not always clear why or how it occurred when it did. For example, there were dozens of programs to bring about change in India in the post-independence era (e.g., the "Barpali Experiment"—Fraser, 1968), but it is not clear why rapid and widespread change took off half a century later. Change related to national development is enormously important but almost completely neglected by Western psychologists (Moghaddam, Bianchi, Daniels, & Harré, 1999).

Traditionally, the "realist" perspective reigned supreme in national development circles, and positive change was assumed to be synonymous with material growth. The dominance of economics in discussions of national development continues (e.g., see Powell, 2007), but since the 1980s particularly the "human" component of development has been given attention (e.g., Haq & Kirdar, 1987), even by some leading economists (e.g., Sen, 1992). It has become clear that new buildings, roads, and bridges do not necessarily translate into progress in the quality of social, cultural, and political life—as reflected, for example, by the situation of Saudi Arabia and some other "oil rich" countries.

"Human development" has come to mean a number of different things. For example, some human development advocates make the point that in addition to the focus on "miles of paved roads," "number of hydroelectric power stations," and other such material criteria, national development must also involve changes in education, health, and social welfare (Goulet & Wilber, 1992). But beyond this, some researchers have proposed that national development is associated with cultural changes (Dube, 1988), and psychologists have argued that national development also involves changes in patterns of thinking and social relations (see readings in Blackler, 1983 and Carr & Schumaker, 1996; Sloan & Montero, 1990). Thus, by the end of the twentieth century there was a more concerted attempt by some psychologists to focus on psychological processes associated with national development.

The most direct intervention on the part of a psychologist in national development processes came through the work of McClelland on *need for achievement*, the personal motivations of individuals toward economic growth (McClelland, 1961; McClelland & Winter, 1969). McClelland's ideas influenced the use of vocational training based on personal goals for post-World War II era projects, primarily in developing countries. But follow-up assessments suggest that such 'bottom up' interventions are not often successful (Blunt & Jones, 1992). Critical assessment of the role of psychology in national development inevitably leads to explorations of the need for change in psychology itself.

CAUSAL VERSUS NORMATIVE CHANGE: REFLECTING BACK ON METHODS

The discussion of national development leads to a more detailed conceptualization of how change comes about. A major distinction is developed between types of change that are causally determined, and those that are normatively regulated. This distinction allows us to reflect back on the state of psychological science in the twenty-first century and to critically assess the assumption of causation in traditional experimental laboratory research. The vast majority of psychological studies are conducted using the laboratory method, and the percentage of studies using psychology undergraduates as participants has increased even in "cross-cultural" journals (Moghaddam & Lee, 2006). The laboratory method using Western undergraduate students to represent "humanity" is highly inappropriate for studying change processes, and it is telling that Reicher and Haslam (this volume) use a television "simulation study," and not laboratory experiments, as a point of departure for exploring change.

We expand the discussion beyond Reicher and Haslam's (this volume) conceptualization of change in three main directions. First, we provide a typology of change and locate Reicher and Haslam's discussion within this typology. Second, within the social identity framework, we argue that art is a centrally important but neglected means through which collective identities are transformed. The focus on art is in line with Reicher and Haslam, we argue, because the best way to make sense of the "BBC Study" is as a piece of drama (for a broader discussion of "experiments as drama," see Moghaddam & Harré, 1992). Third, stepping outside the social identity framework, we examine the role of what we believe to be the most important factor driving change in the contemporary world: technology.

Change: A Partial Typology

In order to better understand change from a psychological perspective, it is useful to first consider the relationship between the discipline of psychology and change. Western psychology has been described as *modulative*, because it emerged and took shape from the latter part of the nineteenth century as part of efforts to "manage" the social and psychological consequences of vast and rapid industrialization and modernization (Moghaddam, 1990). For example, industrial-organizational psychology developed in response to the needs of new industries, educational psychology and counseling emerged to cope with mass education needs, psychological testing and clinical psychology emerged to help cope with the psychological problems of life in new urban communities, war, and so on. In contrast, developing societies have need for a *generative psychology*, one that helps generate the appropriate type of change (Moghaddam, 1990). Thus, the relationship between psychology and change is itself a topic in need of more research attention. Because modern psychology is a product of, and dominated by, Western societies, it is "change" based on needs in Western societies that continues to dominate the discussion (Moghaddam & Taylor, 1986).

Building on the seminal text on change by Watzlawick, Weakland, and Fisch (1974), Moghaddam (2002) formulated a distinction between first-order, second-order, and third-order change. Each type of change takes place within the boundaries of existing sociopolitical conditions. The first type of change, first-order change, takes place in societies where social relationships are unjust and the informal and formal legal system supports unjust relationships. Dictatorships such as Iran and Saudi Arabia are typical of such societies, in which the legal system justifies unequal treatment of large segments of the population, such as women and religious and ethnic minorities, on the basis of their group memberships (of course, such "injustices" may well be integral to fundamentalist and sometimes traditional interpretations of major religions). The second type of change, second-order change, takes place in societies where the legal system has been reformed "on paper," but actual social relationships continue to be unjust. For example, prior to desegregation the United States Constitution, the Bill of Rights, and various other documents promised equal rights to all, but in practice African Americans, women, and various other minorities suffered severe discrimination. Finally, third-order change takes place within the framework of a sociopolitical system in which both actual social relationships and the legal system support just social relationships. Arguably, no society as yet meets these conditions, but the Scandinavian countries probably come closest.

The type of change possible is profoundly different within each of these three societies. First-order change is restricted to within groups, both by formal or "black letter" law, and by the informal social conventions that regulate behavior. For example, in the Islamic Republic of Iran women are prevented from enjoying equal status in legal courts (e.g., women cannot become judges), both because of restrictions set forth in formal law and according to the informal normative system (that is dominated by the masculine power elite). However, a woman can compete with other women and change her status within her gender group. Second-order change takes place mostly within groups, but occasionally it can also take advantage of formal law to force inter-group change. For example, even prior to the 1960s Civil Rights movement, African Americans managed to use "black-letter law" to force changes in the organization of education (as reflected in the famous *Brown vs. Board of Education* decision in 1954). Third-order change takes place both within and between groups, but this kind of open system is seldom achieved in practice.

Transformational Versus Within-System Change

Underlying this discussion of types of change is a foundational distinction between *transformational change*, which involves movement from one system to another, and *within-system change*, which involves change within the limits of the current system. For example, within-system change takes place when one dictator takes over from another within a dictatorship, or a crown-prince becomes king after his father within a hereditary monarchy. In these cases, the change in question sustains the political system (of dictatorship and hereditary monarchy). Revolutions often prove to be within-system changes, but when a revolution results in a movement from one political system to another, such as from dictatorship to democracy, then transformational change has taken place. Examples of transformational change, such as the change from feudalism to capitalism, are fewer (of course, we recognize that the units we are considering are very broad, and there are variations in how societies experience feudalism and capitalism). This typology leads us to the question of what drives change, and by what mechanisms change comes about. We begin with a discussion of how art influences social change, then argue that the methodology of the BBC Study itself is, in fact, an instance of *art-driven change.*

ART-DRIVEN CHANGE

Instances of human art tend to be consistent with social identity theory. In itself, art (like psychology) appears to be both generative and modulative, responding to the social needs of the society and also pushing boundaries and driving change generatively (see also Sayles, this volume). This dynamic is best understood in terms of meaning. Although the importance and nature of "art" varies by culture (Kalmanowitz & Lloyd, 2005), in all cultures art has a role in regulating change and manufacturing meaning.

Meaning and the cultural currency for change may stem not only from the artist's intentions for the artwork, but more powerfully, the interaction of audience interpretations and the social context. Consider for example, that after a 2004 performance of Diane Samuels's play *Kindertransport* during a run at the Octagon Theatre in Bolton, England, one elderly audience member was moved to reveal, for the first time in his life, that he, like the protagonist in the story, had been a kindertransport child.

The play tells the story of a small Jewish girl, Eva, who is sent to England as part of the infamous kindertransport movement, a transport network that smuggled Jewish children out of Germany between 1938 and 1939, unaccompanied by their parents. Eva grows up in England as Evelyn, and keeps her past a secret from her adult family and her daughter Faith. Through the events in the play, Faith discovers her mother's past, and unearths Eva's survivor's guilt as well as anger toward her parents for her abandonment (Samuels, 1995). In a similar fashion, Russian society was rocked by the publication of Aleksandr Solzhenitsyn's *The Gulag Archipelago* (1972-75). Using personal experience, meticulous research and detailed gathering of testimonies, Solzhenitsyn's monumental literary piece revealed the range of horrific situations experienced by Gulag prisoners for the first time, amidst a backdrop of history and ideology. *The Gulag Archipelago* represents the breaking of the silence that pervaded Soviet society. In such cases, witnessing art may instigate personal or collective change, drawing attention to group identity and reducing perceived emotional and social barriers to revealing identity or giving voice to particular narratives.

Ciarán Benson describes the personal impact of art in terms of "aesthetic absorption," where art restores and reimagines relationships by temporarily "taking us out of ourselves" (Benson, 2001, p. 177). In appreciating, participating in or creating art, a state of mind is achieved where there is no notion of "self"—the boundaries between what constitutes as "self" and "other" disappear ("being lost in thought") (Benson, 2001). Benson also distinguishes between the feelings invoked by viewing art that is an imitation of a situation, and the feelings invoked from the actual situation. For instance, when viewing a play where emotions are felt, "there is an emphatic difference between these feelings and their counterparts which I might feel when confronted with similar events in my own daily life. In the first instance, it would be utterly inappropriate for me to act upon my feelings (since this is *only* a play) whereas in the latter case it may be quite inappropriate for me not to act" (p. 188). However, in many cases, plays and other art forms *can* inspire real action. The arts can be seen as "vehicles through which immaterial, transcendent, even spiritual, concerns are revealed, and society as a continuing effort to attain them" (Askew, 2003, p. 610).

Understandably, repressive governments, conservative elements, and dominant groups in various Western and non-Western societies are therefore keen to control national artistic production, whether as a tool to produce political propaganda, or as a perceived threat to neutralize. The fact that artists are sometimes placed under house arrest, threatened, attacked, and sometimes assassinated—from British musician John Lennon to poet Anna Akhmatova to Danish cartoonish Kurt Westergaard—

only underscores that power of art to influence social identity and consciousness, particularly in the form of social commentary. Artistic protest in New York City against the Vietnam War, for example, included effective methods of raising collective awareness (Lippard, 1984). One example is Jeff Schlanger's poster from the 1970s depicting a man's hand extending from a business-suit sleeve, holding a lighter under a child's hand with the caption "Would You Burn a Child?" juxtaposed with an image of a Vietnamese child victim of napalm, captioned "When Necessary" (Lippard, 1987, p. 27). As art critic Lucy Lippard explains, art is "potentially provocative; it makes people think and feel in unexpected ways, focus on real life differently" (p. 34).

Not all art-driven change is explained by social identity theory, however. For example, art sometimes affects change through interaction with biological and physiological responses: war protest art often uses graphic, grotesque, or starkly human images that elicit visceral responses (Goldman, 1994, p. 252). Some types of change are prompted by the act of *creating* art, rather than by the artistic creations themselves. The discipline of art therapy is based on the premise that the alternative expression through artistic (often nonverbal) means can be a healing process (Lumsden, 1997). This can be applied to groups as well, when they engage in collective artistic enterprise such as community mural painting. The power of art to affect change is therefore not simply explained in terms of group differentiation and interactions between groups, but also physical and cognitive responses within individuals and groups.

Moreover, group differentiation does not fully account for the process by which certain symbols, images, and artifacts come to be selected and used. For example, the same work of art may define multiple movements or groups at once, in different places and eras, for different reasons. While the murals of Diego Rivera were created in the context of the Mexican revolution, they also became focal points for indigenous rights and culture, such as the Mexican Mural Renaissance (Goldman, 1994, p. 103). These different uses of art have led some artists to seek increased control over the presentation of their art (Lippard, 1987). Some of this change cannot be explained simply as the result of between-group behavior, but rather points to a broader array of psychosocial processes at play.

Theater and Social Commentary

In many cases, the power of art is to create space: not only imaginative space related to consciousness-raising, but also physical outlets for expression. One powerful illustration is the use of artistic expression in South

Africa during and after apartheid. Theater, music, and visual art played critical roles in both bringing down and upholding apartheid (Olwage, 2008; Peffer, 2009). Theater was a segregated enterprise, forcing a separate development of Black theater that revolved around apartheid discourse (Peterson, 1995). Theater was used as an outlet for protest, and later, resistance (Steadman, 1991). Plays could explore and protest pass laws, the Bantu Education (forced education of Blacks), forced relocations, police brutality, township life, as well as poverty, crime and alcoholism. From a social identity theory perspective, theatre was critical in forming a cohesive anti-apartheid group, exemplified in the last lines of Matsemela Manaka's play *Imbubmda:* "Imbumba, ma-Africa! Imbumba sizwe esimyana! (Unite, unite Africans! Unite Black Nation!" (Wakashe, 1986). However theatre was also one of the few forums in which mixed racial interaction took place, despite the risks. The theater that emerged from these sorts of interaction sought to educate the rest of South Africa and the world about coexistence and a united South African identity (Peterson, 1995). On the flip side, state theater was also very active in upholding the ideals of apartheid South Africa (Graver, 1999). Plays such as *Dingkaka* (1962), *Ipi Tombi* (1975) and *King Africa* (1987) depicted Africans as happy natives and apartheid as a policy of multiculturalism (Peterson, 1990). These plays included traditional African themes and initiatives to foster a sense of celebration of traditional Black culture, overlooking the oppressive government that sought to marginalize these very same traditional cultures (Peterson, 1990). However, leading up to the dismantling of apartheid in 1994, protest and resistance theater also became increasingly propagandistic, relying on apartheid stock-characters and situations which created formulaic, overused performances (Graver, 1999). Art as free expression became commodified and used as propaganda, creating sentimentality in repetition, a "closed loop of feeling" (Benson, 2001, p. 219; Goldman, 1994). Eavan Bolland has called this the "arts of reassurance," describing it as "the protective sense that not only need people not to change but that change itself is undesirable, indeed potentially a betrayal of self" (Benson, 2001, p. 219). Thus, art's power to influence change is not always progressive: some art sustains and defends the status quo.

Post-apartheid theatre struggled to remove itself from this sentimentality trap, and eventually succeeded in adopting new subject material, notably stories that emphasized South Africa as the "Rainbow Nation" (Larlham, 1991). The arts also aided in the national reconciliation process, bringing about healing and personal change with processes that were less institutionalized than the Truth and Reconciliation Commission (TRC). Indeed, several plays covered material from actual TRC testimonials. These plays brought emotionally charged stories to domestic and international audiences. Recalling Benson's loss-of-self that art induces, such performances allowed audiences to empathize with the characters (which were often based on true testimonials, or, in some cases, performed by the actual testifier) (Graham, 2003). While this emotional sharing might not result in outright action, it can contribute to within-person changes, as in the *Kindertransport* example, as well as within-group and between-group change by redefining an emotional landscape. From the perspective of national development, the success of the reconciliation process relies upon this redefinition: shifts from hatred to forgiveness, for example, after apartheid abuses.

In this context, the "BBC Study" is best understood as a piece of televised drama intended to *move* the viewer. The dramaturgical nature of the BBC Study leads us to reflect back on the appropriateness of traditional research methods for the study of social change.

Methodological Implications

An important strength of social identity theory (Tajfel & Turner, 1979, 1986) is that it directly addresses the issue of social change, generally neglected in psychology. For example, the theory postulates the conditions in which group members will attempt to take collective action in order to change the relationship of the in-group with out-group(s). Although some laboratory experiments have attempted to explore individual and collective action (Wright, Taylor, & Moghaddam, 1990), the 1-hour laboratory experiment is not at all suitable for exploring longer term change processes. The BBC Study is telling in that a dramaturgical method, rather than the traditional 1-hour experiment, is adopted to explore change.

Of course, a methodology for studying social change need not use theatre. Working within a social identity theory framework, Brown (1978) conducted 41 interviews over a 6-month period, exploring the impact of wage changes on relations between skilled labor groups at a large American aircraft engineering company. The study examined differentiation strategies using meaningful criteria provided by members of the production team (P) and the development team (D), including labor unions representing them. A third, tool servicing team (T), was also included as a go-between group, playing a complex supporting role to both P and D teams. Brown's analysis found evidence to support Tajfel's (1974) theoretical framework of group distinctiveness, along with evidence that failed to support Muzafer Sherif's (1966) theoretical framework for superordinate goals to unite groups. Brown's (1978) analysis was explicitly situated in cultural context, which included historical considerations of labor and wage relations between the groups under study over a 5-year period. He emphasized:

> It is not intended here to derive the sort of theoretical predictions that one might make prior to a laboratory experiment. The general lack of control over important historical and situational variables would render such an exercise pointless. Therefore, the following propositions are offered more in the way of aids to the interpretation of the data, rather than as precise hypotheses. (p. 410)

While clearly not a laboratory approach, Brown's methodology made the study's findings no less compelling. Indeed, any theory "oriented to social change" (p. 7) should consider relevant historical and social context, or what Muzafer Sherif (1966) called "the heavy hand of the past" (p. 29).

The complexities of social change processes mean that the most successful explorations of change have to step outside the traditional laboratory setting. In an analysis of group-based responses to social change in Russia and Mongolia after the collapse of the Soviet Union, Sablonnière, Tougas, and Lortie-Lussier (2009) propose an integration of relative deprivation theory (Crosby, 1976) and Tajfel's (1974) social identity theory. The authors review a growing body of literature from the social deprivation field, which traditionally includes in-group and out-group comparisons, suggesting that social change is associated with feelings of threat and measured (in terms of degree and pace) by collective relative deprivation (e.g., Beaton, Tougas, & Joly, 1996; Tougas, Sablonnière, Lagace, & Kocum, 2003). Sablonnière and colleagues administered questionnaires to 423 students (age 17-43, mean = 20) in Tyumen, Russia, including 70% women. The questionnaires assessed the degree and pace of social changes perceived, along with questions related to collective esteem, group identity and perceived relative deprivation compared to other groups. In Mongolia, the researchers surveyed 183 adults (age 23-71, mean = 38, 36% men) living in Ulaanbaatar, focusing on degree, pace, and valence of change, along with social collective relative deprivation. When change was perceived to be negative and rapid, participants reported feeling frustrated comparing their group's present situation to an estimated future condition. Such contributions to understanding psychological reactions to social change are difficult, if not impossible, to replicate through a traditional laboratory experiment. To illustrate, we turn to one of the most fundamental macrodrivers of social change: technology.

TECHNOLOGY DRIVEN CHANGE

To understand technology driven changes, we first outline three major theories of social evolution. Second, we focus on the power of technology to restructure social relationships and consciousness without group leaders, a key assumption about the nature of change in Reicher and Haslam's (this volume) discussion of social identity theory. There are two primary manners in which technology can influence ideological change: first, technology already in existence and widely available is used by a social movement to expand and formulate its reach; second, as technology is invented, it acts as a catalyst for new or emerging social movements.

Technology as Catalyst for Social Evolution

The word "technology" is derived from the Greek téchn? (τέχνη), meaning "craft," and is applied to a range of human capacities, from the ability to manipulate heat to make tools, ceramics, and weapons during the Neolithic Era (Shepard, 1980), to the capacity for agricultural food production beginning in the Mesolithic Era (Spencer & Stewart, 1973), to manufacturing abilities in the Industrial Revolution (Toynbee, 1884), to the printing press of the sixteenth century (Loach, 1986), to the ability to produce new knowledge in the Information Technology Revolution (Lyotard, 1984). Indeed, many social evolution theorists regard technological development as the primary driver behind social evolution (e.g., Lenski, 1966; Morgan, 1877; White, 1949). It has facilitated and precipitated radical social shifts. For example, advances in agriculture technology made unprecedented exponential population growth possible in the twentieth century (Kremer, 1993), the Gutenberg Printing Press facilitated the Protestant Reformation through wide-scale reproduction of religious and ideological texts (Loach, 1986), and advances in math and physics helped launch a "nuclear age" with the real possibility of species-wide self-destruction, creating the need for international peacekeeping institutions (Levite, 2009).

On some level, a history of the theories on technology-driven change is a history of theory about social progress, though not without critique (see, e.g., Adas, 1990). Social theorist Lewis Morgan (1818-1881) linked social and technological progress through a study of classic Greek and Roman Sources. Morgan (1877) traced the interplay between the evolution of technology with the evolution of family relations, property relations, advanced systems of governance, and intellectual development. He proposed three stages of social evolution: savagery, barbarism, and civilization, each marked by certain technological milestones. In context,

Morgan's work was within a debate between three nineteenth century theories of social and historical change: sociocultural evolution, the social cycle theory, and Marxist historical materialism (Harris, 1968). Each theory thought of technology as a driver of human evolution.

American anthropologist Leslie White (1900-1975) argued that Morgan's focus on specific technological inventions was too narrow. White grew up in a time of tremendous technological innovation, and witnessed a continued growth in use of natural resources, including gas, oil, and coal, to power new technology. In 1899, the Wright Brothers developed the first airplane. The Model T Ford was introduced when White was 8 years old. In 1898, French physicists Marie Sklodowska-Curie and Pierre Curie discovered a radioactive ore in uranium, raising hopes for the ability to harness energy contained at the atomic level (Rhodes, 1986). White proposed that the primary function of culture, as well as the measure of its advancement, is its ability to harness and control energy (White, 1943, 1949). "Other factors remaining constant," he argued, "culture evolves as the amount of energy harnessed per capita per year is increased, or as the efficiency of the instrumental means of putting the energy to work is increased" (White, 1949, pp. 368-369). Societies that capture more energy and use it more efficiently, according to White, have an advantage over other societies (Peace, 2004).

White's five stages of human development were based on these assumptions about advances in capacity for harnessing energy. The first stage is the use of muscles. In the second stage, energy from domesticated animals is harnessed, enabling long-distance travel by land and more advanced warfare, for example. The third stage is marked by the use of energy from plants, enabling the agricultural revolution. The fourth is the capacity to use energy from natural resources, such as coal, oil, and gas. The fifth is the capacity to harness nuclear energy (Peace, 2004). White published this model in the mid-twentieth century, before the Information Technology Revolution and Green Revolutions.

Garhard Lenski (1924-), on the other hand, published his theory of social evolution at the start of the Information Technology Revolution, then revised it to include ecological theory after the Green Revolution (Lenski, 2005). Lenski argued that White's stages neglect the history of communication, including the relationship between information and technology (Lenski, 1966). In Lenski's four-stage theory, cultural evolution depends upon the quantity of information and knowledge it has, and how that knowledge enables. Technological advances in Lenski's model correspond with advances in economic systems, political systems, distribution of wealth, social inequality, and other spheres of life.

Central in Lenski's model of social change is the history of advances in agricultural technology that have sustained population growth. Capacity for population growth, he argues, is a "profoundly destabilizing force throughout human history and may well be the ultimate source of most social and cultural change" (Lenski, 1987, p. 32). In a macrosociological analysis, technology can therefore affect social change in large scale social systems and populations without any regard whatsoever for between-group relations of the kind highlighted by Reicher and Haslam's account of social identity theory (following Lenski, 1982).

Restructuring Social Relationships

On a level of within-group, between-group, and within-person change, technology's primary contribution to social change is its power to restructure and, at least in some ways, increase flexibility in relationships. This restructuring takes place on three levels, ranging from the micro to the macro: (1) intra- and interpersonal dynamics, including the nature of self-organization; (2) relationships between groups, including conflict and warfare and the nature of economic, political, and cultural relationships; and (3) species-level self-awareness and coordination. This restructuring sometimes overlaps with, but is not encompassed by, social identity theory.

Theories of self-organization in human society range from the intrapersonal (e.g., Rogers, 1961) to the interpersonal (e.g., Luhmann, 1984/1995). The term "self-organization" was first introduced by psychiatrist W. Ross Ashby (1947), who defined the conditions of a "self-organized being" as one of internal causes and ends. Importantly, reliance on outside agency undermines—or at least transforms—self-organization:

> In such a natural product as this every part is thought as owing its presence to the agency of all the remaining parts, and also as existing for the sake of the others and of the whole, that is as an instrument, or organ.... The part must be an organ producing the other parts—each, consequently, reciprocally producing the others.... Only under these conditions and upon these terms can such a product be an organized and self-organized being, and, as such, be called a physical end. (pp. 125-128)

The term was soon adopted by other fields as autopoesis (self-organization) in computer science, particularly important in theories of artificial intelligence (AI) (Pask, 1962), as well as biology (e.g., Maturana & Varela, 1980). Later, Niklas Luhmann (1984/1995) would argue that self-organized systems reproduce themselves through self-production of communications. For Luhmann, the capacity for self-organization is a structural question. In his two-layered model, social consciousness and communication are separate structures that "interpenetrate" each other: human agents ("consciousness") are the environment for systems of social coordination ("communication") (Luhmann, 1984/1995, 1986, 2002). In other words, self-organization does not depend on social consciousness alone, which is the "hardware" of human agency, but rather on the structure of communication, the "software," as it were. In the context of globalization, social groups are increasingly faced with outside communications. The capacity for internal production of information increasingly competes with external production of information. According to Luhmann, a self-organizing system can reproduce itself as long as there is internal, dynamic production capacity.

On an intrapersonal level, however, self-organization is more complex. For example, in a multisensory society, the importance of rote working memory is diminished by ready availability of Internet on a wide array of devices. A British student need not memorize passages from the *Canterbury Tales*, or historic dates from British social history, for example, if she can just as easily Google them on her smartphone using satellite technology.

On an interpersonal level, technology changes the nature of communication, and therefore self-organization. For example older generations who did not grow up with the latest technological advances typically find it difficult to adjust to newer modes of communication. These gaps in generational exposure to technology sometimes cause older generations to be excluded from the production of communication. This weakens capacity for cross-generational socialization, whether between parents and children, or between older and younger generations broadly.

Beyond generational gaps, modern communication devices increase the degrees of freedom in exposure to external sources for socialization. A person in India can decide to become a Spanish-speaker without ever setting foot in a Spanish-speaking community, simply through use of language learning software and videos. A person can learn a trade based on online models without ever apprenticing with a tradesman. Not all influences are positive. A Pashtun youth in Pakistan can look at images of Western pornography using a cell phone, without ever actually meeting Westerners or understanding the cultural context of those images. People can learn to use cell phones, e-mail, and so on, relatively quickly, but need more time to be able to interpret the information and images carried to them by the new electronic communications systems.

The micro-macro rule of change proposes that the maximum speed of change at the macrolevel of political-economic-technological processes is faster than the microlevel of psychological processes (Moghaddam, 2008). Political, economic, and technical changes can take place very quickly. For example, economic and political policy can be changed overnight. New technologies can be introduced quickly. However, the pace of psychological adaptations to these changes tend to be slower. This gap tends to be smaller for younger generations, and larger for older generations.

The second level of technological influence, on relationships between groups, can be both unpredictable and dangerous. In the field of social conflict and warfare, for example, technology has rapidly increased global access to means for violence. This change includes the nuclear armament process of the Cold War in the twentieth century, but also the increased access to power through smaller weapons. For example, the participation of "child soldiers" in warfare depends, in large part, on the availability of AK-47s, Klashnikov guns, and improvised explosive devices (BB-IEDs) that they can carry on their bodies, despite being physically small and ill-equipped for hand-to-hand combat.

Significant shifts in economic relationships between classes, genders, and group identities can be attributed to technology. In Britain, for example, the boom of the Industrial Revolution caused new urban centers to form, creating pressures for electorate reform (Phillips & Wetherell, 1995). These changes led to the Reform Act of 1832, granting seats to new cities in the House of Commons, and taking seats away from boroughs in England and Scotland with small populations. In the process, the Reform Act increased the size of the voting electorate, shifting power away from the land-owning class to a rising class of industrialists (Warham, 1995).

In the twentieth century especially, opportunities for women to participate in the nonmaternal workforce have corresponded with shifts in labor economies from "brawn" to "brains." For example, while the distribution of labor during the Industrial Revolution emphasized strength and power, the resulting surplus of production and the need for specialized skills increased demand for women in service-oriented jobs (Burndette, 2008). By World War II, women in the United States were positioned to assume a wide array of service-oriented jobs. The overcapacity of preserved food production for soldiers after World War II was translated into home economics technology, reducing the amount of time required for cooking and household duties (Elias, 2008). Time surplus at home, in turn, enabled new possibilities for women to organize and work outside the home. Advances in contraception further enabled women to pursue careers and advanced education by through family planning (Riddle, 1999).

Leaderless Movements

Communication technologies have also transformed the nature of group leadership, to create leader-follower roles that are hinted at in the BBC Prison Study. Technology has enabled powerful, decentralized, self-organizing Peer-to-Peer Social Network Services (P2P-SNS) such as Facebook,

MySpace, Friendster, Orkut, and Google Buzz that do not depend upon a leader coordinating followers (Wang & Yaoru, 2008). Decentralized groups such as al-Qaeda use the Internet to recruit members without geographic proximity to them, while the same technology enabled individuals around the world to contribute millions of dollars to Haiti reconstruction after the 2010 earthquake. In effect, technology enables social groups and individuals to relate across long distances, also providing the ability to transport resources across cultural, economic, and political boundaries (Moghaddam, 2002).

The third level of technology-driven change is species-level coordination and self-organization. Technological developments in Western countries in the last two centuries have been parallel to major developments in international coordination, primarily among Western nations, including the Concert of Europe after the Napoleonic wars in the 19th century, the Inter-Parliamentary Union in 1889 and later, the League of Nations and United Nations. To govern armed conflict, nation states established international law through the Hague Conventions (1899 and 1907), and later, the Geneva Conventions following World War II. Advances in technology, including technology for warfare, communication, trade, and economic development, are driving consciousness across nation-states about the need for new means of self-organization and regulation for species-survival. In turn, increasing social consciousness can be a driver of technological development. The words of C. H. Tung, the first Chinese-appointed chief executive of Hong Kong in 1997, provide a useful example: "China was asleep during the Industrial Revolution. She was just waking during the Information Technology Revolution. She intends to participate fully in the Green Revolution" (Friedman, 2010). The metaphor of "waking up" is attributed to national group identity, China's "consciousness"; the cause of the revelation is attributed to past technological revolutions.

Changes in species group consciousness and self-organization can be seen in response to technology-enabled discoveries in science, health, and the treatment of diseases. The threat of transnational, transcontinental spread of diseases and epidemics has created the need for international, coordinated understandings of pathology, containment, and treatment. From ancient discoveries about human anatomy, to Louis Pasteur's discovery of germs in the mid-nineteenth century using his microscope, scientific understandings have often changed or supplemented group-specific understandings of pathology (Diamond, 1997). Superstitions around the pathology of HIV/AIDS may vary across groups at the level of villages, for instance, but international responses to HIV/AIDS uses a coordinated scientific narrative about its origins and treatments.

CONCLUSION

In Western societies, modern psychology evolved as a means of trying to modulate the consequences of rapid change. However, the research methods of modern psychology, particularly the "one hour laboratory experiment" that dominates the field, are not well suited to understanding change processes, or generating the kind of national development change much needed in low-income societies. In the context of art- and technology-driven change, we find the power of the televised, studio-based production of the BBC Prison Study to "change minds" unsurprising: it uses experimental theater rather than experimental psychology. Reicher and Haslam (this volume) have made a valuable contribution by demonstrating, once again, that the dramaturgical approach has considerable potential for influencing change, and that psychologists should give more importance to this approach. Developing dynamic methods of studying and understanding change, in nonlaboratory context, will be a challenge for the next generation of psychologists.

Our discussion also suggests that psychologists should pay more attention to the role of art and also to technology in change processes. Change associated with art and with technology can and often does influence social identity, as part of a far broader impact on individual and collective processes. In these cases the "motor" for change is not identity, initially at least. The monumental changes brought about by electronic communications systems have impacted social relationships in virtually all regions of the world, including how collective movements take place in both Western and non-Western societies, ranging from the *eswarms* in the "leaderless" immigration protests since 2008 in the United States, to the use of electronic texts and images by participants in the prodemocracy Green Movement in Iran today. Indeed, global social conditions and movements have changed radically, yet traditional laboratory methods have failed to predict them.

ACKNOWLEDGMENTS

We are grateful to Rom Harré for comments made on an earlier draft of this chapter.

REFERENCES

Adas, M. (1990). *Machines as the measure of men: Science, technology, and ideologies of Western dominance*. Ithaca, NY: Cornell University Press.

Ashby, W.R. (1947). Principles of the self-organizing dynamic system. *Journal of General Psychology. 37*, 125-128.

Askew, K. M. (2003). As Plato duly warned: Music, politics, and social change in coastal East Africa. *Anthropological Quarterly, 76*, 609-637.

Beaton, A. M., Tougas, F., & Joly, S. (1996). Neosexism among male managers: Is it a matter of numbers? *Journal of Applied Social Psychology, 26,* 2189-2203.

Benson, C. (2001). *The cultural psychology of self.* London: Routledge.

Blackler, F. (Ed.). (1983). *Social psychology and developing countries.* Chichester, England: Wiley.

Blunt, P., & Jones, M. L. (1992). *Managing organizations in Africa.* Berlin, Germany: De Gruyter.

Brown, R. (1978). Divided we fall: An analysis of relations between sections of a factory workforce. In H. Tajfel (Ed.), *Differentiation between social groups* (pp. 395-429). London: Academic Press.

Burndette, J. (2008). *Gender, work, and wages in Industrial Revolution Britain.* New York, NY: Cambridge University Press.

Carr, S. C., & Schumaker, J. F. (Eds.) (1996). *Psychology and the developing world.* Westport, CT.: Praeger.

Crosby, F. (1976). A model of egoistical relative deprivation. *Psychological Review, 83*, 85-113.

Diamond, J. (1997). *Guns, germs, and steel: The fates of human societies.* New York, NY: W. W. Norton.

Dube, S. C. (1988). Cultural dimensions of development. *International Social Sciences Journal, 40,* 505-511.

Elias, Megan (2008) *Stir It Up: Home Economics in American Culture.* Philadelphia, PA: University of Pennsylvania Press.

Fraser, T. M., Jr. (1968). *Culture & Change in India: The Barpali experiment.* Amherst, MA: University of Massachusetts Press.

Friedman, T. (2010) "Who's Sleeping Now?" *The New York Times,* p. 10.

Goldman, S. M. (1994) *Dimensions of the Americas: Art and social change in Latin America and the United States.* Chicago, IL: The University of Chicago Press.

Goulet, D., & Wilber, C. K. (1992). The human dilemma of development. In C. K. Wilber & K. P Jameson (Eds.), *The political economy of development and underdevelopment* (5th ed., pp. 469-477). New York, NY: McGraw-Hill.

Graham, S. (2003). The Truth Commission and post-apartheid literature in South Africa. *Research in African Literatures 34,* 11-30.

Graver, D. (1999). *Drama for a new South Africa.* Bloomington, IN: Indiana University Press.

Haq, K., & Kirdar, U. (Eds.) (1987). *Human development, adjustment, and growth.* Islamabad, Pakistan: North-South Roundtable.

Harris, M. (1968). *The rise of anthropological theory: A history of theories of culture.* New York, NY: Crowell.

Kalmanowitz, D., & Lloyd, B. (Eds.). (2005). *Art therapy and political violence:* with *Art, without illusion.* New York, NY: Routledge.

Kremer, M. (1993). Population growth and technological change: One million B.C. to 1990. *Quarterly Journal of Economics. 108*, 681-716.

Larlham, P. (1991). Theatre in transition: The cultural struggle in South Africa. *The Drama Review, 35*, 200-211.

Lenski, G. (1982). *Human societies: An introduction to Macrosociology*. New York, NY: McGraw-Hill.

Lenski, G. (2005). *Ecological-evolutionary theory: Principles and applications*. Boulder, CO: Paradigm.

Lenski, G. E. (1966). *Power and privilege*. New York, NY: McGraw-Hill.

Lenski, G., & Lenski, J. (1987). *Human societies*. New York, NY: McGraw-Hill.

Levite, A. E. (2009). Heading for the fourth nuclear age (Proliferation Papers). Paris: Institute Francais des Relations Internationales.

Lippard, L. R. (1984). *Get the message? A decade of art for social change*. New York, NY: E. P. Dutton.

Loach, J. (1986). The Marian Establishment and the Printing Press. *English Historical Review, 101*, 135-148.

Luhmann, N. (1995). *Social systems* (J. Bednarz & D. Baecker, trans.) Palto Alto, CA: Stanford University Press. (Original work published in 1984).

Luhmann, N. (1986). The autopoiesis of social systems. In F. Geyer & J. v. d. Zouwen (Eds.), *Sociocybernetic paradoxes* (pp. 172-192). London: SAGE.

Luhmann, N. (2002). How can the mind participate in communication? In W. Rasch (Ed.), *Theories of distinction: Redescribing the descriptions of modernity* (pp. 169-184). Stanford, CA: Stanford University Press.

Lumsden, M. (1997). Breaking the cycle of violence. *SAGE Journal of Peace Research, 34*, 377-383.

Lyotard, J.-F. (1984). *The postmodern condition: A report on knowledge*. London: Manchester University Press.

Maturana, H. R., & Varela F. J. (1980). *Autopoiesis and cognition: The realization of the living*. Dordecht, Netherlands: D. Reidel.

McClelland, D. C. (1961). *The achieving society*. Princeton, NJ: Van Nostrand.

McClelland, D. C., & Winter, D. G. (1969). *Motivating economic achievement*. Glencoe, IL: Free Press.

Moghaddam, F. M. (1990). Modulative and generative orientations in psychology: Implications for psychology in the Three Worlds. *Journal of Social Issues, 56*, 21-41.

Moghaddam, F. M. (2002). *The individual and society: A cultural integration*. New York, NY: Worth.

Moghaddam, F. M. (2008). *Multiculturalism and intergroup relations: Implications for democracy in global context*. Washington, DC: American Psychological Association Press.

Moghaddam, F. M., & Harré, R. (1992) Rethinking the laboratory experiment. *American Behavioral Scientist, 36*, 22-38.

Moghaddam, F. M., & Lee, N. (2006). Double reification: The process of universalizing psychology in the Three Worlds. In A. Brock (Ed.), *Internationalizing the history of psychology* (pp. 163-182). New York: New York University Press.

Moghaddam, F. M., Bianchi, C., Daniels, K., & Harré, R. (1999). Psychology and national development. *Psychology and Developing Societies, 11*, 119-141.

Moghaddam, F. M., & Taylor, D. M. (1986). What constitutes an "appropriate" psychology for the developing world? *International Journal of Psychology, 21*, 253-267.

Morgan, L. H. (1877). *Ancient society*. London: MacMillan.

Olwage, G. (Ed.). (2008) *Composing apartheid: Music for and against apartheid*. Johannesburg: Wits University Press.

Peace, W. (2004). *Leslie A. White: Evolution and revolution in anthropology*. Lincoln, NE: University of Nebraska Press.

Peffer, J. (2009). *Art and the end of apartheid*. Minneapolis, MN: University of Minnesota Press.

Peterson, B. (1990). Apartheid and the political imagination in Black South African Theatre. *Journal of Southern African Studies 16*, 229-245.

Peterson, B. (1995). "A Rain a Fall but the Dirt it Tough": Scholarship on African Theatre in South Africa. *Journal of Southern African Studies 21*, 573-584.

Phillips, J. A.. & Wetherell, C. (1995). The Great Reform Act of 1832 and the political modernization of England. *The American Historical Review, 100*, 411-436.

Powell, B. (Ed.). (2007). *Making poor nations rich: Entrepreneurship and the process of economic development*. Stanford, CA: Stanford University Press.

Pask, G. (1962). A proposed evolutionary model. In H. von Foerster & G. W. Zopf (Eds.), *Principles of self-organization*. New York, NY: Pergamon Press, New York.

Rhodes, R. (1986). *The making of the atomic bomb*. New York, NY: Simon & Schuster.

Riddle, J. M. (1999). *Eve's herbs: A history of contraception and abortion in the West*. Harvard MA: Harvard University Press.

Rogers, C. (1961). *On becoming a person: A therapist's view of psychotherapy*. London: Constable.

Sablonnière, R., Tougas, F., & Lortie-Lussier, M. (2009). Dramatic Social Change in Russia and Mongolia: Connecting relative deprivation to social identity. *Journal of Cross-Cultural Psychology, 40*, 327-348.

Samuels, D. (1995). *Kindertransport*. London: Nick Hern Books Limited.

Sen, A. (1992). *Inequality reexamined*, Oxford, England: Oxford University Press.

Shepard, R. (1980). *Prehistoric mining and allied industries*. New York, NY: Academic Press.

Sherif, M. (1966). *Group conflict and cooperation: Their social psychology*. London: Routledge and Kegan Paul.

Sloan, T. S., & Montero, M. (1990). Psychology in the Third World: A sampler. *Journal of Social Issues, 46*, 1-165.

Solzhenitsyn, Aleksandr (1973) Arkhipelag Gulag, 1918–1956: Opyt knudozhestvennego issledovaniia. Paris: YMCA-Press.

Spencer, J. E., & Stewart, N. R. (1973). The Nature of Agricultural Systems. *Annals of the Association of American Geographers, 63*, 529-544.

Steadman, I. (1991). Theater beyond apartheid. *Research in African Literatures, 22*, 77-90.

Tajfel, H. (1974). Social identity and intergroup behaviour. *Social Science Information, 13*, 65-93.

Tajfel, H., & Turner, J. C. (1986). The social identity theory of inter-group behavior. In S. Worchel & L. W. Austin (Eds.), *Psychology of intergroup relations*. Chigago, IL: Nelson-Hall.

Tajfel, H., & Turner, J. C. (1979). An integrative theory of intergroup conflict. In W. G. Austin & S. Worchel (Eds.), *The social psychology of intergroup relations*. Monterey, CA: Brooks-Cole.

Tougas, F., de la Sablonnière, R., Lagacé, M., & Kocum, L. (2003). Intrusiveness of minorities: growing pains for the majority group? *Journal of Applied Social Psychology, 33*, 283-298.

Toynbee, A. (1884). *Lectures on the Industrial Revolution in England*. Waterloo Place, London: Rivingtons.

Wakashe, T. P. (1986). "Pula": An example of black protest theatre in South Africa. *The Drama Review, 30*, 36-47.

Wang, F., & Yaoru, S. (2008). Self-organizing peer-to-peer social networks. *Computational Intelligence, 24*, 213-233.

Warham, D. (1995). *Imagining the middle class: The political representation of class in Britain, c. 1780-1840*. Cambridge, England: Cambridge University Press.

Watzlawick, P., Weakland, J. H., & Fisch, R. (1974). *Change: Principles of problem formation and problem resolution*. New York, NY: Norton.

White, L. A. (1943). Energy and the evolution of culture. *American Anthropologist, 45*, 335-356.

White, L. A. (1949). *The science of culture: A study of man and civilization*. New York, NY: Grove.

Wright, S. C., Taylor , D. M., & Moghaddam, F. M. (1990). Responding to membership in a disadvantaged group: From acceptance to collective protest. *Journal of Personality and Social Psychology, 58*, 994-1003.

PART II

COMMUNICATING CHANGE

CHAPTER 6

METAPHOR AND STORIES IN DISCOURSE ABOUT PERSONAL AND SOCIAL CHANGE

L. David Ritchie

Barack Obama campaigned on the theme of "change," and as the first African American to win the U.S. Presidency he embodies changes of historical and cultural importance. Central among the changes Obama advocates is his attempt, throughout his campaign, to depart from the "old politics" and keep racial issues in the background. However, at a crucial point in the campaign he was forced to confront these issues when a potentially damaging controversy erupted over a series of comments, widely regarded as unpatriotic, made by his personal friend and spiritual adviser, the Reverend Jeremiah Wright. How Obama dealt with this crisis is a prime example of the role of metaphor and stories in discourse about change, both in promoting and in dealing with change.

According to the standard rationalist prescription, Obama would have been expected to reason with his critics and refute their accusations. A *logical* argument would lay out the issues to be decided in the form of propositions with truth-conditions or questions that can be answered by such propositions.[1] But Obama did not use conventional logic, and he did not spin out explanatory theories or refute alternative theories about the incident (Kuhn, 1991). Obama told stories, and he wove them together with a series of powerful, emotionally-charged metaphors. Using this and other

Culture and Social Change: Transforming Society Through the Power of Ideas, pp. 99–118

examples of public and private discourse, in this essay I argue that the nonpropositional aspects of language use is as important as "content," and that the perceptual, imaginative, emotional, and relational nuances of language use can reveal at least as much about the role of communication in social change as the propositional aspects.

A different sort of crisis, also related to the role of "change agent," confronted then British Prime Minister Tony Blair during the early stages of the 2005 Parliamentary election, when he faced the risk of an intraparty split over his policies that might have cost Labour the election. Here also, the prescriptions of logical argumentation would have called for propositions and rebuttals, theories, and counter-theories. But Blair also chose stories and metaphors, some of them playful, humorous, and whimsical (Ritchie, 2008). In place of reasoned arguments, in his speech to the 2005 Labour Party Conference at Gateshead Blair mixed and transformed familiar metaphors, he told amusingly quaint stories, and Labour won the election.

A crisis of political and cultural change confronted Jo Berry and Pat Magee in a more traumatic and intensely personal way. After her father was killed by a bomb planted by Magee (acting as a member of the IRA), Berry went on a self-described "journey of understanding," seeking to "walk in the footsteps of the bombers" and, when Magee was released in a prisoner exchange, sought him out and engaged him in a series of personal conversations (Cameron, 2007). Here again, traditional views of language and discourse would call for something more like a debate—an exchange of evidence-based facts, views, and carefully reasoned arguments. But here also, what actually occurred was an exchange of stories and metaphors. In her insightful analysis of these conversations, Cameron shows how Berry and Magee overcame their "alterity," their deep political and emotional differences, through use, repetition, and transformation of metaphors and stories to achieve mutual empathy and understanding and to build a relationship of trust and respect.

The subtitle of this volume, *Transforming Society Through the Power of Ideas*, carries a suggestion of *big* changes, brought about through *bold* ideas. In this reading, the role of communication might include transmitting information and ideas and persuading people to adopt and respond to these ideas, replacing previous ideological structures with new ones. All of this would be consistent with a traditional view of language as a *code* in which this kind of information transmission and persuasion is accomplished, and a view of discourse as a chain of facts and opinions expressed in the form of propositions.

I would not deny the value of what Bruner (1987) calls the "paradigmatic" mode of thinking, rational argument based on clear expression of evidence and views, either at the national and global level of politics and institutions or at the more intimate level of interpersonal relationships. However, it does appear from the examples briefly described above, and from examples I will discuss later in this essay, that a complete account of the way people use language in creating or resisting, adapting to or controlling change cannot stop with the propositional aspects of language. A complete account must also address the subtler and possibly more complex uses of language in stories and metaphors—and in word-play, humor, irony, and other examples of what Wilson and Sperber (2004) call "loose" language use. In brief, I will suggest that "narrative" is at least as important as the "paradigmatic" expression of ideas in bringing about and dealing with social change.

In this essay I focus less on the code-like and more on the interactive and relational aspects of language and communication. I focus not only on the large-scale public processes of social and cultural transformation but also on the more intimate, often quite personal processes through which people promote, resist, or accommodate change as they manage their everyday social realities. I analyze discourse about change as it occurs in casual, ordinary conversations as well as in political speeches and organized public events. I approach language use from a cognitive and interactive perspective, and show how attention to the patterns of story-telling, metaphor use and transformation, language play and humor can contribute to our understanding of change-based and change-related discourse.

A COGNITIVE AND INTERACTIVE MODEL OF LANGUAGE

As mentioned in the preceding, Bruner (1987) drew a sharp distinction between what he called the *paradigmatic* or logico-scientific mode of thought and the *narrative* mode, and claimed that these are mutually irreducible. However, Barsalou (1999) demonstrated that it is, in principle, possible to explain even abstract (*paradigmatic*) logic in terms of "perceptual simulations"[2] (by incorporating *introspective* perception of one's own mental processes), thus contradicting Bruner's claim that the two are irreducibly separate. Glenberg (2008) argues that the brain evolved primarily to control action, and produces extensive experimental evidence that language comprehension involves the simulation of action. Other evidence suggests that the computational demands of living in large, complex social groups may have been a more important factor in the evolution of large brains (e.g., see Dunbar & Schultz, 2007). Based on his research with individuals for whom reasoning was separated from emotion because of brain damage, Damasio (1995) argues that emotion is neither coincidental nor antithetical, but an essential part of effective reasoning.

Other evidence suggests that, whatever might be theoretically desirable, people do not naturally engage in the kind of paradigmatic argument advocated by Bruner. In a field experiment testing people's ability to construct and refute alternative explanations of common occurrences, Deanna Kuhn (1991) discovered that the only participants who could reliably satisfy her a priori expectations for constructing an argument, even within their own fields of expertise, were advanced doctoral candidates in philosophy (for detailed discussion see Ritchie, 1994, 2003). In research on political advertising, Cappella and Jamieson (1994) have shown that the verbal content of ads is overwhelmed by the effect of accompanying images.

Traditional code/propositional models of language and associated linear models of communication have recently been challenged from several perspectives. Wilson and Sperber (2004) point out that virtually all language is "loose" in the sense that meanings of words and phrases are underdetermined and require interpretation according to their relevance in a specific context. The fundamental ambiguity of language limits the precision of communication but at the same time greatly increases the expressive power of language. Based on this assessment, Wilson and Sperber claim that metaphor is but an extreme example of this fundamental ambiguity and is processed in exactly the same way as any other language (see also Wilson & Carston, 2006).

Lakoff and Johnson (1980; Lakoff, 2008) argue that metaphors observed in language use are manifestations of underlying *conceptual* metaphors, which develop from associations within perceptual experience and provide the basis for abstract conceptual thought. Lakoff and Johnson claim that commonplace expressions (often regarded as "*dead*" metaphors) such as "a *warm* relationship," "a *close* friend," or "a *big* problem" all originate in and provide evidence of correlations between physical sensations (physical warmth and proximity, perceived size) and more abstract concepts (love and friendship, problem solving).[3] Lakoff and Johnson, along with various collaborators, have identified hundreds of verbal metaphors which, they claim, instantiate underlying conceptual mappings of this sort. Of particular importance are groups of metaphors based on common experiences such as TRAVEL, CONSTRUCTION, and CONFLICT[4] (in addition to those already mentioned).

Gibbs (2006; see also Lakoff, 2008) argues that both metaphorical and literal uses of language activate *simulations* based on *schemas* (interconnected sets of perceptual and motor experience). For example, the word *fire* activates simulations of a set of visual, tactile, and audial perceptions associated with combustion, and the word *up* activates simulations of visual and perhaps visceral perceptions of vertical motion. When we read or hear a metaphorical use of a word, as for example "prices are going *up* again," we experience a *conceptual blend* in which *prices* are understood in terms of *objects* that are in *vertical motion*.[5] Gibbs (1994, 2006; Gibbs & Matlock, 2008) reviews extensive experimental evidence in support of this claim.[6] The idea of simulations goes beyond the conventional idea of imagination: in perceptual simulation, the neural circuits that would be fully activated by direct perception of *fire* or *vertical motion* are partially activated by encountering these concepts in language, either literal or metaphorical (Barsalou, 2007).

Barsalou (2007) acknowledges that language, including metaphorical language, is sometimes processed in terms of connections to other words and phrases (see, e.g., Kintsch, 1998; Landauer & Dumais, 1997). However, he argues that deeper processing of language (and more complex reasoning) is accomplished through perceptual simulations, the partial activation of the same neural groups that would become active in direct perception.[7] Given the constraints of cognitive capacity, the perceptual simulations experienced during language processing and during thought in general are always incomplete (it is easy to imagine, or simulate, the perceived shape of a zebra and its pattern of stripes—but not to count the stripes). Which aspects of a concept are experienced is largely determined by what is most salient in the present context (cf. Giora, 2008; Sperber & Wilson, 1986, 2008).[8]

Metaphors in Obama's Speech

When Obama characterized Reverend Wright's language as "*incendiary*" and referred to the ensuing controversy as a "*firestorm*," according to conceptual metaphor theory hearers would actually experience Wright's language *as* a fire, based on the underlying conceptual metaphor, PASSION IS HEAT. This is a common and familiar conceptual metaphor, expressed in poetry and music[9] as well as everyday usage (e.g., "That *burns me up*"). Perceptual simulations activated by these metaphors are accomplished through partial activation of the neural circuits that would be fully activated by actual perceptions of intense fire. By repeating the metaphors based on FIRE and HEAT, Obama reinforced the underlying conceptual metaphor, intensifying and probably extending the experienced simulations. For some of his listeners, this phrasing may also have evoked other connections with *fire* (both semantic and perceptual), including the biblical allusion used as a title by African American writer James Baldwin, "*The Fire Next Time*," as well as the race riots of the late 1960s that spawned the slogan, "*burn, baby, burn*." Obama picks up the related HEAT metaphor in the phrase "*seared into my genetic makeup*," a phrase that also has the potential to evoke emotionally intense connections with the practice of branding slaves with hot irons.

Obama used repetition and transformation of common metaphors extensively, including metaphors based on JOURNEY. At the beginning of his "*campaign*," Obama set the task to "*continue the long march* of those who *came before* us." The use of this metaphor potentially links the campaign to the *literal* "freedom marches" of the Civil Rights movement as well as to the more conventional "*march of progress*" metaphor. Asserting the need for unity, Obama observes that "we may not have *come from the same place*,[11] but we all want to *move in the same direction*." Referring to the temptation to ignore "the issues that have *surfaced* … that we've never really *worked through*," Obama asserts that "if we *walk away* now … simply *retreat into our respective corners*,[12] we will never be able to *come together* …"

Cameron (2007, 2008) argues that this kind of repetition and transformation of metaphors provides clues to the speaker's underlying patterns of thought and reveals the processes through which the conversation is managed and relationships between participants are developed. In her analysis of the "reconciliation dialogues," Cameron shows how Jo Berry's use of the JOURNEY and HEALING metaphors are picked up, repeated, and transformed by Pat Magee as a sign of his growing empathy for Berry. Cameron argues that Berry's acceptance of Magee's use of metaphors originally introduced by her signals a change in their relationship.

Stories

Examples like those in the previous section illustrate a common but little-discussed aspect of metaphors: They often have the potential to activate *dynamic* schemas, invoking incomplete simulations of familiar stories. I have already alluded to the historical stories that may be activated by some of Obama's metaphors; some of these are drawn from the history of the Civil Rights Movement, some from shared U.S. history. In the reconciliation dialogues, Jo Berry's expression of her wish to "*walk in the footsteps of the bombers*" may remind hearers or readers of relevant aspects of the intersecting stories of the IRA terror campaign and Berry's own search for understanding and healing.

Many of the metaphors in Blair's speech also imply stories. When Blair said he would "welcome lost friends *back into the fold*" he referred to a story about shepherds that has powerful Christian resonance. The choice of Gateshead, in Blair's home district, for the Labour Party conference and Blair's long reference to it early in his speech potentially activated a powerful story of (literal and figurative) "*homecoming*."

Obama also used location to evoke shared stories. He delivered the race speech in Philadelphia's Constitution Center, and quoted from the Preamble to the U.S. Constitution, thereby invoking the shared national story. The phrase, "more perfect union," captures an ideal of perfection as an ideal to work toward, not a state to be achieved for once and for all, an ideal Obama invoked later in the speech by strategic reuse of "*perfect*" in a similarly non-literal sense. Obama immediately invoked a second episode in the shared national history with his paraphrase and transformation of the opening lines of Lincoln's Gettysburg Address, "Two hundred and twenty one years ago ... a group of men ... *launched* America's *improbable experiment* ..."[12] Thus he brought together the central themes of the Civil War and the Constitution which together provided a political and historical (as well as emotional) context for this speech about race relations—and for both bringing about the kind of transformations he sought, and helping his listeners to accept and embrace these transformations.

STORIES AND MEMORY

Schank and Abelson (1995) claim that stories are the primary medium of memory: How we tell something is how we remember it. Their first formulation of this idea implied that the first telling of a story in effect fixes *that* version as the way it is remembered, but they subsequently admitted that different versions of the same story can exist in parallel, and that retelling of the story from a different perspective or in response to a different social situation can alter the way it is remembered. Schank and Abelson do not address the implications of this theory for collective storytelling as a way of establishing and transforming collective memory but their overall account is entirely consistent with Sperber's (1996) ideas about the formation of "cultural representations" through repetition and refining of a common story.

Pasupathi, Weeks, and Rice (2008) describe remembering and retelling as an important process in adult development, both for accomplishing transitions throughout adult life and for accomplishing developmental tasks specific to later life. They include within these developmental functions the maintenance and reinforcement of bonds within intimate relationships that are important throughout adulthood but especially later in life. Pasupathi et al. identify three broad functions of remembering and retelling: those associated with the teller's sense of self, those associated with relationships with others, and those associated with problem solving and goal-achievement. Like Schank and Abelson, Pasupathi et al. emphasize the individual level but their analysis also carries important implications for the collective level of groups and communities, the level at which social transformation is accomplished and encountered. These implications will become particularly evident in a later section in which I analyze a conversation among a group of neighbors about the role of sociability in maintaining a climate of public safety within a rapidly changing urban environment.

After setting the stage by blending the story of the founding of the nation, "two hundred and twenty one years ago," with the story of Lincoln and the Civil War and the story of the present occasion in which he was speaking, Obama proceeded to tell the story of his own Presidential candidacy. This allowed him to set the story of his relationship with Reverend Wright and of the controversy over Wright's language in the context of both the national story and his personal story. He then reframed the Wright story in terms of the Civil Rights story, and the justifiable anger of African Americans at the history of discrimination and deprivation.

Having responded to the controversy over Reverend Wright through a combination of historical and personal themes, Obama turned to stories about ordinary working-class White people, and asserted that *their* anger is also justifiable. This assertion was quite important because, in retelling the familiar stories of enslavement and racial discrimination, Obama ran the risk that different segments of his *national* audience would understand and respond to the stories in different and mutually contradictory ways. By explicitly acknowledging the justified anger of working-class Whites, Obama converted a potentially divisive theme into a potentially uniting theme. He then fused these parallel sets of generic stories into a single story of the current political and economic crisis, linking this composite story to his Presidential campaign, and closing with a final, intensely personal story about two volunteers in his campaign. By retelling these stories and blending them into a single coherent story, he made what was previously "the Black story" and "the White story" become "the American story"; "my" story and "your" story become "our" story—which is one of the fundamental transformations he hoped to bring about.

Jo Berry and Pat Magee were involved in a similar integrative endeavor but on a much more personal level: They were brought together by a single act of violence situated within a long and complex national story. While this act of violence represented a single story it was understood very differently by each of them. Their primary purpose was to "listen to each other's story," and thereby to understand the dual nature of the single story, so it could be blended into one complex and multifaceted story.

STORIES AND PERCEPTUAL SIMULATIONS

Stories are themselves frequently metaphorical, in the broad sense that they lead hearers, or more accurately teller and hearers together, to experience one story or situation in terms of another. Thus, when Blair said, "where we have *lost* old friends, we try to persuade them to *come back to the fold*," he drew on a story that was very likely familiar to most members of his audience ("Jesus is the *good shepherd*"), a story that already had strong metaphorical overtones, and reapplied it in a layered metaphor ("Tony Blair is the *good shepherd*.")

In a more complex example, after reflecting on the early years of his Prime Ministership, Blair alluded to recent intraparty disputes over the Iraq war and other policy issues, then launched into another story: "all of a sudden there you are, the British people, thinking: you're not listening and I think: you're not hearing me. And before you know it you *raise your voice*. And *I raise mine*. Some of you *throw a bit of crockery*. And now you, the British people, have to *sit down* and decide whether you want *the relationship to continue*." Through this metaphorical story Blair reexpressed genuine political differences in terms of a marital spat, with many instantiations in popular culture. This metaphorical story may have worked both to trivialize political objections and to create a shared enjoyment of the humorous image. By retelling the story of the political disagreements as a story of marital dispute—and potential reconciliation—Blair also established a new set of shared memories as the basis for renewed unity. The policy differences could potentially be thereby 'forgotten' or at least suppressed.

The amusing aspect of the "*throwing crockery*" story highlights another important function of language, the creation and reinforcement of social bonds through shared pleasure. Robin Dunbar (1996) refers to this process metaphorically as "*grooming*."

Language and Social Bonding

Noting that about 65% of all talk, among both men and women, is about relationships, and not necessarily concerned with "content" or the accomplishment of informational "tasks" as traditionally construed, Dunbar (1996) argues that language fulfils two fundamentally social purposes, which he labels "grooming" and "gossip." "Grooming," in Dunbar's view, serves an extension and amplification of the social grooming behavior observed in most other primates, that serves to build and maintain "coalitions" necessary for individual animals to maintain their position in the social hierarchy. Conversation can comfortably take place among as many as four people, but it is possible for an animal to groom only one other animal at a time. Hence the substitution of language for grooming greatly increases the size of potential social networks, and enables humans to achieve and maintain much larger primary groups. "Gossip," in Dunbar's view, complements "grooming" by providing information about others' relationships, and about the social behavior of other members of the group (Who is grooming whom? Who can be trusted? Who is a fink?)

The "grooming" view proposed by Dunbar is consistent with the obvious fact that humans, everywhere, take pleasure in conversation. We enjoy talking, and we enjoy hearing other people talk. We especially enjoy listening to other people who talk well, who tell interesting stories and make funny quips—people who entertain us. The shared enjoyment of talk, very likely experienced physiologically as the release of endorphins, may contribute to bonding by associating our conversation partners with pleasure.

Dunbar's account is largely speculative and controversial,[13] but it is evident that people *do* get pleasure from talk, and often engage in talk when there is no evident information-transfer need ("Fine weather we're having, isn't it?"). Given Dunbar's estimate that about 2/3 of our time is spent talking about relationships or building and maintaining relationships through talk, the expression of paradigmatic propositions may not be nearly as important as traditional models of language use imply, and the shared enjoyment of interesting stories, metaphors, and humor may be much *more* important, a central rather than incidental function of language use. Extending this argument, Ritchie and Dyhouse (2008; see also Fazioni, 2008) show that apparently frivolous language play, including novel and apparently meaningless metaphors as well as humor and teasing, may serve important relational functions simply by virtue of the shared pleasure they give speaker and audience.

From this perspective, the corny humor in Blair's "*crockery throwing*" story played a crucial role in the speech. It must have been difficult even for his disgruntled critics to avoid at least a bit of a chuckle in response to the story, to avoid getting at least a bit of pleasure from the story. This bit of corny humor reinforced the impression that much of the speech was not about propositional "content" or arguments at all—it was about "*grooming*," pure and simple. Blair's metaphors and metaphorical stories very likely activated powerful perceptual imagery, and no doubt many listeners could not help experiencing pleasure as they processed these images (*guilty* pleasure perhaps, for some in the audience). Experiencing the same perceptual imagery, and experiencing at least a mild bit of enjoyable humor together, the audience strengthened and renewed their bonds with each other—and with Blair. Only then, with the bonds re-established, did Blair proceed to the more conventional campaign rhetoric—listing the party's campaign promises and excoriating the policies proposed by the opposition.

MANAGING SOCIAL TRANSFORMATION AT A PERSONAL AND COMMUNITY LEVEL

Thus far I have focused primarily on the kind of cultural and political transformations of which epic novels and multivolume histories are made. But people also confront change in the course of their everyday lives, as hopes and dreams materialize or fail to materialize, opportunities emerge or vanish, personal and professional roles change and familiar institutions mature or disappear. In this section I will analyze a conversation in which a group of neighbors used story-telling, thematic metaphors, and occasional bits of humorous teasing both to understand and to reinforce the sense of community that underpins the stability and safety of their neighborhood. Four residents of a single block in a middle-income neighborhood of Portland, Oregon, a midsized city in the Pacific Northwest region of the United States, were invited to discuss concerns about crime and policing. It quickly became clear that the participants had little interest in the topic of policing and more interest in affirming and reinforcing their shared sense of neighborliness and community. In part, the participants were responding to general changes in the composition of the surrounding city and the neighborhood itself, in particular to changes associated with the natural succession of generations in their own neighborhood.

Throughout the conversation, several themes were woven together in a series of metaphors, metonyms, and stories. A central theme of *watchfulness* drew on a metonym, "*eyes on the street*," adapted from urban theorist Jane Jacobs's (1961) classic study of the social matrix of urban neighborhoods. This theme was connected with *sociability*, *mutual caring*, and *children as a resource* in several passages. Consistent with Bayley (1994) and Reed (1998), the primary focus throughout most of this conversation about public safety was not on the role of police agencies, but on the local community, the role of private citizens, both individually and in their ordinary communicative interactions, in maintaining a sense of public safety, and the implications of public safety for everyday activities and particularly for the activities of children.

Some of the stories focused on the contrast between this community and other, less "safe" communities, but many of them focused on the shared history of this community itself, and on affirming the importance of children to the vitality of the community. These stories served (1) to create and perpetuate a consensus about sociability as a basis for the mutual watchfulness that assures the safety of the neighborhood, (2) celebrate "the block" as a place to live that is both socially and physically *comfortable*, and (3) affirm intergenerational solidarity. Intergenerational solidarity was asserted by stories that affirmed the stake of older, childless couples in maintaining the street as a safe place for the children and by stories that affirmed the children themselves as sources of interest and pleasure, as sources of activity that reward the attention and watchfulness that renders the street and the neighborhood safe for them.

Although only one participant in the conversation has children, much of the conversation revolved around children. Children figured both as markers of public safety, a kind of "indicator species" for the health and safety of the community, and as a focus of sociability and watchfulness, sources of interest and liveliness that attract and reward adult attention, and (referring to the older children who live on the next block over) as additional "*eyes on the street*." Thus, children are not only vulnerable people to be protected but also valued resources to be enjoyed, made welcome, and retained in the community: In every instance in which children were mentioned, the vocal tone was warm and affectionate.

Several of the stories described how the four sets of parents on the block collaborate in supervising—and entertaining—their children. Speaking for the other childless participants, Rich asserted that "it's not just the ^parents^[14]... I mean it's the *rest of* us." A few minutes later, Leanne reinforced this idea with a story of her own about walking home from the bus-stop when the kids are home from school, and "they're ^out there^ *having* fun ... and I can talk to them and visit ... walking to our house ..." This segment continued with an account (produced collaboratively with Todd) of how the four sets of parents trade off responsibility for watching the children. From Leanne's story it is evident that the children 'out there having fun' are a source of enjoyment to her. The fact that Todd (the one parent in the group) collaborated with her in telling the story suggests that the exchange successfully produced a "shared reality" (Higgins, 2003).

Leanne made her enjoyment of the children on the street even more evident in a passage, ten minutes later, in which she described an interaction with one of the children who live near the end of the block:

> I was walking *down* the street .. she was sitting there she .. she^ jumps up^ and she said .. I said How are you she said .. Today was the ^first day^ of ^first ^grade^^! ^and it was just ^wonderful^^! And she had on this .. this ^black^ leotard and white tights and little shoes .. and she said .. ^and^ I'm going to be going to ^dance class^ now .. and ^*after*^wards my dad is going to take me to the ^park^ and it's like the ^best^ day of my ^life^! eh heh! .. and she was ^literally^ bouncing up .. and .. down .. I mean she could not ^stay still^ .. she was so excited ... that was just ... ^wonder^ful .. you know? it was just ^fantastic^ to be able to live on a street where you can ^see that^ every day.

Through this and other stories, related in tones of affection and amusement, Leanne and the other childless participants made it clear that they see the presence of young children in the neighborhood as adding value, both because of the social relationships they crystallize and because of their contribution to the liveliness of the street. On the surface, these stories were told to instantiate the sense of security and sociability, and the relationship between sociability and security. But they also appear to have been part of a strategy of building and maintaining the integration of the young families in the community, and securing the continued commitment of the four sets of parents, with Todd as a surrogate, to the neighborhood. More generally, by sharing these pleasant stories, the participants in the conversation strengthened their own social bonds (Dunbar, 1996) and reinforced a shared understanding of the neighborhood as a friendly, safe, and stable environment.

Building and Maintaining Mutual Commitment

The stories, metaphors, and occasional bits of teasing all served to establish, attest, and maintain the mutual understanding that the sociability and mutual caring described in various ways. The childless members of the group used affectionate stories about watching the children, and occasional teasing of Todd for his apparent "over-protectiveness," to establish that children are welcomed and valued, and to reinforce the commitment of the families on the block, as a way of maintaining the values of sociability and mutual stability. Talk about the annual block party (in which the street is closed off for the afternoon and evening while neighbors gather to share food and drink), a metonymic reification of "*The Block*" as a special place, and the recounting of other conversations about the neighborhood all reinforced the shared vision of "*The Block*" as a community of mutual caring and "*watchfulness*." It appears that these metaphorical and metonymic themes, and to an even greater extent the stories told by various participants, fit within a conscious rhetorical strategy of accomplishing and maintaining the sociability and mutual commitment that participants recognized, early in the conversation, as the basis for the sense of safety and security they all enjoy. In brief, the web of stories, metaphors, metonyms, and good-natured teasing was constructed collaboratively as a strategy of maintaining the stability and cohesion of this neighborhood as a mutually protective social unit in the face of change—both the change of generations within the neighborhood and the larger-scale changes in the surrounding city. Some of this may be evident in the informative "*content*" of the discourse,[15] but it is much more evident in the emotional and perceptual dimensions of the stories, metaphors, and teasing that dominated the conversation.

THE ROLE OF NONPROPOSITIONAL TALK IN DISCOURSE ABOUT SOCIAL TRANSFORMATION

At each level—societal, community, and individual—change requires adjustments to what is known and believed, to "knowledge." Part of this knowledge takes a paradigmatic or propositional form, for example, "the difficulties experienced by many African-Americans can be traced to the history of slavery and ante-bellum segregation," "if the Labour Party engages in intra-party feuding we will lose the election," "effective communication with the public and with policy-makers is necessary in order to maintain continued funding for science," and "casual socializing with neighbors helps maintain mutual watchfulness and contributes to safety from crime." But much of the knowledge takes the form of stories about the past, about how things are done in the present, and about hopes and plans for the future. Much of it takes the form of imaginative re-creation of events and experiences, stimulated by repetition of metaphors and stories. And much of it takes the form of inter-personal relationships, a sense of who can and cannot be trusted, feelings of mutual enjoyment, commitment and obligation.

I have shown how this *non*propositional basis for dealing with change is constructed, not through arguments, facts, and reasoning but through metaphors, stories and humor. Obama repeated the old *dividing* stories and metaphors in a way that blended them into new *uniting* stories and metaphors. Blair repeated Biblical stories and blended them with the more particular stories of his years as Prime Minister, then contrasted the blend with a comic story of domestic altercation to highlight the importance and the possibility of unity. The neighbors repeated shared stories of everyday interactions in their neighborhood in the new context of a discussion about public safety as a way of giving new meaning to their sociability and reinforcing their mutual commitment to the community. In each case, understanding the discursive processes and their relationship to the problems and opportunities associated with social change requires attention, not merely to the propositional content of the language, but also to the imagined or simulated experience of perceptions and emotions associated with the metaphors, stories, word-play and teasing.

Conversely, focusing on the propositional "content" and ignoring the simulations (schemas, perceptions, emotions, etc.) and semantic links to other knowledge that are activated by strongly expressive language can contribute to overly simplistic analysis of public discourse. An example occurs in Jensen's (this volume) account of the firing of comedian Bill Maher because of comments made shortly after the September 11 attacks on the World Trade Center. In response to a statement in which President Bush called the attackers "cowards," Maher said "We have been the cowards, lobbing cruise missiles from 2,000 miles away. That's cowardly. Staying in the airplane when it hits the building, say what you want about it, it's not cowardly." According to Jensen's analysis, Maher was the victim of "corporate censorship" resulting from the withdrawal of sponsorship, apparently at least partly in response to "vaguely menacing" statements by White House press secretary Ari Fleischer.

Considering only the propositional content, Bush's statement does seem preposterous, and Maher's remarks seem reasonable. Holding oneself back from personal danger is indeed closer to the conventional definition of "cowardly" than putting oneself in personal danger—even when the intent in the latter case is manifestly both homicidal and suicidal. Bush's use of the word in this context is contradicted by the "dictionary definition" of *cowardice*, and Maher's remarks were consistent with that definition. But when the schemas and emotions activated by the words and phrases are taken into account, things get more complicated. The context, a nation and in particular the families of thousands of victims who were still in the early stages of grieving, must also be considered: The ideas and emotions associated with President Bush's words (however ineptly chosen) were quite consistent with the emotional response to an unprovoked attack on noncombatants engaged in routine daily activities. As such, Bush's words were intended to be, and were in fact comforting not merely to the families of the victims but also to the millions of others who shared their shock and grief.

Conversely the ideas and emotions associated with Maher's words (however *logically* apt) implied *praise* for the attackers and *censure* of the victims. At the time they were spoken, they were like pouring salt in raw wounds. Contrary to the implications of Jensen's analysis, it was not merely the White House Press Secretary and the "Corporate Fat Cats" who controlled ABC's advertising revenues who were offended. Maher's comments were not "politically incorrect" so much as they were emotionally insensitive. It may be possible to construct an argument that this incident exemplifies corporate censorship, but to be convincing, it would be necessary to consider how the associated ideas and emotions interacted with the full context. By focusing on the propositional definition of "cowardly" and ignoring the associated ideas, images, and emotions activated by the uses of the word in this particular context, Jensen's analysis misses an important part of the underlying dynamic.

On the other hand, analysis of associated ideas, images, and emotions supports other aspects of Jensen's analysis. Jensen quotes then White

House press secretary Ari Fleischer's "cautionary and vaguely menacing statement: 'they're reminders to all Americans that they need to watch what they say, watch what they do. This is not a time for remarks like that.' " Here, the *propositional* content does not seem particularly menacing—it is literally true that a time of mourning is *not* the time for praising the attackers. Fleischer's remarks, however, have the potential to activate schemas of "secret police" eavesdroppers, "informers," and "enemies lists" dating back to the Cold War and the Nixon Presidency, and even beyond to 1950s "Red-baiting." It is these associated simulations and schemas, not the propositional content, than render Fleischer's remarks menacing.

It is manifestly true that corporate power is often used to censor views that are either politically unpopular or merely damaging to corporate interests, and censorship may have been a factor here—it certainly seems evident that Bush was already laying the propaganda groundwork for his subsequent war-making and for his outrageous expansion of Presidential power. But there is also a case to be made that Maher's unfeeling remarks, *at the time when he made them,* fit within the widely-accepted "shouting fire in a crowded theater" and "fighting words" exceptions to the principle of free speech. Considering the context and the simulations as well as the propositional content of Maher's remarks, the case can made that Maher deserved censure for the emotional and relational effects of his comments and that his firing from ABC was a reasonable response to his emotional insensitivity. In brief, a complete account of an incident of this sort must include attention to the perceptual simulations, the associated ideas, images, and emotions, as well as to the propositional content of what is actually written or spoken, and in many cases the perceptual simulations may be by far the more important.

CONCLUSION

I have argued for attention to the perceptual and imaginative, the emotional and relational implications of language as well as to the paradigmatic or propositional "content" of discourse related to social change, and for attention to change at the level of individual relationships and small-scale communities as well as at the level of nations and large-scale cultures. I have shown how attention to the non-propositional aspects of language can be at least as revealing as attention to the propositional aspects. Patterns of metaphor use and transformation and patterns of story-telling and transformation are particularly revealing, as is the playful or humorous distortion of familiar metaphors and stories. The transformation and transmission of *ideas* (in propositional form) and the presentation of paradigmatic evidence in well-structured logical arguments is of undoubted importance, but I have argued that the building and reinforcement of relationships and interpersonal commitments through language use is of no less importance. Understanding processes of social transformation at any level requires attention to these interpersonal and relational aspects of society, which in turn require attention to the nuances of language in discourse, both the grand discourse of politicians and thinkers and the casual conversations of ordinary people as they go about their lives.

Politicians are frequently criticized for relying on stories and metaphors instead of paradigmatic reasoning and "well-formed arguments." It is evident from recent press reports of the "moot court" style debates in Obama's cabinet meetings that he is perfectly capable of this style of discourse. But it also seems quite evident that, had he addressed the American voters in that vein on March 18, 2008, with a list of well-formed arguments demonstrating the legitimate basis for Jeremiah Wright's anger toward the United States government and the rightness of his own loyalty to Reverend Wright, he would have lost the election, and the transformations brought about by his election would have been deferred, possibly for another decade or longer. What I hope to have shown in this essay is that metaphors and stories and the perceptual simulations and emotions they activate, the changes in shared memories they bring about, have an important part in the processes of social and cultural transformation—and in our understanding of those processes.

NOTES

1. What Bruner (1987) calls the *paradigmatic* mode of thought, in contrast to the *narrative* mode that characterized the bulk of Obama's speech.
2. The partial activation of the same neural groups that would become active in direct perception or action; perceptual simulation will be discussed in greater detail in a later section of this essay.
3. Notation: I use the convention of marking metaphorical phrases by placing the metaphorical elements in italics and the entire phrase within quotation marks. I refer to the concept that is described or expressed by the metaphor—for example the quality of a relationship—as the "*topic*" of the metaphor, the metaphorical words or phrase—in this case, "*warm*" or "*close*" – as the "*vehicle.*" Following the convention used in the journal, *Metaphor and Symbol,* I put the broader concept underlying the vehicle in small caps, e.g., AFFECTION IS PHYSICAL WARMTH.
4. Throughout this essay I will follow Lakoff and Johnson's inclusive definition of metaphor as experiencing (or expressing) one kind of thing as or in terms of another—thus, "*warm* relationship" is understood as metaphori-

cal because *affection* is experienced in terms of *physical temperature* (see Zhong & Leonardelli, 2008).

5. Lakoff and Johnson (1980) claim that we actually experience prices *as* objects and inflation *as* vertical motion.
6. Lakoff and Johnson include highly-conventionalized or *"dead"* metaphors such as *"big"* problem and *"close"* relationships within this explanation. For criticisms of their position see for example Glucksberg and McGlone (1999), Murphy (1996), and Vervaeke and Kennedy (1996).
7. Direct perception includes *interoception*, perception of one's own bodily state, and *introspection*, perception of one's own thoughts and emotions. As noted in the preceding, abstract reasoning, according to Barsalou, is accomplished through these introspective simulations of cognitive experience.
8. Resolving the question of the relative importance of paradigmatic logic, emotion, and perceptual simulation in cognition is beyond both the scope of this essay and the author's competence. The purpose here is rather to argue for the importance of metaphors and narratives for understanding the actual discursive processes through which people bring about, resist, and accommodate to social change and transformation.
9. A good example is Peggy Lee's masterful version of *Fever*, in which the *"coolness"* of her voice contrasts with and thus emphasizes the *"heat"* of her passion.
10. "we may not have *come from the same place*" can be interpreted literally as well as metaphorically—Obama *comes from* Indonesia and Hawaii as well as Chicago, his mother and grandmother *came from* Kansas, and his father *came from* Kenya. His later reference to relatives "scattered across three continents" reinforces a literal reading.
11. This is clearly a boxing metaphor as well as a MOTION and SEPARATION metaphor.
12. These phrases allude to the opening lines of Lincoln's Gettysburg Address: "Four score and seven years ago our fathers brought forth on this continent, a new nation, conceived in Liberty ..."
13. Dunbar's theory is supported by observed correlations between brain size and the size and complexity of social groups in many mammal and bird species, but it can also be criticized as biological reductionism
14. Transcription: Pauses are indicated by two dots if brief, three dots if longer. Use of louder voice for emphasis is indicated by carets. Thus, in "^best^ day of my ^life^" *best* and *day* are spoken in a louder voice than the other words.
15. One example of propositional content came late in the conversation when one of the participants explicitly cited Jane Jacobs (1961) in support of claims about the importance of a street-centered social life.

REFERENCES

Barsalou, L. W. (2007). Grounded cognition. *Annual Review of Psychology, 59*, 617-45.

Barsalou, L. (1999). Perceptual symbol systems. *Behavioral and Brain Sciences, 22*, 577-609.

Bayley, D. H. (1994). *Police for the future*. New York, NY: Oxford University Press.

Bruner, J. (1987). *Actual minds, possible worlds*. Cambridge, MA: Harvard.

Cameron, L. J. (2007). Patterns of metaphor use in reconciliation talk. *Discourse and Society, 18*, 197-222.

Cameron, L. J. (2008). Metaphor shifting in the dynamics of talk. In M. S. Zanotto, L. Cameron, & M. C. Cavalcanti (Eds.), *Confronting metaphor in use: An applied linguistic approach* (pp. 45-62). Amsterdam: John Benjamins.

Cappella, J. N., & Jamieson, K. H. (1994). Broadcast adwatch effects: a field experiment. *Communication Research, 21*, 342-365.

Damasio, A. R. (1995). *Descartes' error: Emotion, reason, and the human brain*. New York, NY: Quill.

Dunbar, R. (1996). *Grooming, gossip, and the evolution of language*. Cambridge, MA: Harvard.

Fazioni, O. (2008). *The role of humor and play in a workplace interaction*. Portland, OR: Portland State University.

Gibbs, R. W., Jr. (1994). *The poetics of mind: Figurative thought, language, and understanding*. Cambridge, England: Cambridge University Press.

Gibbs, R. W., Jr. (2006). Metaphor interpretation as embodied simulation. *Mind and Language, 21*, 434-458.

Gibbs, R. W., Jr., & Matlock, T. (2008). Metaphor, imagination, and simulations: Psycholinguistic evidence. In R. W. Gibbs, Jr. (Ed.), *The Cambridge handbook of metaphor and thought* (pp. 161-176). Cambridge, England: Cambridge University Press.

Giora, R. (2008). Is metaphor unique? In R. W. Gibbs, Jr. (Ed.), *The Cambridge handbook of metaphor and thought (*pp. 143-160*)*. Cambridge, England: Cambridge University Press.

Glucksberg, S., & McGlone, M. (1999). When love is not a journey: What metaphors mean. *Journal of Pragmatics, 31*, 1541-1558.

Glenberg, A. M. (2008). Toward the integration of bodily states, language, and action. In G. R. Semin & E. R. Smith (Eds.), *Embodied grounding: Social, cognitive, affective, and neuroscientific approaches* (pp. 43-70). Cambridge, England: Cambridge University Press.

Higgins, E. T. (2003). Achieving "shared reality" in the communication game: A social action that creates meaning. In A. W. Kruglanski & E. T. Higgins (Eds.), *Social psychology: A general reader* (pp. 431-444). New York, NY: Psychology Press.

Jacobs, J. (1961). *Death and life of great American cities*. New York, NY: Random House.

Kintsch, W. (1998). *Comprehension: A paradigm for cognition*. Cambridge, England: Cambridge University Press.

Kuhn, D. (1991). *The skills of argument*. Cambridge, England: Cambridge University Press.

Lakoff, G. (2008). The neural theory of metaphor. In R. W. Gibbs, Jr. (Ed.), *The Cambridge handbook of metaphor and thought* (pp. 17-38). Cambridge, England: Cambridge University Press.

Lakoff, G., & Johnson, M. (1980). *Metaphors we live by*. Chicago, IL: University of Chicago Press.
Landauer, T. K., & Dumais, S. T. (1997). A solution to Plato's problem: The latent semantic analysis theory of acquisition induction, and representation of knowledge. *Psychological Review, 104*, 211-240.
Murphy, G. (1996). On metaphorical representation. *Cognition, 60*, 173-204.
Pasupathi, M., Weeks, T., & Rice, C. (2008). Reflecting on life: Remembering as a major process in adult development. *Journal of Language and Social Psychology, 25*, 244-263.
Reed, W. E. (1998). *The politics of community policing: The case of Seattle (Current Issues in Criminal Justice, Vol 25)*. New York, NY: Routledge.
Ritchie, L. D. (1994). Objectivity, doubt, and the two cultures. *Journal of Communication, 44*(1), 65-72.
Ritchie, L. D. (2003). Uncertainty and the fragmentation of knowledge. In B. Dervin & S. Chaffee (Eds.), *Communication: A different kind of horse race. Essays honoring Richard F. Carter.* Cresskill, NJ: Hampton Press.
Ritchie, L. D. (2008). Gateshead revisited: Perceptual simulators and fields of meaning in the analysis of metaphors. *Metaphor and Symbol, 23*, 24-49.
Ritchie, L. D., & Dyhouse, V. (2008). Hair of the frog and other empty metaphors: The play element in figurative language. *Metaphor and Symbol, 23*, 85-107.
Schank, R. C., & Abelson, R. P. (1995). Knowledge and memory: The real story. In R. S. Wyer (Ed.), *Knowledge and memory: The real story* (pp. 1-86). Hillsdale, NJ: Lawrence Erlbaum Associates.
Sperber, D. (1996). *Explaining culture: A naturalistic approach*. London: Blackwell.
Sperber, D., & Wilson, D. (1986; 1995). *Relevance: Communication and cognition*. Cambridge, MA: Harvard University Press.
Sperber, D., & Wilson, D. (2008). A deflationary account of metaphors. In R. W. Gibbs, Jr., (Ed.), *The Cambridge handbook of metaphor and thought* (pp. 84-105). Cambridge, England: Cambridge University Press.
Vervaeke, J., & Kennedy, J. M. (1996). Metaphors in language and thought: Falsification and multiple meanings. *Metaphor and Symbolic Activity, 11*(4), 273-284.
Wilson, D., & Carston, R. (2006). Metaphor, relevance and the "emergent property" issue. *Mind & Language, 21*, 404-433.
Wilson, D., & Sperber, D. (2004). Relevance theory. In L. R. Horn & G. Ward (Eds.), *The handbook of pragmatics* (pp. 607-632). Oxford, England: Blackwell.
Zhong, C.-B., & Leonardelli, G. J. (2008). Cold and lonely: Does social exclusion literally feel cold? *Psychological Science, 19*, 838-842.

CHAPTER 7

THE EARTH, OLYMPUS, AND THE COMMUTER BUS

Carlos Cornejo

I mostly agree with the main thesis of L. D. Ritchie in his chapter, namely that nonpropositional aspect of language use is critical to understand the role of speech in promoting social change. Consequently, I will not try to raise criticisms of what seems to me is true in essence. Instead, I will extend Ritchie's thesis by providing a philosophical framework to better understand the primacy of propositional language in modern psychology. From this framework, the consequences of the point of view he defended will be more evident.

Let me first summarize the arguments presented in his paper. By means of real life examples taken from public discourses, Ritchie convincingly shows that metaphor, stories, and other nonpredicative forms of using language have a strong influence in promoting social change. Metaphors would invoke "perceptual simulations" (in the sense of Barsalou, 1999) more clearly than literal language, often with emotionally intense commitment. Although "conceptual metaphors" (in the sense of Lakoff & Johnson, 1980) are part of perceptual simulations, these include many other semantic and experienced contents. Moreover, argues Ritchie, metaphors have the potential to activate dynamic schemas, invoking partial or incomplete simulations of familiar stories. It is not only an underlying support—conceptual or perceptual—of what is activated by the metaphor,

Culture and Social Change: Transforming Society Through the Power of Ideas, pp. 119–124

but also a general setting to generate new associations and entailments not directly indicated by the expression. Usually, the activated dynamic story is socially shared and emotionally charged, contributing to reinforcing a feeling-based bond that unites people of a certain community. Ritchie underscores that social transformations induced by metaphors and stories operate simultaneously at personal and social levels: possibilities of perception and action induced by given language uses are experienced individually, as well as being observable within communities.

Although I subscribe to most of the preceding statements concerning metaphors and stories, I would like to give closer attention to propositional language, which was not the focus of Ritchie's analysis. While all the statements concerning the role of metaphor in social change are true, experienced simulations may still be understood as phenomena limited to special language uses, typically performed by politicians and rhetoricians. Ritchie's position about this issue is that

> nonpropositional aspects of language use is as important as "content," and that the perceptual, imaginative, emotional and relational nuances of language use can reveal at least as much about the role of communication in social change as the propositional aspects. (Ritchie, this volume, p. 100)

I suggest extending Ritchie's analysis of the embodied functioning of metaphorical expressions to what he calls the "propositional aspect of language use." Since its very beginning as a scientific discipline, Psychology has inherited metaphysical concepts, coming from Epistemology, whose logical existence drastically contrasts with its psychological implausibility. This is the case of the distinction between propositional and non-propositional aspects of language, or, put in psychological terms, between literal and figurative language.[1]

THE CANONICAL VIEW OF LANGUAGE COMPREHENSION

Most psychologists agree with the canonical view of language comprehension. Following this conception, language comprehension requires the processing of the propositional content of the sentences heard or read. This process demands syntactic parsing and lexical knowledge to decode the content of the words and morphemes. The end of this process is the apprehension of the propositional content in the sentence. In some special cases, for example, in real conversations, it can be the case that this propositional content collides with the real context where this proposition is used (e.g., ironies, jokes, and metaphors). In that case, additional processing is required. Then, the cognitive system seeks another interpretation, contextually adequate, temporarily suspending the literal meaning. The description of this second processing is the task of the discipline called pragmatics. As a consequence, the literal meaning or propositional content is logically and temporally prior to any other meaningful interpretation, for example, the metaphorical meaning. Therefore, the cognitive system always expects the literal language as the "default mode" of language use.

Note that the proposition a sentence is transmitting is a result of the composition of several information pieces—the word meanings, whose literality is considered an intrinsic property. Literal meanings and proposition are not a construction of the human mind, but part of an objective structure. The "proposition" is therefore a meaningful unity whose sense does not depend on the language users; they can access them when they correctly use the language. A proposition describes a possible state of the world (e.g., the fact that there is a cat on a mat, or that it rains), but its existence transcends its use. It is irrelevant whether the proposition *The cat is on the mat* is used by a fisherman or by a zookeeper. The propositional content is the same in both cases, just because propositions and literal meanings are not *uses* of language: they are properties of segments of the language *structure*. "Literal meaning" is something that words *hold*, not the resultant process of a subjective act of understanding (Cornejo, 2004). "Proposition" and "literal meaning" emerges as necessary categories when we reflect on the truth conditions of language sentences. They are important items of the epistemological lexicon, used by philosophers of mind performing metaphysical inquiries. But, for the same reason, they are not descriptions of communicative human actions.

Similarly, the very concepts of "sentence" and "word" come from linguistics, not from psychology. The same as the philosophical "proposition" and "meaning" (in the sense of "literal meaning"), "sentence" and "word" are distinctions that follow from an analytical exercise made upon *written* language, not from the observation of language in the moment of its *use*. As a matter of fact, no person emits propositions nor utters sentences; people produce *utterances*. Of course the latter can be analyzed according to whatever criterion, for example, identifying phonemes, words, syntactic phrases or propositions. But this is not equivalent to saying that persons present those units to each other when they communicate. To suppose that when we talk we activate words and literal meanings is a categorical error that leads to a myriad of unsolvable problems. A recent example is the problem of combining linguistic and gesture meaning: Do we have two meaning systems—linguistic and corporal—that combine at some point in sentence processing? Similar puzzles arise when confronting literal meaning versus figurative meaning, lexical knowledge versus world knowledge, semantics versus pragmatics, and propositional content versus nonpropositional aspects of meaning.

Proposition and literal meaning are instruments for solving metaphysical questions, particularly this: How is true knowledge possible at all? They are part of the language of philosophy of mind. Meanings and propositions are also pieces of the Olympus of transcendental entities. They were not developed to be placed in the brain of any particular man, but just to function as representations of an abstract epistemic agent, namely the transcendental subject. However, *human* meaning, which people feel and have in mind, is existent only in real persons. What psychologists *should* investigate is to be found in real interactions occurring on the Earth, where every linguistic unit is an *expression*, before being encrypted by (psycho-)linguists and philosophers into analysis units. Human language is always action. On real interactions, nonused language simply is an oxymoron. It just cannot exist.

THE COMMUTER BUS

Problems of seeing proposition as a model of human comprehension of language are evident whenever we take modes of using language from daily life. The more expressive the utterance, the more inadequate seems the canonical view. This is why metaphor is always a problem for the canonical view of language: Metaphor is a mode of language use, not a deviant mode to put the building blocks of the language structure. A metaphor acquires its entire sense only in the real interaction where it takes place. Its complete sense cannot be reconstructed by means of the static meaningful pieces of semantics. As with many others modes of language use, metaphor has been conceptualized in semantic terms, that is, seeking its richness in the interplay of predefined categories. Usually, this attempt never goes very far (see Cornejo, 2007; Shanon, 1988), basically because metaphor is a phenomenon of the discourse, not of segments of discourse (Ricoeur, 1978). Therefore the *context* of use is fundamental to constitute a metaphor as such (Leezenberg, 2001).

Derrida (1978/2001) noted that *metaphorikos* is the Modern Greek word to design "means of transportation." We can use this remark to say that, in more general terms, the metaphor is in fact transportation, which commutes us from the Olympus of transcendental entities to the living forms of the Earth. Whenever we use metaphors we are transported from the static meanings of the semantics to the living meanings of real interactions. Metaphor is a form of using language and its sense is to be found precisely in the situation of language use. If static meanings are utilized to understand what a metaphor means, its ultimate sense will not be found, not mention its aesthetic value. This is why the metaphorical sense cannot be completely reverted in literal meanings:

> I hold that the endless character of what we call the paraphrase of a metaphor springs from the fact that it attempts to spell out what metaphor make us notice, and to there is no clear end ... I would say the same for any use of language. (Davidson, 1978/2001, p. 263)

Thus, metaphor moves the meaning from the world of perennial entities to the *Lebenswelt*. By revealing that its sense is well understood only in consideration of the conditions and context of use, the metaphor flagrantly evidences that supposing static semantic contents is not the appropriate way to approach the phenomenon of using language.

CONCLUSION: METAPHOR AS A WINDOW TO KNOWLEDGE

Psycholinguists have thought of language as if it were all written language (Olson, 1994). Inserting pieces of language structure to understand language use corresponds to the scientific tendency to reify human verbal expression in objective items. As a consequence, every verbal expression would contain a "propositional aspect," rational and impersonal, which informs us about the objective state of affairs described behind the verbal expression. This canonical conception of language depicts every form of language as primarily satisfying a representative function of the world. However, whenever we come near to real expressions of daily life, we obtain a more complex vision of language: it is not only used to report the state of affairs of the world, but also to express feelings and impressions that can hardly be exhaustively described with concepts. Language also performs an important function of appealing to others to share an emotion or a common view about certain aspects of the world.

Ritchie exposes many of these nonpropositional aspects of language in his description of metaphors and stories. That is because metaphor is one the most extreme examples of the living character of every linguistic expression: it means what it means only within a human and social action. Metaphor transports us from the world of propositions to the world of dynamic meanings. In real life, verbal expressions are completely intertwined with gestures (e.g., Cornejo et al. 2009). They are emotionally charged, socially shared, and have radical consequences in social bonds (see Ritchie, this volume). Therefore, the acute descriptions made by Ritchie, concerning the power of metaphors as promoters of social change can be extended to every language use. Of course, we can meaningfully observe such properties in metaphors. But we can expect that every verbal action produces "perceptual simulations," affective commitment, invoking dynamic schemas, generating entailments, and has the potential to modify possibilities of action at the social and personal levels. In brief, metaphor is a metaphor of every utterance. Or, if one prefers, metaphor is the literal expression of every utterance.

NOTE

1. It is also the case of the distinction between *illocutionary force* and *propositional content* (Searle, 1989), which lacks psychological reality despite its logical clarity (see Hörmann, 1981).

REFERENCES

Barsalou, L. (1999). Perceptual symbol systems. *Behavioral and Brain Sciences, 22*, 577-609.

Cornejo, C. (2004). Who says what the words say?: The problem of linguistic meaning in psychology. *Theory and Psychology, 14*, 5-28.

Cornejo, C. (2007). Review essay: Conceptualizing metaphors versus embodying the language. *Culture & Psychology, 13*(4), 474-487.

Cornejo, C., Simonetti, F., Ibáñez, A., Aldunate, N., Ceric, F., López, V., & Núñez, R. E. (2009). Gesture and metaphor comprehension: Electrophysiological evidence of cross-modal coordination by audiovisual stimulation. *Brain & Cognition, 70*, 42-52.

Davidson, D. (2001). What metaphors mean. In D. Davidson (Ed.), *Inquiries into truth and interpretation* (pp. 245-264). New York, NY: Oxford University Press. (Original work published 1978)

Derrida, J. (2007). The retrait of metaphor. In J. Derrida (Ed.), *Psyche: Inventions of the other* (Vol. 1, pp. 48-80). Stanford, CA: Stanford University Press. (Original work published 1978)

Hörmann, H. (1981). *To mean, to understand.* New York, NY: Springer.

Lakoff, G., & Johnson, M. (1980). *Metaphors we live by.* Chicago, IL: University of Chicago Press.

Leezenberg, M. (2001). *Contexts of metaphor.* Amsterdam: Elsevier.

Olson, D. R. (1994). *The world on paper: the conceptual and cognitive implications of writing and reading*. Cambridge, England: Cambridge University Press.

Ricoeur, P. (1978). The metaphorical process as cognition, imagination, and feeling. *Critical Inquiry, 5*(1), 143-159.

Searle, J. R. (1989). *Speech acts*. Cambridge, MA: Harvard University Press.

Shanon, B. (1988). Semantic representation of meaning: A critique. *Psychological Bulletin, 104*(1), 70-83.

CHAPTER 8

BALANCING STABILITY AND CHANGE

A Neo-Diffusionist Perspective on Cultural Dynamics of Socially Transformative Ideas

Yoshihisa Kashima, Boyka Bratanova, and Kim Peters

Cultural transformation of society abounds. In the same way that ideas of Protestantism, women's suffrage, nationalism, or more generally, culture, have changed the ways in which members of society think and behave, new ideas are changing (and will continue to change) our own thoughts and behaviors. These are *socially transformative ideas*, ideas that have the potential to change society by virtue of being different to the status quo. In a sense, they describe a *possible world* in which members of a society perform a set of new actions that differ from what they do now. Clearly, if we wish to understand cultural transformation of society, we need to understand how socially transformative ideas transform society. At one level, the process seems self-evident: if members of a society adopt a socially transformative idea and perform the new set of associated actions, then society is transformed. However, even this makes clear that the impact of a particular socially transformative idea is far from certain; many will not be adopted widely enough within a society to transform it. One of the critical steps in the cultural transformation of society, then, is

Culture and Social Change: Transforming Society Through the Power of Ideas, pp. 125–144

cultural transmission: the process by which a socially transformative idea is transmitted from one person to another. In this chapter, we seek to shed light on the social circumstances that support the transmission of socially transformative ideas, and hence the cultural transformation of society.

THE GROUNDING MODEL OF CULTURAL TRANSMISSION

In order to understand how (and when) socially transformative ideas may be transmitted between people, we will draw on the grounding model of cultural transmission (Kashima, Klein, & Clark, 2007), which is a variant of neo-diffusionist metatheory of culture. Diffusionism is a metatheory that regards the transmission of nongenetically transmitted information as central to cultural dynamics, namely, the stability and change of culture over time. Nongenetically transmitted information includes not only the propositional content of certain ideations (e.g., the world is round), but also information about how to do things (e.g., how to make an arrow) and how to think about things (e.g., how to solve a differential equation). To the extent that given nongenetic information is more or less shared within a population and transmitted across generations, we call it part of a *culture*. In contrast, we use the term *cultural information*[1] to mean nongenetically transmitted information generally regardless of whether it is shared or transmitted across generations.

The notion that cultural information originates somewhere and spreads from there via various social processes is not new. In fact, nearly a century ago, a diffusionist theory of culture was widely held in British anthropology (e.g., Smith, Rivers) and German ethnology (e.g., Gribner), though it went out of favor partly due to some empirically unsustainable claims (e.g., Smith's claim that every new cultural innovation originated in Egypt and spread around the world). More recently, however, theorists such as Campbell (1975), Dawkins (1976), Cavalli-Sforza and Feldman (1981), Boyd and Richerson (1985), Sperber (1996), and Mesoudi and Whiten (2008) have revived this basic idea in a new form that takes Darwinian mechanisms in cultural evolution seriously. This new form has been termed *neo-diffusionism* (Kashima, Peters, & Whelan, 2008; see Kashima, 2008, for review).

The grounding model of cultural transmission (Kashima et al., 2007) extends a psycholinguistic model of language use (Clark, 1996) to theorise a mechanism for the cultural transformation of society. This model argues that cultural information is transmitted in the course of people's everyday joint activities, such as having lunch with a friend, buying a newspaper or attending a work meeting. In this sense, it is closely aligned with the Vygotskian perspective in cultural psychology (e.g., Cole, 1996; Rogoff, 2003). A joint activity consists of a series of events and actions for a joint goal. It typically involves certain types of people performing certain types of actions (i.e., taking particular roles), has a beginning and an end, and takes place in a certain setting. Cultural transmission can itself be the main goal of a joint activity (e.g., teaching and learning, training and apprenticing); however, it usually occurs as an incidental side effect of joint activity (e.g., aspects of organizational culture may be transmitted in a water cooler conversation that two employees have about a colleague). Therefore, the latter type of cultural transmission can play a significant, though often invisible and implicit, role in cultural dynamics.

According to the grounding model, participants perform a joint activity by carrying out a variety of goal-directed actions that move them closer to their joint goal. However, in order to coordinate their activities to reach their goal, the participants need to establish a *mutual understanding* about the meaning of those actions, such as whether an action is relevant for achieving the joint goal, and if so, what needs to be done next, and so on. The process of establishing a mutual understanding is called *grounding* because it is the process of adding a new mutual understanding to the participants' *common ground*: the collection of information and knowledge that they actually share and suppose they share. According to Clark (1996), it is possible to distinguish between *personal* common ground, which people have accumulated through previous interactions with each other, and *communal* common ground, which accompanies membership of a particular community—such as a community of psychologists or of people living in the same country.

So, in a given joint activity, interactants start with an initial common ground based on their personal and communal common ground, which they update in the course of the activity as they ground new mutual understandings. The common ground that exists at the beginning of a joint activity serves as a resource for grounding any new information. Roughly speaking, common ground can contain *social relational* information, specifying who the interactants are and how they relate to each other (e.g., in terms of their interpersonal relationship, common group membership, or intergroup relationship), and *activity relevant* information, specifying what the interactants know and are perceived to know for the purpose of their joint activity. Similarly, the information that is grounded may be either social relational (e.g., the participants' relationship with another implicated social actor) or activity relevant (e.g., how the joint goal can be achieved). As a consequence of grounding any new social relational or activity relevant information, interactants leave the joint activity with expanded common ground, which is remembered for their next interaction.

However, grounding is not the unproblematic process that the above suggests: it involves one person *presenting* an understanding to another, who then gives some evidence of their *acceptance* of the presenter's understanding *to the extent necessary for the purpose of their joint activity.* If it all goes well, a mutual understanding of cultural information is established, and *some* cultural information is transmitted. However, it often involves a presenter's mistakes, self-corrections, and the like, and accepters often seek clarification, make a counter presentation, and negotiate their understanding. Grounding rarely, if ever, achieves a perfect mutual understanding; it accomplishes a mutual understanding of cultural information *only* to the extent necessary for the joint activity. Thus, the transmission of cultural information is almost always imperfect. Furthermore, grounding leaves open a distinct possibility that there can be a creative process in cultural transmission. That is, participants may end up grounding a mutual understanding of *novel* cultural information in the process of carrying out a joint activity.

THE TRANSMISSION OF SOCIALLY TRANSFORMATIVE IDEAS

The grounding model suggests that if socially transformative ideas are to spread, then these new ideas must be grounded during the joint activity carried out by the interactants. The more often these ideas are grounded, among more interactants, the more widespread and prevalent in society they will become. Importantly, the model also suggests that whether socially transformative ideas will be grounded is likely to depend on the type of joint activities that people engage in because different joint activities tend to be characterized by different prevailing *goals*.

The small group research (e.g., McGrath, 1984) suggests that joint activities involve some degrees of *relational* and/or *task* goals. Obviously, any joint activity is neither purely task nor relationally oriented, and is typically driven by a combination of both. When one is engaged in a discussion about the manufacturing of a new product in a work team, the task goal is to produce a good manufacturing plan. This does not mean one is not concerned about relational goals; there is at least some level of requirement to attend to interpersonal relationships within the team. When people are simply socializing, their main goal may be relational; still, they need to attend to the task of keeping their conversation afloat.

The two goals (task or relational) have important implications for the grounding of socially transformative ideas. If the goal of a joint activity is mainly to carry out the task at hand (*task goals*), then interactants will tend to ground information that is seen to facilitate task performance; if the goal is to establish or maintain relationships (*relational goals*), then interactants will tend to ground information that is seen to facilitate the establishment or maintenance of the desired relationships. Consistent with this, research by Clark and Kashima (2007) has revealed the kinds of information that tend to be seen to facilitate each of these goals. In particular, information that is consistent with the prevailing culture (culture consistent information) tends to be seen as more *socially connective* (i.e., forming or maintaining relationships among interactants) and information that is inconsistent with the prevailing culture (culture inconsistent information) tends to be seen as more *informative* (i.e., providing information that is novel, but harder to understand, and potentially more socially risky).

Given that socially transformative ideas are by definition new, unfamiliar, and inconsistent with the prevailing culture, these findings have clear implications for the transmission of these ideas. In particular, while socially transformative ideas are not likely to be grounded if the joint activity emphasizes relational goals (and a preference for culture consistent information), they have a greater chance of being grounded if relational goals to form new relationships or maintain existing relationships are not so salient, or if the joint activity emphasizes task goals. This suggests that the likelihood of the transmission of socially transformative ideas depends on the type of joint activities that people engage in. By finding out how often people engage in what type of joint activities, we may be able to predict or anticipate the likelihood of the spread of socially transformative ideas. This is the question about *societal distribution of joint activities*. In the next section, we will consider whether there are certain kinds of joint activities that are likely to emphasize relational rather than task goals (or vice versa), and hence whether particular clusters of joint activities are likely to support or hinder the spread of socially transformative ideas.

Joint Activity Clusters and Goals

As we argued above, if we can uncover the *societal distribution of joint activities* that tend to emphasize relational or task goals, this will allow us to theorise the global cultural dynamics of socially transformative ideas. In this regard, recent research on people's conceptions of social groups is helpful. According to this work (e.g., Lickel et al., 2000), people readily classify groups into intimacy groups (e.g., friends, family), task groups (e.g., committees, work groups), and social categories (e.g., ethnic, national groups). Whereas intimacy and task groups tend to be small, involving a great deal of interpersonal interaction, social categories are much larger, and do not involve frequent face-to-face interpersonal interaction. Intimacy and task groups can be distinguished in terms of their goals. Whereas intimacy groups tend to serve socioemotional needs, task groups pursue task goals. Social categories, on the other hand, are not necessarily associated with clear joint goals, but they tend to serve social identity functions.

Drawing on this research, we suggest that people see three general clusters of joint activities in their lives mapping on to these social group categories: private, work and public activities (see Table 8.1). *Private activities* occur among people who have close interpersonal relationships and belong to an intimacy group. To use social network parlance, these people are likely to have strong ties (Granovetter, 1973) through which they communicate frequently about a wide range of topics. They are likely to know each other well, and share personal common ground that contains a large variety of both social relational and activity relevant information. Dinner table conversations at home and conversations with friends at a local pub are examples of private activities.

Work activities occur among people who belong to a task group. They are likely to know each other, although their social relationships will be limited to the narrow range and limited duration of their task relevant activities (though some of these relationships may develop into more personal ones). Therefore, the personal common ground that they share will largely be restricted to task relevant information. Work groups are primary examples of a task group. If one works at a manufacturing company, whether one is in sales, production, or any other branch, one is likely to belong to a team of colleagues. Most activities that occur there are constrained by the overall task goal: be it a sales planning meeting or a water fountain conversation, they are probably best characterized as work activities.

Public activities occur among people who belong to a social category. They tend not to know each other well, have weak ties (Granovetter, 1973) if any, and do not have a great deal of personal common ground. This is the type of joint activity in which we engage as members of a community, such as a friendly chat with one's neighbors, an exchange of a few words with a shop keeper at a local corner shop, and a conversation with someone who hap-

Table 8.1. Activity Clusters and Transmission of Socially Transformative Ideas

Activity	*Group Types*	*Goals*	*Common Ground*	*Transmission Likelihood*
Private	Intimacy	Compound	Personal	Most likely
Task	Task	Task	Personal	Possible if task relevant
Public	Social Category	Relational	Communal	Least likely

pens to occupy the next patch of sand at a public beach. To the extent that there is some social engagement and interaction, from the perspective of the grounding model, shared social categories act as general cultural markers of communal common ground; that is, people who belong in a certain social category tend to share communal common ground, which tends to contain certain types of information (e.g., if you are a psychologist, you are likely to know something about Freud) and a social identity to go with it (e.g., social identity as a psychologist). Society—typically people's national community—is arguably one such social category.

Joint Activity Clusters and the Transmission of Socially Transformative Ideas

We argue that each of the activity clusters will be differentially likely to support the spread of socially transformative ideas, with public activities the least likely of all. Under ordinary circumstances, public activities are characterized by the general relational goal to be "civil" or "polite," although the degree to which politeness norms are observed and enforced varies across different public activities. Whether public activities are characterized by task goals may vary somewhat, depending on whether they pertain to economic transactions (e.g., buying or selling an item at a shop or in a market) or other sorts of chance meetings with acquaintances or strangers in public places. However, while economic transactions have definite task goals, they are unlikely to facilitate the transmission of socially transformative ideas.

So, generally, while being informative is not a priority in all public activities, being socially connective is. Without attempting to be at least minimally socially connective, public activities like polite conversations with one's acquaintances cannot happen. This means that socially transformative ideas, which are less socially connective, are less likely to be communicated here because they are socially risky. Instead, people may communicate culture consistent information that affirms the communal common ground, as this may be more polite (Brown & Levinson, 1986) and may serve a social integrative function by maintaining the fabric of the community defined by a social category. In support of this claim, Clark and Kashima (2007) found that culture inconsistent information (in their case, stereotype inconsistent information in a story) was unlikely to be communicated through a communication chain of people who were unacquainted, but shared a social category as students, because it was seen to be a less socially engaging thing to say.

On the other hand, private activities are perhaps most amenable to the transmission of socially transformative ideas. A number of factors contribute to this. First, although relationships are very important in private activities, they are likely to be preexisting and part of their personal common ground. Therefore, there is no need to improve them; interactants only need not harm them. With this comes a greater tolerance for any reductions in interpersonal understanding and smoothness, leaving people free to discuss a wide range of topics, from very culture consistent to very culture inconsistent. Second, people who engage in private activities have extensive personal common ground, which means that they tend to know what they mutually know. As a consequence, exchanging platitudes is not sufficient, and the communication of informative (and potentially more entertaining) culture inconsistent information may actually be encouraged. Third, when people interact with each other for private activities, they are more likely to have the time that is needed to discuss, argue about, or clarify culture inconsistent ideas. So, in all, socially transformative ideas may have a greater chance of being transmitted and grounded in people's private activities. Consistent with this line of reasoning, Ruscher, Santuzzi, and Hammer (2003) found that people were more willing to share novel, culture inconsistent information with friends than with strangers.

Finally, work activities fall somewhere between public and private activities in that socially transformative ideas may be transmitted here if they are task relevant. Far more than public or private activities, work activities are characterized by task goals, which tend to support the sharing of more informative, culture inconsistent information. Arguably, R&D (research and development) teams are the epitome of task groups whose main activities are the generation and transmission of novel ideas. Moreover, entrepreneurial activity can be defined as the creation of the new in the economic domain, and researchers are increasingly emphasizing the link between entrepreneurial activity and social and cultural change (e.g., Rindova, Barry, & Ketchen, 2009; Calás, Smircich, & Bourne, 2009). Therefore, in these contexts the transmission of socially transformative ideas should be facilitated.

However, even in work activities, relational goals can come into play. Where they do, they will create a tension with task goals that partially account for the finding that groups tend to focus on information that all group members have in common (akin to culture consistent information) rather than unique (culture inconsistent) information (e.g., Stasser & Titus, 1985; see Stasser & Titus, 2003 for a review). This means that even where interactants have explicit task goals, they are only more likely to transmit potentially socially transformative ideas when they are not inhibited by relational concerns. In line with this, Mann (2009) noted the striking importance of the so-called "soft" factors including the interpersonal climate in R&D teams. Participative safety (openness to ideas without being ridiculed or criticized) and support for innovation (supportiveness to pursue innovative goals by advice giving and resource sharing) are among the more important factors that facilitate creativity in R&D teams (West & Anderson, 1996; see Mann, 2005).

Interim Summary

Socially transformative ideas are culturally new—they are necessarily unfamiliar to many and are often downright inconsistent with the cultural consensus. Drawing on the grounding model, we suggest that people are most likely to transmit socially transformative ideas while engaging in joint activities that are less characterized by the relational concerns that present barriers to the transmission of these socially risky ideas and are more characterized by the task goals that facilitate the transmission of innovative ideas. In the contemporary world, people appear to organize their joint activities into three broad clusters: private, public, and work. Each of these is characterized by different levels of relational and task goals. The consequence of this is, we suggest, that socially transformative ideas are most likely to be reproduced in private activities, least likely to be reproduced in public activities, and somewhat likely to be reproduced in work activities depending on their task relevance. The cultural dynamics surrounding the spread of socially transformative ideas in broader society, then, is a function of the distribution of these three types of activities in that society. In the next section, we will discuss how the distribution of these joint activities is a sociocultural system that makes possible the simultaneous stability and change of culture.

CULTURAL DYNAMICS OF SOCIALLY TRANSFORMATIVE IDEAS

Balancing Stability and Change

To consider the implications of the foregoing discussion, let us conduct a thought experiment. First, imagine a hypothetical community of people whose social engagement mainly consists of private activities. Perhaps they are "angry young men" who do not frequently partake in public activities or even avoid them vehemently; instead, they primarily talk among themselves within small and intimate groups (or "gangs"). According to the above analysis, they will freely generate and disseminate socially transformative ideas among themselves. As a result, their private activities may become a hot bed of innovative, and perhaps even radical, ideas. To the extent that they can break their existing habits, and coordinate their activities, these ideas may even transform their social actions and may transform their portions of the society. However, if these people do not engage in public activities and transmit these socially transformative ideas more widely, the social transformation remains local.

In contrast, imagine another hypothetical community, whose members engage mainly in public activities, and few, if any, private ones. Perhaps it is a community of "Good Samaritans," who are compassionate, polite, and community minded. They engage in socially connective joint activities with any member of the community. It may sound like an ideal community to live in. Ironically, however, the foregoing analysis suggests that socially transformative ideas are least likely to spread in this community because such ideas may disturb the social integration of the community. Rather, information that is consistent with the prevailing culture of the community is more likely to spread, which will tend to maintain the status quo.

In fact, all communities consist of people whose joint activities are differentially divided between the public and private spheres. Most of us engage in both types of activities although some do more of one than the other. In so doing, we are likely to be contributing to the social integration and maintenance of a large community (based on a social category) through public activities and the dissemination and incubation of potentially socially transformative ideas through private activities within small intimacy groups. This duality – and what some may label duplicity—may be a highly adaptive social mechanism that strikes a balance between stability and change in society (Kashima & Bratanova, in press).

The society that we describe here is one consisting of small world networks (Milgram, 1967; Watts, 1999). Here, individuals are connected to each other by strong ties within a small group. These ties are highly clustered among themselves, and constitute a close knit group (intimacy groups). However, these individuals are at the same time connected to others who belong to other such clustered networks via weak ties. Therefore, this society is characterized by a high degree of local clustering of social networks, coupled with short distances on average to connect any two members of the society (recall the movie, *Six Degrees of Separation* by Guare, 1990). In this type of society, socially transformative ideas may be nurtured within the local clusters of closely connected individuals, but will not circulate beyond them. At the very least, this enables a large number of people to maintain a level of stability in their public activities, while keeping innovative ideas alive in their close circle. However, as we will describe, this may have important psychological and social implications.

Mechanisms of Public-Private Dissociation

Individuals in this type of society are likely to have developed a cognitive dissociation between their macropublic and microprivate spheres of life (Kashima & Bratanova, in press), whereby they regard the wider community (based on a social category) and the close circle of their friends and family as quite different from each other. There is some evidence for this public-private dissociation in people's perceptions of the effects of the media. In particular, research has shown that people often believe that the wider community is more likely to be influenced by mass media than they themselves are (third person effect, Davison, 1983; see Duck, Hogg, & Terry, & 2000, for a review) and indeed as being at higher risk from negative mass media contents, such as alcohol (the impersonal impact hypothesis; Tyler & Cook, 1984).

More generally, mass media may play an important role in the formation of a cognitive representation of a large scale group based on a social category as an entity separate from the private sphere of life. For instance, a well known political historian, Benedict Anderson (1991), has famously argued that a nation state—arguably one of the most significant social categories in the modern era—was enabled in part by the construction of a shared representation of the nation as a unique political entity, which was in turn enabled by the establishment of a national language and a nationally circulated print media that helped people to construe the nation state as an "imagined community."

Again, the grounding model can help us understand how mass media communication can exacerbate the public-private cognitive dissociation. In particular, when people receive a mass media communication about an event, such as a government announcement, a public health campaign or a news item about a world event, they are likely to assume that it is a part of their nation's communal common ground. However, it is only when people themselves have a conversation with others about this event that it can become part of their shared reality (Hardin & Higgins, 1996). This is because until the event is grounded in their personal common ground with another, there is always uncertainty about whether others did receive the communication, and whether they reacted to it in the same way - did they react to it favorably or unfavorably? There is evidence to suggest that it is when people find out they share similar views about a media communication that the message has strong psychological effects (e.g., Dunlop, Wakefield, & Kashima, 2008; Morton & Duck, 2001, 2006). Therefore, impersonal mass media often acts as a reminder of the potential difference between the public and the private, the national communal common ground and the personal private common ground.

One of the more pernicious symptoms of the public-private cognitive dissociation is pluralistic ignorance[2] (Miller & McFarland, 1987; Miller, Monin, & Prentice, 2000, for review). This is a cognitive illusion where people believe that a wider community holds a norm that differs markedly from the attitudes they or their close others hold. Ironically, the private attitudes that most people believe are unique to themselves are in fact much more widely held—perhaps even by a majority of the community. Pluralistic ignorance may act as a barrier to the circulation of socially transformative ideas. For instance, Noelle-Neumann's (1993) spiral of silence theory points to this possibility in political public opinion dynamics suggesting that people may not express their opinion because they are afraid a majority may disagree. In social psychology, Lyons and Kashima (2003) showed that people preferred to transmit stereotype consistent rather than inconsistent (socially transformative) information when they thought the stereotype was widely endorsed in their community, but that this tendency was attenuated when they thought that the community did not endorse the stereotype. Similarly, Clark and Kashima (2007) found that people felt stereotype consistent information was less socially connective and therefore were less likely to communicate it when they did not think that the stereotypes were endorsed by the community than when they did.

Thus, this research suggests that people's perception of the community endorsement of a socially transformative idea may moderate its circulation through their public joint activities. In particular, we have argued that people's perception that their community may not endorse a socially transformative idea may inhibit its transmission. However, this mechanism can be reversed, potentially facilitating the circulation of socially transformative ideas. In other words, if people are led to believe that their community in fact *endorse* a socially transformative idea, they may think it is more socially connective, and then may transmit it more. Consistent with this insight, recent research by Miller and Morrison (2009) found that people were more willing to express deviant opinions (i.e., potentially socially transformative ideas) when they believed that their views were endorsed by the majority of their community.

In addition, the research on diffusion of innovations (e.g., Rogers, 1995) is consistent with this line of reasoning. One of the most robust findings about the temporal dynamics of the spread of new technological (or other types of) innovations is the S-shaped adoption curve. When one plots the percentage of people within a population that adopts a new technology against time after its invention, the initial uptake of the invention is usually slow, but it begins to increase sharply, and then eventually its increase slows and reaches a plateau. Henrich (2001) showed that the S-shaped adoption curve obtains if people exhibit a conformist tendency—the tendency to adopt what a majority of the population adopts. Consistent with this, the diffusion of innovations has been modeled within a deterministic framework of differential equations by Bass (1969) as a combination of the two processes, the independent learning and adoption of an innovation, and the imitation of those early adopters by others. This latter process reflects the tendency for people to adopt (or publicly endorse) an innovation. Intriguingly, the time course of the diffusion of innovations can be understood as a process akin to biological evolution. Bass's model is mathematically equivalent to the evolutionary dynamics of a stochastic pure birth process in the population size of infinity (Niu, 2002).

Therefore, while pluralistic ignorance may act as a barrier to the transmission of socially transformative ideas, if there are visible cues that members of a society do in fact endorse the idea—in the form of early adopters, some kinds of mass media information (like opinion polls), or claims that a leader may make in a speech—then the public-private dissociation may be broken, leading to rapid adoption of the socially transformative idea.

Work Activities

So far, we have considered the cultural dynamics of socially transformative ideas while focusing on public and private joint activities. What about joint activities at work? Do they facilitate or inhibit the circulation of socially transformative ideas? It is hard to make a broad generalization about this sphere. The likelihood of their transmission through work activities depends on their task relevance. For instance, in highly unionized work places, a socially transformative idea that aims to change the management practice may be likely to spread, but another that aims to reduce domestic violence may not (unless the union makes domestic violence its policy item). On the other hand, the idea of equal rights would be highly pertinent for social workers employed by local governments, but may not be for bankers in the central business district. Nonetheless, this sphere of activities can potentially act as a third channel through which socially transformative ideas can be circulated in society, and thus adds to the complexity of their cultural dynamics.

One speculation can be offered about the effect of dissociation of work activities from the other two spheres, and from private activities in particular. There is cross-cultural variation in the extent to which work is dissociated from nonwork. Sanchez-Burks and his colleagues (Sanchez-Burks, 2002; Sanchez-Burks, Lee, Choi, Nisbett, & Zhao, 2003) have shown that Anglo Americans draw a much clearer distinction between work and nonwork activities when compared to Latin Americans or East Asians. Quoting

Hampden-Turner and Trompenaars's (1993, p. 133) memorable passage, "[For the Protestant,] the world is split between the machine and the suburban garden, producing and consuming. No intimacy, affection, brotherhood, or rootedness is supposed to sully the world of work," Sanchez-Burks (2002) argued that the Protestant asceticism—highlighted by Weber (1904-1905/1958) as a cultural underpinning of the capitalist economy—was also responsible for a North American emphasis on professionalism and the normatively sanctioned inattention to interpersonal relational matters at work. Dubbed the Protestant relational ideology, the relational goals of private activities are quarantined from work activities in North America. In contrast, relational goals are integral to joint activities at work in non-Protestant societies. If Sanchez-Burks's analysis is right, and if private activities tend to tolerate the voicing of culturally novel or radical ideas as we suggested, a weaker dissociation between work and nonwork may facilitate the circulation of socially transformative ideas.

Recapitulation, Caveats, and Concluding Remarks

Our analysis has drawn on a neo-diffusionist perspective, particularly on the grounding model of cultural transmission, to explore and speculate on its implications for the cultural dynamics of socially transformative ideas. Based on Clark and Kashima's (2007) situated functional model, we suggested that the relative importance of relational and task goals and perceived consequences of transmitting a socially transformative idea in joint activities would affect the likelihood of its spread, generally suggesting that the relative emphasis on relational goals to form or maintain social relationships tend to promote the transmission of culturally conservative ideas. Further, we suggested that there are three clusters of joint activities, namely, private, public, and work, and the likelihood of diffusion of a socially transformative idea in a large scale collective depends on the distribution of these types of activities. Private activities are most facilitative, public activities are least facilitative, and work activities may be quite contingent.

Our analysis suggests that this tripartite system of joint activities may give us an adaptive mechanism of the production and reproduction of cultural information in a population. The public-private dissociation may strike a balance between the reproduction of culturally conservative ideas in the public sphere and the production of culturally innovative ideas in the private sphere. At the same time, this mechanism facilitates the social integration of a large scale collective, while ensuring the constant generation of culturally novel and potentially socially transformative ideas. The cognitive dissociation between the public and private spheres, with pluralistic ignorance as its symptom, may inhibit the introduction of innovative, and potentially radical ideas, into the public sphere of joint activities; however, this process may be reversed when people perceive the community endorsement of the culturally conservative ideas has waned and public support of more innovative ideas has increased, thus accelerating the circulation of socially transformative ideas when public sentiment is seen to have reversed.

In addition, we have discussed the impact of work activities on the circulation of novel ideas in society. They act as a third channel through which socially transformative ideas can spread. If they are relevant for the task, socially transformative ideas can be transmitted while people engage in their joint activities at work. The specific nature of the task and joint activities to go with it can affect this process, and it can be facilitative or inhibitory. Nonetheless, we speculated that the separation between work and private activities may cast a broad constraint on the flow of socially innovative ideas. In particular, in the presence of cultural ideas that emphasize the work-private dissociation (e.g., Protestant cultures), socially transformative ideas may be less likely to circulate through work activities.

Before closing, we must note down a few caveats. First, we defined socially transformative ideas as ideas that describe a possible world in which people perform a set of actions that differ from what they do. However, there is an obvious difference in the amount of societal change that those ideas imply. Take an example of women's suffrage. This idea describes a world in which women have the right to cast a vote in the political process. It transformed society from the one in which women did not to the one in which women do. Nonetheless, its implications are much broader and deeper than the simple change in voting behavior. The societal change it has effected is *broad* in that it has affected a number of other social actions and institutions and *deep* in that it has affected the circulation of a number of other ideas. In the present analysis, however, we have treated all socially transformative ideas as ideas that are contrary to the prevailing majority culture. Obviously, the breadth and depth of social transformation that a socially transformative idea requires would impact on the difficulty it is likely to encounter; the broader and deeper it is, the more resistance it would face. This aspect of cultural transformation of society was not discussed here, and requires further consideration.

Second, when a new socially transformative idea is transmitted to people and adopted by them, it is still likely to encounter at least two types of inertia. One is intraindividual inertia based on their habit. If the socially transformative idea is to have them stop a set of actions that they have performed habitually, and to get them to start on a set of new actions instead, the old habit is likely to interfere with the new idea and to make it more difficult to switch over (Wood & Neal, 2007). The other is interindividual inertia based on the requirement of social coordination. If the new actions can be performed completely by individuals on their own accord, this type of inertia is least likely. However, many socially transformative ideas require people in different social roles to perform new actions as well (including new institutional arrangements), and those actions need to be coordinated with each other. The requirement of social coordination is likely to present another source of inertia for cultural transformation of society. Nonetheless, these inertial considerations were not included in the current analysis. Both of these issues require a great deal of discussion, which we cannot provide in this chapter.

In conclusion, an idea can transform society. To do so, however, it needs to be encoded into a communicable form, transmitted to a number of people in the society, and adopted by them for implementation. The process of cultural diffusion is a *sine qua non* of cultural transformation of society. Its dynamics, however, are greatly shaped by the distribution of joint activities in the society—more often than not culture diffuses as a side effect of people interacting with each other for some other purpose. The main act is those joint activities. While people intentionally and purposefully engage in what they jointly try to achieve, cultural information is passed along without them noticing it. This is not to say that people do not consciously transmit cultural information. Obviously they do. Education, teaching, and training are all such instances. Yet, it may be those mundane joint activities, a far cry from the auspicious and high minded occasions of imparting knowledge, that play a far greater role in the production and reproduction of culture, and the formation, maintenance, and transformation of society. Those rare socially transformative ideas that enter into the unnoticed public flow of cultural information can eventually make a difference to society, for better or for worse.

NOTES

1. Note that cultural information differs from the concepts such as beliefs, attitudes, and values. Philosophers typically characterize such psychological concepts as propositional attitudes, that is, psychological "attitudes" directed towards some propositional content. For instance, when someone is said to believe that the world is round, the propositional content is that "the world is round," and this person is said to have an attitude towards it of "believing." The propositional content of "the world is round" is a kind of cultural information, but this person's attitude of "believing" is not. However, propositional contents of propositional attitudes do not exhaust all that is cultural information. Cultural information may be information about how to do things or how to think about things. This type of information is typically not coded as propositions, but rather as something like a "know how" or what some cognitive psychologists call procedural knowledge. In using any of these psychological concepts, one must make a theo-

retical commitment to a certain type of cognitive metatheory. We use the generic term 'cultural information' to avoid it.

2. There are other types of biases in perception of public opinion distribution. Among them is a false consensus bias, in which those who have a certain opinion tend to estimate the proportion of others in society who agree with their opinion to be greater than those who do not. Although this may appear to contradict pluralistic ignorance, false consensus and pluralistic ignorance are two different effects, which can coexist largely independently of each other (e.g., Monin & Norton, 2008). Generally speaking, pluralistic ignorance is indicated by a difference between one's own opinion and perceived opinion of the average other, whereas false consensus is indicated by a correlation between one's own opinion and perceived opinion of the average other across perceivers.

REFERENCES

Anderson, B. (1991). *Imagined communities*. London, England: Verso.

Bass, F. M. (1969). A new product growth for model consumer durables. *Management Science, 16*, 215-227.

Boyd, R,. & Richerson, P. J. (1985). *Culture and the evolutionary process*. Chicago, IL: University of Chicago Press.

Brown, P., & Levinson, S. C. (1987). Politeness: Some universals in language usage. Cambridge, England: Cambridge University Press.

Calás, M. B., Smircich, L., & Bourne, K. A. (2009). Extending the boundaries: Reframing "entrepreneurship as social change" through feminist perspectives. *Academy of Management Review, 34*, 552-569.

Campbell, D.T. (1975). On the conflicts between biological and social evolution and between psychology and moral tradition. *American Psychologist, 30*, 1103-1126.

Cavalli-Sforza, L. L., & Feldman, M. W. (1981). *Cultural transmission and evolution*. Princeton, NJ: Princeton University Press.

Clark, A. E., & Kashima, Y. (2007). Stereotype consistent information helps people connect with others: Situated-functional account of stereotype communication. *Journal of Personality and Social Psychology, 93*, 1028-1039.

Clark, H. H. (1996). *Using language*. New York, NY: Cambridge University Press.

Cole, M. (1996). *Cultural psychology: A once and future discipline*. Cambridge, MA: Harvard University Press.

Dawkins, R. (1976). *The selfish gene*. Oxford, England: Oxford University Press.

Davison, W. P. (1983). The third-person effect in communication. *Public Opinion Quarterly, 47*, 1-15.

Duck, J. M., Hogg, M. A., & Terry, D. J. (2000). The perceived impact of persuasive messages on "us" and "them." In D. J. Terry & M. A. Hogg (Eds), *Attitudes, behavior, and social context* (pp. 265-291). Mahwah, NJ: Lawrence Erlbaum.

Dunlop, S. M., Wakefield, M., & Kashima, Y. (2008). The contribution of anti-smoking advertising to quitting: Intra- and interpersonal processes. *Journal of Health Communication, 13*, 250-266.

Granovetter, M. (1973). The strength of weak ties. *American Journal of Sociology, 78*, 1360-1380.

Guare, J. (1990). *Six degrees of separation*. New York, NY: Random House.

Hampden-Turner, C., & Trompenaars, A. (1993). *The seven cultures of capitalism: Value systems for creating wealth in the United States, Japan, Germany, France, Britain, Sweden, and the Netherlands.* New York, NY: Doubleday.

Hardin, C. D., & Higgins, E. T. (1996). Shared reality: How social verification makes the subjective objective. R. M. Sorrentino & E. T. Higgins (Eds.), *Handbook of motivation and cognition* (Vol. 3, pp. 28-84). New York, NY: Guilford Press.

Henrich, J. (2001). Cultural transmission and the diffusion of innovations: Adoption dynamics indicate that biased cultural transmission is the predominate force in behavioral change. *American Anthropologist, 103*, 992-1013.

Kashima, Y. (2008). A social psychology of cultural dynamics: How cultures are formed, maintained, and transformed. *Social and Personality Psychology Compass, 2*, 107-120.

Kashima, Y. & Bratanova, B. (in press). Situated sociality and cultural dynamics: A puzzle of necessary dependency and perceived dissociation. In G. Semin & G. Echterhoff (Eds.), *Grounding sociality: Neurons, minds, and culture.* New York: Psychology Press.

Kashima, Y., Klein, O., & Clark, A. E. (2007). Grounding: Sharing information in social interaction. In K. Fiedler (Ed.), *Social communication* (pp. 27-77). New York: Psychology Press.

Kashima, Y., Peters, K., & Whelan, J. (2008). Culture, narrative, and human agency. In R. Sorrentino & S. Yamaguchi (Eds.), *Handbook of motivation and cognition across cultures* (pp. 393-421). San Diego, CA: Academic Press.

Lickel, B., Hamilton, D. L., Wieczorkowska, Lewis, A., Sherman, S. J., & Uhles, A. N. (2000). Varieties of groups and the perception of group entitativity. *Journal of Personality and Social Psychology, 78*, 223-246.

Lyons, A., & Kashima, Y. (2003). How are stereotypes maintained through communication? The influence of stereotype sharedness. *Journal of Personality and Social Psychology, 85*, 989-1005.

Mann, L. (2005). *Leadership, management, and innovation in R&D project teams*. Westport, CT: Praeger.

Mann, L. (2009). *Social psychology of creativity and innovation: Teams and their leaders*. Australia: The University of Melbourne, Department of Psychology.

McGrath, J. E. (1984). *Groups: Interaction and performance*. Englewood Cliffs, NJ: Prentice-Hall.

Mesoudi, A., & Whiten, A. (2008). The multiple roles of cultural transmission experiments in understanding human cultural evolution. *Philosophical Transaction of the Royal Society, B, 363*, 3489-3501.

Milgram, S. (1967). The small-world problem. *Psychology Today, 1*, 61-67.

Miller, D. T. & McFarland, C. (1987). Pluralistic ignorance: When similarity is interpreted as dissimilarity. *Journal of Personality and Social Psychology, 53*, 298-305.

Miller, D. T., Monin, B., & Prentice, D. A. (2000). Pluralistic ignorance and inconsistency between private attitudes and public behaviors. In D. J. Terry & M. A. Hogg (Eds.), *Attitudes, behavior, and social context* (pp. 95-113). Mahwah, NJ: Lawrence Erlbaum.

Miller, D. T., & Morrison, K. R. (2009). Expressing deviant opinions: Believing you are in the majority helps. *Journal of Experimental Social Psychology, 45*, 740-747.

Monin, B. & Norton, M. I. (2008). Perceptions of a fluid consensus: Uniqueness bias, false consensus, false polarization, and pluralistic ignorance in a water conservation crisis. *Personality and Social Psychology Bulletin, 29*, 559-567.

Morton, T. A., & Duck, J. M. (2001). Communication and health beliefs: Mass and interpersonal influences on perception of risk to self and others. *Communication Research, 28*, 602–626.

Morton, T. A., & Duck, J. M. (2006). Enlisting the influence of others: Alternative strategies for persuasive media campaigns. *Journal of Applied Social Psychology, 36*, 269-296.

Niu, S. -C. (2002). A stochastic formulation of the Buss model of new-product diffusion. *Mathematical Problems in Engineering, 8*, 249-263.

Noelle-Newmann, E. (1993). *The spiral of silence: Public opinion—our social skin* (2nd ed.). Chicago, IL: University of Chicago Press.

Rindova, V., Barry, D., & Ketchen, D. J. (2009). Entrepreneuring as emancipation. *Academy of Management Review, 34*, 477-491.

Rogers, E. M. (1995). *Diffusion of innovations* (4th ed.). New York, NY: Free Press.

Rogoff, B. (2003). *The cultural nature of human development*. Oxford, England: Oxford University Press.

Ruscher, J., B., Santuzzi, A. M., & Hammer, E. Y. (2003). Shared impression formation in the cognitively interdependent dyad. *British Journal of Social Psychology, 42*, 411-425.

Sanchez-Burks, J. (2002). Protestant relational ideology and (in)attention to relational cues in work settings. *Journal of Personality and Social Psychology, 83*, 919-929.

Sanchez-Burks, J., Lee, F., Choi, I., Nisbett, R., & Zhao, S. (2003). Conversing across cultures: East-West communication styles in work and nonwork contexts. *Journal of Personality and Social Psychology, 85*, 363-372.

Sperber, D. (1996). *Explaining culture*. Oxford, England: Blackwell.

Stasser, G., & Titus, W. (1985). Polling of unshared information in group decision making: Biased information sampling during discussion. *Journal of Personality and Social Psychology, 57*, 67-78.

Stasser, G., & Titus, W. (2003). Hidden profiles: A brief history. *Psychological Inquiry, 14*, 304-313.

Tyler, T. R., & Cook, F. L. (1984). The mass media and judgments of risk: Distinguishing impact on personal and societal level judgments. *Journal of Personality and Social Psychology, 47*, 693-708.

Watts, D. J. (1999). *Small worlds*. Princeton, NJ: Princeton University Press.

Weber, M. (1958). *Protestant ethic and the spirit of capitalism* (T. Parsons, Trans.). New York, NY: Scribner. (Original work published 1904-1905)

West, M. A., & Anderson, N.R. (1996). Innovation in top management teams. *Journal of Applied Psychology, 81*(6), 680-693.

Wood, W., & Neal, D. (2007). A new look at habits and the habit-goal interface. *Psychological Review, 114*, 843-863.

CHAPTER 9

THE MEETING OF IDEAS

Diffusion, Dialogical Interaction, and Social Change

Brady Wagoner

Kashima, Bratanova, and Peters (this volume, Chapter 8) develop a "neo-diffusionist" perspective on intrasocietal cultural dynamics, exploring the conditions under which stability or change takes place in society. They argue that social change occurs when "socially transformative ideas" are sufficiently diffused in society. Diffusion takes place in situated joint activities, through a process of establishing intersubjective understanding and the coordination of action, which they call "grounding." Certain kinds of activity contexts (i.e., private rather than public) are said to be more conducive to transmission of socially transformative ideas, because they are focused on task goals rather than relational goals, which may be jeopardized by radical new ideas. I am sympathetic to Kashima et al.'s overall approach, especially their interest in reviving concepts and concerns from diffusionism, their "grounding" approach that situates ideas in the space of interaction between individuals and in cultural practices, and their exploration of social change through processes of communication. In this chapter I will discuss and evaluate Kashima et al.'s ideas against the backdrop of early diffusionist thinkers, particularly Bartlett, foregrounding what I see as a central point for critique and development, namely, their

Culture and Social Change: Transforming Society Through the Power of Ideas, pp. 145–159

over objectification and mechanical treatment of ideas and their transmission. Along these lines, I will make a number of critiques, particularly at the level of research methodology.

At the outset, a clarification of the phrase "socially transformative ideas" is needed to avoid circularity: What ideas are socially transformative? We cannot simply say it those ideas that transform society. I assume that what Kashima et al. (this volume) means is that certain ideas conceive an alternative social reality that challenges those who hold positions of power. Socially transformative ideas may or may not come to transform the structures of society; but they have the potential to do so. As Kashima et al. point out ideas are usually accepted as normative ideals first and second they need to be implemented in concrete social practices (although I would also argue that social practices can also be changed directly without the mediation of new ideas). Moreover, the adoption of an idea at the level of discourse does *not* necessarily mean the associated actions will follow (see Jensen & Wagoner, 2009).

A second caution is that if Kashima et al's (this volume) approach is adopted as a research program, communication risks being reduced to the study of the likelihood of an idea being transmitted. Such a conceptualization would miss other essential features of communication, such as *transformation in transmission, rhetoric, positioning in relation to the message, elaboration of meaning,* and more generally a study of *the concrete process by which information is grounded and contextualized.* We would hold a distorted image of communication as a unidirectional transfer of fixed entities, instead of as a negotiation and reconstruction of a message between the sender and receiver (see Cornejo, this volume, Chapter 7; Valsiner, 2007). Positioning in relation to communication is a complex social process: An idea can be transmitted successfully without being accepted by an interlocutor, or alternatively it might be accepted but understood differently by them (this important distinction between "transmission" and "acceptance" is not developed Kashima et al.'s framework). Moscovici (1991) has also shown that radical ideas are often explicitly rejected; yet aspects of them are implicitly accepted in our worldview through an unconscious "sleeper effect." In all these cases, we find a generative tension between two or more perspectives on an idea, forming a triad, which some theorists have considered to be a primary unit of analysis in social psychology (see Cornish, this volume, Chapter 3; Marková, 2003)

Third, it needs to be kept in mind that social change most often occurs as part of a *cultural struggle*. This does not clearly appear in Kashima et al.'s (this volume) analysis. During a cultural struggle, individuals take positions (pro- this or anti- that) aligning themselves with the ideas and projects of certain social groups. These group positions exist vis-à-vis other positions within a broader societal framework. Thus, there is a need to take a more "social" social psychological perspective (Greenwood, 2004) in our analysis, so as to situate psychological processes within the social positions and meaning systems of the *particular* societies in which they occur. Cultural battles for woman's suffrage, to take an example from Kashima et al. (this volume), involved consistently linking the then normatively accepted idea of EQUALITY to particular social practices. Those arguing against this social change would have to employ "yes, but ..." argumentative tactics, whereby the ideal of EQUALITY is accepted but its application to particular practices is rejected (see Castro & Batel, 2008). In short, "communal grounding" (as a process of meaning coconstruction) cannot adequately be studied in the abstract but instead needs to be studied in the process and content of real groups' communications within particular cultural contexts.

In this commentary, I expand on these critiques in order to further develop a neo-diffusionist approach to understanding the communicative processes and social conditions through which radical ideas become normative in society. To do this, I first look more closely at some of the theoretical resources available to us in the diffusionist approach to culture; second, I turn to social representations theory for an illustrative example of research on communication and social change to shed light on diffusionist principles and apply them to the dynamics of contemporary societies; and finally, I explicitly theorize the transmission of ideas as part of a dialogical exchange in which self and other are seen as interdependent opposites in tension.

DIFFUSIONISM: PAST AND PRESENT

Diffusionism gained ground in the first decades of the twentieth century, as an alternative to the cultural evolutionists (e.g., Comte, Spencer, Wundt, Fraser, and Tylor), who saw societies internally unfolding through different qualitatively distinct cultural stages. For the diffusionists, by contrast, there was only a quantitative distinction to be made between the mentalities of "primitive"[1] and "advanced" cultural groups—the later simply being more complex, though the former were also considered complex. Even more, the diffusionists believed that social change was most often the result of the contact of cultures, rather than by changes originating internally, as the evolutionists argued. The complexity of a group's culture was a sign of a diverse history of cultural contacts. For example, Rivers (1914) argued that the numerous different ways Melanesians disposed of their dead signaled that they had been in contact with a variety of other groups. Whenever contact occurs between groups, foreign cultural elements become assimilated into the cultural patterns of the recipient group. Those selected cultural elements are shaped into the new context—a process that came to be called "conventionalization" (Rivers, 1912).

The diffusionists outlined different kinds of cultural contacts—for example, war, colonialism, trade, migration, cohabitation in a certain territory, and so on—, which led to greater or lesser adoption of the other group's culture. When, for example, one group is *dominant* and the other *submissive*, as often happened in European colonialism, the transfer will be rather one-sided. In all cases however there are certain aspects of culture more resistant to change than others—Bartlett (1943, 1946) calls these the "hard" as opposed to the "soft" features of culture. What aspects are "hard" will depend on the particular customs, values and beliefs of different social groups. However, across cultures, social structure is one of the most stable features (i.e., least likely to be altered by contact), whereas certain forms of technology are readily abandoned for more advanced varieties.

Among the early diffusionists were the leading anthropologists Boas, Haddon, and Rivers, to name just a few. Though the movement had its radicals (e.g., Smith and Perry), who believed all innovations diffused from ancient Egypt, the central premises of the approach were quite solid, and have affinities with a number of well-known contemporary theories. Diamond (1997), for example, has argued in a similar spirit that one of the major reasons that Europe conquered the Americas, rather than vice-versa, was that the geography of Eurasia and Northern Africa was much more conducive to transmission of cultural innovations than the Americas, because its horizontal axis enabled trade across similar climates, whereas the vertical axis of the Americas meant movement between diverse climates and through physical boundaries, such as mountains and deserts. Certain technological innovations, such as writing which was useful for the accounting practices in expanding administrative centers, were probably only independently invented 2-4 times (in Sumer, Mesoamerica, and possibly in Egypt and/or China), but spread quickly in Eurasia.

In the following subsections, I will focus in on Bartlett's diffusionist analysis in elaborating Kashima et al.'s (this volume) framework. Bartlett develops diffusionist ideas of his anthropologist mentors at Cambridge (e.g., Haddon and Rivers) into a coherent theoretical framework, filling in missing aspects with new concepts, such as "social constructiveness." He is also the most psychological of the diffusionists. Kashima is well acquainted with Bartlett's work on cultural dynamics (see Kashima, 2000), but I will argue that he and his colleagues' approach can still be further developed with the help of a number of Bartlett's core ideas—mainly, (1) dialectical interdependence of stability and change, (2) "social constructiveness," by which a group creatively constructs culture along the lines it is developing, and (3) the need to build theory by way of a careful analysis of particular social groups and the customs, traditions and values specific to them. I will consider each feature in turn.

The Dialectical Interdependence of Stability and Change

In Bartlett and Rivers' work "conservation" and "plasticity" (their terminology for "stability" and "change") are interdependent. As Bartlett (1923) put it, "it is because the group is selectively conservative that it is also plastic" (pp. 151-152). In order to make sense of this statement, we need to be cognizant of two general assumptions about culture: First, cultures are conceptualized as being in a process of continual change and second, cultural elements can only be artificially separated from the whole culture to which they are a part and from which they receive their meaning (cf. Bourdieu, 1994). Given these assumptions, the conservation of particular cultural elements does not ensure that they will retain the same meaning and function. For example, interventions to "preserve" parts of a group's culture necessarily change what is preserved. Gillespie (2006) has discussed how tourism essentially saved indigenous Ladakhi culture (e.g., traditional clothing and dances) by providing positive recognition from the outside, but in so doing it has become a spectacle for tourists and as such has lost its status as an everyday "living" cultural practice.

While stability turns out to be closely allied to change, so too is change dependent on stability. For example, Bartlett (1925) describes how years after the Spanish conquest of New Granada and conversion of its inhabitants to Christianity, shrines were discovered offering Christian paraphernalia (e.g., a friar's cap, a rosary, a priest's biretta, a prayer book, etc.) to the "overthrown" deities. The culture of the Spanish conquerors had been adopted by the people of New Granada, but in the process the meaning given to the foreign cultural practices changed so as to preserve the New Granada cultural patterns at a deeper level. Likewise, in contemporary globalizing societies franchises like McDonalds have to adapt themselves to local conditions if they are to be successful in the new context—a process cleverly named "glocalization" by combining globalization and localization (Robertson, 1992). They need to be assigned a location and thus meaning within the recipient culture, which will give a particular social status to the received cultural element, helping to fortify already existing distinctions in the recipient culture (see e.g., Pigg, 1996). The process of "globalization" itself is always confronted with the opposite tendency toward "localization." The two tendencies require each other, work in concert and as such need to be conceptualized together (Hermans & Dimaggio, 2007). With the globalization of "fast food" franchises, such as McDonalds, the "slow food" counter movement has developed, which aims to promote local culinary traditions and crops. Here too we see change and stability working side-by-side.

Bartlett's model of culture as actively developing patterns, which both assimilate and accommodate the new, finds an analogue at the individual level in his concept of "schema," which he defined as "an active organization of past reactions, or of past experiences" (Bartlett, 1932, p. 200). Commentators on Bartlett's work have generally overlooked this parallel as a result of neglecting the social dimensions of his corpus and by turning schema into a kind of static knowledge structure in the head, which is studied by counting the number of separate "units" remembered, forgotten or distorted. The methodological approach of counting units of information (at the expense of systemic relations between units) leaves the researcher completely blind to the properties of memories as wholes and their qualitative transformations (Wagoner, 2010), just as labeling information culture consistent OR inconstant (in Kashima et al.'s framework) hides important features of cultural transmission. By conceptually separating stability from change (even if their frequency is balanced), rather than treating them as interdependent opposites in tension, Kashima et al. has missed the study of change in its dependence on (relatively) stable meaning in cultural transmission, though at the theoretical level their "grounding model" points to such an approach. Let us now look more closely at the issue of how individuals and groups use an evolving system of reference to actively appropriate AND transform culture.

Social Constructiveness

The dialectical interdependence of cultural conservation and change is aptly illustrated by the fate of cultural elements during cultural contact. When cultural elements pass from one group to another a process of "conventionalization" ensues, whereby they change until they have reached a stable form in the recipient culture. Bartlett (1932, Chapter 16) says this occurs by way of assimilation, simplification, retention of apparently unimportant details, and by social constructiveness. The first three in this list help us to understand the small innovations introduced into cultural forms whenever they communicated or acted upon (as his famous experiments on remembering are powerfully demonstrated), while the last in this list (i.e., social constructiveness) highlights a more radical reconstructive process. Social constructiveness points to the fact that cultural elements are not only changed in the direction of the existing culture (i.e., towards conservation) but also *along the line in which the social group happens to be developing* (i.e., towards the innovation of genuinely new cultural forms). Bartlett called this future orientation the group's "prospect."[2] The important point to keep in mind here is that groups are not simply determined by their past (e.g., their traditions), but are also capable of creatively constructing something new in moving towards the future. The new cultural form is constructed by welding "together elements of culture coming from diverse sources and having historically, perhaps, very diverse significance" (Bartlett, 1932, p. 275). Again, we find an analogue with Bartlett's theorizing at the level of the individual: The mind is said to be "constructive" not so much because it uses "schemas" (to perceive, imagine, remember, and think), but rather as a result of its capacity for actively building together elements coming from diverse sources in a new synthesis.

If the concept of social constructiveness is accepted then we need a methodology that goes deeper than a study of the likelihood of new ideas being accepted or rejected in a given context. More importantly, we need to study how new ideas can stimulate creative change from within. This requires a "developmental" framework, by which I do not mean "child psychology," but rather the older meaning of "development" as a system's construction of novelty in its movement toward an indeterminate future (Valsiner, 2007). A genuinely developmental methodology does not concern itself with prediction. Such efforts can only be probabilistic. Development at the level of the single case cannot be predicted; it can only be observed as it unfolds. A developmental methodology concentrates on the *present-to-future* movement to study how a person or group actively adapts themselves to the future with the resources of the past (Valsiner, 2001). Thus, the framework brings back a focus on agency and the uniqueness of single cases, in the place of establishing cause-effect relationship between variables. The need to develop general theory about cultural dynamics from the complexities of single cases was central to Bartlett's (1923) approach and will be elaborated in the next section.

Studying Social Groups in Their Complex Particularity and Generality

The word "social" (as in "social contructiveness") had a specific meaning common to thinkers in the early decades of the twentieth century, but not widely understood today. It meant those properties of groups (e.g., their values, norms, and customs) irreducible to the aggregation of individuals in them (see Farr, 1996; Greenwood, 2004). A social psychological study was one that investigated and compared the distinctive mentalities of different social groups. For example, in Murchison's (1935) *A Handbook of Social Psychology* there are separate chapters on the psychology of the "negro," "red man," "white man," "yellow man" and even chapters on the social behavior in insects, birds, and primates.[3] Bartlett is very upfront about his advocacy of a more "social" social psychology. He argues that an adequate theory of cultural dynamics should be developed through an analysis of ethnographic studies of particular societies around the world. In his book *Psychology and Primitive Culture* he illustrates this strategy with extensive discussions of examples of culture change from field studies in the Americas, Africa, and Southeast Asia. Bartlett (1923) works with each society in its uniqueness to develop principles for describing and explaining cultural contact and culture change in general.

The single case approach to theory building was shared with a number of other important psychologists at this time (e.g., Vygotsky, Lewin, and even F. Allport) and is recently making its way back into psychology (e.g., see Salvatore and Valsiner's (2008) *Yearbook of Idiographic Science,* now in its fourth volume). This approach recognizes that the reporting of data in aggregate statistics (without other forms of data) tells us nothing about how different factors are actually organized within whole single cases. Lewin (1933) comments, "The laws of falling bodies in physics cannot be discovered by taking the average of actual falling movements, say of leaves, stones, and other objects, but only by proceeding from so-called "pure" cases" (p. 559). This critique will be of even greater importance when dealing with social systems, which unlike physical systems have different histories, meaningful patterns of self-organization and a "prospect" (see above).

THE MOVEMENT OF IDEAS IN CONTEMPORARY SOCIETIES

In this section, the above outlined principles of Bartlett's diffusionist theory are applied and extended to understand the communication of ideas in contemporary society. Bartlett thought that the increase of complexity in contemporary societies (in terms of heterogeneity of social groups, culture and contacts) was coeval with the increase of freedom and constructiveness (at both individual and group levels). The frequent and diverse cultural contacts between social groups in contemporary societies provided many resources for the construction of new ideas and the stimulation of social change. However, this process does not occur without controversy (see also Jensen, this volume, Chapter 10 on "scientific controversies"). Social groups have different projects for themselves and will construct ideas to advance them, which come in conflict with other groups' ideas. Moscovici eloquently expresses this in relation to how ideas constructed in the scientific community stimulate constructive changes within popular thinking:

> When a new idea of scientific knowledge penetrates into the public sphere, the cultural life of a society, then you have a real *kulturkampf*, cultural struggles, intellectual polemics and opposition between different modes of thinking.... There is a drama involved in the process of transformation and the birth of a new social representation. (Moscovici, 2000, p. 229)

The "drama" Moscocivi speaks of is not isolated to scientific ideas, but any new ideas advanced in society. Still, it will be helpful to consider Moscovici's (2008) own study of the assimilation of psychoanalysis (science) into French society as an illustrative example of how to approach contemporary cultural dynamics from a perspective akin to Bartlett's diffusionism.

The second Part of Moscovici's *Psychoanalysis: Its Image and Its Public* is a content analysis of French press, exploring the process by which psychoanalysis was assimilated into the fabric of French society through different social groups' media communications. In the 1950s, when his study was conducted, the French Press was differentiated into three main media sources: the liberal, catholic and communist press. Each social group had its own aims, constructed its own image of psychoanalysis, and used its own "communication genre" to do so, which in turn lead to different psychological outcomes (see Table 9.1).[4] The *liberal press* had as its principle aim attracting readers, and oriented its communication to pleasing the audience. As such there was symmetry between author and audience in the communication—Bartlett (1923) would say this was a relation of "comradeship," which is highly conducive to the blending of cultures. In support of its aim of attracting readers, the liberal press used irony, reservations about psychoanalysis, humor, diverse perspectives and references to specialists to distance itself from psychoanalysis. As such, this genre of communication encourages the development of individual *opinions* about psychoanalysis.[5] Moscovici calls this communication genre "diffusion."

In contrast to "diffusion," the two other communicative genres Moscovici identifies lead to ideas being held "socially"—that is, as a member of a social group rather than as an individual—and also to the creation of "semantic barriers" to try to block the influence of new ideas from other

Table 9.1. A summary of Moscovici's (2008) Content Analysis of the French Press

Media	*Communication Genre*	*Relationship*	*Psychological Outcomes*
Liberal press	Diffusion	Symmetrical	Opinions
Catholic press	Propagation	Authoritative	Attitudes
Communist press	Propaganda	Authoritarian	Stereotypes

groups. The *Catholic press* authoritatively accepts some aspects of psychoanalysis (e.g., potential therapeutic benefits) but rejects others (e.g., Freud's image of man). It uses the communicative genre of "propagation" to advance a particular representation of psychoanalysis and behavior towards it. The result is structured group *attitudes* towards psychoanalysis, rather than individual *opinions*. Finally, the *communist press* uses "propaganda" to reinforce its group's dichotomized worldview, in which communist, soviet, rational and science are good, and American, irrational, pseudo-science, bourgeois and individualist are bad. The terms in each grouping become interchangeable through repeated communication: Psychoanalysis is always prefixed with one of these other adjectives in the bad side, such that clusters of associations are formed (i.e., *prejudices*). Whereas the Catholics let themselves be partially influenced by psychoanalysis there is little elaboration on the new idea of psychoanalysis by the communists, only an attempt to neutralize it. In both "propagation" and "propaganda" there is an asymmetrical relationship between sender and receiver. Bartlett's (1923) would say that the sender is "dominant" and the receiver "submissive" (as opposed to e.g., "comradeship"), a relationship that leads to high acceptance of the message. "Propagation" and "propaganda" differ in that the former is authoritative but not authoritarian, as is the latter—"propagation" is flexible but firm in its command of authority.

Comparing Moscovici's (2008) approach to Kashima et al.'s (this volume) a number of interesting differences come into view. First, we are studying real historically situated social groups and comparing their distinct mentalities. All three groups would fall under Kashima et al.'s "public" activity group and yet they all transmit the radical new idea to a certain extend (and the liberal and catholic press do so in a "socially constructive" fashion), though they position themselves in relation to it in distinctive ways. Second, looking at real groups allows us to explore the concrete *process* (e.g., the communicative genre) and *content* (i.e., specific image of psychoanalysis) of communication. All groups transmit the idea of psychoanalysis but do so through different tactics and construct their own image of it. Thus, we can speak of different representations of psychoanalysis for liberals, Catholics, communists, Americans, French, and so on. Third, in exploring the content of messages, we find the representation of a potentially competing group's representation from within a social representation. Gillespie (2009) suggests these "alternative representations" are straw men used to either dialogue with or dismiss another group's point of view. The effect of the interaction between the two positions can lead to the construction of new ways of thinking—an outcome authoritarian groups try to suppress. Groups protect their representations from this kind of dialogical change by constructing what Gillespie calls "semantic barriers," such as creating rigid opposites (as discussed above with the Communist group), stigmatizing the other and undermining their motive. The Communist Press, for example, said people who go to psychoanalysts are "fashionable women" and psychoanalysts are just in it for the money (pp. 386-387). In sum, ideas become part of dialogical exchanges between different groups' perspectives. On the one hand, this enhances social constructiveness, but on the other, it stimulates groups to create barriers to dialogue in order to limit this process. In the next section, I will further elaborate on the dialogical dynamics of ideas.

A DIALOGICAL THEORY OF COMMUNICATION

Kashima et al. (this volume) mention two contemporary approaches to communication, which they say are akin to his own—Vygotskyian approaches and memetic approaches. Though both approaches deal with cultural transmission, their assumptions about the processes involved are radically different. First, from a Vygotskyian perspective, culture is a psychological tool (or "sign") used by a person to regulate him or herself or another (Vygotsky & Luria, 1930/1994). The locus of causality—what Heider and Simmel (1944) called the "causal center"—is the person performing the action. By contrast, in memetics, "memes" (a combination of "mime" and "gene") are said to "infect minds" (like a virus) and are thus themselves granted causal agency. Second, in the last sections we already explored a number of processes by which culture is transformed in transmission. Memeticians are reluctant to acknowledge that in the realm of culture transmission transformation of message is the rule rather than the exception. In contrast, Vygotskian approaches make creative transformation of culture in the process of its "appropriation" or "internalization" a focus of analysis.[6] Third, there is little in memetics to distinguish human imitation from imitation in other animals. Human beings do not only imitate but also mock, ventriloquate, lie, and pretend. These activities presuppose the ability to take another's perspective towards oneself. It should be clear that only the Vygotskian approaches are compatible with the diffusionist principles outlined above. Kashima et al.'s theoretical model of grounding seems to be in accord with a Vygotskian approach, but methodologically they come much closer to memetics.

At a general level the contrast hangs on the treatment of human beings as objects (in memetics), rather than as meaning-making subjects (in the Vygotskian approach). Following Rommetveit (2003), we can say this is the difference between seeing human beings from a third or second person psychology. The second person psychology starts with the assumption that "you" are intelligible to "me" because we are cohabitants of an immanently meaningful world. As such one cannot adequately approach the study of human beings as one would physical laws or even the behavior of non-human animals—that is, from the outside. Instead, understanding others is also a process of self-understanding, of knowing/working on one's own mind and view of the world (Gadamer, 2004). Kashima et al. call this intersubjectively shared world human beings live in the "communal ground," through which we can communicate with one another. Yet they do not adequately position themselves as subjects sharing a meaningful world with the people they study. Instead, other people are approached purely from a third person perspective (of predicting likelihood of transmission—as if an idea were simply a physical object) rather than exploring communication and cognition from within the meaningful world of subjects. This enables them to speak very abstractly about the diffusion of ideas without "grounding" it within the lifeworlds of particular subjects and societies.

What might they find if they approached the diffusion of "socially transformative ideas" by treating people as subjects rather than objects? Approached from within one's own lifeworld we know that revealing a belief (acceptance of a certain idea) to another is a tension filled act of social positioning, which can result in failure, rejection or worse (see Moscovici, 1986). This is so because ideas are not free floating entities but linked to social positions—being pro-this or anti-that, within a social landscape. Privately held ideas are typically still situated in social life, in that they are formed in interaction with others and carry those others with them—even if we tell no one about our belief we are still aware of the way it positions us vis-à-vis others. Put bluntly, ideas are always situated between two or more people. As such, an idea can be thought of as a certain social perspective on the world, which I represent as being shared with some and not others.

The intersubjective nature of ideas gives rise to new complexities: I not only believe that others share an idea but also that they believe I share the same idea with them, and even more that they believe I believe they share the same idea. Kashima et al.'s concept of "pluralistic ignorance," whereby multiple people share an idea but believe that others do not clearly alludes to a similar phenomenon. Yet levels of complexity can easily be added to their concept: I might think that others also share my socially transformative belief, but do not think that they believe that I share the same belief with them. Thus, there is still an obstacle to group organization and mobilization. The power of crowd demonstration is in showing that we know that others believe that we believe—thus paving the way to social change (see Drury, Reicher, & Scott, this volume, Chapter 2 on the rationality of crowds). In sum, the spread of socially transformative ideas is not enough for social change to occur; additionally these ideas must become part of an intersubjectively shared worldview.

CONCLUSION

In this chapter, I have extended Kashima et al.'s (this volume) ideas towards a more constructive, social and dialogical theory of communication and social change. The chapter began by reexamining early diffusionist theories, especially those put forward by Frederic Bartlett, extracting three key methodological principles: (1) conceptualizing stability and change as dialectically interdependent concepts, (2) recognizing that cultural transmission also involves constructive changes being made to the material, and (3) studying social groups in their complex particularity and generality. Moscovici's study of psychoanalysis was then used as a case study to illustrate and advance diffusionist ideas in the context of cultural transmission in contemporary society. In Moscovici's framework "diffusion" is only one of three "communication genres" used to transmit new ideas and is the most permissive of the three. The others, "propagation" and "propaganda," set up "semantic barriers" to block the free dialogue with the new ideas that promotes social constructiveness. Last, ideas were situated within dialogical interaction, whereby ideas are intersubjective perspectives on the world that position us vis-à-vis others. It is only by taking these additional notions into account that we can fully understand the multitude of ways an idea can be held, shared and resisted, and the processes enabling it to be acted upon for the purposes of social change.

ACKNOWLEDGMENTS

I would like to thank Julian Oldmeadow and Eric Jensen for their helpful comments on earlier drafts of this chapter.

NOTES

1. The word "primitive" was not used in a derogatory sense.
2. Social representations theorists have developed a similar concept, called a group's "project" (Bauer & Gaskell, 1999).
3. What has frequently been described as the first social psychology study—Triplett's (1898) early experiment demonstrating the presence of another person can increase productivity—was not at the time believed to be a study in social psychology at all, but instead an experiment in physiology. Floyd Allport created the myth that Triplett's experiment was the first social psychology study, in order to advance his own version of social psychology, which was very explicitly a psychology of individuals. His version of social psychology has remained with us until this day, though recently there have been a number of efforts to return to earlier concerns of the

subdiscipline (e.g., social representations theory, social identity theory, and cultural psychology).

4. Moscovici (2008) is clear that each group might employ a different communicative genre to communicate about another topic. Thus, we cannot separate communication processes from the content of the social representation.
5. It should be noted that a content analysis of the press does not in itself allow us to legitimately make claims about audience reception. In Part I of Moscovici's (2008) study, he conducts interviews and administers questionnaires but these date sources are, by his own admission, not systematically linked to his analysis of the French Press.
6. It should, however, be noted here that early twentieth century theorists who attempted to model cultural transmission on Darwin's evolutionary perspective (e.g., Baldwin) discussed "innovation" alongside "imitation" (see Jahoda, 2002)

REFERENCES

Bartlett, F. C. (1923). *Psychology and Primitive Culture.* Cambridge, England: Cambridge University Press.

Bartlett, F. C. (1925). The social functions of symbols. *Astralasian Journal of Psychology and Philosophy, 3,* 1-11.

Bartlett, F. C. (1932). *Remembering: A study in experimental and social psychology.* Cambridge, England: Cambridge University Press.

Bartlett, F.C. (1943). Anthropology in reconstruction. *Journal of the Royal Anthropological Institute* 72: 9-16

Bartlett, F. C. (1946). Psychological methods for the study of "hard" and "soft" features of culture. *Africa, 16,* 145-155.

Bauer, M. W., & Gaskell, G. (1999). Towards a paradigm for research on social representations. *Journal for the Theory of Social Behaviour, 29*(2), 163-186.

Bourdieu, P. (1994). Social space and symbolic space. In P. Bourdieu (Ed.), *Practical reason* (pp. 1-13). Stanford, CA: Stanford University Press.

Castro, P., & Batel, S. (2008). Social representation, change and resistance: On the difficulties of generalizing new norms. *Culture & Psychology, 14*(4), 475-497.

Diamond, J. (1997). *Guns, germs, and steel: The fates of human societies.* New York, NY: W. W. Norton.

Farr, R. M. (1996). *The roots of modern social psychology.* Oxford, England: Blackwell.

Gadamer, H. (2004). *Truth and method* (2nd ed.). London: Continuum.

Greenwood, J. (2004). *Disappearance of the social in American social psychology.* Cambridge, England: Cambridge University Press.

Gillespie, A. (2006). *Becoming other: From social interaction to self-reflection.* Charlotte, NC: Information Age.

Gillespie, A. (2009). Social representations, alternative representations and semantic barriers. *Journal for the Theory of Social Behaviour, 38*(4), 376-391.

Heider, F., & Simmel, M. (1944). An experimental study of apparent behavior. *American Journal of Psychology, 57,* 243-259.

Hermans, H. J. M., & Dimaggio, G. (2007). Self, identity, and globalisation in times of uncertainty: A dialogical analysis. *Review of General Psychology, 11*(1), 31-61.

Jahoda, G. (2002). The ghosts in the meme machine. *History of the Human Sciences, 15*(22), 55-68.

Jensen, E., & Wagoner, B. (2009). A cyclical model of social change. *Culture & Psychology, 15*(2), 217-228.

Kashima, Y. (2000). Recovering Bartlett's social psychology of cultural dynamics. *European Journal of Social Psychology, 30*(3), 383-403.

Lewin, K. (1933). Environmental forces in child behavior and development. In C. Murchinson (Ed.), *A handbook of child psychology* (pp. 590–625). Worcester, MA: Clark University Press.

Marková, I. (2003). *Dialogicality and social representations.* Cambridge, England: Cambridge University Press.

Moscovici, S. (1986). The Dreyfus affair, Proust, and social psychology. *Social Research, 53,* 23-56.

Moscovici, S. (1991). Experience and experiment: An intermediate step from Sherif to Asch. *Journal for the Theory of Social Behavior, 21*(3), 253-268.

Moscovici, S. (2000). *Social representations: Explorations in social psychology.* New York, NY: New York University.

Moscovici, S. (2008). *Psychoanalysis: Its image and its public.* Cambridge, England: Polity Press.

Murchison, C. M. (Ed.) (1935). *A handbook of social psychology.* Worcester, MA: Clark University Press.

Pigg, S. L. (1996). The credible and the credulous: The question of "villagers' beliefs" in Nepal. *Cultural Anthropology,* 11(2), 160-201

Rivers, W. H. R. (1912). Conventionalism in primitive art. *Reports of British Association for the Advancement of Science* (Sección H), 599.

Rivers, W. H. R. (1914). *The history of Melanesian society.* Cambridge, England: Cambridge University Press.

Robertson, R. (1992). *Globalization: Social theory and global culture.* London: Sage.

Rommetveit, R. (2003) On the role of "a psychology of the second person" in studies of meaning, language and mind. *Mind, Culture and Activity, 10*(3), 205-218.

Salvatore, S., Valsiner, J., Strout-Yagodzynski, S., & Clegg, J. (Eds.). (2008). *Yearbook of Idiographic Science: Volume 1.* Rome, Italy: Firera & Liuzzo Group.

Triplett, N. (1898). The dynamogenic factors in pacemaking and competition. *American Journal of Psychology, 9,* 507-533.

Valsiner, J. (2001). Process structure of semiotic mediation. *Human Development, 44,* 84-97.

Valsiner, J. (2007). *Culture in minds and societies.* New Dehli: SAGE.

Vygotsky, L., & Luria, A. (1994). Tool and symbol in child development. In J. Valsiner & R. van der Veer (Eds.), *The Vygotsky Reader* (pp. 99-174). Oxford, England: Blackwell. (Original work published in 1930)

Wagoner, B. (2012). Culture in constructive remembering. In J. Valsiner (Ed.), *Oxford handbook of culture and psychology.* Oxford, England: Oxford University Press.

CHAPTER 10

SCIENTIFIC CONTROVERSIES AND THE STRUGGLE FOR SYMBOLIC POWER

Eric Jensen

Symbols are implicated in the production of knowledge and the communication of information across all domains of professional life, and the sciences are no exception. The sciences pride themselves on communicating technical meanings based upon objective empirical observations. However, there can be no doubt that scientific knowledge takes on symbolic and even metaphorical meanings, especially when it is communicated to publics outside of a specialist subfield (Jensen & Weasel, 2006; Wagoner & Jensen, 2010; Weasel & Jensen, 2005). Some scientists resist the extension and symbolization of scientific meaning in the public sphere, while others accept or even embrace it as a necessary dimension of science communication (Holliman & Jensen, 2009). In either case, scientific institutions and individual scientists intervene in the process of signification connecting socially constructed and arbitrary signs or symbols to their technical referents within scientific practice (Saussure, 1990). Such interventions promote symbols reflecting and reinforcing materialist and empiricist definitions of the sciences' roles in contemporary society. At the same time, public awareness of risks inherent in techno-scientific development has increased alongside resistance to particular aspects of scientific development, alongside a nascent institutional reflexivity that challenges the

Culture and Social Change: Transforming Society Through the Power of Ideas, pp. 161–183

grand metanarrative of scientific progress from within (Beck, 1992; Select Committee on Science & Technology, 2000). The resulting struggles over symbolic representation of new scientific developments can determine levels of acceptance or resistance that emerge in public discourse (Jensen & Wagoner, 2009). This chapter elucidates the process of symbolization of scientific ideas in the public sphere, with particular emphasis on high profile controversies in the life sciences. Although there are other means of communicating science outside the mass media industries, "there is one forum that overshadows all others.... *General-audience mass media provide a master forum*" (emphasis added), comprising "*the* major site of political contest because all of the players in the policy process assume its pervasive influence (whether justified or not)" (Ferree, Gamson, Gerhards, & Rucht, 2002, p. 10). As such, there is a special focus in this chapter on theorizing the role of mass media publicizing scientific ideas.

The power to mould symbolic representations of a given scientific development when it becomes public is unequally distributed amongst various stakeholders under conditions of "normal science." For example, government officials, scientists, and other experts are disproportionately influential in shaping mainstream journalistic coverage (Fishman, 1980; Herman & Chomsky, 1988), and thereby the public agenda (e.g., McCombs & Shaw, 1972). Activists and other non-routine sources for news media have only second tier access to journalistic coverage of the sciences, thereby disadvantaging their voices unless they are re-broadcast by powerful expert institutions (Jensen, 2010b). These technocratic forces maintain their power through greater access to economic, social and cultural capital to support a set of symbols comprising the dominant Enlightenment myth of "science" as "progress" in the grand quest for objective Truth and technological and medical utopia (Jensen, E., 2008b; Lyotard, 1984). The political dominance of this ideological position is reproduced in part through its affinity with the demand for continual economic growth that fuels modern capitalism. However, I will argue in this chapter that controversies can unhinge the predominately technocratic social order governing the symbolization of scientific issues in the mediated public sphere. Whereas scientific ideas and issues being constituted in the public sphere as "normal" and uncontroversial are frequently addressed in institutions such as museums and news media with deference to the epistemological superiority of scientific expertise, scientific controversies are often defined by the unmasking of human, processual and even ideological identity of the sciences and scientific expertise. Such subjective dimensions of scientific practice are typically well-hidden by symbolic rituals such as peer review, which reconstruct and consecrate scientific practice as an inductive, organized, logical, and linear endeavor. Indeed this unrealistic representation of the sciences is the Shibboleth required by scientific journals and university presses for entry into the hallowed ground of institutionally sanctioned scientific truth. Under normal conditions of uncontroversial scientific ideas and issues, the dominant Enlightenment myth of the sciences gives academic and industry scientists a relatively free hand in developing their research with an implied public consensus that the sciences have earned their autonomy by way of delivering technological advances and concomitant economic value (Beck, 1992).

Scientific controversies "combine moral argument with extensive use of scientific expertise" (Nelkin, 1992, p. xviii), which often play out in news media. Such controversies can be viewed as a struggle to define the terms, scope and dominant framing of a scientific issue. Recent scientific controversies include human cloning, embryo research, genetically modified crops, bovine spongiform encephalopathy (BSE or "mad cow disease") and foot and mouth disease. In the wake of technological disasters such as Chernobyl, Fukushima and other examples of "risky" sciences and technologies, Beck (1992), Giddens (1991, 1994) and others have argued that expert systems such as the sciences have lost much of their authority in "late" or "second" modernity. However, I argue that these claims about the sciences' changing status in contemporary societies should be more narrowly focussed on the impacts of scientific controversies. Indeed, I contend that controversies are a major source of disruptions in the dominant public symbolism of the sciences. Specifically, the control exercised by techno-scientific institutions such as the American Association for the Advancement of Science and the Royal Society, corporations and government over the prevailing symbols for scientific development is weakened during heated scientific debates in the public sphere. While these powerful interests maintain privileged access to news media during controversies, I suggest that they lose the power to assert their preferred framing of the issue *unchallenged.* During controversies, news media allow nonroutine sources such as protest groups, dissenting or "fringe" scientists and "ordinary citizens" temporary access; thus, new symbolic meanings and metaphorical source domains are introduced to challenge ascendant scientific definitions of the issue. Although these new scientific symbols are unquestionably influential, the longevity of this disruption in the structure of symbolic power is unclear. This essay considers whether such symbols emerging during scientific controversies are robust to shifting news media and citizen interests. In other words, controversies yield long-term social change in cultural representations of the sciences?

In this chapter, I argue that indeed controversies overturn the normal symbolic order in mediated science communication, and not necessarily on a temporary basis. As such, I contend that scientific controversies play an important- if variable- emancipatory role, democratizing the sciences by shifting the linguistic landscape from a near monopoly of the dominant myth of "scientific progress" to a more open range of symbols emerging primarily from the communicative rationality of the lifeworld (Habermas, 1987), which are equally accessible to scientists and nonscientists alike (also see Collins & Evans, 2002). To develop these arguments, I briefly consider scientific controversies with clear struggles for symbolic power and ideological dominance between institutionally sponsored scientific experts and dissenting scientists, activists and citizens. The struggle within and between scientific, religious and activist forces over definitions and prevailing conceptual metaphors for controversial sciences offers insights into the punctuated equilibrium of scientific symbolization in the public sphere.

THEORETICAL BACKGROUND

This chapter examines the transformation of conventional public meanings for scientific concepts or issues. Typically, such meanings are propounded through largely uncontested symbolic power exercised by expert media sources and institutions, framing a newly publicized scientific idea using the symbolism of scientific progress. Yet, a dynamic struggle occasionally breaks out in the mediated public sphere when competing cultural meanings are introduced.

The "capacity to intervene" and successfully promote one's definition of an issue "by means of the production and transmission of symbolic forms" is known as *symbolic power* (Thompson, 1995, p. 17). This chapter centers on *symbolic valorization*.

> "Symbolic valorization" … is the process through which symbolic forms are ascribed a certain "symbolic value" … that objects have by virtue of the ways in which, and the extent to which, they are esteemed, … praised or denounced, cherished or despised. (Thompson, 1990, pp. 154-155)

Thompson (1990, p. 155) emphasizes that symbolic valorization is a contested process, structured by the uneven distribution of economic, cultural and symbolic capital among the participants in this struggle. Different strategies of symbolic valuation are employed by those in dominant, intermediate, or subordinate positions within the field of symbolic interaction (Thompson, 1990, p. 158).[1] "In exercising symbolic power, individuals draw on various kinds of resources." The most important resources are the "means of information and communication," including myths and symbols designed to impose a preferred definition of a concept in the public sphere.

In analyzing this process, cultural theorist Roland Barthes' (1973) distinction between the literal, or "denotative" meaning of an image, text or sound on the one hand, and the symbolic or "connotative" meaning on the other is key. Connotative meanings are culturally bound and, according to Barthes, structured within myths that reinforce the dominant position of economic elites within society. A text is encoded with often subtle signals that activate knowledge, beliefs, and stereotypes constitutive of cultural myths, which function by masking the constructedness and contingency of these ideas (Barthes, 1977). Crucially, such myths are taken for granted as common sense (Barthes, 1973). Indeed, once a myth is fully "naturalized" in this way, it can be difficult to detect because it is no longer recognized as a subjective belief, but instead has become an intersubjective "social fact" within the culture.

Regardless of their mythical or "naturalized" status, Saussure (1990) argues that the arbitrariness of signs opens them up to the possibility and indeed inevitability of change over time. He contends that shifts in meaning occur through a gradual reorientation of the relationships between concepts. In the context of conceptual relationships, Lakoff's (1993) conceptual metaphor theory is instructive. One component of Lakoff's theory is that metaphors can carry over meanings from source domains to target domains (see also Cornejo, this volume). Thus, for example, when the conceptual metaphor "*LIFE IS A JOURNEY*" is activated, certain meanings and signifiers associated with "journeys" (e.g., pathways, roads, orienteering) are recognized as relevant (Sperber & Wilson, 1986) and temporarily transferred from the *source domain* "journey" to the *target domain* of "life" (cf. Ritchie, 2003, 2006; Vervaeke & Kennedy, 1996). There are a wide range of possible conceptual metaphors that could be applied to a given scientific concept. For example, human cloning has been connected to source domains such as "Xerox copying," "baby manufacturing," and "abortion" (Jensen & Weasel, 2006). Genetically modified crops have been characterized with metaphorical frames such as "*seeds of disaster*" or "*forbidden fruit*" (Nerlich, Clarke, & Dingwall, 2000, p. 235). I will argue that the ascendance of particular metaphorical source domains meaning are of central importance to the connotative symbolic valuation of newly publicized scientific issues.

SYMBOLIC SIGNIFICATION AND VALUATION DURING "NORMAL SCIENCE"

> Normal science, the activity in which most scientists inevitably spend almost all their time, is predicated on the assumption that the scientific community knows what the world is like. Much of the success of the enterprise derives from the community's willingness to defend that assumption, if necessary at considerable cost. (Kuhn, 1960, p. 5)[2]

Ideas associated with new technological or scientific developments can remain largely sequestered[3] within a relatively closed speech community of specialist scientific experts indefinitely (cf. Collins & Evans, 2002), where symbolization is constricted. When such concepts become known outside of the specialist subfield, they attract an increasing range of symbolic meanings from contact with broader scientific communities. However, as long as the concept remains within academic and industrial scientific fields, the range of possible meanings is restricted by the ascendant positivist epistemology, instrumental rationality and materialist values (Burchell, 2007). Most scientific ideas remain primarily technical and nonsymbolic for their entire life cycle, never leaving the small specialist subfield in which they were originally conceived. A small percentage of these ideas will achieve a high enough profile to be noticed within broader scientific communities. A small percentage of these concepts are "consecrated" through publication in a top journal such as *Science* or *Nature*. These journals will in turn promote a subset of their articles to science journalists and other media stakeholders, who will select "newsworthy" stories based on journalistic news values and organizational norms (Jensen, 2010a).

Under normal conditions, media coverage of scientific journal articles is perhaps best described as "compliant." Scientists tend to be the only sources consulted, and their claims about the benefits of their research are typically taken at face value. Indeed most of the scientific ideas discussed in the press are given a treatment some science journalists refer to as a "study says" story. "Study says" news stories simply recount the findings of a given journal article, using scientists or "scientific press officers" as sources (Gregory & Miller, 1998, p. 109). Such news stories reinforce the symbolism of scientific progress, for example the "breakthrough" and "milestone" frames (e.g., Brown, 2000). This symbolism promotes the symbolic valorization of scientific ideas by pointing to their benefits and downplaying their drawbacks (e.g., Gutteling et al., 2002). For example, "study says" stories regularly employ the conceptual metaphor, "*scientific research is forward motion in space*" (i.e., scientific progress), emphasizing the techno-scientific development's instrumental utility and downplaying risk.

The Dominant Myth of Science

Conventional meaning is not predetermined in the case of new scientific ideas emerge from a scientific field. Rather, the process of conventionalization and symbolic valuation begins in earnest when scientific ideas reach a wide public audience, often via mass media. A fundamental contention in this essay is that upon entrance into the public sphere the technical, denotative meaning of a scientific issue becomes submerged. As Barthes (1973, p. 109) notes, "every object in the world can pass from a closed, silent existence to an oral state, open to appropriation by society." Once in this public domain, scientific concepts become "adapted to a certain type of consumption, laden with literary self-indulgence, revolt, images, in short with a type of social usage which is added to pure matter" (p. 109). In this socially defined realm, nontechnical, symbolic meanings immediately begin to overlay the original denotative scientific meanings. These new symbolic meanings are "connotative" in Barthes' (1977) terms.

When science enters the public realm it is invariably "filtered" through the lens of mass media (see Herman & Chomsky, 1988), although today mass media include a range of "new media." In science news, journalistic norms and writing conventions structure the presentation of science. For example, journalists select metaphors, characters and framing devices based on their conceptualization of audience interests and their own "news sense" about the best way to represent or "accommodate" scientific knowledge for a lay audience. As Fahnestock (1993, p. 19) argues, "scientific accommodations are overwhelmingly epideictic; their main purpose is to celebrate rather than validate.... The work of epideictic rhetoric in science journalism requires the adjustment of new information to the audiences' already held values and assumptions." For example, the techno-scientific establishment constructs scientific advances as comprising an inexorable march towards enlightenment (i.e., "scientific progress"). Symbolically—or mythologically (Barthes, 1973)—this proscience framing of the new scientific concept includes metaphorical phrases such as scientific "advance," "remarkable feat," "breakthrough" (Brown, 2000), "technological fix," "scientific milestone" and "important step on the road to a cure" (e.g., Hellsten, 2000; Weasel & Jensen, 2005). These framing devices "accommodate" technical, esoteric concepts to more universal audience knowledge using conceptual metaphors related to the notion of science as a journey, competition, or tool (Lakoff, 1993). Such conceptual metaphors point to the underlying myth of scientific progress, a myth that reached its apotheosis for most twentieth century Americans when astronaut Neil Armstrong landed on the moon and declared that he was taking "One small step for man; One giant leap for mankind." Such framing devices reinforce the dominant myth of science in Western culture:

> The dominant myth of science presents it as humankind's ability to adapt nature to our needs, to improve ... our standard of living, to celebrate our achievement. Science is seen as objective, true, and good. (Fiske, 1990, p. 90)

In addition to demonstrating control over nature, there is also an aura of utopian hope that surrounds many new scientific technologies. Nuclear power, for example, was bathed in this utopian aura when it was first promoted as a permanent solution to the world's energy needs in postwar America and Britain. Mulkay (1997, pp. 70-71) identified a similarly prophetic "rhetoric of hope" in the U.K. embryo research debate of the 1980s: "The primary message ... was that the use of science-based techniques offered hope.... In these texts, the future accomplishments of embryo research become strangely tangible." Indeed, hyping the imminence of a technological or medical marvel is a long-standing phenomenon in European history (e.g., Toumey, 1996). Haran, Kitzinger, McNeil, and O'Riordan (2007, p. 47) describe this prophetic framing as a form of "temporal contraction," that is, "discursive renderings involving the condensation of the timelines for curing through technoscien[ce]."

THE SYMBOLIC SIGNIFICATION AND VALUATION OF CONTROVERSIAL SCIENCE

Particular scientific issues are not static in terms of their symbolic valuation in the public domain. Today's symbolically uncontested science can become controversial science tomorrow. Only a minority of the scientific ideas that are made public are connected to some form of risk, disaster or moral transgression that qualifies them as "controversial" for certain publics. For example, a longitudinal study of U.K. press content found about 25% of science news is devoted to controversies of this type (Bauer, Durant, Ragnarsodottir, & Rudolphsdotir, 1995). Scientific controversies can open the door to counter-myths which challenge the supremacy of the dominant myth of science.

> But the counter-myth [of science] is also very strong. This sees science as evil [... and] scientists [as] selfish and short-sighted, in pursuit of our own material ends. (Fiske, 1990, p. 90)

Fiske identifies the tendency for these (counter-)myths and to reside in different media forms.

> In popular culture both myths are represented. The factual side of television, news, current affairs, [...] tends to show more of the dominant than the counter-myth; fictional television and cinema, on the other hand, reverse the proportions. (pp. 90-91)

Fiske's description above is valid in the case of uncontested scientific developments. However during controversies, the "factual side" of television (i.e., primarily news) sometimes incorporates counter-myths grounded in allusions to science fiction such as *Frankenstein* or *Brave New World* (cf. Kitzinger & Williams, 2005). For example, in factual coverage of the human cloning controversy, Hellsten (2000) identified a tension between the dominant myth of scientific progress and an oppositional reading which framed human cloning as "progress" towards a dangerous or even apocalyptic destination. Moreover at times of controversy, newspapers may mention "*Franken*food" or "embryo hatcheries" to describe a position opposed to the dominant myth, thereby reinforcing the most powerful and culturally grounded counter-myth: That is, the *Frankenstein*-inspired notion of hubristic, myopic science leading to ultimately self-destructive unintended consequences. Like scientific utopianism, apocalyptic visions frequently accompanying *Frankenstein* scenarios are characterized by "temporal contraction," which frames the dangers of techno-scientific development (Jensen, E., 2008b). Moreover, apocalypticism of this type has a long history in Western thought. Of course the most notable apocalypticist in the Western tradition is Jesus of Nazareth, who exemplified this temporal contraction by cryptically predicting almost 2,000 years ago that the world would end within the lifetimes of his contemporaries:

> And [Jesus] said unto them, "Verily I say unto you, That there be some of them that stand here, which shall not taste of death, till they have seen the kingdom of God come with power." (Mark 9:1, King James Bible)

Indeed, apocalypticism is a deeply embedded narrative in western thought. Since the ascent of Christianity, elements of every generation have come up with their own doomsday stories that were believed to be destined to come about in their lifetimes.

DOMAIN SHIFTING

> There is no fixity in mythical concepts: they can come into being, alter, disintegrate, disappear completely. (Barthes, 1973, pp. 110, 120)

Domain shifting from uncontroversial to controversial science[4] becomes possible when there is some form of negative incident or disaster associated with a particular aspect of public science. By itself, however, an incident is not sufficient to yield a scientific controversy. Rather, a disastrous event or disclosed risk merely renders a science or technology as "discreditable." For controversy to attach however, the additional requirement is that the narrative or "story" of this negative incident must be compelling, intelligible and relatable to the public. These criteria align with the requirements of professional news production as well. Indeed, context and the processes of news production are key mediating factors in the shift into the domain of controversial science. At the same time, public representations of controversial sciences also rely in large part on the availability of previously extant cultural symbolism that can be adapted to articulate the risks inhering in this aspect of techno-scientific development. For example, it is no accident that permutations of the *Frankenstein* narrative are so ubiquitous in the framing controversial sciences (Bloomfield & Vurdubakis, 2003; Mulkay, 1996; Turney, 1998). Below, I examine two sources of symbolism constitutive of scientific controversies: (1) science fiction providing stock characters and familiar narratives that can be grafted onto a discreditable domain of techno-science and (2) a "risk" frame accessing deep societal unease with uncontrollable hazards unleashed by scientific development.

Fictive Source Domains: The Cultural Genealogy of Science

New symbols that emerge during controversies tend to stay close to previously established conventional meanings and narratives, frequently drawing upon stock characters and themes from science fiction. In particular, the *Frankenstein* myth is key to opposition symbolism in numerous scientific controversies (Mulkay, 1996; e.g., Turney, 1998). Mary Shelley's *Frankenstein* is deeply embedded in the genealogy of Western culture. Symbolically, it represents the folly of science, and the unforeseen dangers that can emerge from well-meaning scientific development. During the GM controversy, genetically altered crops were branded "*Frankenfood*" by opponents. In the human cloning debate, contemporary science fiction films such as *The Sixth Day* replicated the *Frankenstein* story, providing second order allusions to its generative narrative of scientific hubris (Jensen, 2008b).

"Widely disseminated images and narratives have real effects, regardless of their relationship to the technical details of the scientific work. They shape the way people think about new technologies, assess their impacts, and develop ways to control them" (Nelkin & Lindee, 2001, p. 91). Mulkay (1996) similarly identified the importance of symbols from science fiction in the struggle over the symbolic valuation of embryo research in the 1980s. The Wellcome Trust (1998) commissioned focus group research to gather public perspectives on human cloning, finding that respondents frequently drew upon science fiction films and books as source domains to communicate their understandings of the technology. For these respondents, science fiction stories stood as free-standing symbols capable of instantly communicating an entire dystopian narrative about human cloning through allusion (Wellcome, 1998). In other words, "popular culture motifs filled in the gaps in meaning" in the human cloning controversy (Gerlach & Hamilton, 2005, p. 90; Peterson, Anderson, & Allan, 2005), thereby providing the symbolic materials that could be used to contest the dominant myth of scientific progress.

The Wellcome Trust audience research suggests that science fiction-based symbolism strikes a chord with the public, giving concrete form to dystopian concerns about new scientific technologies. Indeed, such concerns may be difficult to articulate without reference to a shared cultural genealogy of symbols constructed through popular literature and films (Jensen, 2008b; Nerlich et al., 2000; Weasel & Jensen, 2005). Mulkay (1996) contends that such fictional symbols are an inevitable feature of debates over scientific development:

> When speculating about the development of new, science-based technologies, participants cannot rely entirely on what they take to be the established facts. While they think and argue about the shape of things to come, they have no alternative but to create some kind of story that goes beyond these facts.... In the course of public appraisal of science and technology, the conventional boundary between fact and fiction ... become[s] blurred. (p. 158)

Moreover, Tudor (1989, p. 589) argues that cultural texts such as dystopian science fiction films channel the "changing popular images of what is threatening about science and scientists" into relatable narratives and symbols. That is, science fiction-based symbolism can be used to communicate the deep misgivings some feel about the entire project of techno-scientific development.

> Stories of mad scientists ... constitute an extremely effective antirationalist critique of science ... under the premise that scientists are dangerous. Untrue, perhaps; preposterous, perhaps; low-brow, perhaps. But nevertheless effective. (Toumey, 1992, p. 434)

Likewise, Bloomfield and Vurdubakis (2003, p. 1) contend that

> figures of occidental folklore such as Frankenstein ... or *Brave New World* ... [are] a convenient shorthand for articulating unease with the direction and pace of technological development, or even voicing a loss of confidence in the modernist technological project of instrumental control.

For example, in the U.K. embryo research debate, symbolism from science fiction "reminded recipients forcefully of the dangers of scientific development" (Mulkay, 1996, p. 169). In this way, journalistic use of "literary devices and techniques, including the employment of evocative stereotypes, symbols, terminology or metaphors ... [can] connect readers with complex matters, assisting them to understand the unfamiliar and to imagine the possibilities that lay ahead" (Peterson et al., 2005, p. 343). These media processes are central to the struggle over the symbolic valuation of newly publicized scientific concepts, within the context of societal resistance to certain aspects of scientific development.

Scientific Disasters Symbolize the "Structure of Feeling" in Risk Society

Symbols associated with the *Frankenstein*-inspired counter-myth of science are clearly derived from the cultural genealogy of science. However I contend that these cultural representations of science are coextensive with symbols associated with real life scientific disaster. Disaster symbols are based on historical events that tap into a deep reservoir of discontent with the "side effects" (Beck, 1992, 1999) and "wasted lives" (Bauman, 2004) inevitably produced by the modern project of techno-economic development. Social theorist Ulrich Beck (1992) argues that Western nations have moved from a stage of "first modernity" that he labels *industrial society* to one of "second modernity," or *risk society*. Today, risks are uncontrollable, uninsurable and unseen, yielding pervasive uncertainty in society. Risk society is defined by the increasing ubiquity of globalized risks and "low probability, high consequence" hazards produced by modern industrialized societies such as BSE/CjD, pollution, nuclear disaster and genetic engineering. These risks cannot be controlled at the level of individual nation-states and their consequences spread with limited regard for national borders. According to Beck (1994), awareness of the catastrophic potential inherent in techno-scientific development has prompted restless reflexivity across society.

I will argue that certain high-profile techno-scientific disasters stand as symbols for the broader reflexive concern Beck describes. Given the deep structure of contemporary unease with certain aspects of techno-scientific development such as human cloning (e.g. Kass, 2004), many people grasp for symbols capable of expressing their feelings of concern (Weasel & Jensen, 2005). One way of expressing the shared concerns of risk society is by allusions to specific high-profile disasters such as Chernobyl.

In the 1950s, nuclear power was heralded as the quintessential symbol of scientific progress, heralding the dawn of a utopian "atomic age" of unlimited energy. However nuclear disasters have fundamentally altered this early symbolization of nuclear power plants. New symbols were introduced into the public sphere around the Chernobyl disaster, including images of dying and deformed bodies. Such images powerfully influenced the process of symbolic valuation for nuclear power. Even before Chernobyl, the ever present danger of total nuclear annihilation during the cold war cast a pall over all things nuclear, with the image of the mushroom cloud increasingly overtaking sketches of clean, brightly lit cities as the dominant symbol of even civilian nuclear energy for many citizens. Today, industry's and governments' continued promotion of nuclear power in the interest of economic expansion faces significant resistance in certain quarters, resistance which is underpinned by these powerful disaster symbols. There are renewed attempts to frame nuclear power as a panacea that will save the environment by obviating fossil fuels. However, efforts to reassert the grand narrative of progress in this field must contend with negative visual symbols ranging from mushroom clouds to Chernobyl's victims to three-eyed fish swimming in the waters surrounding the Springfield Nuclear Power Plant in *The Simpsons*.

The BSE crisis in the U.K. similarly encapsulated the generational structure of feeling in risk society through stark visual imagery, with video footage of mad cows and notions of "polluted" food accessing deeply unsettling themes in the modern psyche. These images were disseminated through the mass media and incorporated into the "structure of feeling" (Williams, 1961) of the generation that witnessed these events. The images symbolize the broader cultural experience of being "at risk" and uncertain about whether something as innocuous as one's food will turn out to be the instrument of unseen, manufactured danger. Moreover, these incidents are examples of scientific hubris leading to disaster just as the cultural genealogy warns. Indeed, incidents such as Chernobyl, 3-Mile Island and "mad-cow disease" can be wielded as symbols interchangeably with rhetorical devices from *Frankenstein* and *Brave New World* by activists protesting newly emerging, unproven techno-science. Together these symbols give activists symbolic power in the struggle over the valorization of controversial science in public sphere.

Indeed, resistance to the dominant myth of science can take the form of a controversy when the material conditions of risk society become so clearly hazardous that symbols of techno-scientific progress cannot sustain their legitimacy, even within commercial news media. The ensuing influx of opposition (e.g., scientific disaster) symbols underpinned by counter-myths of science such as *Frankenstein* represent an authentic rollback of hegemonic power, which cannot be wholly discounted as an "inoculation" strategy. That is, this pattern is not simply what Barthes (1973, p. 150) identifies as the bourgeoisie "admitting the accidental evil of a class-bound institution [such as science] the better to conceal its principle evil." While science fiction could be partially classified as such a "small inoculation of acknowledged evil" or as displaying "localized subversions" of science (p. 150), the symbolism of technological disasters constitutes a fundamental challenge to the myth of scientific progress.

SYMBOLIC VALORIZATION: A CASE EXAMPLE

> Popularisation or public acceptance of a particular type of science, far from being a linear process of overcoming "resistance[,]" is a process of translation and negotiation. Genetics is a locus of contestation in which special interest groups and professional groups are involved in designing the hegemonic meaning of [science]. (Dijck, 1998, p. 334)

Recent debates around therapeutic cloning and embryonic stem cell (ESC) research exemplify the way in which various interest groups struggle for dominance in the process of scientific symbolization. At issue in this debate was the use of somatic cell nuclear transfer technology (SCNT; i.e., human cloning) famously developed to create Dolly the sheep in combination with the medical use of cloned embryonic stem cells. The derivation of stem cells from a cloned embryo requires its destruction, thus drawing protests from antiabortion activists in addition to more general ethical concerns about biomedical and genetic manipulations.

When the scientific idea of therapeutic cloning ascended into public view, it underwent symbolic valorization by scientists and science journalists who framed it as a harbinger of utopian therapeutic possibilities (Jensen, 2008b, 2008c; Radford, 2006). Promoted by the biotechnology industry, the promise of cures for diseases from Parkinson's to cancer to Alzheimer's quickly drew support from patient advocacy groups and key politicians. The technical scientific definitions of SCNT and ESC research were immediately supplanted by connotative symbolic meanings connected to cures and scientific progress in the public realm. Moreover cures were discussed as though they already existed, and were simply awaiting the scientific funding and political support to bring about the promised medical benefits. Mulkay (1997, pp. 70-71) identified this prophetic "rhetoric of hope" in the U.K. embryo research debate of the 1980s, wherein "The primary message ... was that the use of science-based techniques offered hope.... In these texts, the future accomplishments of embryo research become strangely tangible." In their study of the human cloning debate, Haran et al. (2007, p. 47) describe this practice as "temporal contraction," that is, "discursive renderings involving the condensation of the timelines for curing through technoscientific cloning." One key visual symbol of this utopian vision was a government-sponsored postage stamp released in South Korea where therapeutic cloning researcher Hwang Woo-Suk was reporting remarkable breakthroughs on a yearly basis.[5] This stamp (Figure 10.1) visually contracts the timeframe for basic research, clinical testing, and so on. Moreover, it redacts the inherent uncertainties of such research to construct a symbol supporting the dominant myth of scientific and medical progress.

Source: Image obtained from from http://www.australasianbioethics.org/Images/2005_images/183-stamp.jpg

Figure 10.1. South Korean postage stamp depicting curative power of therapeutic cloning research.

Overall, this kind of symbolism associated with promissory science was very successful in garnering support in the United Kingdom. However, the political context in the U.S. includes powerful support for counter-myths opposing the grand narrative of scientific progress. In particular, evangelical Christians comprising almost one third of the U.S. population constituted a key opposition force opposing therapeutic cloning. This opposition was constructed out of existing symbolism related to the moral controversy over abortion in the United States and the Frankenstein counter-myth of the life sciences.

In contrast to the dominance of scientific utopianism in the United Kingdom, the greater symbolic power of the antiabortion and evangelical Christian lobbies in the United States, and the power of religiously conservative President Bush delivered political defeat for therapeutic cloning funding at the national level from 2001-2008.[6] Indeed, a remarkable range of dystopian tropes were employed in former President Bush's public statements against human cloning of any kind.

> Allowing cloning would be taking a significant step toward a society in which human beings are grown for spare body parts, and children are engineered to custom specifications. (Bush, 2002)

Meanwhile, antiabortion and evangelical groups marshalled existing symbolic resources in the form of conceptual metaphors linking human cloning to concepts such as "murder" and "unnatural." I have argued that this rhetorical strategy helped to rally conservative religious forces against human cloning in the United States (Jensen & Weasel, 2006):

> Cloning has attracted the same type of "death" rhetoric that characterises much of Christian fundamentalists' communication about abortion per se. Over time, repeated use of the conceptual metaphor "human cloning is abortion," combined with a strong tendency to view human cloning as a fundamentally religious issue (Evans, 2002b), could establish the long-term rhetorical framework for large-scale political mobilization of Christian fundamentalists against any form of human cloning technology (including cloning for therapeutic or research purposes). The establishment of a strong conceptual link connecting abortion and human cloning would lead most Christian fundamentalists to the clear moral prescription for opposition to human cloning. (Jensen & Weasel, 2006, p. 318)

While these conceptual links likely remain intact for evangelicals at the time of writing (2011), the Obama Administration has signaled that it will privilege the "cures" and "hope" conceptualizations of therapeutic cloning research. This can be seen in Obama's first speech on this topic as President.

> Scientists believe these tiny cells may [...] help us cure, some of our most devastating diseases and conditions: to regenerate a severed spinal cord and lift someone from a wheelchair; to spur insulin production and spare a child from a lifetime of needles; to treat Parkinson's, cancer, heart disease and others that affect millions of Americans and the people who love them. (Obama, 2009)

As can be seen in the extract above, the dialectical symbolism of hope/fear is continuing to frame this issue under a new Presidency, even if U.S. policy has changed.

CONCLUSION

This chapter has outlined the transformative power of scientific controversies in shaping the mythologizing and symbolic valuation of the sciences in the public sphere. Under normal conditions, scientific institutions tend to be in a dominant position in the symbolic valorization of scientific technologies in the mediated public sphere by virtue of their privileged access to symbolic, cultural, and media capital (Jensen, 2008a). Moreover, in addition to promoting the dominant Enlightenment myth of scientific progress, scientific institutions tend to employ a "strategy of distinction" to valorize scientific judgments as superior to lay opinions and a "strategy of derision" which regards, for example, works of dystopian science fiction as "brash, gauche, immature or unrefined" (Thompson, 1990, pp. 158-159). However, as this chapter has shown, those in subordinate positions during this symbolization process can employ a "strategy of rejection" by ridiculing controversial scientific developments (p. 160). In such cases of controversy, rejection strategies seek the symbolic devaluation of particular scientific developments in the public sphere. In this process, the cultural genealogy of a scientific issue provides symbolic materials that can be used to resist the dominant Enlightenment myth of the sciences.

The public realm holds both rewards and dangers for scientists (see, e.g., see Weasel & Jensen, 2005). Although individual scientists and institutional press officers can exercise substantial control over the timing, placement and format of publicity in most cases, they are also made vulnerable to rejection or controversy by the very fact of their visibility. At the same time, symbolic capital, media capital (fame), funding, and influence are among the spoils to be won through the successful manipulation of scientific symbolization in the mediated public sphere.

The debate over embryonic stem cell research funding in the U.S. exemplifies this combination of rewards and dangers stemming from a high level of visibility in the mediated public sphere. For example, $3 billion in research funding was allocated for embryonic stem cell research in the state of California alone through a democratic initiative with wide public support. This special dispensation of economic capital was obtained through effective management of symbols defining embryonic stem cell research in the public sphere. However, in playing the media game there are also dangers for the scientific field. Once publicized, a scientific domain may be rejected by publics who demand regulation, legal bans or protest against individual scientists and their institutional sponsors. This has occurred, for example, with scientific issues bordering on one of the most fundamental and contentious of all moral controversies in the United States, the abortion debate (Jensen & Weasel, 2006). In the United Kingdom, animal researchers have faced personal and institutional protests and even attacks from activist groups when their work became visible. Moreover, social research has revealed that resistance to controversial sciences can actually stiffen with increased subject knowledge and public exposure (Irwin & Wynne, 1996; Michael, 1996). Overall then, merely being public does not presage either positive or negative consequences for the technological or scientific field, although it does raise the stakes significantly (see Holliman & Jensen, 2009; Jensen & Wagoner, 2009).

The dominant framing of scientific controversies' role in public life is that they are detrimental, dangerous outbreaks of public discord (e.g., Select Committee on Science & Technology, 2000). Typically rejecting authentic upstream public engagement (Rogers-Hayden & Pidgeon, 2007), governments and the scientific community instead seek to stave off future controversies by gauging public reactions to new scientific developments in advance and adjusting their language accordingly (Holliman & Jensen, 2009; Irwin, 2006). Such attempts to circumvent public dissent recalls Hannah Arendt's (1958, p. 220) contention that the institutions of modernity view pluralistic forces in society as a threat to the social order and profitability because of their inherent "haphazardness" and perceived "moral irresponsibility." Indeed, controversies are feared by scientific institutions because they destabilize the aura surrounding the dominant Enlightenment myth of science. The inability of the sciences to offer final answers becomes salient, making clear the need for a plurality of perspectives in democratic decision-making about scientific issues.

Contrary to the negative view of controversies' destabilizing power, I contend they promote democratic engagement precisely because they occasion disorderly displays of dissensus. Specifically, controversies breach the normally entrenched linguistic structures that scientists and their allies have imposed upon scientific issues, laying them bare for pluralistic symbolic contestation, particularly in news media (Jensen, 2010b). What can emerge in scientific controversies is akin to Zygmunt Bauman's ideal notion of the public realm as a "territory of constant tension," "tug-of-war," and "dialogue, co-operation or compromise" where the "communal search for the common good" (Bauman, 1999, pp. 87, 167) can be discussed under more pluralistic conditions than normal. There are certainly dangers and limitations in such open and agonistic struggles over scientific meaning (e.g. Collins & Evans, 2002),[7] some of which have been identified in previous studies of scientific controversies (e.g. Jensen, 2008b, 2008c; Weasel & Jensen, 2005). For example, Jensen and Weasel (2006) have argued that abortion rhetoric in American human cloning coverage carried the risk of a dysfunctional moral controversy spilling over into the realm of biomedicine and inhibiting productive dialogue. However, given the democratic imperative for pluralistic public discourse (Benhabib, 2002; Gould, 1996; Young, 2000), scientific controversies could be viewed as necessary, if imperfect, opportunities for the emergence of active scientific citizenship and authentic democratic engagement with scientific developments.

ACKNOWLEDGMENTS

The author would like to thank Professor Alan Irwin and Dr Richard Holliman for their insightful comments on an earlier draft of this chapter.

NOTES

1. Although the "dominant" group is clearly in a powerful position, Thompson (1990, p. 160) emphasizes that there will still be resistance in most cases.
2. The use of Kuhn's concept of "normal science" in this essay is a creative and indirect extension of his idea for the present topic, not a faithful application of his original ideas.
3. Some contact with the outside, at least semipublic domain is usually required, at least to legitimate one's funding or promotion within a university. Even when such decisions are made by peer review, the influence of economic and political considerations is never altogether absent.
4. While this chapter focuses on domain shifting from uncontroversial to controversial science, clearly shifts in the opposite direction are also possible. To reframe a controversial science as uncontroversial, the main required ingredient is *time*. As Saussure (1990, p. 78) argued, "If one looked at the community of speakers without taking the passage of time into account, one would not see the effect of social forces acting upon the language." Indeed, there are a number of examples of once controversial scientific technologies that have now become largely 'normalized', including heart transplants and in vitro fertilization.
5. These reports were later revealed as fraudulent however.
6. On the other hand, certain individual states voted to fund embryo research directly, and attempts to pass a federal ban on human cloning through Congress were unsuccessful.
7. One danger of open debate over science is that dystopian and utopian hype can distract from the real issues at hand (Jensen, 2008b). Moreover, journalistic hype represents an abdication of the historical ideal of a critical, "fourth estate" press that could challenge the claims of the powerful in society (Jensen, 2010a).

REFERENCES

Arendt, H. (1958). *The human condition*. Chicago, IL: University of Chicago Press.

Barthes, R. (1973). *Mythologies*. London: Granada.

Barthes, R. (1977). *Image-music-text*. London: Fontana.

Bauer, M. W., Durant, J., Ragnarsodottir, A., & Rudolphsdotir, A. (1995). *Science and technology in the British press, 1946-1990*. London: The Science Museum.

Bauman, Z. (1999). *In search of politics*. Stanford, CA: Stanford University Press.

Bauman, Z. (2004). *Wasted lives: Modernity and its outcasts*. Cambridge, MA: Polity.

Beck, U. (1992). *Risk society: Towards a new modernity*. London: SAGE.

Beck, U. (1994). The reinvention of politics: Towards a theory of reflexive modernization. In U. Beck, A. Giddens, & S. Lash (Eds.), *Reflexive modernization: Politics, tradition and aesthetics in the modern social order* (pp. 1-55). Cambridge, MA: Polity Press.

Beck, U. (1999). *World risk society*. Cambridge, MA: Polity.

Benhabib, S. (2002). Political geographies in a global world: Arendtian Reflections. *Social Research, 69*, 539.

Bloomfield, B. P., & Vurdubakis, T. (2003). The curse of Frankenstein: Visions of technology and society in the debate over new reproductive technologies. *Lancaster University Management School Working Papers Series*. Retrieved from www.lums.co.uk/publications

Brown, N. (2000). Organising/disorganising the breakthrough motif: Dolly the cloned ewe meets Astrid the hybrid pig. In N. Brown, B. Rappert & A. Webster (Eds.), *Contested futures: A sociology of prospective science and technology* (pp. 87-110). Aldershot: Ashgate.

Burchell, K. (2007). Empiricist selves and contingent "others": The performative function of the discourse of scientists working in conditions of controversy. *Public Understanding of Science, 16*(2), 145-162.

Bush, G. W. (2002). *President Bush calls on Senate to back human cloning ban: Remarks by the President on human cloning legislation.* Retrieved from http://www.whitehouse.gov/news/releases/2002/04/20020410-4.html

Collins, H. M., & Evans, R. (2002). The third wave of science studies: Studies of expertise and experience. *Social Studies of Sciences, 32*(2), 235-296.

Dijck, J. V. (1998). *Imagenation: Popular images of genetics*. New York, NY: New York University Press.

Fahnestock, J. (1993). Accommodating science: The rhetorical life of scientific facts. In M. W. McRae (Ed.), *The literature of science—perspectives on popular scientific writing* (pp. 17-36). Athens, GA: University of Georgia Press.

Ferree, M. M., Gamson, W. A., Gerhards, J., & Rucht, D. (2002). *Shaping abortion discourse: Democracy and the public sphere in Germany and the United States*. Cambridge, England: Cambridge University Press.

Fishman, M. (1980). *Manufacturing the news*. Austin, Texas: University of Texas Press.

Fiske, J. (1990). *Introduction to communication studies* (2nd ed.). London: Routledge.

Gerlach, N., & Hamilton, S. N. (2005). From mad scientist to bad scientist: Richard Seed as biogovernmental event. *Communication Theory, 15*(1), 78-99.

Giddens, A. (1991). *Modernity and self-identity: Self and society in the late modern age*. Cambridge: Polity Press.

Giddens, A. (1994). Living in a post-traditional society. In U. Beck, A. Giddens, & S. Lash (Eds.), *Reflexive modernization: Politics, tradition and aesthetics in the modern social order.* Cambridge, MA: Polity Press.

Gould, C. C. (1996). Diversity and democracy: Representing differences. In S. Benhabib (Ed.), *Democracy and difference: Contesting the boundaries of the political* (pp. 171-186). Princeton, NJ: Princeton University Press.

Gregory, J., & Miller, S. (1998). *Science in public. Communication, culture, and credibility.* New York, NY: Plenum Press.

Gutteling, J. M., Olofsson, A., Fjaestad, B., Kohring, M., Goerke, A., Bauer, M. W., & Rusanen, T. (2002). Media coverage 1973-1996: Trends and dynamics. In M. W. Bauer & G. Gaskell (Eds.), *Biotechnology: The making of a global controversy* (pp. 95-128). Cambridge, England: Cambridge University Press.

Habermas, J. (1987). *The theory of communicative action: Lifeworld and system: A critique of functionalist reason* (Vol. 2). Cambridge, MA: Polity Press.

Haran, J., Kitzinger, J., McNeil, M., & O'Riordan, K. (2007). *Human cloning in the media: From science fiction to science practice*. London: Routledge.

Hellsten, I. (2000). Dolly: Scientific breakthrough or Frankenstein's monster? Journalistic and scientific metaphors of cloning. *Metaphor and Symbol, 15*, 213-221.

Herman, E. S., & Chomsky, N. (1988). *Manufacturing consent: The political economy of the mass media*. London: Vintage.

Holliman, R., & Jensen, E. (2009). (In)authentic science and (im)partial publics: (Re)constructing the science outreach and public engagement agenda. In R. Holliman, E. Whitelegg, E. Scanlon, S. Smidt & J. Thomas (Eds.), *Investigating science communication in the information age: Implications for public engagement and popular media* (pp. 35-52). Oxford, England: Oxford University Press.

Irwin, A. (2006). The politics of talk: Coming to terms with the "new" scientific governance. *Social Studies of Science, 36*(2), 299-320.

Irwin, A., & Wynne, B. (1996). Conclusions. In A. Irwin & B. Wynne (Eds.), *Misunderstanding science? The public reconstruction of science and technology* (pp. 213-221). Cambridge, England: Cambridge University Press.

Jensen, E. (2008a). *Anglo-American press coverage of therapeutic cloning: A grounded discourse analysis of news production and content* (PhD dissertation, University of Cambridge).

Jensen, E. (2008b). The Dao of human cloning: Hope, fear and hype in the UK press and popular films. *Public Understanding of Science, 17*(2), 123-143.

Jensen, E. (2008c). Through thick and thin: Rationalizing the public bioethical debate over therapeutic cloning. *Clinical Ethics, 3*, 194-198.

Jensen, E. (2010a). Between credulity and scepticism: Sightings of the fourth estate in 21st century science journalism. *Media, Culture & Society, 32*(4), 615-630.

Jensen, E. (2010b). Mediating subpolitics in US and UK science news. *Public Understanding of Science*.

Jensen, E., & Wagoner, B. (2009). A cyclical model of social change. *Culture & Psychology, 15*(2), 217-228.

Jensen, E., & Weasel, L. H. (2006). Abortion rhetoric in American news coverage of human cloning. *New Genetics and Society, 25*(3), 305-324.

Kass, L. (2004). The wisdom of repugnance: Why we should ban the cloning of humans. In G. McGee & A. Caplan (Eds.), *The human cloning debate* (4th ed., pp. 137-172). Berkeley, CA: Berkeley Hills Books.

Kitzinger, J., & Williams, C. (2005). Forecasting science futures: Legitimising hope and calming fears in the embryo stem cell debate. *Social Science & Medicine, 61*(3), 731-740.

Kuhn, T. S. (1960). *The structure of scientific revolutions* (2nd ed.). Chicago, IL: University of Chicago Press.

Lakoff, G. (1993). The contemporary theory of metaphor. In A. Ortony (Ed.), *Metaphor and thought* (2nd ed., pp. 202-251). Cambridge, England: Cambridge University Press.

Lyotard, J.-F. (1984). *The postmodern condition*. Manchester, England: Manchester University Press.

McCombs, M. E., & Shaw, D. L. (1972). The agenda-setting function of mass media. *Public Opinion Quarterly, 36*(2), 176-187.

Michael, M. (1996). Ignoring science: discourses of ignorance in the public understanding of science. In A. Irwin & B. Wynne (Eds.), *Misunderstanding science? The public reconstruction of science and technology* (pp. 107-125). Cambridge, England: Cambridge University Press.

Mulkay, M. (1996). Frankenstein and the debate over embryo research. *Science, Technology, & Human Values, 21*(2), 157-176.

Mulkay, M. (1997). *The embryo research debate: Science and the politics of reproduction*. Cambridge, England: Cambridge University Press.

Nelkin, D. (1992). Science, technology, and the political conflict: Analyzing the issues. In D. Nelkin (Ed.), *Controversy: Politics of technical decisions* (3rd ed., pp. ix-xxv). Newbury Park, CA: SAGE.

Nelkin, D., & Lindee, M. S. (2001). Cloning in the popular imagination. In A. J. Klotzko (Ed.), *The cloning sourcebook*. New York, NY: Oxford University Press.

Nerlich, B., Clarke, D., & Dingwall, R. (2000). Clones and crops: The use of stock characters and word play in two debates about bioengineering. *Metaphor and Symbol, 15*, 223-239.

Obama, B. (2009). *Obama's remarks on stem cell research*. Retrieved from http://www.nytimes.com/2009/03/09/us/politics/09text-obama.html

Peterson, A., Anderson, A., & Allan, S. (2005). Science fiction/science fact: Medical genetics in news stories. *New Genetics and Society, 24*(3), 337-353.

Radford, T. (2006). Hype, hope, and hair-raising: How the British press saw it (S. S. A. H. Centre for Research in the Arts, Trans.) *Talking embryos: Interdisciplinary conversations exploring the social roles of the embryo*. Cambridge, England: King's College, University of Cambridge.

Ritchie, D. (2003). "Argument is war"—Or is it a games of chess? Multiple meanings in the analysis of implicit metaphors. *Metaphor and Symbol, 18*(2), 125-146.

Ritchie, L. D. (2006). *Context and connection in metaphor*. Basingstoke, England: Palgrave-Macmillan.

Rogers-Hayden, T., & Pidgeon, N. (2007). Moving engagement 'upstream'? Nanotechnologies and the Royal Society and Royal Academy of Engineering inquiry. *Public Understanding of Science, 16*, 345-364.

Saussure, F. D. (1990). *Course in general linguistics* (R. Harris, Trans.). London: Duckworth.

Select Committee on Science & Technology. (2000). *Science and society*. London: Author.

Sperber, D., & Wilson, D. (1986). *Relevance: Communication and cognition*. Cambridge, MA: Harvard University Press.

Thompson, J. (1990). *Ideology and modern culture: Critical social theory in the era of mass communication*. Cambridge, MA: Polity.

Thompson, J. B. (1995). *The media and modernity: A social theory of the media*. Stanford, CA: Stanford University Press.

Toumey, C. P. (1992). The moral character of mad scientists: A cultural critique of science. *Science, Technology & Human Values, 17*(4), 411.

Toumey, C. P. (1996). *Conjuring science: Scientific symbols and cultural meanings in American life.* New Brunswick, NJ: Rutgers Univerity press.

Tudor, A. (1989). Seeing the worst side of science. *Nature, 340*, 589-592.

Turney, J. (1998). *Frankenstein's footsteps: Science, genetics and popular culture.* New Haven, CT: Yale University Press.

Vervaeke, J., & Kennedy, J. M. (1996). Metaphors in language and thought: Falsification and multiple meanings. *Metaphor and Symbolic Activity, 11*, 273-284.

Wagoner, B., & Jensen, E. (2010). Science learning at the zoo: Evaluating children's developing understanding of animals and their habitats. *Psychology & Society, 3*(1), 65-76.

Weasel, L. H., & Jensen, E. (2005). Language and values in the human cloning debate: A web-based survey of scientists and Christian fundamentalist pastors. [submitted for peer review]. *New Genetics and Society, 24*(1), 1-14.

Wellcome, T. (1998). Public perspectives on human cloning *Medicine in Society Program.*

Williams, R. (1961). *The long revolution.* London: Columbia University Press.

Young, I. M. (2000). *Inclusion and democracy.* Oxford, England: Oxford University Press.

CHAPTER 11

THE STRUGGLE FOR SCIENTIFIC CONSENSUS

Communicating Climate Science Around COP-15

Richard Holliman

Jensen (this volume) provides an account of the struggle for symbolic power in relation to scientific controversies by exploring mass media portrayals, mainly involving news reports of the life sciences. In so doing he argues that media portrayals that are professionally produced for consumption in the public sphere (e.g., as news, documentaries, books, and films) continue to hold particular significance in terms of framing what is controversial, who is a credible expert, and what counts as reliable and valid knowledge (see also Allgaier & Holliman, 2006; Holliman, 2004; Holliman & Scanlon, 2009; Nisbet & Scheufele, 2009). As Habermas (2006) argues:

> the *dynamics* of mass communication are driven by the power of the media to select, and shape the presentation of, messages and by the strategic use of political and social power to influence the agendas as well as the triggering and framing of public issues. (p. 415, emphasis in original)

Culture and Social Change: Transforming Society Through the Power of Ideas, pp. 185–207

Science news reports can also perform what Gieryn (1995) describes as "boundary work," sometimes explicitly but often implicitly defining what does not count as reliable and valid knowledge and expertise. Jensen (this volume) goes on to argue that the struggle for symbolic power in the public sphere is rarely confined to discussions about scientific findings and experimental procedures. For example, media portrayals of "life science" controversies can explore social, ethical, economic, and political issues in relation to scientific information. In so doing, media portrayals have the potential to both reflect on, and contribute to, the impact of scientific research within society. In essence, media portrayals can be indirect (and sometimes direct) agents of social change, but the outcomes of such exposure in the public sphere are not necessarily predictable. This argument is exemplified by a number of environmental and lifestyle issues, many of which continue to generate media coverage and public debate, but only sometimes resulting in social change. Examples include: ongoing attempts to reduce biodiversity loss; debates about the effects of "acid rain"; the reduction in the use of chlorofluorocarbons (CFCs) in aerosols; the shift to unleaded petrol and concomitant "greening" of oil companies; the reduction in organochlorine pesticide use; the recent popularity of locally sourced and organic foods; and the shifting practices of waste management (e.g., reuse, recycling, free cycling, and composting).

The thesis that media representations of controversy can act as a catalyst for social change can be explored in relation to areas of scientific enquiry other than the life or environmental sciences, such as symbolic representations of controversy in the physical sciences, planetary and space sciences, and so on. But how might they apply if the scholarly focus shifted away from ideas about controversy to explore the symbolic struggle for scientific consensus and its relation to social change? Given that ideas about consensus are valued within the scientific community, how might scientists and scientific institutions seek to communicate it, and to what purpose? Furthermore, what might be gained from broadening the scholarly focus from news media accounts produced by professional journalists to examining representations of scientific consensus in a wider range of mediated communication in the public sphere?

This chapter takes a complementary approach to Jensen's (this volume) through an exploration of the symbolic struggle by a range of actors to destabilise (and by others to repair) representations of the scientific consensus of anthropogenic climate change. The focus for this brief examination is the United Nations Copenhagen Summit (also known as "COP-15," where COP stands for Conference of the Parties) in December 2009. COP-15 provided a focus for news organizations around the world.[1] The fact that this high-profile event was scheduled in advance gave news editors the opportunity to commission supplements, podcasts and features, record interviews, and so on. Newsrooms committed reporters, photographers, camera crews, and so on, to this event. These preparations were disrupted, however, by several challenges to the scientific consensus of anthropogenic climate change. Analyses of two examples of these challenges form the basis of this chapter. Specifically, I will begin by reviewing the nature of scientific consensus and how it can be communicated, then introduce COP-15 and analyze a collaboratively authored newspaper editorial. I then examine attempts to question the validity and reliability of scientific interpretations of temperature data following the publication of e-mails from the Climatic Research Unit at the University of East Anglia (as reviewed by House of Commons Science and Technology Committee, 2010; Oxburgh et al., 2010; Russell et al., 2010). Furthermore, I will explore challenges to the validity and reliability of data related to the rate of decline of the Himalayan glaciers from the fourth report of the Intergovernmental Panel on Climate Change (IPCC, 2007, 2010).

In addressing these examples I argue that COP-15 became an important focus in the public sphere for the symbolic struggle for the scientific consensus of anthropogenic climate change, and demands for political action to mitigate its effects. Various actors, some of whom were climate scientists, worked strategically to promote, maintain, destabilize, and repair the scientific consensus at this time.[2] In this chapter I argue that both consensus and controversy lie at the very heart of scientific progress. As such, representations of consensus and controversy, both within the scientific community and in the wider public sphere, can have important implications for social change. To fully understand how a scientific controversy relates to ideas about social change requires some consideration of the scientific consensus at that time, and vice versa. In this instance, the struggle for the scientific consensus of anthropogenic climate change, which preceded COP-15 and has continued after this event, was a very public one. A wide range of actors, whether they argued "for" or "against" ideas about anthropogenic climate change, valued the concept of a scientific consensus and what it represented in the public sphere. Indeed they valued the ideal of consensus sufficiently to either contest/challenge or promote/defend it via a range of communication channels: social media (e.g., blogs and microblogs), professional media (e.g., broadcast news and newspapers), using freedom of information legislation, and so on. In so doing, these actors drew on coordinated and sophisticated communication strategies, using the rhetoric, methods, and methodologies of climate science, to make their respective cases.

SYMBOLIZING SCIENTIFIC CONSENSUS

Scientific consensus is an elusive yet apparently desirable property. Speak to any academic research scientist and they are likely to value the *ideal* of scientific consensus. It can be hard fought for and represent the bedrock of a scientific discipline. And yet there are no hard and fast rules about what constitutes a scientific consensus in practice and how it might be represented, either among scientists, or in the wider public sphere. As part of their enculturation into the practices of the sciences, trainee research scientists are taught about the importance of working to a "scientific method" that generates reliable and valid evidence that is initially checked via peer review, and then again via attempts to replicate published findings. Following from the oft-cited Popperian (1935) view of what this "scientific method" *should* look like,[3] the theory goes that as more work is completed and published in peer reviewed journals, other scientists try to disprove it. By this iterative mechanism of 'falsification' and self-correction a scientific consensus may emerge. And yet a scientific consensus is never complete. Scientists tend to value scepticism as much as the ideal of consensus, as evident in the aftermath of COP-15 when over 250 scientists signed an open letter published in the journal *Science*.

> There is always some uncertainty associated with scientific conclusions; science never absolutely proves anything. When someone says that society should wait until scientists are absolutely certain before taking any action, it is the same as saying society should never take action....
>
> Scientific conclusions derive from an understanding of basic laws supported by laboratory experiments, observations of nature, and mathematical and computer modeling. Like all human beings, scientists make mistakes, but the scientific process is designed to find and correct them.
>
> This process is inherently adversarial—scientists build reputations and gain recognition not only for supporting conventional wisdom, but even more so for demonstrating that the scientific consensus is wrong and that there is a better explanation. That's what Galileo, Pasteur, Darwin, and Einstein did. But when some conclusions have been thoroughly and deeply tested, questioned, and examined, they gain the status of "well-established theories" and are often spoken of as "facts." (Gleick et al., 2010, p. 689)

This idea that "science never absolutely proves anything" (p. 689) is crucial to understanding how scientific consensus is challenged in the public sphere. In short, acceptance of the scientific norm of scepticism gives licence to those who define themselves as scientists, or actors with epistemologically equivalent expertise, to draw on the methodologies and rhetoric of scientific investigation to attempt to challenge a scientific consensus (Allgaier & Holliman, 2006). In essence then, a scientific "fact" can never be proven. It is always open to challenge.

So, what might a scientific consensus look like in practice? Scientific consensus can be communicated in a number of different forms. For example, it is possible to generate consensus among scientists as the result of specially convened meetings such as the Asilomar conference from the mid-1970s where, at the height of this public controversy, the future of recombinant DNA (deoxyribonucleic acid) was deliberated by over 100 scientists and other stakeholders. As a direct result of this meeting a set of voluntary guidelines was agreed about future experimental work and the potential implications of this research for public health (see Berg, 2008; Turney, 1999 for discussion). It follows that scientific meetings can have an important role for deliberating and directing social change, and communicating consensus.

In a similar vein it is possible to generate some level of scientific consensus from the result of a vote by members of a professional body following debates among scientists, and this can drive social change. This was the case in August 2006 when the International Astronomical Union (IAU) reclassified Pluto as a "Dwarf Planet" (IAU, 2006). This decision had important implications within the astronomy community, but also in the wider public sphere, not least within science classrooms where pupils are now taught about the eight planets that constitute our solar system (as opposed to nine, which the previous generation learned about), but also about dwarf planets. As happened in the 1960s with the acceptance of the science of plate tectonics among Earth scientists, an agreement such as this has repercussions in the wider sphere, requiring that science teachers are provided with new knowledge and resources to teach the emergent scientific consensus. Indeed, we might add scientific curricula, textbooks and other teaching resources as further forms that communicate scientific consensus, as driven by professional bodies, scientific institutions, market concerns, policy imperatives, and the like.

A more routine route to consensus within the scientific community involves peer review. This process is clearly valued by scientists, as part of the process of establishing valid and reliable knowledge (Wager, 2009),[4] but is this in itself sufficient in generating a new, or shifting the boundaries of an existing, scientific consensus and therefore driving social change? Moreover, can a single peer reviewed paper generate "ready-made science" (Latour, 1987) within a scientific discipline, or does this require multiple papers arguing for a similar theoretical explanation, scientific "fact," and so on, perhaps as the result of a meta-analysis of a number of related papers over a period of time (e.g., Oreskes, 2004)? In some instances, and with the benefit of hindsight, it is possible to argue that a single scientific paper has acted as a catalyst that has driven the process whereby a new consensus has emerged. Watson and Crick's (1953) generative paper about the now infamous double helix structure of DNA is a high-profile case in point for the life sciences. Once this paper had been supported by other work it fundamentally changed how life scientists work and led to new areas of scientific research, but it also changed the perception of human genetics in the public sphere, for example, following the publication of popular science books (Watson, 1968; see Lewenstein, 2009 for discussion), and textbooks. Thus, the original paper by Watson and Crick, alongside the supporting evidence that followed, had a role in driving social change. The Asilomar conference, for example, would not have been required without Watson and Crick's discovery. Hence, scientific papers have a role in communicating consensus with the potential to drive social change, either through meta-analyses of large numbers of papers, or, very occasionally, via single generative texts, the latter gaining support from subsequent peer reviewed papers that fail to falsify the original.

Authorship can provide another measure of consensus. There is some evidence to suggest that the number of authors listed on scientific papers has increased over time (Green, 2007; Valiela, 2001), evidence itself of social change in the ways that science is organized and communicated. For example, compare Watson and Crick (1953) with the papers produced by the public- and privately-funded teams reporting the completion of working drafts of the human genome sequence. The combined authorship of the two more recent papers was over 500, representing over 20 research groups, institutions, and companies (International Human Genome Sequencing Consortium, 2001; Venter et al. 2001). Examples such as these illustrate how the sciences can be funded as collaborative "big science" projects (de Solla Price, 1963), the findings of which can be communicated by multiple authors. They also illustrate that scientists, scientific institutions, research funders, politicians, and academic journals are well aware of the instrumental benefits of communicating the results of research specifically for the public sphere, via coordinated promotional campaigns, information subsidies, and so on (see Bauer & Bucchi, 2007; Holliman, 2004; Nerlich, Dingwall, & Clarke 2002; Holliman et al. 2001, 2002 for discussion). Of course, not all areas of science generate consensus statements for circulation specifically in the public sphere. When this happens it tends to be in response to challenges to the symbolic authority of the science in question, enacted via the scientific norm of scepticism and the methodologies and rhetorical strategies of scientific investigation. In other words, consensus is enacted in response to attempts to destabilise it, and these attempts to destabilise consensus are often linked to a desire for social change or the status quo. In this way a scientific consensus may only become visible in the public sphere when it is challenged and requires defending or repairing. So, for example, scientific consensus has been represented symbolically in the form of:

- Open letters, petitions and declarations with multiple signatories, such as the Durban Declaration on the link between HIV and AIDS (Abdool Karim et al., 2000; see Holliman, 2002 for discussion). This declaration was signed by over 5,000 scientists, medical professionals and other stakeholders. It was published on the web and in the journal *Nature* to coincide with the 13th International AIDS conference, held in South Africa, July 2000. In essence, the Durban Declaration was an attempt to defend an existing scientific consensus; that HIV (Human Immunodeficiency Virus) causes AIDS (Acquired Immune Deficiency Syndrome). It was generated in response to challenges to this scientific consensus by a small number of scientists and other stakeholders. The Durban Declaration also served to support calls for social change at the time of this international conference by shoring up support for action to combat HIV/AIDS, particularly in sub-Saharan Africa.
- Textbooks, and science curricula in schools and universities. A long running example of the struggle for scientific consensus in the United States, and more recently in U.K.-based science education, relates to school biology lessons. Many life scientists argue that evolutionary theory by natural selection is a well-established scientific consensus, and they have actively defended this position in public debates and via news media representations (Allgaier & Holliman, 2006). And some U.K.-based science journalists agree to the extent that they are willing to override the journalistic norms of impartiality and balance to support this scientific consensus (Allgaier & Holliman, 2006).

  Mediated communication arguing for this scientific consensus has been published in response to those who support the teaching of creationist accounts and ideas about intelligent design in school biology lessons as epistemologically equivalent explanations to that of evolutionary theory. In part, this struggle for consensus has emerged because of the symbolic value attributed to school science curricula and school science education more generally, and how it has long been perceived to drive social change in terms of how children and young people frame their understanding of the life sciences. In the United Kingdom at least there is some evidence to suggest that school curricula have been revised to support the existing scientific consensus. Such changes have come about, at least in part, because of related media representations and public debate (Allgaier & Holliman, 2006).

In these various ways, then, acts of communication can be used to codify some level of consensus among scientists for circulation in the wider public sphere. These symbolic acts of consensus are generated to either drive social change, shore up support for the status quo, or direct calls for political action. How then might these issues apply to the scientific consensus of climate change?

THE SCIENTIFIC CONSENSUS OF CLIMATE CHANGE

The Earth's climate is changing. Few climate scientists doubt that this is the case. Scientific evidence from proxy data such as ice cores, tree rings and lake sediments indicates that the Earth's climate has changed throughout its history. But the evidence relating to climate change can be complex and difficult to interpret.

The key questions to which scientific data and interpretations can provide some answers are: what are currently the main drivers causing the Earth's climate to change; to what extent are these changes the result of human activity or "natural" fluctuations; at what rate is the Earth's climate warming; should efforts be made to mitigate the effects of climate change, and if so, what should be done, by who, and when?

These related questions continue to generate significant levels of discussion in a whole range of mediated communication, involving scientists and scientific institutions, politicians and officials, media professionals, activists, nongovernmental organizations (NGOs), citizens and various other stakeholders. In part, this is because the answers to them have the potential to drive social change. These questions were also the focus of discussion and debate at COP-15, and in a range of professional and social media generated around the time of this event.

COP-15: The United Nations Climate Change Conference 2009

The United Nations Climate Change Conference 2009, also known as COP-15, was the 15th meeting of the parties to the United Nations Framework Convention on Climate Change (UNFCCC) and the fifth meeting since the negotiation of the Kyoto Protocol ("CMP5"). Held in Copenhagen Denmark from December 7-9, 2009, this summit involved delegations from 192 countries, who were charged with the production of an agreement to reduce emissions of greenhouse gases, lower energy demands, and mitigate the worst effects of climate change.

Given the high-profile nature of this scheduled event, it is hardly surprising that COP-15 was represented internationally in various media and genres, committing a range of actors to produce, access, analyze and respond to acts of mediated communication. Broadly speaking, these acts of mediated communication can be characterized as:

1. "social," "citizen" or "user-generated" media (blogs, microblogs, social networking sites, etc.). The significance of these forms during COP-15 is partly evidenced by the links to several online platforms on the official conference website (see also Vidal, 2009, December 6).[5] They are also evident in the "climategate" example discussed later in this chapter.
2. "professional" media outlets, such as print and online newspapers, and "broadcast" media (radio, television and associated online news and current affairs).[6] (Of course, professional media outlets sometimes provide opportunities for readers, listeners and viewers to contribute user-generated content.)

In this chapter, I examine only a very small selection of communicative acts produced to coincide with COP-15. In this respect, the chapter does not attempt to provide a systematic analysis of relevant content; given the complexity and longevity of the issue of climate change to do so would require significantly longer than a single chapter. Rather, the focus of this chapter is the examination of scientific consensus and how it can be communicated, in this instance exploring how various actors represented the evidence for the scientific consensus of anthropogenic climate change. How did various actors work to reinforce and repair, or destabilise and challenge, the scientific consensus to coincide with COP-15?

The global nature of the mediated communication related to this scheduled event, alongside the desire for social change by some actors, is evidenced in part by a collaboratively-authored editorial published by 56 newspapers in 20 languages in 45 different countries (Editorial, *The Guardian*, 2009, p. 1). This editorial was drafted by a team working for the elite U.K. national newspaper *The Guardian*, in consultation with editors from more than 20 of the newspapers that eventually published it (Katz, 2009). It was published on the opening day of COP-15 as the only story on the front page of *The Guardian*, including a headline, the agreed text, and the logos of the 56 newspapers above this.

The following extracts from this editorial illustrate how media professionals used the scientific consensus of anthropogenic climate change as the foundation to drive social change at COP-15.

> ... Now the facts have started to speak: 11 of the past 14 years have been the warmest on record, the Arctic ice cap is melting [...]. In scientific journals the question is no longer whether humans are to blame, but how little time we have got left to limit the damage....
>
> The science is complex, but the facts are clear. The world needs to take steps to limit temperature rises to 2C, an aim that will require global emissions to peak and begin falling within the next 5-10 years. [...] *The controversy over emails by British researchers that suggest they tried to suppress inconvenient data has muddied the waters but failed to dent the mass of evidence on which these predictions are based.* (Editorial, *The Guardian*, 2009, p. 1, my emphasis)

This example illustrates how newspapers had prepared for this high-profile event. It is an unprecedented "call to action" on the part of the newspapers involved.[7] Journalistic norms of balance and impartiality are not in evidence. Rather, this is a direct appeal for a political consensus to drive social change, based on the rhetoric of science, the authority and reliability of scientific evidence, and the scientific consensus of anthropogenic climate change.

With one exception this joint editorial was printed in all 56 newspapers as per the agreed text, subject to the constraints of newspaper formatting (Katz, 2009). However, the final sentence in this extract (see my emphasis) was not part of the agreed text. Rather, it was considered to be optional as it was only added at the last minute. It is evidence that at least one newspaper—*The Guardian*—was prepared to counter attempts to destabilise calls to action for social change, to repair the consensus of anthropogenic climate change. The episode in question, described in some newspapers as "climategate," is the subject of the next section of this chapter.

"Climategate"

"Climategate"[8] is a story of "private" and "public" communication, of freedom of scientific information and illegal hacking, all delivered via peer reviewed scientific papers, IPCC (and other) reports, websites, the blogosphere and professional news media. This story has the potential to introduce profound changes in the ways that scientists work and communicate with each other, and with other stakeholders and members of the public. It may also change the ways that scientific knowledge is produced, verified and archived, and what information and data are required to be circulated in the public sphere when a peer reviewed paper is published.

In mid-November 2009 (just prior to COP-15) a back-up server at the Climatic Research Unit at the University of East Anglia was accessed. Over 160Mb of data was copied without the permission of the Climatic Research

Unit or the University of East Anglia, consisting of over 1,000 e-mails and more than 3,000 documents (House of Commons Science and Technology Committee, 2010). This information was published on a website called "RealClimate" and announced via a blog post on "the Air Vent" (House of Commons Science and Technology Committee, 2010).[9] The information had been produced primarily by scientific researchers working at the Climatic Research Unit (CRU). This communication was "private." It had not been produced for dissemination in the public sphere. Rather, it was produced and circulated among CRU-based scientists and peers during research activities and the preparation of scientific manuscripts for publication in peer reviewed academic journals and other reports, including the assessment reports produced by the IPCC. In effect, the private communication of several climate scientists was made public, but without the knowledge or permission of the scientists involved or their institutions. It is worth noting, however, that scientists working at the Climatic Research Unit had received a number of requests under the terms of the UK's Freedom of Information Act (FoIA), in particular in July 2009 (House of Commons Science and Technology Committee, 2010).[10]

Following publication of the Climatic Research Unit e-mails and documents bloggers who were critical of the scientific consensus posted arguments to the effect that the climate scientists involved were guilty of withholding or manipulating data, and attempting to influence the peer review process and preparation of IPPC reports, to promote evidence of anthropogenic climate change. Extensive news media coverage reported these issues, both in the United Kingdom and internationally. News reports and bloggers placed particular emphasis on extracts, italicized in the following quote, from an e-mail sent in 1999 by Professor Phil Jones, Director of the Climatic Research Unit.

> I've just completed Mike's Nature *trick* of adding in the real temps to each series for the last 20 years (ie [sic] from 1981 onwards) amd [sic] from 1961 for Keith's *to hide the decline*. (as cited in House of Commons Science and Technology Committee, 2010, p. 19, my emphasis)

The "trick" in question relates to the "hockey stick" graph, which was published a year earlier in the journal *Nature* (Mann, Bradley, & Hughes, 1998). The "trick" refers to a solution to the challenge of interpreting proxy data from tree rings. This solution had been explained in that earlier paper (Mann et al. 1998).[11]

Three reviews were instigated to assess the claims made against the Climatic Research Unit and the University of East Anglia (House of Commons Science and Technology Committee, 2010; Oxburgh et al., 2010; Russell et al., 2010). The reviews are discussed below with respect to the wider implications for the communication of scientific consensus and its relation to social change.

The University of East Anglia instigated two of the three reviews (Oxburgh et al., 2010; Russell et al. 2010). In so doing, they emphasized the independence of the respective members of the panels. It is worth noting, therefore, that the membership of both panels was contested. For example, the impartiality of two prospective members of the em@il review (Russell et al. 2010) were challenged. One of these panel members, Philip Campbell (editor of the journal *Nature*), stepped down following the publication by a blogger of a radio interview where Campbell appeared to support the CRU-based scientists (Batty & Adam, 2010). Furthermore, as the chair of the scientific review, Oxburgh was accused of having a conflict of interest because he had interests in companies that might profit from policies that attempt to address climate change. He did not resign and fulfilled his role as chair of this review. These examples illustrate the contested nature of the review process and the ways that critics used social media ("fifth estate"; Holliman, 2008) to bring issues to the attention of professional media (fourth estate). In so doing, critics of the scientific consensus challenged the review process before the panels had begun work.

Having survived a challenge to his position, Oxburgh et al. (2010) chaired the scientific review, which also involved contributions from The Royal Society. Their remit was to examine the scientific methodologies applied by Jones and colleagues "to assess the integrity of the research published by the Climatic Research Unit" (p. 1). As such, this panel examined *processes* by which the scientific evidence was analyzed and interpreted. They made no comment on the *products* of this research. Similarly, the Russell et al. (2010, p. 10) review made it explicit that they offered "no opinion on the validity of their [CRU's] scientific work." Rather, they studied the "honesty, rigour and openness with which the CRU scientists acted" (p. 10) In effect, both panels argued that it was the job of peers to attempt to falsify the scientific findings through further scientific research.

All three reviews cleared the CRU scientists of any significant wrongdoing, but they also included criticisms in their reports, primarily focussing on issues of openness and transparency in terms of handling climate science data, and responding to FoIA requests. For example, the House of Commons Select Committee (2010) cleared the Climatic Research Unit scientists of malpractice, in particular arguing that the language used in the leaked e-mails was "colloquial." Similarly, the em@il review found that the "rigour and honesty" of the CRU scientists "are not in doubt," and that the leaked e-mails did not undermine the conclusions of the IPCC assessments (Russell et al., 2010, p. 11). However, both these committees raised concerns about the ways that the University of East Anglia had responded to FoIA requests (House of Commons Select Committee, 2010; Russell et al., 2010). For example, the House of Commons Science and Technology Committee argued that the University of East Anglia were resistant to disclosing data following these requests, adding that the U.K.'s Deputy Information Commissioner had argued that the University of East Anglia may have been in breach of the FoIA (House of Commons Select Committee, 2010). Similarly, Russell et al. (2010) offered criticism of the CRU for being unhelpful in responding to these requests, potentially also for deleting e-mails that might have been requested under the FoIA.

In the scientific review Oxburgh et al. (2010) reviewed 11 peer reviewed scientific papers published by Climatic Research Unit scientists over a period of 20 years. They found "no evidence of any deliberate scientific malpractice" (p. 5), arguing that relevant caveats were included in peer review papers, such as those relating the distinction between direct measurements of temperature, and those derived from proxy data. However, these caveats were not always transferred into subsequent IPCC reports and news media accounts. In effect, the data and interpretations in these mediated accounts, including those used in AR3, would have appeared to be more "certain" than the original accounts. The em@il review was more critical of the CRU scientists on an analogous issue, arguing that their preparation of a graph for a 1999 World Meteorological Organization was "misleading," because the way it had been produced was not clearly described in the associated caption (Russell et al., 2010, p. 13).

Russell et al. (2010) conducted their own analysis of raw data and reached similar conclusions to the CRU scientists and the scientific consensus. Oxburgh et al. (2010) also commended the Climatic Research Unit researchers for self-correcting their work in line with findings published by peers, whilst noting that other studies had, broadly speaking, replicated the findings in these papers. In effect, these further scientific papers were crucial in supporting the original work and establishing a scientific consensus. Among a number of pertinent issues raised by this panel was the need to work with expert statisticians when assessing complex sets of secondary proxy data, and to be more organized and consistent in record keeping (Oxburgh et al., 2010). The em@il review raised a related issue in terms archiving and curation of research data and information, notably how research councils should provide advice, resources and funding for these activities (Russell et al., 2010).

Oxburgh et al. (2010) raised concerns about the availability of relevant data sets to facilitate openness and transparency through sharing of information, also how unresolved questions remained about the application of FoI legislation in academic contexts. In a similar vein, Russell et al. (2010) raised a number of relevant issues about scientific research in the digital age, and they called for further discussion about some of these issues. It follows that "Climategate" raises some important issues of relevance to the communication of scientific consensus and its relation to social change that are worthy of further study, including: who "owns" versus who "holds" data; who has the legal rights to make data publicly available; what should be archived, by who, with what resources, and where; how much of this data is already publicly available versus what should be (re)published alongside newly published papers; how should scientists respond to e-mails from critics; and whether freedom of scientific information enacted via policies of greater openness and transparency will reduce conflict and contest or hinder and delay scientific research.

Given these issues, it is interesting that one of the recommendations of the House of Commons Select Committee (2010) was to promote openness and transparency, a proactive and comprehensive approach to how data, methodologies, findings and interpretations about climate science should be made public. In short, this committee argued that all raw data and computer codes should be made available proactively on the web when peer reviewed papers are published. This raises interesting questions about what should be published so that peers can assess the validity and reliability of scientific data and interpretations. In effect, the implicit assumption that underlies this recommendation is that a peer reviewed academic paper is insufficient to ensure that climate science is "irreproachable" and that there "should be enough information published to allow verification" (House of Commons Select Committee, 2010, p. 19). In other words, the facilitation of falsification requires full disclosure of data sets, methodologies and, where relevant, computer codes, requiring a fundamental shift in how climate science research is produced and circulated. Acceptance of this recommendation by climate scientists, and Russell et al. (2010) caution against such a change before further deliberation, would have important implications for the publication of peer reviewed papers and the compilation of future IPCC reports.

THE ROLE OF THE IPPC, AR4, AND THE CASE OF THE HIMALAYAN GLACIERS

The Intergovernmental Panel on Climate Change (IPCC; ipcc.ch) was established in 1988, through the United Nations Environment Programme and the World Meteorological Organization (IPCC, 2007). The mandate of the IPCC is to produce policy-relevant assessment related to climate change, drawing on relevant scientific, technical and socioeconomic information. As such, the IPPC manages the process of reviewing existing research via a small secretariat, drawing on a network of authors and reviewers.

Since its instigation, the IPCC, itself symbolically represented as a series of assessment reports, has become one of the very few institutional bodies routinely cited as embodying a scientific consensus. As such, it has also become a focal point for attacks by those who wish to challenge this consensus, contesting whether human activity is at least partly responsible for global climate change. In essence, this scientific consensus is based on a series of assessment reports produced under the auspices of the IPCC, the fourth of which was published in 2007.[12] Under the chairmanship of Rajendra Pachauri, this fourth assessment report, also known as AR4, involved more than 500 lead authors and 2,000 expert reviewers (IPCC, 2007).[13] The report is over 3,000-pages long and consists of four volumes: a synthesis volume and three further volumes from working groups that examine "The physical science basis," "Impacts, Adaptation and Variability," and "Mitigation of Climate Change," respectively.

In the weeks immediately preceding COP-15, data about the rate of retreat in the Himalayan glaciers was discussed in scientific journals (e.g., Bagla, 2009), represented in news media reports, and debated via social media, including blogs.[14] The evidence in question was published in the Asia chapter of the second volume of AR4 where it was claimed that:

> Glaciers in the Himalayas are receding faster than in any other part of the world [the supporting data is shown in the same section of the report (p. 494) in Table 10.9] and, if the present rate continues, the likelihood of them disappearing by the year 2035 and perhaps sooner is very high if the Earth keeps warming at the current rate. Its total area will likely shrink from the present 500,000 to 100,000 km^2 by the year 2035 (WWF, 2005). (Cruz et al., 2007, p. 493)

Following the publication of a discussion paper produced for the government of India, the IPPC-cited data on the rate of recession and disappearance of Himalayan glaciers was questioned, and any direct links to climate change were argued to be premature (Raina, 2009).The sources of the data in the IPPC report were also questioned, because they had not undergone peer review.

In response to these concerns the IPCC accepted that a mistake had been made in relation to this data. They issued a short statement where they reinforced the overall conclusions of AR4 in relation to water resources. The IPCC statement goes on to argue that:[15]

> It has ... recently come to our attention that a paragraph in the 938-page Working Group II contribution to the underlying assessment[2] refers to poorly substantiated estimates of rate of recession and date for the disap-

pearance of Himalayan glaciers. In drafting the paragraph in question, the clear and well-established standards of evidence, required by the IPCC procedures, were not applied properly. (IPCC, 2010)

[Footnote 2 states:] The text in question is the second paragraph in section 10.6.2 of the Working Group II contribution and a repeat of part of the paragraph in Box TS.6. of the Working Group II Technical Summary of the IPCC Fourth Assessment Report. (IPCC, 2010)

This episode illustrates how the scientific norm of scepticism and the methodologies and rhetorical strategies of scientific investigation were used to successfully challenge the Himalayan glacier data from AR4. Specifically, this episode placed in question the processes whereby scientific data were selected and checked before inclusion in AR4, thereby indirectly challenging the scientific credibility of those involved in producing the IPCC reports. This is further evidenced by the calls that were made for the chair of the IPCC, Rajendra Pachauri, an important symbol for the scientific consensus of anthropogenic climate change, to resign. He resisted and is currently (January 2012) chairing production of the Fifth Assessment Report (AR5), which is due to be published in 2013 and 2014.

This example further illustrates the contested nature of the consensus of anthropogenic climate change. In successfully challenging the data on the Himalayan glaciers, critics questioned the processes by which AR4 had been produced, enacting the scientific norm of scepticism and the methodologies and rhetorical strategies of scientific investigation. Securing the clarification of this data from the IPCC was symbolically important, as was the timing. This challenge was timed to coincide with the run up to COP-15. In effect, this episode partly undermined the scientific case for anthropogenic climate change, potentially damaging the chances of building a political consensus to drive social change.

CONCLUSION

Mediated communication can be an important factor in the emergence, framing, duration and closure of representations of scientific consensus in the public sphere. And, as with news media accounts of scientific controversies (Jensen, this volume), representations of scientific consensus in the public sphere can have profound, if unpredictable, implications for social change. Such representations develop out of different forms, involving collaboratively authored reports, meta-analyses of peer reviewed papers, textbooks, science curricula, the outcomes from conferences and meetings, open letters, petitions and declarations, press conferences, press releases, blog postings, even graphical representations such as the "hockey stick" graph (Mann et al., 1998). By its very nature the symbolic struggle for scientific consensus involves challenge and contestation, sometimes over an extended period of time, and occasionally played out in the public sphere. In this way consensus and controversy are dynamically opposed, but closely related.

A scientific consensus may only become visible in the public sphere when it is challenged and becomes "controversial." Through the dynamic processes of generating, defending, repairing, adapting, and partially revising the data and interpretations on which a consensus is based, scientific ideas, explanations, theories, and so on change over time, with potentially profound implications for social change. In the examples discussed in this chapter, scientists, journalists, and activists communicated via a number of forms, including professional media (e.g., broadcast and print news) and social media (e.g., blog posts). These examples illustrate how digital forms of communication are changing at least some of the ways that the sciences are communicated, and democratic processes are enacted.

Particular attention in the run up to COP-15 was paid to questions about e-mails sent during the production of peer reviewed papers, freedom of information requests, and the selection and checking of data for inclusion in AR4 (IPCC, 2007), respectively. Furthermore, the work of the Director of the Climatic Research Unit at the University of East Anglia, and the chair of the IPCC, were scrutinised. Following COP-15 the membership of the independent reviews set up to review "climategate" were also challenged. These examples document how critics of the scientific consensus of anthropogenic climate change challenged various aspects of the processes that underpinned the production of symbolic representations of the scientific consensus of anthropogenic climate change. In so doing, these critics used various forms of social media (e.g., blogs) to inform professional media (e.g., newspapers and broadcast news), as well as more traditional routes of science communication.

The outcomes of the communication of scientific consensus around COP-15 may have profound implications for how climate science is produced and circulated in the future. The calls for proactive openness and transparency in comprehensively communicating raw data, methodologies, findings and interpretations reflect ongoing discussions about trust, (in)access to information and the authentic practices of digital scholarship (Borgman, 2007). Such developments are not without challenges, however. At the same time the diversity of mainly digital forms via which scientific and politically motivated communication was enacted around COP-15 raises interesting questions about the role of mediated communication in the public sphere, and its relation to deliberative politics and social change (Habermas, 2006). The examples discussed in this chapter illustrate that there is an emerging role for a "fifth estate" (Holliman, 2008), which is increasingly important in informing how the established fourth estate frame issues of scientific consensus and controversy.

Within this wider context the symbolic struggle for the scientific consensus of anthropogenic climate change is ongoing and the long-term effects of the examples described in this chapter remain to be seen. However, it is clear that events such as COP-15, the work of the IPCC in producing AR3 and AR4, and the scientific information upon which future reports such as AR5 are based, will continue to generate some level of consensus, but also challenges, contest and controversy. This begs the question of whether it is possible to maintain a scientific consensus about the causes of climate change, much less a political and social consensus for how to act in the light of a changing climate, in an age where digital communication circulates so freely and speedily, and conspiracy theories abound.

In conclusion, Jensen (this volume), drawing on the work of Beck (1992) and others, argues that the sciences have lost some of their authority as epistemologically superior sources of knowledge in the public sphere. At the same time, however, the "risk society" has also become ever more reliant on these forms of expertise. Scientific experts may have lost some of their authority, in part because of episodes such as "Climategate" and the Himalayan glaciers, but they are no less popular among media professionals (Jensen, 2008) and politicians as a result. Indeed, reporting of scientific consensus (and controversies) relies on various forms of expertise, many of whom are advocates for particular scientific theories, political ideologies, worldviews, and so on, whilst politicians routinely recite the need for evidence-based policy. What has changed, however, is the emergence of social media, and its attendant social practices. The proliferation of digital media forms facilitates archiving, searching and sharing of data sets. It has also increased the number of channels to produce and circulate content, disagree, form alliances, and so on. The blogosphere provides almost unlimited capacity to communicate where disagreement, controversy and conspiracy theories abound. Disruption of a scientific consensus, enacted via strategies whereby social media are used to inform professional media, alongside the use of freedom of information requests and other related strategies, may be sufficient to further delay action to mitigate the effects of climate change. In this emerging context openness and transparency should be guiding principles for those who support the scientific consensus. But these concepts must apply equally to critics of anthropogenic climate change. Similarly, the limitations of evidence-based policy, where scientific uncertainties and complexity are in evidence, should be acknowledged. Taking into account this wider context, calls for social change in how we respond to a changing climate may be more effectively sought via the rhetoric of precaution.

NOTES

1. Similarly, scientists, scientific institutions, politicians, economists, business people, nongovernmental organizations (NGOs), activists, and so on, were also well prepared to communicate before, during and after this event.
2. Of course, the scientific consensus of anthropogenic climate change is inextricably enmeshed with ongoing efforts to generate and maintain a global political consensus. This was evident at COP-15, exemplified by attempts to negotiate international agreement on decreases in emissions of "greenhouse" gases and reductions in energy requirements, and how best to mitigate the effects of climate change.
3. Sociologists of scientific knowledge (e.g. Latour, 1987) argue that ethnographic research exploring the authentic practices of knowledge production can provide valid accounts of how scientists work.
4. Peer review also has a role in determining which research grants to fund, which may have the effect of supporting or challenging an existing scientific consensus. It has an additional function for indirectly representing science in the public sphere, because peer reviewed publication, via the use of 'information subsidies' and other promotional work (Bauer & Bucchi, 2007; Kiernan, 2006), provides journalists seeking a newsworthy science story with what they consider to be reliable source material (Holliman, 2004). Similarly, publishers often use peer review to assess proposals for new books.
5. See unfccc.int/meetings/cop_15/items/5257.php for the official website of COP-15.
6. Vidal (2009, December 6) notes that 5000 journalists from 180 countries received accreditation in advance of COP-15, so many that applications were closed prior to the event. The applications for media accreditation were themselves a focus for contest as many were received from advocates of charities, NGOs, pressure groups and industry. This illustrates the importance that these actors attributed to mediated communication and its potential to influence social change. Gaining access via media accreditation was considered as an important step in influencing perceptions of COP-15 in the public sphere, and how debates developed during this event.
7. Notably, only one U.S.-based newspaper (*Miami Herald*) officially signed up to this editorial, although other U.S. nationals expressed informal support (Katz, 2009). This suggests that national U.S.-based newspapers were unwilling to publish a call to action of this nature. In the same way that *The Guardian* were appealing to their readers, we can infer that this decision was made, at least in part, because of concerns about upsetting some of the readers of these U.S.-based publications.
8. Jensen (this volume) talks of the importance of conceptual metaphors in how scientific phenomena are described in the public sphere. In a classic example of journalistic shorthand, some news reports framed the leaking of e-mails from the Climatic Research Unit at the University of East Anglia as an example of suppressed evidence by describing it as "climategate," This

shorthand made links to the impeachment of the U.S. President Richard Nixon in the 1970s following a break-in at the Watergate office complex.

9. For the "RealClimate" site, see realclimate.org. For "the Air Vent" blog, see noconsensus.wordpress.com.
10. See ico.gov.uk/what_we_cover/freedom_of_information.aspx for further information about the U.K.'s FoIA.
11. Following publication in 1998 the 'hockey stick' graph was also challenged. It was subject to a National Research Council (NRC) investigation, at the request of the U.S. Congress. The NRC broadly supported the original findings of Mann et al. (1998) and several peer reviewed studies have broadly replicated the original analysis and interpretations. However, the graph caused considerable debate as to whether it should feature in the 2001 IPCC report (AR3). In the end it did, but without the uncertainties that had appeared in the original peer reviewed paper. Notably, this graph has featured in popular media, including the feature-length documentary *An Inconvenient Truth.*
12. In that same year the IPCC were jointly awarded (along with Al Gore) the Nobel Peace Prize: "for their efforts to build up and disseminate greater knowledge about man-made climate change, and to lay the foundations for the measures that are needed to counteract such change." This provided symbolic recognition of the work of the IPCC and reinforced the significance of AR4.
13. The three previous reports were published in 1990, 1995, and 2001, respectively.
14. The Himalayan glaciers hold particular significance because they contain the largest mass of ice and snow outside the poles. Indeed, they have been described as the "third pole" (e.g., see Bagla, 2009).
15. The World Wildlife Fund also issued a correction, which has been added to the start of the relevant report (WWF, 2005).

REFERENCES

Abdool Karim, Q., et. al. (2000). The Durban Declaration, *Nature, 406,* 15-6.

Allgaier, J., & Holliman, R. (2006). The emergence of the controversy around the theory of evolution and creationism in UK newspaper reports. *Curriculum Journal, 17,* 263-279.

Bagla, P. (2009). No sign yet of Himalayan meltdown, Indian report finds. *Science, 326,* 924-925.

Batty, D., & Adam, D. (2010, February 10). Climate emails review panellist quits after his impartiality questioned. *Guardian.co.uk*. Retrieved from guardian.co.uk/environment/2010/feb/12/climate-change-climategate-nature-global-warming

Bauer, M., & Bucchi, M. (Eds.). (2007). *Journalism, science and society: Science communication between news and public relations*. Abingdon and New York: Routledge.

Beck, U. (1992). *Risk society: Towards a new modernity.* London: SAGE.

Berg, P. (2008). Asilomar 1975: DNA modification secured. *Nature, 455,* 290-291.

Borgman, C. (2007). *Scholarship in the digital age: information, infrastructure and the Internet*. Cambridge, MA: MIT.

Cruz, R. V., Harasawa, H., Lal, M., Wu, S., Anokhin, Y., Punsalmaa, B., et al. (2007). *Asia. Climate Change 2007: Impacts, Adaptation and Vulnerability.* In M. L. Parry, O. F. Canziani, J. P. Palutikof, P. J. van der Linden, & C. E. Hanson (Eds.), *Contribution of Working Group II to the Fourth Assessment Report of the Intergovernmental Panel on Climate Change*, Cambridge, England: Cambridge University Press. Retrieved from ipcc.ch/pdf/assessment-report/ar4/wg2/ar4-wg2-chapter10.pdf

de Solla Price, D. (1963). *Little science, big science ... and beyond.* New York, NY: Columbia University Press.

Editorial (2009, December 7). Fourteen days to seal history's judgment on this generation. *The Guardian*, p. 1. Retrieved from guardian.co.uk/commentisfree/2009/dec/06/copenhagen-editorial

Gieryn, T. (1995). Boundaries of science. In S. Jasanoff, G. Markle, J. Petersen, & T. Pinch (Eds.), *Handbook of science and technology studies* (pp. 393-443). Thousand Oaks, CA: SAGE.

Gleick, P., et al. (2010). Climate change and the integrity of science. *Science, 328,* 689-670.

Green, M. (2007). The demise of the lone author. *Nature, 450,* 1165.

Habermas, J. (2006). Political communication in media society: Does democracy still enjoy an epistemic dimension? The impact of normative theory on empirical research, *Communication Theory, 16,* 411-426.

Holliman, R., & Scanlon, E. (2009). Interpreting contested science: Media influence and scientific citizenship. In R. Holliman, E. Whitelegg, E. Scanlon, S. Smidt, & J. Thomas (Eds.), *Investigating science communication in the information age: Implications for public engagement and popular media* (pp. 254-73). Oxford, England: Oxford University Press.

Holliman, R. (2008). Communicating science in the digital age—issues and prospects for public engagement. In J. MacLennan (Ed.), *Readings for technical writers* (pp. 68-76). Toronto, Canada: Oxford University Press.

Holliman, R. (2004). Media coverage of cloning: A study of media content, production and reception. *Public Understanding of Science, 13,* 107-130.

Holliman., R. (2002). HIV/AIDS: a global pandemic. S802 *Science and the public.* Milton Keynes: The Open University.

Holliman, R. Trench, B. Fahy, D. Basedas, I. Revuelta, G. Lederbogen, U., & Poupardin, E. (2002, December). *Science in the news: A cross-cultural study of newspapers in five European countries.* Proceedings of the 7th International Public Communication of Science and Technology Conference—*Science Communication in a Diverse World*, Cape Town, South Africa.

Holliman, R., Donovan, C., Scanlon, E., Yates, S., & Macqueen, H. (2001). *Media coverage of the Human Genome Project.* Paper presented at the British Sociological Association Conference—*A Sociological Odyssey,* Manchester Metropolitan University.

House of Commons Science and Technology Committee. (2010, March 24). *The disclosure of climate data from the Climatic Research Unit of the University of East Anglia* (Eighth Report of Session 2009-10). London: HMSO.

IAU (International Astronomical Union) (2006). *Resolutions B5 and B6: Definition of a planet in the solar system and Pluto.* Retrieved from iau.org/static/resolutions/Resolution_GA26-5-6.pdf

International Human Genome Sequencing Consortium. (2001). Initial sequencing and analysis of the human genome. *Nature*, 409, 860-921.

IPCC. (2007). Climate Change 2007: Synthesis Report. In Pachauri, R. K & Reisinger, A. (Eds.), *Contribution of Working Groups I, II and III to the Fourth Assessment Report of the Intergovernmental Panel on Climate Change.* Geneva, Switzerland: Author. Retrieved from ipcc.ch/publications_and_data/publications_ipcc_fourth_assessment_report_synthesis_report.htm

IPCC. (2010, January 20). *IPCC statement on the melting of Himalayan glaciers*. IPCC, Geneva, Switzerland: Author. Retrieved from ipcc.ch/pdf/presentations/himalaya-statement-20january2010.pdf

Jensen, E. (2008). *Anglo–American press coverage of therapeutic cloning: A grounded discourse analysis of news production and content.* (Unpublished PhD thesis). University of Cambridge.

Katz, I. (2009, December 6). How the climate change global editorial project came about. *Guardian.co.uk: Environment.* Retrieved from guardian.co.uk/environment/2009/dec/06/climate-change-leader-editorial

Kiernan, V. (2006). *Embargoed science*. Urbana: University of Illinois Press.

Latour, B. (1987). *Science in action: How to follow scientists and engineers through society.* Milton Keynes: Open University Press.

Lewenstein, B. (2009). Where do books fit in the information age? In R. Holliman, J. Thomas, S. Smidt, E. Scanlon, & E. Whitelegg (Eds.), *Practising science communication in the information age: Theorising professional practices* (pp. 151-65). Oxford, England: Oxford University Press.

Mann, M., Bradley, R., & Hughes, M. (1998). Global-scale temperature patterns and climate forcing over the past six centuries. *Nature, 392,* 779-787.

Nerlich, B., Dingwall, R., & Clarke, D. (2002). The book of life: How the completion of the Human Genome Project was revealed to the public. *Health, 6,* 445-469.

Nisbet, M., & Scheufele, D. (2009). What's next for science communication? Promising directions and lingering distractions. *American Journal of Botany, 96,* 1767-1778.

Oreskes, N. (2004). The scientific consensus on climate change. *Science, 306,* 1686.

Oxburgh, R., Davies, H., Emanuel, K., Graumlich, L., Hand, D., Huppert, H., & Kelly, M. (2010, April 10). *Report of the International Panel set up by the University of East Anglia to examine the research of the Climatic Research Unit.* Retrieved from uea.ac.uk/mac/comm/media/press/CRUstatements/Report+of+the+Science+Assessment+Panel

Popper, K. (1935). *The logic of scientific discovery.* London: Hutchinson.

Raina, V. (2009). *Himalayan glaciers: A state-of-art review of glacial studies, glacial retreat and climate change*. Ministry of Environment and Forests Discussion Paper, Government of India. Retrieved from moef.nic.in/downloads/public-information/MoEF%20Discussion%20Paper%20_him.pdf

Russell, M., Boulton, G., Clarke, P., Eyton, D., & Norton, J. (2010, July). *The independent climate change emails review.* Retrieved from http://www.cce-review.org/pdf/FINAL%20REPORT.pdf

Turney, J. (1999). The recombinant DNA debate. In E. Scanlon, R. Hill, & K. Junker (Eds.), *Communicating science: Professional contexts* (pp. 289-303). London: Routledge.

Valiela, I. (2001). *Doing science: Design, analysis and communication of scientific research.* Oxford, England: Oxford University Press.

Venter, J. et al. (2001). The sequence of the human genome. *Science, 291,* 1304-1351.

Vidal, J. (2009, December 7). A perfect storm. Independent twitterers, bloggers, activists and diverse interest groups will outnumber the media at the Copenhagen summit. *MediaGuardian,* p. 3. Retrieved from guardian.co.uk/media/2009/dec/07/copenhagen-summit-media-army

Wager, E. (2009). Peer review in science journals: past, present and future. In R. Holliman, J. Thomas, S. Smidt, E. Scanlon & E. Whitelegg (Eds.), *Practising science communication in the information age: Theorising professional practices* (pp. 115-130) Oxford, England: Oxford University Press.

Watson, J. (1968). *The double helix.* London: Weidenfeld and Nicolson.

Watson, J. D., & Crick, F. (1953). A structure for Deoxyribose Nucleic Acid. *Nature, 4356,* 737-738.

World Wildlife Fund. (2005, March). *An overview of glaciers, glacier retreat, and subsequent impacts in Nepal, India and China.* World Wildlife Fund, Nepal Programme. Retrived from assets.panda.org/downloads/himalayaglaciersreport2005.pdf

PART III

SOCIETIES IN TRANSITION

CHAPTER 12

MEDIATING SOCIAL CHANGE IN AUTHORITARIAN AND DEMOCRATIC STATES

Irony, Hybridity, and Corporate Censorship

Eric Jensen

Only jokes that have a purpose run the risk of meeting with people who do not want to listen to them

—Freud (1905/1991, p. 132)

The development and cultural appropriation of social change is never straightforward or simple. In Western democratic societies, transformations in cultural representations and practices may initially develop within an agonistic and pluralistic public sphere. However, there are always institutional and systemic forces in such societies that resist social and cultural change through more subtle, behind-the-scenes and passive aggressive means. Louis Althusser (1971) has argued that ideological state apparatuses such as education and propaganda are the primary means by which the existing capitalist system is reproduced in contemporary democratic societies. In contrast, authoritarian regimes supplement ideological state

Culture and Social Change: Transforming Society Through the Power of Ideas, pp. 211–221

apparatuses with overt repression of the population through the threat of coercion and censorship of potentially subversive political speech. Yet, I will argue that the presumed differences between democratic and authoritarian systems when it comes to quashing dissident political speech are greatly exaggerated. In the interests of maintaining the ideological and material status quo, attempts to transform society through the power of new or challenging ideas are routinely subjected to harsh reprisals under both systems of government. In Western democracies, reprisals target dissidents' economic, symbolic or political standing, and media corporations are a primary if unofficial instrument of censorship. In authoritarian societies such as China or Saudi Arabia, government bureaucrats act as officially sanctioned censors with the repressive power of the government underpinning their activities. In this chapter, I will draw upon two case studies to develop my argument that under both authoritarian and democratic regimes humor and irony are two of the most effective tools for introducing into the public realm any fundamental rhetorical challenges to the existing social order. At the same time, stepping outside the cloak of irony and humor raises the risk of reprisals under both systems, a point which is illustrated by the post-September 11 censorship of American television comedian Bill Maher.

CASE STUDY 1: SOCIAL CHANGE AND SAUDI TELEVISION

Given its emanating influence across the Middle East, Saudi Arabian television has become a key forum for social and political change in the postcolonial era. The content of Saudi national broadcasts offers insights into shifting cultural (self-)representations. This essay considers the ascendance of more critical and ironic accounts of Saudi society through a brief analysis of the long-running comedy and current affairs program *Tash Ma Tash*. A 2006 episode[1] featuring a parody titled "Terrorist Academy" is considered as a case example of the role this program plays in indirectly challenging authoritarian governance by bringing controversial issues into the mediated public sphere in Saudi Arabia and throughout the Middle East.

Tash Ma Tash is a hybrid media product that defies categorization as either "news and current affairs" or "entertainment" programming. In this essay, I argue that this popular and iconoclastic programme draws its influence and maintains its ability to operate from its "in-betweenness." As Homi Bhahba (1994, pp. 1-2) pointed out in his analysis of colonial power, the "in-between spaces provide the terrain for elaborating strategies of selfhood—singular or communal—that initiate new signs of identity, and innovative sites of collaboration, and contestation, in the act of defining the idea of society." In the context of authoritarian government control over the media, perspectives that challenge the dominant-hegemonic worldview in the nation can only be expressed indirectly and ambiguously. By treating serious issues in a satirical manner, *Tash Ma Tash* subtly weaves its perspective into the cultural interstices of Saudi society, giving public voice to many critical views that would otherwise remain unspeakable without reprisal.

Airing nightly during the holy month of Ramadan annually since 1993, *Tash Ma Tash* (in Arabic, طاش ما طاش) defies categorization. It is controversial, drawing protests and religious invectives, and at the same time extremely popular with consistently high audience ratings year on year. It is absurd, using slapstick comedy and outrageous exaggeration, but simultaneously building a subtle critique of the religious establishment and the paradoxical absurdities of everyday life within Saudi Arabia through satire and parody.[2] The program engages with subjects of varying significance, including ridiculing societal norms, traditions, beliefs and customs. *Tash Ma Tash* has even dealt with issues of gender equality.

Though it originated on Saudi terrestrial television, the program is produced privately with the approval of the Saudi ministry of information to tackle sensitive social topics. 20-25 episodes are broadcast each year throughout the region on the Middle East Broadcast Channel (MBC). Satellite channels such as MBC have rolled back the state's censoring power over the media by providing a transnational source of information and critical public discourse. While *Tash Ma Tash* continues to be aimed at the national audience in Saudi Arabia, its influence is boosted through satellite broadcasts, which are popular with audiences throughout the Middle East.

Hybridity, Humor, and Resistance

Jensen and Wagoner (2009) have argued previously that social change follows a complex, dynamic, and processual cycle within which it is possible for new ideas to become the dominant representations in a given domain. However, the struggle to have ideas accepted in theory and practice is greatly complicated by the rules of the game within an authoritarian state such as the Kingdom of Saudi Arabia. Clashes of opinion regarding core public policy cannot become publicly visible in an authoritarian context without fear of reprisal. Dissent is suppressed, dispersed, and confined to the sphere of private conversations. Moreover, the public sphere in Saudi Arabia is restricted even further by the strict gender segregation and inflexible gender role definitions, which exclude women from any discussions of public policy or participation in political life.

Finally, the strict oligarchy in the Kingdom is underwritten by religious authorities who simultaneously maintain the existing power structure and engage daily in the work of reproducing existing norms and practices within Saudi society.

Given such inclement conditions for the development of new representations of Saudi life and public policy, it is unsurprising that progressive social change has been extremely slow in coming to Saudi Arabia. The limited segment of the population that is empowered to engage in discussion about public policy dared not speak against the official position of the ruling family, nor their beneficiaries and enablers in the religious establishment. How then can new representations be introduced and cultivated in such a closed political system? In this essay, I point to the potential of hybrid media forms as an important platform for raising political issues in an indirect, ironic and humorous manner. Rather than directly confronting the shortcomings of the Saudi royal family and religious authorities directly, they can be displayed by demonstrating the comedic foolishness of certain positions and the absurdity of traditional gender inequality and Islamic extremist ideology, amongst other issues.

Terrorist Academy

I now turn to a specific episode of *Tash Ma Tash* titled *Terrorist Academy* to illustrate my argument about the power of humor and irony in an authoritarian context. As the title suggests this episode is a parody of the Western reality show *Star Academy*. It borrows some of the props of this Western programme to illustrate how Islamic terrorists have resorted to using Western publicity techniques to promote *Jihad* (holy war) against the West. However the main line in this episode involves the terrorists citing a number of aspects of Western influence in the Middle East as threats to Islam. In particular the terrorist characters in the parody decry cultural imperialism, depicting television as a powerful tool for the corrupting influence of Western liberal values on Muslim beliefs and moral conduct. Thus, the terrorist characters portray Muslims as passive dupes of the West, given to signs of decadence and immorality. The terrorist characters use this portrayal of cultural imperialism to paint Americans and the West more generally as leading a new twenty-first century crusade. They explicitly conjured the Crusades of the Middle Ages, seeking to tap into deep historical ethnic identities as means of rallying Muslims for a renewed *Jihad* (e.g., see Smith, 1986). The terrorists in this episode called for violence against the *infidels* (nonbelievers, or non-Muslims) posing this ideological threat of cultural imperialism.

The ironical nature of the terrorists' diatribe can be identified in part through the fact that the writers for the show did not highlight what could be viewed as more legitimate concerns such as the Israeli-Palestinian conflict, the war in Iraq, or the colonial legacy as the basis of terrorists' hatred of the West. Rather, the terrorists' appeared to be advocating an irrationally extreme response to mere television shows. The folly of the terrorists' outlook was identified most explicitly in the final scene. An explosive suicide-bomber belt is presented to the winner of the Terrorist Academy contest. The belt explodes on stage, implicitly suggesting the self-defeating nature of the extremist ideologies espoused by the terrorists on the show.

The exaggerated and ironic nature of this final scene makes it difficult to identify it as an unambiguous criticism of Islamic extremism. However, this ambiguity is precisely what allows the subtle critique to slip past with government censors. Moreover, the comedic dimensions of this episode invite viewers to let down their guard and laugh with the programme at the absurdity of the terrorists' self-defeating position. An explicit discussion of the fallacies of extremism that is largely supported by the religious establishment within Saudi Arabia would have certainly been censored, but this hybrid form of political parody delivered this message just the same.

Tash Ma Tash: Giving Voice to Saudi Subalterns

Episodes such as *Terrorist Academy* utilize the hybridity of *Tash Ma Tash* as a media format to develop a critique of Saudi societal structures, which speaks directly to subaltern Saudi publics that have long been without a voice in public sphere. Homi Bhabha's definition of subaltern groups applies to Saudi publics because of their authoritarian government and religious authorities. Given the high level of social control exercised on the Saudi population by the government and religious authorities, the majority of the nation could be viewed as oppressed, their freedoms strictly circumscribed. The popularity of *Tash Ma Tash* aligns with Bhabha's (1996) argument that subaltern groups desire to subvert the discursive hegemony of their oppressors. Its subtle criticisms undermine hegemonic efforts to impose a "common sense" understanding of Saudi society that supports elite and institutional interests (Hall, 1998). I contend that the fundamental criticisms the programme offers regarding the fabric of everyday life within Saudi society contributes a great deal to subverting the authority of religious and government authorities, even though the Saudi royal family is never addressed directly. Mockery of the existing system of religious control in *Tash Ma Tash* could be viewed as undermining the very ideology that allowed the Saudi royals to claim, maintain and legitimize their power.

Notably, the pattern established by the *Tash Ma Tash* example can also be seen in the rise of web-based broadcasting in Saudi Arabia. Shows such as *On the Fly* and *La Yekthar* or ("Zip It" in English) broadcast ironic and humorous programming with socially relevant content on Youtube. The following extract from a *New York Times* article describes the kinds of social issues that *On the Fly* has taken on through humor:

> It ran with a sardonic news report, which the writers described as a gift, of a judge's defending himself publicly against accusations of graft by saying that the devil possessed him. It also reported the news that a member of the religious police stabbed a man, possibly with nail clippers, after the two fought over a remark that the man's wife should cover her face. The most popular episode, released in February [2011] amid the upheaval in Egypt and elsewhere, received more than 635,000 hits. (MacFarquhar, 2011, p. A14)

However, as with *Tash Ma Tash*, the fundamentals of the existing Saudi system of power and legitimation are still largely off limits to criticism, even online.

> The shows avoid mentioning the royal family and the absence of the Arab Spring in the kingdom ... and they rarely touch on the judiciary system or other bastions of Islamic puritanism. (MacFarquhar, 2011, p. A14)

Thus, the dynamics of censorship in this authoritarian state continue to hold true as broadcasting expands into the online sphere.

CASE STUDY 2: TOO POLITICALLY INCORRECT?

In the wake of the September 11 attacks, political speech was severely restricted in the United States. In this context, some television comedians became an unlikely critical voice within the public sphere, communicating messages challenging government policy in a way that few other professional groups could during this time. However, even this group was not immune from harsh reprisals when criticisms or alternative points of view were expressed without the cloak of irony. For example, Bill Maher, an iconoclastic television comedian and host of the long-runnng U.S.-based ABC show *Politically Incorrect with Bill Maher* faced censorship and exclusion from the public realm for challenging President George W. Bush's statement that the terrorists who attacked the World Trade Center were "cowards." Maher made the following statement a week after the September 11 attacks: "We have been the cowards, lobbing cruise missiles from 2,000 miles away. That's cowardly. Staying in the airplane when it hits the building, say what you want about it, it's not cowardly." The subsequent controversy over this statement included then White House press secretary Ari Fleischer making made the cautionary and vaguely menacing statement: "they're reminders to all Americans that they need to watch what they say, watch what they do. This is not a time for remarks like that." However, it was the withdrawal of powerful corporate advertisers such as Sears Roebuck that resulted in the network canceling Maher's show in 2002.

One key theoretical and philosophical problem revealed by this example is the conventional definition of censorship in Western political philosophy, which only counts *state action* and not the "private" actions of corporations or individuals to suppress unpopular speech that challenges the existing capitalist and corporatist system in the United States, United Kingdom, Australia, and other "democracies." Thus, Maher's unpopular statement and subsequent dismissal was not defined as "censorship" under the mainstream definition of that word. Being outside this definition meant that Maher was unable to effectively draw upon the accumulated symbolic resources in American cultural history focused on, for example, the celebration of First Amendment protections against state censorship of the press. Not only did this categorical exclusion of corporate censorship legitimate Maher's expulsion from network television, it reveals the typically invisible censorship that pervades commercial media. This invisible censorship drives journalists and others in the media away from discussing systemic sources of inequality and suffering in Western democracies in favour of superficial and episodic framing of public affairs (Herman & Chomsky, 1988; Iyengar, 1994).

The corporate censorship of Maher shows the danger facing even comedians, even in supposedly free societies, and even on a show titled *Politically Incorrect*. Actors on the public stage cannot be too direct in their dissent from the dominant state messages about terrorism and war, nor in their challenges to common sense assumptions about society. Moreover, this case also shows the power of corporations to limit the range of opinions given airtime in the mediated public sphere to a narrow sliver of the political spectrum. For example, even the most innocuous suggestions of "the rich paying their fair share" or "helping those who can't help themselves" by U.S. politicians such as President Barack Obama were met with an instant barrage of epithets such as "communist" and "socialist."

Of course, even the power of corporate censorship is bounded by the even greater power of corporate greed. Bill Maher's politically incorrect speech got him fired from the mainstream broadcast network ABC, but the subscription cable network HBO saw profit potential in Maher's show and hired him in 2003. His show was rebranded *Real Time with Bill Maher* and he was freed from corporate censorship by virtue of the fact HBO has no advertisers or corporate sponsors, only individual or institutional subscribers. Maher's new show has been running each year since (in its sixth season at time of writing) despite expressing dissenting and highly controversial opinions about a wide range of topics, including arguing the American food and pharmaceutical companies are the largest contributors to poor public health in the United States. Such anticorporate arguments are never expressed so directly in mainstream advertiser-funded commercial media.

CONCLUSION

This chapter examined the similarities of censorship and resistance in authoritarian and democratic regimes. The main difference was that censorship operates primarily through the state's repressive power in authoritarian societies versus the power of the corporate purse to censor dissent in Western democracies. In both cases, the key to introducing dissenting ideas was to maintain the cover of humour and irony; to avoid stating explicitly one's opposition to the dominant assumptions in one's society. Indeed the importance of such indirectness can also be seen from the example of philosopher Jean-Jacques Rousseau who was perceived as criticizing religion too directly in his book *Emile* and was chased out of his home city of Geneva as a result. Commenting on this turn of events, Scottish philosopher David Hume said he was unsurprised at the harsh response given that Rousseau

> has not had the precaution to throw any veil over his sentiments; and, as he scorns to dissemble his contempt for established opinions, he could not wonder that all the zealots were in arms against him. The liberty of the press is not so secured in any country ... as not to render such an open attack on popular prejudice somewhat dangerous. (Gay, 1969, p. 72)

Rousseau's contemporary Voltaire maintained his high standing in French society by using satire and parody rather than direct criticisms to communicate his views on the religious establishment of his day. To paraphrase Hume, this precaution of "dissembling one's contempt for established opinions" can be seen in the *Tash Ma Tash* episode explicated above, as well as the general approach of this program.

Tash Ma Tash, and similar subsequent humor-based programming brings into the light many social issues and practices within Saudi society that would otherwise never be openly criticized or even analyzed in the Saudi Arabian public sphere. Without such interventions, the powerful in Saudi society are able to exercise influence unfettered by critical public debate that could call their actions to account (e.g., see Habermas, 1989; Mill, 1858/1992; Milton, 1644). That is, Saudi media do not offer a space for a "public of private people making use of their reason" (Habermas, 1989, p. 51) in order to openly challenge the government. Given that media are frequently viewed as the "main tool through which organized citizens can limit power and hold powerful actors accountable" (Young, 2000, p. 174), government censorship represents a major limitation on Saudi publics' ability to mobilize, develop intersubjective discursive positions and to actively demand reform. However, *Tash Ma Tash* and some of its successors on broadcasting on YouTube can be seen as platforms for satire and criticism militating against censorship by maintaining their liminal status as entertainment programmes that humorously and ironically addresses current affairs issues. It could be argued that such programmes present a critical perspective on Saudi social structure that subaltern Saudis are currently unable to express themselves for fear of government or religious reprisal. Of course there have been reformists in the Saudi exile or diasporic communities demanding the overthrow of the Saudi state and religious power structure. What is remarkable about *Tash Ma Tash* is that it is being broadcast with the consent of the government through the national media. Operating within the existing hegemonic system, the programme would seem to have a better chance of exacting "concessions" from the government (see Gramsci, 1971).

Peter Berger (1997) argues that laughter emerges from the incongruities and contradictions that permeate human existence. He goes on to contend that satire is the use of humour to develop a rhetorical attack. Indeed, *Tash Ma Tash* employs satire to undermine the status quo in Saudi society. Although the plotlines routinely center on the absurd, there may also be a profundity in the subtle cultural critiques they develop. Stated grandly, if as Albert Camus (1942/2005) once argued, meaning emerges through recognizing the absurdities of daily life, then *Tash Ma Tash* through satire, parody and even slapstick may be viewed as laying bare the essential character of everyday life within Saudi society. Yet it is important to remain circumspect in evaluating the role of humor in different cultures. As Voltaire (1733/1894) once observed, "the delicacy of the humour, the allusion, the *à propos*—all these are lost to a foreigner.... True comedy is the speaking picture of the follies and ridiculous foibles of a nation; so that he only is able to judge of the painting who is perfectly acquainted with the people it represents."

NOTES

1. The factual information in this essay regarding the television program *Tash Ma Tash* is drawn from English language news sources available online. As such the details of the case may not be fully reliable. However, this case can be considered as an ideal type which is indicative of the role hybrid media can play in authoritarian regimes.
2. Notably, the wide ranging critiques within this programme still avoid the topic of the Saudi royal family and their current decisions regarding foreign policy.

REFERENCES

Althusser, L. (1971). Ideology and ideological state apparatuses (B. Brewster, Trans.) *Lenin and philosophy and other essays*. London: New Left Books.

Berger, P. (1997). *Redeeming laughter: The comic dimension of human experience*. New York, NY: Walter de Gruyter.

Bhabha, H. K. (1996). Text and nation: Cross-disciplinary essays on cultural and national identities. In L. G. -M. A. P. C. Pfeiffer (Ed.), *Unsatisfied: Notes on vernacular cosmopolitanism* (pp. 191-207). Columbia, SC: Camden House.

Bhahba, H. K. (1994). *The location of culture*. London: Routledge.

Camus, A. (2005). *The myth of Sisyphus* (J. O'Brien, Trans.). London: Penguin. (Original work published 1942)

Freud, S. (1991). *Jokes and their relation to their unconscious* (Vol. 6). Harmondsworth: Penguin. (Original work published 1905)

Gay, P. (1969). *The enlightenment: The science of freedom*. New York, NY: W. W. Norton.

Gramsci, A. (1971). *Selections from prison notebooks*. London: Lawrence & Wishart.

Habermas, J. (1989). *The structural transformation of the public sphere* (T. Burger & F. Lawrence, Trans.). Cambridge, MA: MIT Press.

Hall, S. (1998). The rediscovery of "ideology." In J. Rivkin & M. Ryan (Eds.), *Literary theory: An anthology*. London: Blackwell.

Herman, E. S., & Chomsky, N. (1988). *Manufacturing consent: The political economy of the mass media*. London: Vintage.

Iyengar, S. (1994). *Is anyone responsible?: How television frames political issues*. Chicago, IL: University of Chicago.

Jensen, E., & Wagoner, B. (2009). A cyclical model of social change. *Culture & Psychology, 15*(2), 217-228.

MacFarquhar, N. (2011, June 12). In Saudi Arabia, comedy cautiously pushes limits. *New York Times*, p. A14.

Mill, J. (1992). *Political writings* (T. Ball, Trans.). Cambridge, England: Cambridge University Press. (Original work published 1858)

Milton, J. (1644). *Areopagitica: A speech for the liberty of unlicensed printing*. Retrieved from http://onlinebooks.library.upenn.edu/webbin/gutbook/lookup?num=608

Smith, A. D. (1986). *The ethnic origins of nations*. Oxford, England: Blackwell.

Voltaire. (1894). Letters on England. In D. Price (Eds.), *Letter XIX: On comedy.* (Original work published 1733). Retrieved from http://www.gutenberg.org/dirs/2/4/4/2445/2445-h/2445-h.htm

Young, I. M. (2000). *Inclusion and democracy.* Oxford, England: Oxford University Press.

CHAPTER 13

SUBVERSIVELY FUNNY

Critical Humor in Art

Lisa Taylor-Sayles

Laughter is the most beautiful form of boundary transgression.

—Curator Anna Tilroe

Eric Jensen (this volume, Chapter 13) argues that humor and irony can be a vehicle with which to address taboo political subjects in a way that avoids or mediates censorship, in both democratic and authoritarian societies. While Jensen looks primarily at the use of humor in media contexts, the principle may also be applicable to other contexts. In this chapter, I will argue that not only has humor played a central role in the social-political art of the last century, but also humor merits more serious consideration as a distinctive form of political discourse that is particularly well suited to the task of challenging accepted ideological structures and introducing alternative or dissident ideas, in both verbal and visual contexts.

From the time before Plato, to the Stalinist regime in the Soviet Union, to Senator Jesse Helms, efforts to shape public perception and behavior have often involved an attempt to control or influence both the content and style of art (Edelman, 1995). Fathali M. Moghaddam, Zach Warren, and Rhea Vance-Cheng (this volume, Chapter 5) argued, "Art is a cen-

Culture and Social Change: Transforming Society Through the Power of Ideas, pp. 223–239

trally important but neglected means through which collective identities are transformed" (p. 77). This occurs through multiple, distributed actions, as works of art in all genres, supply, according to political scientist Murray Edelman (1995), the "models, scenarios, narratives, and images" that embody and activate cultural ideologies (p. 1). Edelman likewise has contended that

> contrary to the usual assumption—which sees art as ancillary to the social scene, divorced from it, or, at best, reflective of it—art should be recognized as a major and integral part of the transaction that engenders political behavior. (p. 2)

The role that art plays in the formation of public opinion and behavior is yet to be fully determined; nevertheless, throughout history, leaders and regimes have recognized art as a potential threat to the social order. Even so, art, like humor, is employed in the service of both conservative and progressive politics. The art field emphasizes the progressive or the avant-garde potential of art, yet the subversive use of humor in art over the last century has received little consideration (Higgie, 2007).

WHAT HUMOR IS AND DOES

Humor comes in a variety of forms (e.g., irony, satire, parody, and ridicule) and usually involves an element of incongruity, surprise, or contradiction (Isaak, 1996; Roukes, 1997; Robinson & Sith-Lovin, 2001; Sorensen, 2008). Interestingly, while there may at times be a correlation between humor appreciation and the shared opinions of the humorist and the audience (Stillion & White, 1987), some humor theories and empirical evidence indicate that humor appreciation has more to do with message qualities like incongruity and surprise, than congruence of opinion (Nabi, Moyer-Guse, & Byrne, 2007). Sorensen (2008) stated, "Generally, what causes amusement is when things are turned upside down or when things are no longer as we usually perceive them" (p. 171). Consequently, rather than merely "preaching to the choir," humorists can potentially influence an audience that is either neutral or opposed to their opinions (Nabi et al., 2007; Sorensen, 2008).

Because humorous discourse is not regulated to the same degree as other forms of communication, humor can open up opportunities for individuals and groups to bypass social systems of control in order to redefine themselves and their social reality (Bing, 2004; Case & Lippard, 2009; Goffman, 1959; Higgie, 2007). Majken Jul Sorensen's (2008) theory of humor as a mode of nonviolent resistance evolved most notably from his case study of the Serbian Otpor movement in which humor was used to directly resist oppression. Sorensen's theory involves three major components that inform this discussion of the use of humor in the visual arts as a resistance strategy, primarily by minority groups in Western culture. These include (1) outreach to and mobilization of those outside the movement, (2) creating a "culture of resistance" and solidarity inside the movement, and (3) "turning the oppression upside down" or changing "the relationship between the oppressor and the oppressed" (p. 175). Consequently, humor can play a critical role in the success of subversive movements.

However, according to Michael Billig (2005) humor more often than not serves a conservative role in the social order. Billig argued that humor is both less important and more important than is currently thought. Less important because an emphasis has been misplaced on the secondary issues related to humor, for example the moral values of having a "good" sense of humor, or possible psychological or physiological benefits, rather than the more important or primary role that humor fulfills in maintaining social structures. Building on Irving Goffman's theory of embarrassment, which posits that social actors are motivated to conform to social rules and norms in order to avoid embarrassment or save face,[1] Billig argued that humor, specifically in the form of ridicule (both real and anticipated), is the mechanism that threatens embarrassment and therefore performs a disciplinary function in social life. Furthermore, Billig contended that rebellious humor, humor that violates social norms and seeks to undermine the social order, is often only superficially rebellious because it functions as a form of carnival,[2] a temporary release valve that in the end actually serves to maintain existing social structures. While it is likely that humor is playing a more central, conservative role in the maintenance of social structures than was previously understood, this chapter argues that a reversal of terms is possible, namely that humor can be and is being used to challenge social norms, opening up the possibility for progressive social change.

VISUAL HUMOR AND IRONIC ART

Since antiquity, humor has been employed as a critical form of political discourse. However, the last thirty years have seen a growing interest in humor's subversive potential amongst feminists and other underrepresented or oppressed groups, across a variety of contexts, and specifically in the arts[3] (Roukes, 1997). According to Case and Lippard (2009), "Humor can be a subversive and empowering tool for women and feminists in the ideological battle to symbolically redefine gender roles, attitudes, and stereotypes" (p 240). Martha Rosler's (1975) video short titled *Semiotics of the Kitchen*, commences with Rosler donning a kitchen apron and stating with an exaggerated yet deadpan expression "APRON." She then begins picking up kitchen tools, naming them and then demonstrating their use, albeit with overstated, sometimes angry gestures that belie both normative uses of kitchen tools and her calm exterior.

While humorous, the video calls attention to frustrations associated with the performance of rigid gender roles. May Stevens produced a series of paintings from 1967-1976 whose central figure is a character she called "Big Daddy." In the painting titled *Big Daddy Paper Doll* (1967) (Figure 13.1), which Stevens suggests is the key image in the series, sits a smug, middle-aged, unnaturally white, naked male paper doll. Sitting on Big Daddy's lap is an equally pompous and corpulent bulldog. The characters are flanked on either side by two sets of paper doll clothes; to the right a police uniform and butcher's attire, and to the left a military uniform and executioner's garments, each with matching outfits for the bull dog (Hills, 2005). Stevens' Big Daddy character personifies the patriarchal social and political structure of the United States and how that power structure plays out in multiple roles throughout social spheres, both within U.S. culture and abroad. This ironic visual depiction calls into question the legitimacy and reach of the dominant power structures. Indeed, Rosler and Stevens are among a number of artists and artist groups who in the 1960s and 70s began to use humor, irony, and satire to call into question structures of power and the social construction of gender roles (Higgie, 2007; Klein, 2007; Reckitt & Phelan, 2001).

The Guerilla Girls are a group of anonymous women artists who since the 1980s have used humor and irony to fulfill their self-appointed role as the "conscience of the art world." Their poster titled "*The Advantages of Being a Woman Artist*" sardonically lists items such as "Not having to be in shows with men, not being stuck in a tenured teaching position," and "not having to undergo the embarrassment of being called a genius" (Guerilla Girls, 1998, p. 9). In response to the conspicuously low number of women artists included in exhibitions at museums such as the Metropolitan Museum in New York, another poster asked, "Do Women have to be naked to get into the Met?" (Figure 13.2). Wearing guerilla masks in public, their version of the masked Lone Ranger, they stage protest events, produce humorous but sharply critical books, posters, and handouts filled with statistics and sometimes scathingly sarcastic wit in an effort to combat sexism and racism (Guerilla Girls, 1998; Guerilla Girls, 2010; Higgie, 2007). In 2003 the Guerilla Girls extended the scope of their work to the arts in other forms, such as the disparity between the number of women portrayed in Hollywood media in contrast to the number of women producers, writers, and directors (Hoban, 2004). The Dyke Action Machine

Figure 13.1 May Stevens. *Big Daddy Paper Doll,* 1970. Acrylic on canvas, 72 x 168 in. Brooklyn Museum. © artist or artist's estate. Courtesy of the artist and Mary Ryan Gallery, New York.

(DAM!) also uses humor and interventionist tactics; however DAM!, formed in 1991 by Carrie Moyer and Sue Schaffner, addresses contemporary issues specifically relevant to lesbians. DAM!s campaigns include bombarding New York City streets with images of lesbians in mock media-style advertisements and interactive websites in an effort to reveal "how lesbians are and are not depicted in American popular culture" (Atkins 2001; Dyke Action Machine!, 1994; Moyer & Schaffner, n.d., para. 2). Their movie poster *Straight to Hell* envisions an action movie about lesbians of color that seek revenge for being expelled out of the military as a result of Clinton's Don't Ask, Don't Tell policy. Art critic Donald Kuspit suggests

> [humorous] art today exists to preserve the possibility of "another" interpretation of life-the possibility of a continuing view from the margin, if not the correct one, then the correcting one, reminding us that the totality of the truth about life and art itself, is hardly in the possession of any supposed mainstream" (as cited in Roukes, 1997 p. 20)

Indeed, numerous artists employ humor or irony in their effort to communicate a "view from the margin."

In addition to satirizing sexism, artists have wielded ironic visual representations to challenge racial stereotypes, such as those of the "American Indian" or other native peoples. In this vein, Allan Ryan

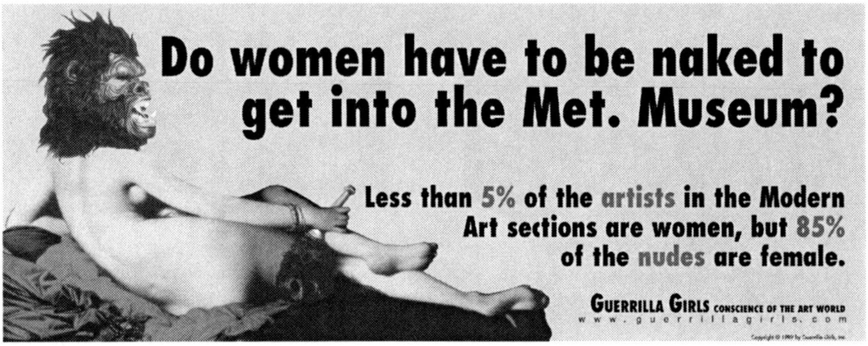

Figure 13.2. Guerilla Girls. *Do women have to be naked to get into the Met. Museum?* 1989. Poster. Copyright © by Guerrilla Girls, Inc., Courtesy www.guerrillagirls.com

Figure 13.3. Dyke Action Machine (DAM!), *Straight to Hell,* 1994. Poster.

describes an old Native paradigm he calls the Trickster Shift, which is influencing the work of contemporary native artists. Cree writer Tomson Highway suggests that the "Trickster" is just as central to the spiritual lives of native cultures as Jesus Christ is to Christianity. The contemporary "Trickster" uses humor and irony in combination with "subversive practice, aesthetic production, spiritual truth, and cultural wisdom" in order to address native stereotypes or issues (Ryan, 1999, p. 3). Jimmie Durham's 1986 installation *On Loan from the Museum of the American Indian* is a parody of the ethnographic spectacle surrounding "Indian" art and artifacts and a refusal to conform to the categorical boundaries of native art. Durham's found and partially constructed objects like, an Indian Leg Bone, and Pocahontas' red-feathered underwear, are displayed in an official, museum-like arrangement of historical Indian artifacts. Durham's playful mockery holds stereotypes of "Indians" up to ridicule while commenting on the colonizing practice of collecting and marketing Indian art (Durant, Snauwaert, Mulvey, & Durham, 1995; Fisher, 1992; Shiff, 1992). Jaune Quick-To-See Smith's collage painting titled *Trade (gifts for trading land with white people) 1992* consists of a collaged canoe painted on canvas with a rope strung across the top from which hang a number of items that stereotype Indians; Red Man chewing Tobacco, a plastic Indian doll, a Redskins baseball cap, and so on, ironically referencing both the unjust dealings of the past and the persistent stereotypes of Native Americans in the present (Juane Quick-to-See). For many native artists, humor and irony are part of a rich cultural tradition that is being envisioned anew in order to contest worn out and well rehearsed social constructions and myths of "Indians" (Ryan, 1999).

During the 1980s, the artist collective *Gran Fury*, which originated from ACT UP (AIDS Coalitions to Unleash Power), produced a wide range of advertising style media such as billboards, posters, subway, and bus signs, videos and staged projects, in order to confront problems related to the AIDS crisis and homophobia. Humor and playfulness were central characteristics of their work. A one day project involved a massive march organized in New York in which protesters confused the local law enforcement when, instead of picketing, yelling or lying down in the street, the participants all started kissing (Kalin, Nesline, & Lindell, 2010). More recently, Erwin Wurm's photograph *Looking for a Bomb 3* from the series *How to Be Politically Incorrect 2002-2003* (Figure 13.4) depicts a man on his knees sticking his arm through the fly of another man's trousers, all the way up to his elbow, presumably in an effort to find a bomb. With this ironic artistic representation, Wurm not only highlights issues related to security, fear and individual freedoms after 9-11, but also homophobia (Molon & Rooks, 2005). Bollards, rigid barriers made of concrete and steel, have been erected in increasing numbers since 911 in an effort to protect public buildings or spaces, specifically from terrorist attack. Conversely, Jesse Kahn's (2009) *24 Camouflage Bollards with Chains* (Figure 13.5) are constructed with soft ultra suede fabric. Some of Kahn's elongated, phallic-shaped bollards almost stand upright, and others droop, nearly touching the floor. In what seems to be an optimistic gesture, Kahn has refused to allow the bollards to fulfill their intended purpose. Bollards are a reoccurring motif in Kahn's art; they are metaphors for the boundaries between public and private space, control and accessibility. Kahn, whose craft-based practice addresses issues related to gay male sexuality, explains the intended message embedded in his ironic art:

> The images that are on display here expose our sexual lives, propose how we live and who we look to for inspiration, show how playful we can be and suggest how painfully aware we are of the tenuous nature of our civil rights and liberties. (Kahn 2009 p. 5)

As with the controversial political messages discussed in Jensen's (this volume) chapter, contentious art that does not contain overtones of irony and humor is at greater risk of censorship. A key example of this pattern is Robert Mapplethorpe's controversial homoerotic photographs that were a

Figure 13.4. Erwin Wurm, Instructions on how to be politically incorrect, *Looking for a bomb 3*, 2003, c-print, 126 x 184 cm; Photograph prepared by: Studio Wurm.

Figure 13.5. Jesse M. Kahn, *24 Camouflage Bollards With Chains,* 2007, ultra suede and sewing notions, 31" x 8" diameter (each), installed dimensions variable. Used by permission.

part of an exhibition entitled "The Perfect Moment" which ran from 1989-1991 in various cities in the United States (Kammen, 2006). Mapplethorpe employed art historical conventions of beauty in a direct portrayal of homosexuality and marginality, without the use of humor or irony. Three male nude torsos line up in profile across the page of Mapplethorpe's 1982 *Derrick Cross & Friends*. A light skinned male is sandwiched tightly between two dark skinned males in what appears to be a graceful, almost dancelike, albeit erotically charged pose. In an *ARTnews* interview in 1988 Mapplethorpe stated, "I don't like that particular word 'shocking.' I'm looking for the unexpected ... I was in a position to take those pictures. I felt an obligation to do them" (as cited in The Robert Mapplethorpe Foundation, n.d., para. 4). While many of Mapplethorpe's photographs are of flowers and innocuous figures, a number of the photographs contain explicit homosexual acts or references to the S&M underground, including photographs of Mapplethorpe himself in leather S&M style clothing. As a result, his work received harsh negative reactions (including legal action), with the controversy covered widely in the media (Hickey, 1998). The traveling exhibition was eventually shut down, an art director was put on trial for showing the work and members of the U.S. Congress threatened to shut down the entire

National Endowment for the Arts program. As a result of this and other controversies, the U.S. government no longer supports individual artists with grants or fellowships (Katz, 2009).

In explaining this fierce backlash to Mapplethorpe's work, art critic Dave Hickey (1998) argued "it was the *celebration* [of homosexuality] and not the marginality that made these images dangerous. So, it was not that men were making it, then, but that Mapplethorpe was 'making it beautiful' " (p. 23). Hickey stated, "all this litigation to establish Robert Mapplethorpe's 'corruption' would have been unnecessary had his images somehow *acknowledged* that corruption, and thus qualified him for our forgiveness. But they did not" (p. 24). Mapplethorpe's dramatic lighting is reminiscent of the Baroque period; his photographs are technically and esthetically exquisite. Evidently, beauty does not protect an artist from censorship. All of the media attention on the controversy increased the public's curiosity and boosted the artist's notoriety, but in the end the public's attitudes about nudity and homosexuality remained unchanged (Kammen, 2006). If, like the previous artists, Maplethorp had employed humor, might the outcome have been different?

DOES IRONIC HUMOR CREATE SOCIAL CHANGE?

One possible distinction between the use of humor in the context of art as discussed here and media context discussed by Jensen (this volume) is that social norms or conventions may cue the viewer to have different expectations about their engagement with each field. Calling something art sets up expectations related to an enlightened or educated state of being, or what Carol Duncan (1995) calls a *liminal* experience. Whereas the media, while valued ideologically in a participatory democracy, are often associated with less lofty activities like commercial advertising, the persuasive appeal of a corporation or political group, or escapism. Walter Benjamin (1935) argues that the reproducibility of mass media takes away the specialness or "Aura" of its creation, yet, the lines between art and other social spaces, like media, have become increasingly blurred as artists and groups like the Guerilla Girls, DAM! and Gran Fury, occupy multiple and overlapping spheres. Furthermore, there is a wide range of meanings and interpretive positions possible in all communicative contexts, to include both art and media. Stuart Hall (1991) maintains that viewers can accept the way a message is encoded (preferred), partially accept the message (negotiated), or reject a message completely (oppositional). However, when humor is used as a subversive strategy it may increase the likelihood that a message will be accepted rather than rejected regardless of the context.

Humor increases liking and credibility, strengthens arguments, increases the motivation to listen and attend to information and minimizes bias. This increase in attention and motivation to listen is thought, however, to be offset by the audience's tendency to discount the content of humorous messages. A joke is perceived as fictional, something not to be taken seriously, which therefore reduces its persuasive effect (Nabi et al., 2007). Indeed, according to measurements taken shortly after exposure to both serious and humorous messages, Nabi et al. noted that the humorous messages were no more persuasive than nonhumorous ones. However, when respondents were assessed just a week later, a difference between the two groups emerged; there was a significant gain in attitude change and persuasive effect over time from the humorous message. This is called a sleeper effect. Additional research is needed on both the sleeper effect and the specific conditions that limit or exploit the use of humor for serious messages (Nabi et al., 2007). Moreover, this social psychological research does not tend to take into account the more sociological observations made by Jensen (this volume), such as the fact that some ideas might never be uttered if not for the protective cloak of humor. Janet Bing (2004) states "If a joke allows a new message to be received rather than ignored or not perceived at all, that joke is indeed subversive" (p. 30). Furthermore, Sorensen's (2008) theory of humor as a form of nonviolent resistance suggests additional benefits that result when humor is used as a subversive strategy; outreach outside the movement, increased solidarity within the movement and a change in power dynamics.

Outreach Outside the Movement

Many artists direct their efforts to social hierarchies within the art field and only indirectly reach those outside this sphere. However, in an effort to reach a larger audience, directly reference or critique another field, or establish a new set of art values, a growing number of artists are working across social boundaries or forgoing art world venues entirely.[4] The Guerilla Girls note, "We started doing work about the art world because that's the world we knew best, but we quickly branched out to other social and political issues" (Raizada, 2007, p. 54). Interestingly, the Guerilla Girls (2010) did not start out using humor, however they "found out quickly that humor gets people involved" (para. 9). According to Phoebe Hoban (2004) of the *New York Times*, the Guerilla Girls have become "cultural icons" (p. 1). Paula Shutkever from *Everywoman Magazine* affirms "Making those in power accountable, raising public awareness and inspiring other groups to do the same, the Guerilla Girls are not only making waves in the art world, they're making the F-word[5] fashionable again" (as cited in Guerilla Girls, 2010, p. 1). Similarly Gran Fury's influence reached far beyond the art field and opened up a space within public discourse to address multidimensional problems related to AIDS. Gran Fury member Tom Kalin recalls, "We went from being wheat-pasting hooligans to suddenly having real resources and opportunities and a platform from which to speak" (Crimp, 2008, para. 30). In addition to the kissing protest event, one of Gran Fury's most well known public-art projects reached multiple audiences when they placed posters on buses and subway platforms in San Francisco, New York, Washington D.C., and Chicago which stated "Kissing doesn't kill; Greed and Indifference Do" with images of a diverse range of heterosexual and homosexual couples kissing under the text heading (Crimp, 2008; Kalin et al., 2010). Whether artists position their work within the art world or outside of it, humor can play a central role in a group's ability to connect with and mobilize people outside their respective groups or movements.

Creating a Culture of Resistance

Jo Anna Isaak (1996) suggests that collective positions or identities are never homogenous, nor is the "margin" a fixed place; rather they constitute "an agency of intervention" that destabilizes centered discourse (p. 4). By confirming shared values and experiences, humor can help establish in-groups and create group solidarity (Bing, 2004) and what Sorensen (2008) calls a "Culture of Resistance." In reference to DAM!'s movie poster *Straight to Hell* (1994), Becky Bivens (2009) confirms "getting the joke is great, because it leads to a certain amount of intellectual camaraderie, to an experience of shared pleasure. Humor can create community amongst people, between the us who get the joke (me, you, dykes)" (para. 6). Carrie Moyer of DAM! notes, "We get tons of fan mail from people saying how great it is to see themselves and their feelings represented in the world" (Atkins, 2001, para. 8). Correspondingly, Jimmie Durham's multilayered and humorous artwork is often literally inscribed with private jokes; puns written in Cherokee and therefore comprehensible only to a specific Native American community (Shiff, 1992). Furthermore, process-oriented artists may use humor to build a sense of community through their creative process in addition to or instead of an artistic product. Jesse Kahn's (2009) craft and sewing based artwork is created in part during a weekly stitching circle for queer men called *Nine Inch Needles* which Kahn explains "is loosely based in the tradition of sewing bees and lesbian feminist working groups and consciousness raising circles" (p. 3). The members of *Nine Inch Needles* generate a supportive community through artistic production that is embedded in discussions about the issues they face as queer men and fiber arts education. Such group solidarity generates a momentum that provides internal strength to an opposition movement as members begin to actively support one another and overcome both political and individual apathy (Sorensen, 2008).

Changing Power Dynamics

It has been well established that humor is often used to maintain and reinforce existing hierarchies (Billig, 2005; Bing, 2004; Case & Lippard, 2009; Robinson & Smith-Lovin, 2001). For example, in the feminist context Case and Lippard note that "historically, men and male-dominated institutions have controlled the dissemination of humor and determined what is and is not acceptable as humorous discourse" (p. 240). Early feminist artists like Martha Rosler and May Stevens renegotiate power dynamics by challenging patriarchal control of humorous discourse. Rosler's video (1975) *Semiotics of the Kitchen* is among a number of works produced by Rosler, which posits women's experiences and roles as sources of humorous content, and for rebellious purposes. Stevens' (1970) *Big Daddy Paper Doll* series inverts the status quo by making men's roles and male-dominated institutions the targets of visual humor. Indeed, the artists discussed in this chapter use humor to challenge, in various degrees, the social constructions of gender, ethnicity, or sexuality by expanding the range of issues and representations deemed acceptable for humorous discourse, including previously taboo subjects and imagery. In so doing, underrepresented groups often gain a stronger voice in public discourse, increased representation and visibility, and increased opportunities.

Moghaddam et al. (this volume) differentiates between *within-system change,* which takes place within an existing social system, and *transformational change*, which constitutes a change from one type of system to another system. Although a number of artists and art groups seek transformational system change by working outside art world venues, or producing primarily ephemeral works or projects that do not fit easily within the current art world economy, most artists work within the existing art field system (*within-system change*), rather than striving to transform or overturn the current system (*transformational change*). While there have been significant gains, for example, since the early 1970s the number of women artist's exhibitions has doubled; nevertheless, that still only brings women to the point where they have approximately one opportunity to every four that open up to men in the arts and these numbers have been declining since the 1990s (Davis, 2007; Heartney, Posner, & Princethal, 2007). It is not yet clear whether *within-system change* is enough to secure comprehensive or sustainable changes in power relations, within or outside of the art world.

It is important to acknowledge that humor can be a useful tool for both dominant and subordinate groups. Because humor is a complicated and context specific tool, it may only be effective under certain conditions, or what Hart and Bos (2008) called a "political opportunity structure" (p. 13). Specifically, Hart and Bos suggested that in order for humor to be effective as a tool for social protest movements there should be a clear division between hierarchical groups, other sympathetic groups, an independent "public sphere," and a degree of political instability. Additionally, rebellious humor can actually serve to maintain social hierarchies rather than subvert them. In this way humor acts as a form of carnival, making people feel like they are being rebellious, when there are no rebellious effects, so that a degree of subversion actually helps to maintain the status quo (Billig, 2005). Moreover, modes of humor are culturally specific and comic meaning changes over time (Reaves, 2001). Whereas this chapter looks at the use of humor in Western contexts, an exploration into the use of humor in non-Western contexts would greatly inform this area of inquiry, especially taking into consideration Michael Billig's (2005) argument that all social subjects that are language driven use humor and ridicule as a form of social control.

Finally, humor can serve as a real and powerful way to express opposition to dominant power structures and potentially change power dynamics across a variety of social contexts. In looking at a number of examples of social protest movements that involved the use of humor, Hart and Bos (2008) concluded, "Humour and laughter can serve as a powerful tool in social protest" (p. 1). Like Sorensen (2008), they suggest that humor can be an effective way for marginalized groups to gain attention to their cause, increase solidarity among protesters and undermine social hierarchies. Humor has played a central role in politically oriented art movements of the last century such as Dada, Surrealism, Fluxus, and Feminist Art and continues to constitute an important form of political discourse for contemporary artists determined to introduce a dissonant strain of thought into the body politic (Higgie, 2007; Klein, 2007). Dam! contends, "Humor has always been the best delivery method for aggression and transgression" (Raizada, 2007, p. 49).

NOTES

1. See Goffman, E. (1967). *Interaction Ritual.* New York. Pantheon Books.
2. Mikhail Bakhtin's study *Rabelais and His World* (1967) discusses the carnival or carnivalesque as a form of controlled social uprising during the Middle Ages.
3. The artists and art collectives discussed here do not constitute an exhaustive list of artists using humor as a subversive strategy, nor is the range of work representative or meant to suggest a cannon of ideal approaches or styles.
4. Recent trends in contemporary art include socially engaged art practices, also known by the terms new genre public art (Susan Lacy), connective aesthetics (Suzi Gablik), dialogic art (Grant Kesler), social acupuncture (Darren O'Donnell, and Relational Aesthetics (Nicholas Bourriaud). See Reyes, (2009).
5. F-word refers to feminism

REFERENCES

Atkins, R. (2001). Girls with wheatpaste and web space. *The Media Channel.* Retrieved from http://www.robertatkins.net/beta/witness/public/girls.html

Benjamin, W. (1935). *The work of art in the age of mechanical reproduction.* Retrieved from http://walterbenjamin.ominiverdi.org/wp-content/workart.pdf

Billig, M. (2005). *Laughter and ridicule: Towards a social critique of humour.* Thousand Oaks, CA: SAGE.

Bing, J. (2004). Is feminist humor an oxymoron? *Women and Language, 27*(1), 22-33.

Bivens, B. (2009). The F in FWART. *Gender across borders: A global feminist blog.* Retrieved from http://www.genderacrossborders.com/2009/12/18/the-f-in-fwart/

Case, C. E., & C. D. Lippard (2009). Humorous Assaults on Patriarchal Ideology. *Sociological Inquiry, 79*(2), 240-255.

Crimp, D. (2008). Gran fury talks to Douglas Crimp. *ArtForum.* Retrieved from http://howtowin.visitsteve.com/research/gran-fury-talks-to-douglas-crimp

Davis, B. (2007). White walls, glass ceiling. *Artnet.* Retrieved from http://www.artnet.com/magazineus/features/davis/davis3-12-07.asp

Duncan, C. (1995). The art museum as ritual. In D. Preziosi (Ed.), *The art of art history: A critical anthology* (pp. 473-485). Oxford, England: Oxford University Press.

Dyke Action Machine! (1994). *Straight to hell.* Retrieved from http://www.dykeactionmachine.com/index.html

Edelman, M. (1995). *From art to politics: How artistic creations shape political conceptions.* Chicago, IL: University of Chicago Press.

Fisher, J. (1992). "Inauthentic": Disturbing signs in contemporary Native American art. *Art Journal, 51*(3), 44-50.

Goffman, E. (1959). *The presentation of self in everday life*. New York, NY: Doubleday.
Guerilla Girls. (2010). *Guerrilla girls: Re-inventing the "f" words—feminism.* Retrieved from http://www.guerrillagirls.com/info/blurbs.shtml
Guerilla Girls. (1998). *The guerilla girls' bedside companion to the history of Western art.* New York, NY: Penguin Books.
Hall, S. (1991). Encoding\decoding*. In S. Hall, D. Hobson, A. Lowe, & P. Willis (Ed.), *Culture, media, language*. New York, NY: Routledge.
Hart, M. T., & Bos, D. (Eds.). (2008). *Humour and social protest. International Review of Social History Supplements.* New York, NY: University of Cambridge Press.
Heartney, E., H. Posner, & N. Princethal (2007). After the revolution: Women who transformed contemporary art. New York, NY: Prestel.
Hickey, D. (1998). Enter the dragon: On the vernacular of beauty. In B. Beckley & D. Shapiro (Ed.), *Uncontrollable beauty: Toward a new aesthetics* (pp. 15-24). New York, NY: Allworth Press.
Higgie, J. (Ed.). (2007). *The artist's joke. Documents of contemporary art.* London: Whitechapel.
Stevens, M. (1970). Big Daddy Paper Doll. In P. Hills., May Stevens.(2005). Petaluma, CA: Pomegranate Communications.
Hoban, P. (2004, January 4, 2004). Art, masks still in place, but firmly in the mainstream. *New York Times.* Retrieved from http://www.nytimes.com/2004/01/04/theater/art-masks-still-in-place-but-firmly-in-the-mainstream.html
Isaak, J. A. (1996). *Feminism and contemporary art: The revolutionary power of women's laughter.* New York, NY: Routledge.
Kahn, J. (2009). *Faggotstitch.* Los Angeles, CA: College Art Association.
Kalin, T., Nesline, M., & Liindell, J. (2010). A presentation: Gran Fury. In W. Gradley & C. Eshe (Ed.), *Art and social change: A critical reader.* London: Tate Publishing and Afterall.
Kammen, M. (2006). *Visual shock*. New York, NY: Vintage Books.
Katz, J. (2009). Imperfect moments: Mapplethorpe and censorship twenty years later. *Institute of Contemporary Art.* Retrieved from http://www.icaphila.org/news/pdf/mapplethorpe_pr.pdf
Klein, S. (2007). *Art & laughter.* New York, NY: I. B. Tauris.
Molon, D., & M. Rooks (2005). *Situation comedy: Humor in recent art.* New York, NY: Independent Curators International.
Moyer, C., & S. Schaffner. (2009). Dyke Action Machine. Retrieved from http://www.dykeactionmachine.com/index.html
Durant, M., Snauwaert, A. D., Mulvey, L., & Durham, J. (Eds.). (1995). *Jimmie Durham (Contemporary Artists).* New York, NY: Phaidon Press.
Nabi, R. L., Moyer-Guse, E., & Byrne, S. (2007). All joking aside: A serious investigation into the persuasive effect of funny social issue messages. *Communication Monographs, 74*(1), 29-54.
Quick-to-See Smith, J. (2010). *Trade (Gifts for Trading Land with White People).* Retrieved from http://www.brooklynmuseum.org/eascfa/feminist_art_base/gallery/Quick_to_See_Smith.php?i=1553
Raizada, K. (2007). An interview with the guerrilla girls, dyke action machine (DAM!) and the toxic titties. *Feminist Formations, 19*(1), 39-58.
Reaves, W. W. (2001). The art in humor, the humor in art. *American Art, 15*(2), 2-9.

Reckitt, H., & P. Phelan (Eds.). (2001). *Art & feminism.* New York, NY: Phaidon Press.

Reyes, J. D. (Ed.). (2009). *We need to know where we've been to know where we are going: A collaboratively written history of art and social practice.* Portland, OR: Portland State University.

Robinson, D., & Sith-Lovin, L. (2001). Getting a laugh: Gender, status, and humor in task discussions. *Social Forces, 80*(1), 123-158.

Robinson, D. T., & Smith-Lovin, L. (2001). Getting a laugh: Gender, status, and humor in task discussions. *Social Forces, 80*(1), 123-158.

Rosler, M. (1975). *Semiotics of the kitchen.* New York, NY: Electronic Arts Intermix.

Roukes, N. (1997). *Humor in Art: A celebration of Visual Wit.* Worcester, MA: Davis Publications.

Ryan, A. J. (1999). *The trickster shift: humour and irony in contemporary native art.* Seattle, WA: University of Washington Press.

Shiff, R. (1992). The necessity of Jimmie Durham's Jokes. *Art Journal, 51*(3), 74-80.

Sorensen, M. J. (2008). Humor as a serious strategy of nonviolent resistance to oppression. *Peace & Change, 33*(2), 167-190.

Stillion, J. M., & H. White (1987). Feminist humor: Who appreciates it and why. *Psychology of Women Quarterly, 11,* 219-232.

The Robert Mapplethorpe Foundation. (n.d.). *Biography.* Retrieved www.mapplethorpe.org/biography/

CHAPTER 14

ASSESSING SOCIAL CHANGE THROUGH SOCIAL CAPITAL

Local Leadership and Sociopolitical Change in Bolivia

Martín Mendoza-Botelho

A permanent challenge for scholars across the spectrum of the social sciences has been the measurement of abstract and complex processes of social change, however we define those. Moreover, social change happens in a myriad of ways and is not necessarily a gradual evolution of societies but instead a dynamic, sometimes radical, process of transformation. But what is behind these processes of "social change?" What different factors accelerate or hinder social transformation? One of these factors is leadership; this is the committed work of individuals that assume responsibilities on behalf of their communities towards the achievement of specific social and/or political goals. The dilemma, again, becomes in how to assess the role that this other abstract concept, leadership, plays in larger and much more complex processes of social transformation. A proposed way to address these issues is interpreting leadership as a particular manifestation of social capital, defined here as "stretching social capital" and building on the extensive work developed in this particular theoretical direction. Evidently, social capital—like any other theoretical concept—

Culture and Social Change: Transforming Society Through the Power of Ideas, pp. 241–262

has multiple strengths, potentials and limitations as well as many supporters and detractors. The aim of this chapter, therefore, is not to focus on the ongoing debate around this concept but instead focus on alternative and innovative ways to use this theoretical proposition to further our understanding of some of the many factors behind processes of social transformation. In the pursuance of this theoretical objective, I will use recent evidence from Bolivia's emblematic process of state decentralization, or *Popular Participation* as it is widely known, in order to link these seemingly abstract ideas with ongoing colorful and vibrant processes of social change in the Andes.

INTERPRETING SOCIAL CAPITAL

In order to link the notion of social capital to that of leadership, and subsequently to the overarching idea of social change, first it is important to layout some basic notions relevant relevant to this discussion, starting with social capital.

For many social and political scientists social capital (hereafter also SC) is just a new way to (re)interpret an old idea. According to several scholars,[1] while Loury (1977) introduced the term social capital into modern social science research, Coleman's (1988) study placed it at the forefront of research in sociology. Perhaps the most important contribution of the latter was the identification of SC's three main forms: (1) obligations and expectations (notion of trust); (2) information-flow in social structures (interaction among agents); and (3) norms accompanied by sanctions (social action). Coleman (1990) also differentiated the effects of SC at the individual and collective levels. In the former SC is mainly related to the network of "social relationships," the interaction with other individuals and the expected reciprocity. But this capital is also a collective good and as such it allows multiple interactions between "diverse individuals," which evidently affects its overall level in a given society. Its "public" use, through public mobilization and collective action (cf. Olson, 1965; and Ostrom, 1990), can also create public (intangible) goods that would not be achieved in its absence. In other words, what SC "is" (a set of relationships) and what it "produces" (e.g., collective action) (cf. Portes, 1998). Although Coleman's works provided some of the theoretical foundations for this concept, the subsequent works of Robert Putnam popularized its use in the political and social sciences.

Putnam expanded Coleman's definition by adding aspects such as social interaction and civic participation. Putnam's study on regional governments in Italy (Putnam, Leonardi, & Nanetti, 1993) suggested that the relative superior performance of institutions in the north was explained by apparent higher levels of civic involvement ("*civic-ness*") and SC in the form of "trust," enforceable (collective) norms and values, denser social networks and public participation. In a subsequent work Putnam (2000) explained further his reading of SC, stating that:

> Whereas physical capital refers to physical objects and human capital refers to the properties of individuals, social capital refers to connections among individuals—social networks and the norms of reciprocity and trustworthiness that arise from them. In that sense social capital is closely related to what some have called "civic virtue." The difference is that "social capital" calls attention to the fact that civic virtue is most powerful when embedded in a dense network of reciprocal social relations. A society of many virtuous but isolated individuals is not necessarily rich in social capital. (p. 19)

Of particular relevance, therefore, is his observance of "civic virtue" or the aggregate behavior of individuals following certain social norms of trust and reciprocity, which varies from informal attitudes (such as how people take care of each other and of public property) to formal forms of public behavior (such as the payment of taxes) and where the common element is that all these factors contribute to the overall well-being of society, and following preestablished norms and cultural patterns (what society envisions as "good" civic behavior). Another key element of Putnam's argument is the "level of association." A society with diverse organizations that fulfill many roles is one that has the capacity to act cooperatively, creating networks and spaces for dialogue and all sorts of internal synergies. This last idea suggests, therefore, that societies that foster gregarious cultural practices are in a more advantaged position to exploit firmly their embedded social capital.[2]

Interpersonal Trust and System Trust

Trust and reciprocity, as interpreted in SC theory, allow effective mobilization for collective action and the production of certain intangible public goods. Significant trust is needed to ensure cooperation and production of "public goods," particularly in large organizations where people do not face each other regularly. Without trust, and the expected reciprocity, people would not have enough confidence in each other to form coherent groups/organizations. Trust also facilitates the decision of people in engaging (or not) in collective actions, easing the resolution of conflicts among competing interests, enforcing collective norms and reducing fears of free-riding.

An important basic distinction, therefore, is the difference between "interpersonal trust" or trust among individuals which mostly denotes "behavior" and "system trust" or trust in strangers and complex forms of organization which are mainly "attitudes" (Luhmann, 1979). This distinction, however, can be subtle as sometimes people trust institutions not because of their validity but because they trust the people that represent them. On this issue, Giddens (1990, pp. 85-86) provides an alternative perspective with the concept of "*face-work*" or the trust expressed in individuals that represent interest groups. The correlation between trust in individuals and institutions, therefore, seems sound because although institutions may represent more abstract and complex forms of social organization, ultimately they are composed of individuals.[3] Moreover, according to Putnam et al. (1993) the levels of interpersonal trust and social participation are intrinsically related (their notion of "*civicness*"). Their evidence for Italy showed that individuals that show higher levels of inter-personal trust are more willing to create associations and collaborate with others (including public institutions), thus strengthening SC. At the same time, higher levels of social interaction and organization strengthen interpersonal trust, producing "a virtuous circle between civic participation and interpersonal trust" (Seligson et al., 2006, p. 63).

Social Norms

Norms and their **enforcement** are also important elements not only of SC but also of cultural patterns and relevant to the notion of social change.[5] In settings where agreements tend to be informal (due to lack of formal mechanisms such as a judiciary system) social norms become the only "tool" to make people comply with their side of a bargain. If a person does not fulfil an agreement, the social sanction can be loss of prestige, marginalization, isolation and/or other social punishments depending on the strength of the norm. Norms are also related to collective values and moral conceptions. For example, social punishments might be harsher against someone that defects from an agreement with the church than to someone that defects from a commercial transaction. According to Coleman (1988), norms are forms of SC and "when a norm exists and is effective, it constitutes a powerful, though sometimes fragile, form of social capital." In certain cases, however, norms can restrain or restrict innovation, something that is particularly valid in societies with polarized values. The arts provide a good example, where the creativity of some artists is constrained by social norms and values, or what society may consider appropriate or morally correct.

Negative Aspects

Most of the literature describes SC as something positive for society, perhaps due to the idea that socialization per se is a good thing and only good things can emerge out of it, however, there are many potential negative consequences associated with this concept and its role in any process of social change. Portes (1998) identifies four manifestations of negative SC. The first one is **restrictive or selective membership** (closed groups). A common example is ethnic groups that exploit their SC for the advancement of members, but at the expense of other groups. But ethnicity is only one of the many potential "common denominators" for people.[6] Another negative form is the **excess claims on group members,** in others words how successful/diligent persons might be approached by others interested in sharing their success with little or no effort (free-riding), something that could dissipate a community's SC. Other negative manifestation is the **restriction on individual freedoms.** Communities with values and norms strongly enforced might be less tolerant with members that disagree with them. These "independent-minded" members might decide to leave the community rather than staying in the hopes of changing some of the norms, something that weakens social structures and hinders larger processes of social change. **Downward leveling norms**, or the forcing of members to adapt to a groups' values (even if those are damaging), is another negative form of SC and in many cases might worsen social conditions for the rest of society.

Social capital can also be exploited for **nefarious purposes**, affecting negatively a community/society's overall well-being.[7] Gambetta (1993) provides an excellent example in his insightful study of the Sicilian Mafia. According to him, the sort of "private protection" provided by the Mafia is the logical consequence of a social necessity in a setting with scarce trust and ineffective enforcement of formal laws. As a result, the Mafia becomes the institution that provides that kind of protection needed for the informal enforcement of social contracts. To achieve this purpose the Mafia relies heavily on the SC of its members, which is built on their trust in each other and a very selective membership; but whose purposes are dishonest, such as providing protection (often forced) to those seen in need of this service. Gambetta concludes that although the Mafia's arrangements were not a fair solution to a social need—because protection is not egalitarian (nor universal) and often leads to abuses of power, violence and other vices—this social model worked efficiently for centuries due to its cohesiveness and is a good example of the resistance to social change by certain social forces.

STRETCHING SOCIAL CAPITAL

The concepts discussed above provide some of social capital's fundamental ideas; however, in order to link them to the overarching theme of social change, and more precisely the role of leadership behind this processes, it is necessary to introduce a theoretical proposition: the notion of "stretching social capital."

Social capital is applicable to different contexts, differentiating individual notions (networks) with those at the community and other aggregated levels (cf. Portes, 2000). Evidently, collective SC is not necessarily the aggregation of individual capitals but instead the manifestation of communal behavior. In certain circumstances, however, individual(s) social capital(s) can undermine the collective one. A classic example is the use of personal contacts (i.e., closed networks) for individual advantages in detriment of the overall benefit to society. For students of this form of capital there are important distinctions between the way people interact with family and friends, people with dissimilar characteristics (social, economic, ethnic, etc.) and in formal settings (such as those with people representing institutions/groups and in positions of power).[8] A common characterisation defines three main forms of SC:[9]

- **Bonding** refers to "strong" ties (exclusive) among people with common social features or similar characteristics (such as kinship, friendships, community/neighborhood relations, people with the same ethnicity, etc).
- **Bridging** refers to "weak" ties (inclusive) established by people who do not share many characteristics but have a common social objective (e.g., professional associations, clubs, etc.).
- **Linking** refers to the kind of relationships with people in positions of power or representing some form of authority, something more common in formal settings, such as the interaction of citizens with their public officers (bureaucrats, police, authorities, political parties, etc.) or with those of the private sector.

According to Woolcock (1999), the optimal combination of these three elements is dynamic and changes as society evolves and develops. Also, the scale of the relationships also matters. For Putnam (2000, pp. 23-24), while bonding SC "constitutes a kind of sociological superglue" bridging "provides a sociological WD-40" or the capacity to facilitate group interaction, recognizing that these "are not interchangeable." Noteboom (2007) adds that while in small and tight communities most trust relationships can be highly personalized, the complex interactions between large and varied groups tend to be more abstract and depersonalized. This differentiation locates "bonding" in one extreme (small groups with close and personalized ties); "bridging" in the middle (group interaction); and "linking" in the other (complex, more distant and impersonal interaction). Woolcock adds that while "bridging" reflects a horizontal type of relationship (interaction between peers), "linking" denotes a vertical one (asymmetry of powers or different scales).

Although bonding, bridging and linking provide a solid foundation for the understanding of SC in different contexts, these interpretations and their proponents have not yet explored extensively its aggregate manifestations. Perhaps a missing element not captured by these dimensions, therefore, is how SC aggregates in formal scenarios and is "*stretched*" to represent individuals' and communities' collective actions and desires for social change, particularly by local formal and informal forms of leadership. This is particularly relevant when relationships are carried out in semi-formal and formal scenarios, and in situations where collective actions - and the aggregate SC, norms and values that these embody—are negotiated by specific individuals "on behalf" of a larger group (e.g., by local leaders), thus "stretching" local SC to reach other instances.

Stretching social capital, therefore, can be understood as the ties that certain individuals (particularly local leaders) establish on behalf of the communities/groups that these represent with other groups and institutions. Like any other types of SC, this concept is bounded by essential elements such as trust and reciprocity, norms, and so on. The difference lies in the use of "represented" forms of SC by certain individuals, rather than their own (such as the delegated "trust"), and with the purpose of pursuing collective action goals, thus "stretching" the community's outreach in search for social change. Evidently, stretching cannot go beyond specifically assigned roles as this form of SC will break easily if leaders do not embody the overall level of trust expressed by their communities, their norms and values or if they fracture this trust.

Figure 14.1 helps to visualize the interpretation of the different forms of SC. The small circles represent individuals (I) and their interactions, while solid lines represent "thick" trust and dotted lines "thinner" trust. Within each group (G) there are all sorts of interactions but these groups interact also with other groups. Institutions and formal forms of organizations are represented by the square (Inst), but are also composed by individuals. Finally, local leaders (L) represent group interests in specific formal scenarios. As seen in the graph, the differences between bonding, bridging, linking and stretching will vary according to the type and purpose of particular relationships and interactions.

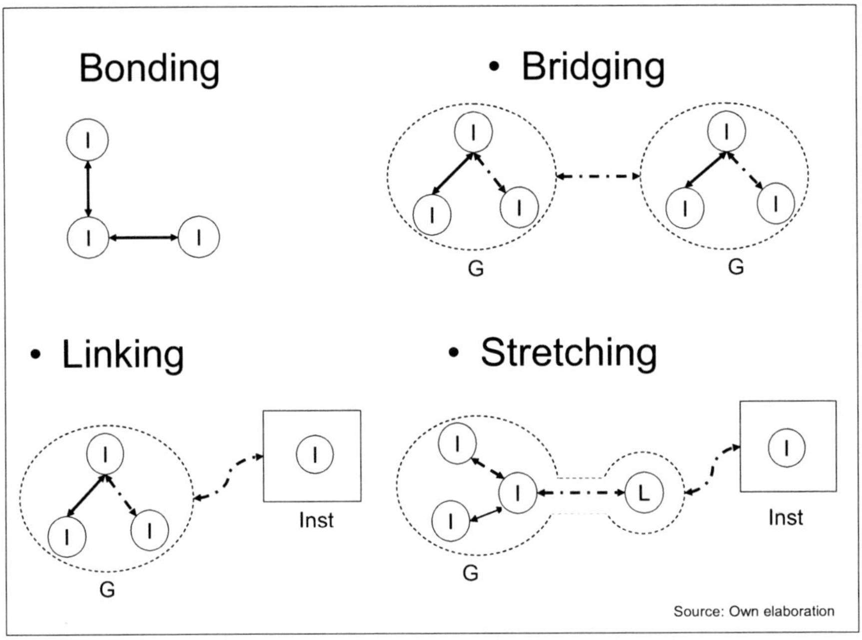

Figure 14.1. Different forms of social capital

Social Change, Leadership, and Social Capital

Leadership is more than an interpersonal human capital skill and another important element embedded in the notion of SC. However, the interaction of people or the mere exchange of information does not constitute SC; to become such it needs a higher purpose of mutual benefit. Leaders play a key role making explicit the benefit of such exchange for a group, facilitating in the process social change, therefore, in this context leadership can be interpreted as a some sort of functional, and perhaps the most representative, form of "stretching social capital."

Leadership can also partly be understood as a concept that helps to explain "power relationships" (Australian Bureau of Statistics, 2004). A leader might convince other people to contribute to the common good or to join a particular cause, thus mobilizing existing SC in a community/society and helping to raise the overall level of trust. The successful mobilisation of SC, therefore, will depend, to a certain degree, on good leadership "conferred on individuals or groups on the basis of personal characteristics and experience, or through tradition and/or position occupied" (p. 82). Religious organizations are good examples, where people gather for the production (and consumption) of an intangible public good that is not provided by the state. The success of these movements lies mainly in trust and effective leadership, but as Lehmann (2007, p. 6) points out, with a careful interpretation of the kind of "trust" expressed by followers "in individuals, not guaranteed or protected by an institutional apparatus governing the exercise of their authority as leaders." Evidently, the larger the religious group the more complex the networks of trust and religious hierarchy required to attain certain goals.[10] This same logic can also be applied to other groups, such as political parties (cf. Uslaner, 2004) and even nongovernmental organizations (NGOs). As Durlauf and Fafchamps (2004) comment

> good leaders may also improve efficiency ... by fostering altruistic behavior and concern for the common good; favoring group identification; preaching good behavior and making free-riders feel guilty; encouraging mimicry of good behavior through role models and the manipulation of group symbols and representations (e.g., religion, ideology).

In another study on Andean communities in South America, Bebbington (1997) describes how certain individuals (community outsiders) played a critical role in the development of communities, bringing not only ideas "but more importantly ... networks of contacts that helped bridge the gaps between the locality and non-local institutions and resources," thus demonstrating how leadership facilitates group interaction. In a study of 69 Indian villages, Krishna (2002) argues that "social capital matters significantly for political participation, and the capacity of new leaders adds to (and also multiplies) the effects of social capital" (p. 453).

The kind of effective leadership that emerges from networks with relatively "abundant" SC, therefore, is one that not only knows how to "read" people's aggregate preferences and behaviors/attitudes but also one that knows how to "represent" them. In other words, local leaders are not only good examples of the kind of social networks (and the embodied SC) that they represent, but also some sort of "valve" that regulates the flow of "social energy" (cf. Hirschman, 1984) and the one that facilitates processes of social change.

FROM COMMUNITY ACTIVISM TO POLITICAL INTERVENTION: LOCAL LEADERS AND SOCIAL CHANGE IN BOLIVIA

In 1994, Bolivian President Gonzalo Sánchez de Lozada's introduced Law No. 1551 of Popular Participation (PP) to the parliament as "the most important redistribution of political and economic power since the revolution of 1952" (Grindle, 2000, p. 120). This reform was one of the most comprehensive and innovative state-led initiatives in Latin America in recent times and one that foster a large process of social and political transformation.[11] Perhaps PP's first article describes best the spirit of this reform:

> The present Law acknowledges, promotes, and consolidates the process of Popular Participation, incorporating the indigenous communities, indigenous peoples, rural communities and urban neighbourhoods in the juridical, political and economic life of the country. It is aimed at improving the quality of life of Bolivian women and men, through a fairer distribution and better administration of public resources. It strengthens the political and economic means and institutions necessary for perfecting representative democracy, incorporating citizens' participation in a process of participative democracy and guaranteeing equality of representation at all levels between women and men. (Gobierno de Bolivia, 1994. Translation by Altman & Lalander, 2003)

The implementation of PP brought immediate social, political and economic transformations. While some readjustments were merely cosmetic, some other changes had a deep impact in society. Although it would be difficult to summarize all the changes brought by this process, some of the most important changes were:

- ***Municipalization of the entire country.*** Extension and creation of the municipal jurisdiction, allowing the incorporation of previously unrepresented rural areas and social groups. Creation, practically overnight, of 250 new municipalities to increase the number of municipalities to 309 (currently 327). In addition, "districts" were introduced as sub-administrative units in order to allow indigenous and other groups to gain limited control over the administration of their territories and communal lands.
- ***Consolidation of representative democracy at the local level.*** In 1995, mayors and municipal councilors were elected throughout the country for the first time. This was an enormous political step in this traditionally centralist country and a clear sign that a new institutional order was in place. Interestingly, in this election 27% of all councilors elected claimed to be of indigenous origin (437 out of 1,625); marking a new trend in the participation of indigenous peoples in formal Bolivian politics.
- ***Creation of participatory democratic structures.*** Institutionalization of social participation mechanisms in public affairs (watchdog organizations). As Booth (1997) argues, the creation of a new layer of elected local government and representative social groups allowed

PP to blend Western representative democracy with Andean participatory ancestral practices.

- ***Transfer of public responsibilities and resources.*** Increase in municipal and departmental public responsibilities and resources for health, education, infrastructure and productive activities.
- ***Opening up of a space for new forms of leadership.*** PP opened an institutional window that allowed existing and emerging leadership to enter formal politics. Groups that had little (or no) representation and participation in the past became active players in the process.
- ***Reemergence of ethno-political groups.*** Decentralization allowed certain ethnic and social groups to gain local spaces of 'formal' representation, particularly in municipalities where these were in the majority (cf. Van Cott, 2005). This situation also favoured the creation of social and political movements with national aspirations, such as Bolivia's current president Evo Morales' party Movement Toward Socialism (*Movimiento al Socialismo*, MAS).

Social Change in Bolivia: The Role of the Emerging Local Leadership

One of the important contributions of PP, and one that certainly has accelerated the process of social change, has been the promotion of new forms of local leadership, this is the stretching of SC embedded in Bolivian society to reach higher instances of power. Prior to PP, most local leaders emerged during their mandatory community service but with limited possibilities to project themselves beyond the local sphere. Decentralization, via the election of thousands of local authorities, changed local leadership practically overnight. Leaders were not only given specific functions as part of PP's institutional design but most importantly they received formal recognition by the state as mayors, community representatives, indigenous-authorities, and so on. It was not a coincidence, therefore, that since the beginning of this process most elected local and national authorities had a long experience serving as community leaders.

This emerging local leadership, however, had to compete fiercely with local political elites and their "clienteles," most of them resistant, or at least reluctant, to change and with all the negative manifestations of SC. As the process consolidated, political leadership mixed with the abundant social leadership. In some cases, however, local elites were successful at "capturing" powers, something that is partly explained by the novelty of the process, their interest in controlling resources for their own benefit and the relative attractiveness of municipal posts and their associated benefits (i.e., salary, prestige, political visibility, and advancement, etc.). As some scholars argue, these elites were represented at the local level in the form of male, semieducated *mestizos*, something that Ayo (1997) describes as the "masculinization and de-indigenization" of municipal governments. Although the participation of women was restricted to the minimum established by law at the initial stages, partly explained by the "*machista*" character of Bolivian society that relegates women to minor roles, eventually women gained higher political participation. The seemingly "revolutionary" ideas brought by PP reforms, therefore, fostered a large process of social change altering deeply embedded cultural patters that relegated indigenous citizens and women to subordinate positions in society, thus questioning a whole system of norms and values that was practically unaltered for centuries.

This sort of "silent revolution" promoted by PP reforms triggered a large process of social change and made manifest many forms of emerging leadership. As a result, Bolivian society was finally able to unleash part of its repressed social capital into the political arena thanks to the efforts of an army of local leaders that effectively *stretched* this type of capital to reach previously inaccessible circles of power. For instance, the large number of available elective positions (i.e., councilors and mayors) attracted a large number of people with little or no previous political experience. Furthermore, political parties recognized the importance of local leadership as a means to keep a local presence and incorporated community leaders into their ranks. Promptly, local leaders adjusted to this new scenario, realizing that they were in a more powerful position than political parties in terms of popularity and electoral attractiveness. If political parties did not agree with their conditions they could either switch parties or leverage local resources to build local support. As a result, parties saw their capacity to co-opt local leaders diminished. Traditional forms of power and organization were also suddenly transformed into formal structures recognized by the state (e.g., the election of indigenous leaders as municipal authorities).

Some Theoretical Considerations on Bolivia's Local Leadership

The arrival of new forms of leadership promoted by PP represented a new event in Bolivian politics and clearly the beginning of a large process of social change. In rural areas, local leadership originates at the very base of political structures, in the communities, and responds to two main sources. The first one can be seen as **"circumstantial leadership,"** resulting from the expected community service assignments (i.e., *cargo* system), for a fixed period of normally one year, and delegated to most young male members—although in recent times there is an increasing participation of women. This type of leadership provides the human resources necessary to fulfil the multiple positions demanded by PP. Grootaert and Narayan (2000, p. 23) found that unlike other countries, people of low socioeconomic status in Bolivia managed to take up leadership positions, empirically confirming the strength of the rotation of leadership positions and the contribution of PP in reducing economic barriers for political participation. Circumstantial leadership, however, lacks the strength and legitimacy of traditional leadership, which is normally exercised by people with higher authority (and normally older), such as indigenous authorities.

A second stream of leadership, therefore, is **"charismatic and evolutionary,"** where local leaders are elected by communities following democratic and ancestral practices, which grants them certain legitimacy. Because this type of leaders do not necessarily represent a specific political discourse or ideology, it is easy for people to "empathize" with them, thus strengthening "trust" bonds between them and their communities. This kind of leadership is present in formal political scenarios, through the election of mayors and councilors, and in informal ones, through traditional forms of community and indigenous leadership.

Clearly, the differences between these two types of leadership are sublte, as each one can lead to another and it is also possible to exercise both at the same time. For instance, circumstantial leadership becomes legitimized when communities manifest their support through voting. In any event, what is important is that both kinds of leadership regulate the interaction between social groups as some sort of social valve. According to the national expert Oscar Montes, local leaders are essential to "promote solidarity inside and outside the community, something that varies in each locality." Local leaders also represent that "collective voice" that not only transmit local demands but also allow the flow of information and ideas back to the communities. This same concern is expressed by Honorata Flores, an indigenous female councilor of the rural/indigenous municipality of Ravelo (pop. 20,000). As she argues "we elect leaders so they can work for the benefit of the community, so they can bring back something concrete, a specific project. That is why we elect them." Community leaders, therefore, can mobilize social resources for collective actions and collaboration between groups, drawing from available SC resources. And indeed they do, as the empirical evidence of more than 15 years of the implementation of PP seems to confirm in many ways, from thousands of elected local authorities, including indigenous and women leaders, to the permanent work at the grassroots of individuals committed to their communities.

The emerging leadership can be seen, therefore, as the engine that has been driving the process of social change in Bolivia resulting from the institutional re-engineering of PP, and more importantly as a clear manifestation of an effective (and positive) form of stretching social capital. In this regard, local leaders have the responsibilities of harmonizing diverse and competing interests, minimizing the lack of trust between groups ("bridging"), bringing social objectives and social demands to the attention of local governments ("linking") and representing the aggregated behavior/values of their communities ("stretching").

The main characteristics of this emerging leadership (Figure 14.2) are: (1) **Circumstantial active** as most leaders assume temporary positions based on community obligations, (2) **Legitimized** by communities' delegated trust, (3) **Counter-hegemonic** as it creates a counterbalance to local dominant elites, (4) **Progressive** as it builds on previous experiences, (5) **Recurrent** as many leaders return to their communities of origin to serve them, and (6) **Ascending** as it progressively gains higher instances of power at the regional and national level.

Local leaders, however, can also exacerbate differences, particularly in groups with high social and ethnic entry barriers (the negative aspects of SC). Also, they can use the embodied trust for personal gains, thus ignoring their role stretching their communities' social capital. The legitimacy of local leaders, therefore, relies heavily on contextual elements that define collective goals. For example, it is likely that communities will

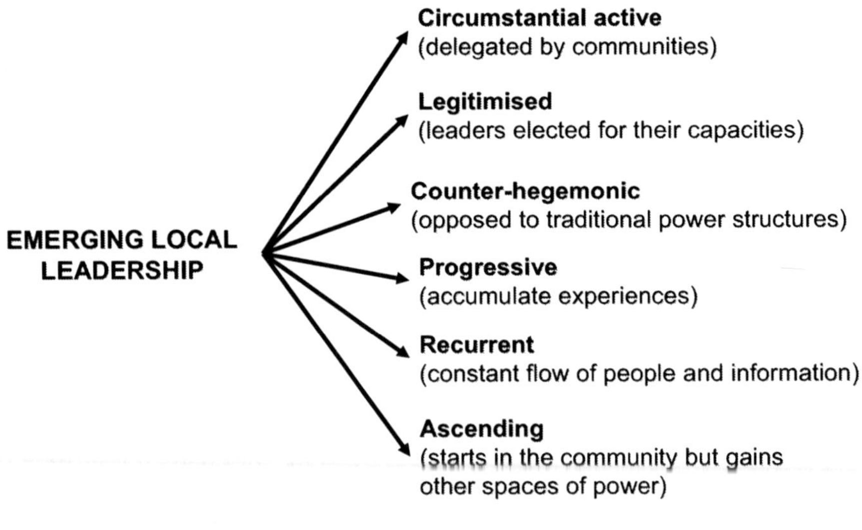

Source: Own elaboration.

Figure 14.2. Emerging local leadership in Bolivia.

mobilise and follow the directives of local leaders if there are pressing needs, such as ousting a corrupt mayor. However, when prospective rewards of embarking on collective actions are lower than participation costs, it is unlikely that people will follow their leaders with the same devotion. For instance, in issues where there is no consensus. But local leadership also has other limitations. According to the local expert Oscar Montes "in many areas local leaders are 'passive' and the efforts of mobilizing communities are left to external actors such as NGOs." As Durlauf and Fafchamps (2004) argue, although

> community leaders often play a crucial role in fostering the creation of social capital—e.g., membership drive—that they can harness for a particular goal ... in many small localities good leadership could be scarce and leadership is much harder to replicate than groups. (p. 44)

The proposed notion of "stretching social capital" provides some theoretical explanations. PP forced the creation of hundreds of bureaucratic/administrative municipal units and their respective political forms of democratic representation; however, it also incorporated civil society to this process through many formal and informal roles. People could actively participate in this process by expressing their political preferences through voting, attending local meetings, or transmitting their demands to local leaders so they could act on their behalf. The substantial difference lies in the fact that while voting tends to be an individual exercise (or at least that is what is normally expected); the representation by local leaders entails processes of confrontation, negotiation, and agreement, where SC places a fundamental role. This is precisely the kind of social change fostered by PP ideas within the cultural constrains of Bolivian society. The support that leaders might harness from the community is based not only on how good (or bad) their ideas might be but also on their reputation, their suspected intentions/motivations; and how much they are believed to represent the community's norms and values. The mandate that local leaders receive and bring with them to municipal instances of negotiation, therefore, is not entirely "their own" but a reflection of a complex process of social negotiation and to a great extent a value system in which SC plays a fundamental role. In other words, in order to be successful, leaders need to find a way to effectively "stretch" the SC of their communities to those instances of power where decisions are made. As this process evolves, those leaders believed to embody community ideals are empowered and supported to reach higher instances of power, fostering ultimately a process of social change.

Ascending Leadership

The previous observations suggest that PP created adequate conditions for social change at the grassroots level; but perhaps the big question is if PP succeeded in terms of fostering a large/national process of transformation beyond the local sphere. In this sense, the swift and expedite way in which local leaders built their political careers (from the bottom-up) is a good example of the extent (and projection) of this process of social change. The municipal arena became the training ground for future regional and national leaders. As the decentralization expert Miguel Urioste observes (in Ayo, 2004, pp. 345-346):

> None of the indigenous people in the parliament today [in 2002] would have achieved that level if it would not have been through the PP process ... furthermore, I am certain that most of them were *union* leaders, leaders of social movements; then they became municipal councillors, mayors or members of CVs and later they became congressmen.

Urioste's initial hypothesis was tested observing the composition of the Bolivian parliament elected in 2005 and his early observations were partly validated (Figure 14.3). While only a small fraction of congressmen had some sort of formal municipal experience serving either as mayors or councilors, most of them had previous experience as community leaders (84%), peasant/worker unions (*sindicato*) representatives (44%) and/or coordinating social movements (18%). As Edgar Peñarrieta, the mayor of the municipality of Ravelo (pop. 10,000), explains "if you are a good community leader, people at the top [i.e., national level] look at you and you can climb in your career, but only if you are a good local leader."

Other interesting cases of "ascending leadership" can be found in Bolivia's highest levels of the executive and in the Constituent Assembly, the legislative body that was responsible for rewriting Bolivia's constitution. The former is exemplified by the President himself. Evo Morales began his political career as a sports delegate under the *cargo* system in the Chapare region and later became a community leader for *cocalero* farmers.[12] Eventually Morales gained national visibility and higher instances of power when he became a national congressman in 1997 but he had always received strong support not only from grassroots *cocalero* organizations but also from some of the municipalities that this movement controls in this region. Part of the stand and appeal of Morales is that he embodies many of the norms and values of grassroots and indigenous organizations in a country that ignored those for centuries. The dynamic character of his presidency (currently serving a second term) has transformed him into an international and emblematic symbol of social change. Morales has not only managed to *stretch*

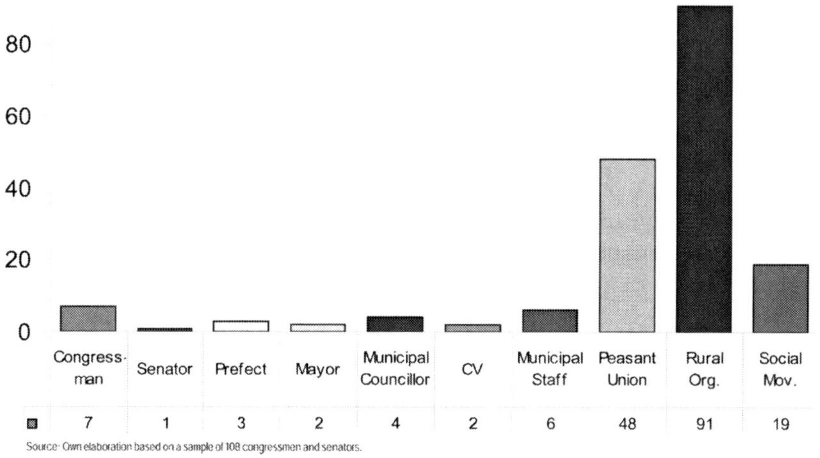

Figure 14.3. Previous experience of Bolivian congressmen/senators, 2006 (author's own data).

the social capital of the thousands of communities and minority groups that he represents to reach the highest levels of power in this society; but he has also been relatively successful at promoting a larger process of social change through a pseudo-socialist model of governance (with the complicity of social movements) that is finally transforming and challenging a previously static society.

Another representative example is that of the former President of Bolivia's Constituent Assembly (2006-2008) and close ally of Morales, Mrs. Silvia Lazarte. Lazarte is an indigenous *Quechua* woman who was forced to quit school at the age of 12 as her family could not afford her education. She surmounted gender prejudice and discrimination and at the age of 18 she became a community representative to a women's organization in her locality in the Chapare. Following a long trajectory as social leader, which included the position of Executive Secretary of the National Federation of Peasant Women of Bolivia "Bartolina Sisa" (1999-2001) (the largest women peasant organisation in the country) Lazarte was elected councilor for the municipality of Chimoré (2001-2003). In 2006, she was elected as a representative to the Constituent Assembly and soon after became its President and a symbol of the arrival of minority groups into power and of a long waited and urgent process of social change. Bolivia's new constitution (ratified by the population in 2009), that praises the multiethnic and pluri-cultural character of this society, is perhaps one of the most clear examples of the social change that has took roots in this highly complex and diverse country, something that would not have been possible without the permanent and committed work of local leaders such as Lazarte.

CONCLUSIONS

Despite its recent popularity social capital remains a concept under construction. A common element in the many definitions, however, is that SC facilitates the pursuance by society of common objectives, through interpersonal networks and/or associations and involving essential values such as trust and reciprocity. The common classification of "bonding," "bridging" and "linking" are also useful at the time of differentiating the sociological, political, institutional, and cultural elements of this concept. However, there is a distinctive element of this form of capital that has not been explored yet which is the ties that certain individuals (such as local leaders) establish on behalf of the communities/groups that they "represent" with other groups and institutions, embodying aggregated forms of this type of capital, norms and values that are not entirely their own. Because social change happens at the grassroots it is of enormous importance to understand what kind of factors foster or hinders this process. For this reason, this chapter introduced the concept of "stretching social capital" or how aggregated forms of social capital are "stretched" to reach multiple spaces of social and political power.

So, how does leadership affect social change? If we understand social change as a readjustment of collective norms and behavior, then leadership, again interpreted as "stretching social capital," is the crucial element that allows the transformation of aggregate manifestations of social norms/values and collective trust into powerful social forces that nourish the change itself. Without the constant activism of local leaders, and in many cases with the involvement of governments through their institutions, any process of social change would be restricted to individual and perhaps weak and lengthy processes of change. Committed leadership, therefore, not only accelerates social change through dissemination of ideas but also facilitates the "formalization" of this process. Both ad-hoc leaders (that emerge in response to particular social needs) as well as those leaders formally recognized by society (such as elected public officers) play a pivotal role in transmitting, contesting and negotiating informal social norms; and ultimately helping to transform these into formal mechanisms of social control through laws and legislation. Good leadership therefore does not act entirely alone or by instinct, but instead it operates "on behalf" of the communities, people and aggregated social capital, norms and values that it represents, where trust, reciprocity and accountability must be present.

Bolivia's process of state decentralization, or Popular Participation as it is widely known, was used to illustrate the role of local leadership in a large process of social transformation. The constant activism of local/ indigenous and women leaders at the grassroots, was the main mechanism in which political participation finally reached historically marginalized social groups. Popular Participation, therefore, was more than just the reshuffling of public institutions and it became a process of social change that contested a longstanding and rigid system of norms and values. This is precisely the contribution of PP to this society as political ideas moved from design into action, altering in the process seemingly static cultural and institutional norms.[13] Although this process is still far from reaching large goals and democratic ideals of full and equal social and political participation, at least is evident a process of social change has begun. Only time will tell if this emerging leadership in Bolivia is capable of altering some deeply embodied cultural patterns that have dominated this society for centuries, but in the meantime these leaders are working toward that goal.

NOTES

1. Cf. Woolcock (1998), Putnam (2000), Durlauf and Fafchamps (2004) and Edwards et al (2006). Also many mention the pioneer work of Pierre Bourdieu (1985).
2. Related relevant discussions can be found in Fukuyama (1997 and 1999), Portes (1998), Uphoff (2000), Woolcock (2000), Lin (2001), OECD (2001), Durlauf and Fafchamps (2004) and Lewandowski (2006).
3. See also Granovetter's (1985) concept of "'*mbeddedness.*"
4. Cf. Narayan and Pritchett (1997), Krishna (2002), Halpern (2005), Edwards et al. (2006), Lewandowski (2006), Arneil (2006, pp. 134-139) and Conrad (2007).
5. Cf. Narayan and Pritchett (1997), Krishna (2002), Halpern (2005), Edwards, Franklin, & Holland (2006), Lewandowski (2006), Arneil (2006, pp. 134-139) and Conrad (2007).
6. For other examples see Sen's (2006) work on identity, Putnam (2000 and 2007) and Field (2003).
7. Streeten (2002) labels this distortion as 'unsocial capital'.
8. Cf. Portes (1998), Woolcock (1999), Lin (2001), Szreter (2002) and Ramos-Pinto (2006).
9. To my knowledge, the initial definitions of "bonding" and "bridging" can be attributable to James Coleman and 'linking' to Michael Woolcock.
10. For SC and religion see Putnam (2000), Halpern (2005), Lehmann (2007) and Putnam (2008).
11. For a detailed description of this process see Mendoza-Botelho (2008).
12. A social movement that represents the interests of coca leaves producers in this region, where part of this activity is considered illegal.

13. These ideas are congruent with Jensen and Wagoner's (2009) description of the cycles of social change, in particular Transcendent to Immanent, or how "institutions and organizations are mobilized to create norms and practices that align with the ascendant transcendent representations", considering also that "change is highly contingent, non-linear and culturally bound" (p. 219).

REFERENCES

Altman, D., & Lalander, R. (2003). Bolivia's Popular Participation Law: An Undemocratic Democratisation Process? Decentralisation and Democratic Governance: Experiences from India, Bolivia and South Africa. A. Hadenius. Stockholm, Expert Group on Development Issues (EGDI), Swedish Ministry for Foreign Affairs.

Arneil, B. (2006). *Diverse communities: the problem with social capital.* Cambridge, England: Cambridge University Press.

Australian Bureau of Statistics (ABS). (2004). Measuring social capital: An Australian framework and indicators. *Information Paper No. 1378.0.*

Ayo, D. (1997). Las élites de la Participación Popular: Las mujeres, los indígenas y campesinos como autoridades locales, municipales y departamentales [Popular participation elites. Women, indigenous and peasants as local, municipal and departmental authorities]. *Análisis Político. Revista Especializada* Año 1, (No .2).

Bebbington, A. (1997). Social Capital and Rural Intensification: Local Organizations and Islands of Sustainability in the Rural Andes. *Geographical Journal, 163*(2), 189-197.

Ayo, D. Ed. (2004). *Voces Críticas de la Descentralización: Una Década de la Participación Popular. Serie Descentralización y Participación No. 7* [Critical Voices of Decentralization. A Decade into Popular Participation. Series Decentralization and Participation No. 7]. La Paz, Bolivia, Fundación Friederich Ebert e Instituto Latinomericano de Investigaciones Sociales (ILDIS). Plural Editores.

Booth, D. (1997). *Popular participation. Democratising the state in the rural Bolivia.* Stockholm, Sweden: Stockholm University.

Bourdieu, P. (1985). The forms of capital. In J. G. Richardson (Ed.), *Handbook of theory and research for the sociology of education.* New York: Greenwood Press.

Coleman, J. S. (1988). Social capital in the creation of human capital. *American Journal of Sociology, 94,* S95-S121.

Coleman, J. S. (1990). *Foundations of social theory.* Cambridge, MA: Belknap Press of Harvard University Press.

Conrad, D. (2007). Defining social capital. *Electronic Journal of Sociology* .

Durlauf, S. N., & M. Fafchamps (2004). Social capital. *Working Paper 10485.* Cambridge, MA: National Bureau of Economic Research

Edwards, R., J. Franklin, Holland, & J. Eds. (2006). *Assessing social capital: Concept, Policy, Practice.* Newcastle, England: Cambridge Scholars Press.

Field, J. (2003). *Social capital.* London: Routledge.

Fukuyama, F. (1997). Social Capital. Tanner Lecture on Human Values., Brasenose College, Oxford (12-15 May, 1997).

Fukuyama, F. (1999). *Social capital and civil society.* Paper presented at the IMF Conference on Second Generation Reforms, Washington, DC. Retrieved from http://www.imf.org/external/pubs/ft/seminar/1999/reforms/fukuyama.htm.

Gambetta, D. (1993). *The Sicilian Mafia: the business of private protection.* Cambridge, MA: Harvard University Press.

Giddens, A. (1990). *The consequences of modernity.* Stanford, CA: SUP.

Gobierno de Bolivia [Government of Bolivia]. (1994). Ley de Participación Popular, La Paz, Bolivia. Ley No 1551 Del 20 de abril de 1994 [Law No. 1551 of Popular Participation. April 20, 1994].

Granovetter, M. (1985). Economic action and social structure: The problem of embeddedness. *American Journal of Sociology, 91*(3), 481-510.

Grindle, M. S. (2000). *Audacious reforms: Institutional invention and democracy in Latin America.* Baltimore, MS: Johns Hopkins University Press.

Grootaert, C., D. Narayan, et al. (2000). Measuring social capital: An integrated questionnaire. *Working Paper No. 18.* Washington, DC: The World Bank.

Halpern, D. (2005). *Social capital.* Cambridge, England: Polity.

Hirschman, A. O. (1984). *Getting ahead collectively: Grassroots experiences in Latin America.* New York, NY: Pergamon Press.

Jensen, E., & Wagoner, B. (2009). Continuing commentary: A cyclical model of social change. *Culture & Psychology, 15*(2), 217-228.

Krishna, A. (2002). Enhancing political participation in democracies. What is the role of social capital? *Comparative Political Studies, 35*(4), 437-460.

Lehmann, D. (2007). The miraculous economics of religion: An essay on social capital (Unpublished essay). Cambridge, England.

Lewandowski, J. D. (2006). Capitalising sociability: Rethinking the theory of social capital. In R. Edwards, J. Franklin, & J. Holland (Eds.), *Assessing social capital: Concept, policy, practice.* Cambridge, England: Cambridge Scholars Press.

Lin, N. (2001). *Social capital. A theory of social structure and action.* Cambridge, England: Cambridge University Press.

Loury, G. (1977). A dynamic theory of racial income differences. In P. Wallace & A. LeMund (Ed.), *Women, minorities, and employment discrimination.* Lexington, KY: Lexington Books.

Luhmann, N. (1979). *Trust and power,* Chichester, England: Wiley.

Mendoza-Botelho, M. (2008). *Decentralisation, social capital and social change in the Andes: The case of Bolivia.* (Doctoral Dissertation for the degree of Ph.D. in Political Science). Faculty of Social and Political Sciences. University of Cambridge, England.

Narayan, D., & L. Pritchett (1997). Cents and sociability: Household income and social capital in rural Tanzania. *Work Bank Policy Research Working Paper No. 1796.* Washington, DC: The World Bank.

Noteboom, B. (2007). Social capital, institutions and trust. *Review of Social Economy, LXV*(1), 29-53.

Olson, M. (1965). *The logic of collective action; public goods and the theory of groups.* Cambridge, MA: Harvard University Press.

Organization for Economic Co-operation and Development (OECD). (2001). The Wellbeing of Nations: The Role of Human and Social Capital, Education and Skills. Paris, France, OECD Centre for Educational Research and Innovation.

Ostrom, E. (1990). *Governing the commons: The evolution of institutions for collective action*. Cambridge, England: Cambridge University Press.

Portes, A. (1998). Social capital: Its origins and application in modern sociology. *Annual Review of Sociology, 24,* 1-24.

Portes, A. (2000). The two meanings of social capital. *Sociological Forum, 15*(1), 1-12.

Putnam, R. D., Leonardi, R., & Nanetti, R. Y. (1993). *Making democracy work: civic traditions in modern Italy*. Princeton, NJ: Princeton University Press.

Putnam, R. D. (2000). *Bowling alone: The collapse and revival of American community*. New York, NY: Simon & Schuster.

Putnam, R. D. (2002). *Democracies in flux: the evolution of social capital in contemporary society*. Oxford, England: Oxford University Press.

Putnam, R. D. (2007). *E Pluribus Unum*: Diversity and community in the twenty-first century. The 2006 Johan Skytte Prize Lecture. *Scandinavian Political Studies, 30*(2), 137-174.

Putnam, R. D. (2008). American grace: The changing role of religion in American civic life (Unpublished book). Cambridge, MA.

Ramos-Pinto, P. (2006). Social Capital as a Capacity for Collective Action. In R. Edwards, J. Franklin & J. Holland (Eds.), *Assessing social capital: Concept, policy, practice*. Cambridge, England: Cambridge Scholars Press.

Seligson, M. A., Cordova, B. A., Donoso, J. C., Morales M. D., Orcés, D., Blum, V. S. (2006). *Democracy Audit: Bolivia 2006 Report*. La Paz, Bolivia, Catholic University of Bolivia and U.S. Agency for International Development (USAID).

Sen, A. K. (2006). *Identity and violence: The illusion of destiny*. New York, NY: W. W. Norton.

Streeten, P. (2002). Reflections on social and antisocial capital. *Journal of Human Development, 3*(1).

Szreter, S. (2002). The State of social capital: Bringing back in power, politics, and history. *Theory and Society, 31*(5), 573-621.

Uphoff, N. (2000). Understanding social capital: Learning from the analysis and experience of participation. P. Dasgupta & I. Serageldin (Eds.), *Social capital: A multifaceted perspective*. Washington DC: The World Bank.

Uslaner, E. M. (2004). Political parties and social capital, political parties or social capital (Manuscript). University of Maryland–College Park.

Van Cott, D. L.(2005). *From movements to parties in Latin America: The evolution of ethnic politics*. Cambridge, England: Cambridge University Press.

Woolcock, M. (1998). Social capital and economic development: Toward a synthesis and policy framework. *Theory and Society, 27,* 151-208.

Woolcock, M. (1999). *Managing risk, shocks and opportunity in developing economies: The role of social capital.* Washington, DC: The World Bank, Development Research Group.

Woolcock, M. (2000). Social capital in theory and practice: Where do we stand? (Development Research Group, The World Bank). *21st Annual Conference on Economic Issues The Role of Social Capital in Determining Well-Being: Implications for the Teaching and Practice of Development and Environmental Economics.* Department of Economics, Middlebury College, Vermont.

CHAPTER 15

SOCIAL INFLUENCE AND SOCIAL CHANGE

States and Strategies of Social Capital

Gordon Sammut, Eleni Andreouli, and Mohammad Sartawi

The concern with identifying the factors that bind social groups together and that mobilize them to pursue collective action is a long-standing one in the social sciences. This concern goes back to the very roots of social inquiry, and various concepts, such as social cohesion, social solidarity, and others, have been articulated in an effort to address this concern. In recent years, the concept of social capital captured the scholarly imagination and led to widespread research (Shortt, 2004). Its operationalization in terms of civicness has generated a wealth of empirical research (Campbell, Cornish, & McLean, 2004; Gregson, Terceira, Mushati, Nyamukapa, & Campbell, 2004; Maloney, Smith, & Stoker, 2000; Muntaner, Lynch, & Smith, 2000; Woolcock, 1998; Woolcock & Narayan, 2000). Nevertheless, the conceptualization of social capital as well as its measurement has come under constant critique (Campbell, Williams, & Gilgen, 2002; Grix, 2001; Lochner, Kawachi, & Kennedy, 1999; Schuller, Baron, & Field, 2000; Shortt, 2004) and some have questioned whether it might not be worth disinvesting in social capital altogether (Foley & Edwards, 1999). Such critiques have been accompanied with calls for further theoretical elaboration, conceptual development, and methodological refinement.

Culture and Social Change: Transforming Society Through the Power of Ideas, pp. 263–273

The chapter by Mendoza-Botelho (this volume) is a laudable attempt at addressing some of the conceptual nuances of the concept. Mendoza-Botelho does this by modeling the three definitions of social capital that have been postulated in the literature, that is, bonding, bridging, and linking. The author makes a further decisive contribution by adding a fourth element, introducing the notion of 'stretching social capital' to the other three. Mendoza-Botelho argues that leadership provides a strategy for communities to maximize the returns of whatever social capital lies at their disposal. This, according to Mendoza-Botelho, takes place through community representation by community leaders in decision-making bodies in which the community's own interests are at stake. Such representative leadership is termed stretching social capital. This chapter furthers Mendoza-Botelho's contribution by locating it within the broader framework of social influence. Social influence is a social psychological process that underlies intergroup relations in the public sphere, as individuals and communities strive to establish legitimacy for their own worldviews over those of others. Social influence is exercised through a number of modalities (Sammut & Bauer, 2011), including leadership. Le Bon's (1896/2006) classical work on the psychology of crowds set a key agenda for the study of social influence through leadership. A directing function is a basic characteristic of any group (Counselman, 1991; Cranach, 1986) and this fact has led to a sustained interest in the study of effective leadership (Chemers, 2001; Hogg, 2007; Lord, Brown, & Harvey, 2001; Lord & Hall, 2003) that aims to identify its various features.

In any modality (including leadership) social influence can serve a dominant group to retain its views and practices as normative. Sidanius (Haley & Sidanius, 2005; Pratto, Sidanius, & Levin, 2006; Sidanius, Mitchell, Haley, & Navarrete, 2006; Thomsen, Green, & Sidanius, 2008) has demonstrated how societal institutions serve to preserve the societal structure that enables a dominant group to exercise power over subordinate groups in an effort to preserve its own status. Social influence is also exercised by subordinate groups in their attempts to legitimate their ways of life and institute their own practices, as opposed to those established by a dominant group as normative. Moscovici (1976) has demonstrated how minority influence can serve to bring about social change by challenging normativity through behavioral consistency (Faucheux & Moscovici, 1967), and establishing legitimacy for its own views and practices. In this chapter we argue that stretching social capital represents a form of minority influence by which communities gain a stake in the wider circle of institutional power at the societal level. In stretching social capital, communities gain a seat at the decision-making table that enables them to enter into social relations with dominant groups who garner power within a society, and to further their aims through legitimate forms of social influence. While such negotiation can both succeed or fail, representation in and of itself yields dividends in social capital due to the fact that it comes with recognition, or in terms of social capital, the recognition that the resources embedded within a given social network have value for others. And recognition, as Moscovici notes, in and of itself legitimates a minority groups' project.

STATES AND STRATEGIES OF SOCIAL CAPITAL

Theories of social capital have posited that social networks constitute a valuable resource for individuals or groups enabling them to gain access to resources that serve the advancement of their own interests. Consequently, social networks serve not merely the human need for affiliation, they provide a gateway to valuable resources that the individual or group might not have at their immediate disposal but that they might nevertheless be able to access through accessing the right channel. As Woolcock and Narayan (2000) argue, social capital captures the common aphorism of: *It's who you know.* For this reason, social networks are repositories of value that can be drawn on to acquire resources, that is, capital. Particularly in Bourdieu's (1986) work, social capital is a repository of value that in times of need can be converted to other forms such as cultural capital (knowledge, skills, etc.) or economic capital (financial resources). Gittel and Vidal (1998) have distinguished between two forms of capital, bonding and bridging, which have also been used by Putnam (2000). In Gittel and Vidal's conception, bonding social capital refers to intracommunity ties amongst people who share similar goals and interests, while bridging social capital refers to extracommunity ties, that is, ties that exist across social groups, such as those between different communities or communities and public services (Campbell, Cornish, & McLean, 2004; Woolcock & Narayan, 2000).

Societal dynamics are infinitely more complex than those represented by an orthogonal distinction between inter- and intracommunity ties. Further conceptions of social capital have thus been postulated to capture other ways by which a community can profit from social networks. Linking social capital refers to relations between individuals or groups that traverse hierarchical power, status, and wealth strata in society (Office for National Statistics [ONS], 2001). And in Mendoza-Botelho's formulation, stretching social capital refers to community representation in decision-making circles where power and access to resources are wielded. Whilst these two further conceptions of social capital extend our understanding of the term and enable a more nuanced conceptualization of it, they nevertheless describe some characteristically different features than the bonding/bridging distinction. In an effort to better articulate their characteristically different features, we distinguish between social capital states and strategies. In fact we go a step further and propose that bonding/bridging and linking/stretching are qualitatively different conceptions of social capital that need to be treated as such. On the one hand, bridging/bonding social capital are structural elements of social groups. On the other hand, linking/stretching are processes enabled by social capital structures that serve to further group interests through either establishing links with, or seeking representation in, institutions of power. Linking and stretching social capital can also become states, in that a group may establish stable links with institutions that fossilize association with powerful agents or representation. However, for the purposes of this chapter, we will focus on stretching and linking as strategies in order to stress their role in social change processes whereby a group tries to enhance its position within a social system.

Bonding and bridging social capital reflect *states* of social capital. A given community will have some level, or state, of bonding social capital that reflects its internal cohesion. Its state of binding social capital, that reflects its ties with other communities or entities, can also be described at any given point in time. Either or both can be high or low. Communities can be cohesive but insulated, or they can be cohesive but well connected with other communities. Alternatively, communities can display little internal organization but can similarly be more or less well connected. Elsewhere, the four quadrants of bonding and bridging social capital that ensue from a two-dimensional conception of social capital representing internal and external community relations have been linked to Berry Poortinga, Segall, and Dasen (2002) acculturation model that similarly represents inter- and intracommunity ties in the context of migration (Sammut, 2011). Bonding and bridging social capital thus refer to the state of each of these levels of social capital that exists in a given community at a given point in time. As such, bonding social capital, for example, may increase or decrease over time depending on whether community cohesion strengthens or weakens.

On the other hand, linking and stretching are better conceptualized in this context as social capital investment *strategies*. Through association with power-wielding agents or through representation in decision-making circles, social capital serves as a foundation upon which a community can promote its interests. These strategies, over time, might enable a community to improve its status vis-à-vis other groups and better serve its needs and interests. Alternatively, the breakdown of relations with powerful agents, or the dissolution of representation, may lead to a devaluation in the status of the group therefore preventing them from meeting their interests and minimize their access to resources. Linking and stretching social capital can variably serve as social capital maximizing strategies.

MINORITY INFLUENCE

The proposition to treat linking and stretching social capital as strategies for maximizing a community's resources locates their operation within the general framework of social influence. More specifically, linking and stretching social capital are forms of minority influence that serve subordinate groups to legitimate and institute their own ways. Subordinate groups may thus seek either political affiliation or representation in their effort to challenge their relative status in a given society. Dominant groups, on the other hand, may strive to repress such strategies in their effort to subdue a deviant group and maintain conformity (cf. Sammut & Bauer, 2011).

The study of minority influence emerged in the works of Moscovici (1974, 1976) as a critique of the dominant paradigm of conformity studies in social influence. Social influence is not simply a matter of social control by dominant and more powerful groups imposing their own practices as normative. Minority groups, or subordinate groups, engage in processes of deviance and minority influence to garner allies and further their cause (Paicheler, 1988). Deviance is thus an innovative and creative enterprise that seeks to topple the existent social order and establish itself as a legitimate concern. At the point where such deviance institutionalizes itself, the tipping point of public opinion (Gladwell, 2000), a subordinate community institutes social change by naturalizing its own community ways. Sammut and Bauer (2011) have termed this process of normative social change the cycle of common-sense. The treatment of deviance is a central concern in this cycle. A disenfranchised community that comes together seeking emancipation to institute its own ways in a social order in which it is not recognized is deviant de facto. For it to gain emancipation, it needs to gain the right to have a voice and to propose it as a legitimate, rather than a deviant, one. It is in this way that communities, through strategies of linking and stretching social capital, gain for themselves the very right to exist and to be recognized. The recognition of minority perspectives is fundamental in processes of social change. Indeed, recognition in communicative practices is a fundamental condition for innovation (Duveen & Psaltis, 2008; Psaltis & Duveen, 2006), ergo social change. The critical aspect of this cycle is that, initially, a subordinate community requires support for a deviant cause. Before such a community gains a critical mass that reaches a tipping point for its ways, it requires the support of allies who put their trust in the community's deviant cause. Social capital, as Fukuyama (1999) notes, is the crucible of trust. For a community to bring about any change in the social order, it needs to come together, garner support, and build social capital. It needs to gain the trust of its own members as well as that of others. Minorities acquire status and support incrementally. They originate as deviant; over time they can attract newcomers and bring about social change. To be influential, a minority needs to be perceived as offering a clear and distinct alternative to the status quo. In order to be convincing, minorities need to appear consistent in their cause (Faucheux & Moscovici, 1967). In this sense, bonding social capital can be a useful resource for minority influence. On the other hand if the minority is perceived as isolated then it can be psychologized as eccentric or perverse, delegitimizing its cause (Papastamou, 1986). Links with others groups are, thus, also a condition for successful minority influence. Therefore, *both* bonding and bridging social capital are a prerequisite in order for stretching social capital, as conceptualized by Mendoza-Botelho, to be established.

A strategy of stretching social capital through directive leadership can serve a community to precipitate social change in its favor. Legitimacy alone is sufficient to ensure success over time. When a minority or subordinate group gains legitimacy for its own perspective, its voice remains possibly dissident but no longer deviant. It finds itself in a position where it can recruit others to its cause—legitimately, through persuasion. Stretching social capital grants a community the opportunity for social influence. In time, even if in aggregate its position remains in minority, its perspective nevertheless becomes a reasonable, rather than a deviant, alternative. This is sufficient for it to enter the cycle of common-sense, and at the point where a critical mass is recruited, it succeeds in institutionalizing itself and fulfilling its aims.

CONCLUSION

Mendoza-Botelho (this volume) draws our attention to a very important question regarding the relationship between social capital and action framed within the issue of social change. Action can take place either at the individual or collective level. Therefore, in terms of social capital, the question that also arises is whether social capital represents individual or collective resources. In relation to the present chapter, we contend that it is necessary to view social capital as both. At the group level cultural symbols, meanings, and norms maintain social bonds and material resources, and reproduce social structures. In seeking recognition and representation these resources form the bedrock for social change with regard to the group. If, as Mendoza-Botelho is arguing, we are interested in the formation of ties between groups and individuals that are (in linking), or are made to be (in stretching), in a position of status in order to act in the group's interest, then we are also interested in individual resources.

In addition, according to the classic social capital approach, individuals or collectives may take action either to a) *maintain* valued resources or b) *gain* valued resources (Lin, 2001). With regards to action and social capital, perspectives seem to vary as to whether an individual utilizes collective resources for personal gain (Lin, 1982), or whether social capital as a maintained and reproduced group asset enhances the lives of its members (Bourdieu, 1986; Coleman, 1988, 1990; Putnam, 1993, 1995, 2000). Therefore, the focus on the former is on individual motivations and purposive action, while the latter sees individual action in terms of the opportunities afforded by social structures. The former is a view with a focus on agency while the latter adopts a structural approach. Mendoza-Botelho is interested in the actions of individual members on behalf of the group that utilize existing collective assets in order to *gain* valued resources through linking and stretching. His approach is in itself a 'bridging' of various approaches in conceptualizing social capital and action. However, in highlighting the issue of structure and opportunity, one also needs to consider the issue of constraint (Bourdieu & Passeron, 1977). This becomes especially relevant to the present case where groups strive for recognition and for representation by individuals. As opportunities and constraints are decisive for purposive action, we must turn our attention to the fundamental issue of power.

In his discussion of social capital and action, Lin (2001) notes that in order for resources to be recognized as valuable, three processes of social influence may be exercised: persuasion, petition, or coercion. The struggle for recognition is always a power dynamic. Nye (1990, 2004) explicates how the resolution of social struggle can be resolved through "hard power," that is, coercion and violence, or "soft power," through persuasion (or petition). The means for both achieving as well as retaining power is social influence. Social influence serves a dominant group to retain its own, often hard-won practices as normative. It also serves minorities to mount challenges to that normativity, topple the status quo, and establish social order according to its own ways. It is for this reason that the strategies of linking and stretching social capital are rooted in the access to, and exercise of, power. Linking social capital provides a community with access to figures in whom power is vested, and who hold the capacity to exercise their power in ways that further the community's own interests. Stretching social capital provides a community with representation in decision-making circles wherein power is wielded. Social change is an event of successful social influence by which certain individuals or groups acquire the power to institute their own ways. In so doing, they further their community's interests, amass support, and extend their sphere of influence. In other words, they acquire social capital—bonding and/or bridging. The political question that ensues is who should be granted stretching social capital. Ought every community to be afforded the possibility of stretching social capital? At face value, it might seem that representation itself is commendable and that any social change that might accrue from democratic participation could only ever be for the better. Mendoza-Botelho's chapter portrays representative leadership as a successful emancipation strategy. However, representation is a two-sided coin that comes with recognition, and recognition legitimates a minority's cause, as noted above. Recognition and legitimation offer a minority the possibility to engage in influence tactics to institutionalize its own ways. "Extending minorities" stretching social capital also extends them "soft power." And clearly, many would argue against granting certain groups any form of power, even soft power. The contemporary recognition of the Palestinian National Liberation Movement (Fatah) in the Israeli-Palestinian conflict, and the corollary negation of recognition by Western powers of the democratically elected Islamic Recognition Movement (Hamas) in Gaza, is a case-example of extending stretching social capital to a community but negating it to another, for the reason of legitimating a cause and denouncing another. The granting of stretching social capital is in itself a political game that involves, itself, the exercise of soft power to serve the interests of some against those of others.

REFERENCES

Berry, J. W., Poortinga, Y. H., Segall, M. H., & Dasen, P. R. (2002). *Cross-cultural psychology: Research and applications*. Cambridge, England: Cambridge University Press.

Bourdieu, P. (1986). The forms of capital. In J. G. Richardson (Ed.), *Handbook of theory and research for the sociology of education* (pp. 241-248). New York, NY: Greenwood Press.

Bourdieu, P., & Passeron, J. -C. (1977). *Reproduction in Education, Society and Culture*. Richard Nice (tr.). London: SAGE. (Original work published 1970)

Campbell, C., Cornish, F., & McLean, C. (2004). Social capital, participation and the perpetuation of health inequalities: obstacles to African-Caribbean participation in 'partnerships' to improve mental health. *Ethnicity and health, 9*, 305-327.

Campbell, C., Williams, B., & Gilgen, D. (2002). Is social capital a useful conceptual tool for exploring community level influences on HIV infection? An exploratory case study from South Africa. *AIDS Care, 14*, 41-54

Chemers, M. M. (2001). Leadership effectiveness: An integrative review. In M.A. Hogg & R.S. Tindale (Eds.), *Blackwell handbook of social psychology: Group processes* (pp. 283-310). Oxford, England: Blackwell.

Coleman, J. S. (1988). Social Capital in the creation of Human Capital. *The American Journal of Sociology, 94*, S95-S120.

Coleman, J. S. (1990). *Foundation of social theory.* Cambridge, MA: Harvard University Press.

Counselman, E. (1991). Leadership in a long-term leaderless women's group. *Small group Research, 22*, 240-257.

Cranach, M. von (1986). Leadership as a function of group action. In C. F. Graumann & S. Moscovici (Eds.), *Changing conceptions of leadership* (pp. 115-134). New York, NY: Springer Verlag.

Duveen, G., & Psaltis, C. (2008). The constructive role of asymmetries in social interaction. In U. Mueller, J. Carpendale, N. Budwig & B. Sokol (Eds.), *Social life and social knowledge: Toward a process account of development* (pp. 183-204). Mahwah, NJ: Lawrence Erlbaum.

Faucheux, C., & Moscovici, S. (1967). Le style de comportement d'une minorité et son influence sur les réponses d'une majorité. *Bulletin du C.E.R.P. 16*, 337-360.

Foley, M.W., & Edwards, B. (1999). Is it time to disinvest in SC?. *Journal of Public Policy, 19*, 141-173

Fukuyama, F. (1999, November). *Social Capital and Civil Society.* Paper prepared for delivery at the IMF Conference on Second Generation Reforms, IMF Institute and the Fiscal Affairs Department, Washington, DC.

Gittell, R., & Vidal, A. (1998). *Community organizing: Building social capital as a development strategy.* California: SAGE.

Gladwell, M. (2000). *The tipping point: How little things can make a big difference.* Boston, MA: Little Brown.

Gregson, S., Terceira, N., Mushati, P., Nyamukapa, C., & Campbell, C. (2004). Community group participation: can it help young women to avoid HIV? An exploratory study of social capital and school education in rural Zimbabwe. *Social science and medicine, 58*, 2119-2132.

Grix, J. (2001). Social capital as a concept in the social sciences: The current state of the debate. *Democratization, 8*, 189-210

Haley, H., & Sidanius, J. (2005). Person-organization congruence and the maintenance of group-based social hierarchy: A social dominance perspective. *Group Processes and Intergroup Relations, 8*, 187-203.

Hogg, M. A. (2007). Social psychology of leadership. In A. W. Kruglanski & E. T. Higgins (Eds.), *Social psychology: A handbook of basic principles* (2nd ed., pp. 716-733). New York, NY: Guilford

Le Bon, G. (2006). *The crowd: A study of the popular mind.* West Valley City, UT: Waking Lion Press. (Original work published 1896)

Lin, N. (1982). Social resources and instrumental action. In P. V. Marsden & N. Lin (Eds.), *Social Structure and Network Analysis* (pp. 131-145). Beverly Hills, CA: SAGE.

Lin, N. (2001). *Social capital: A theory of structure and action.* Cambridge, England: Cambridge University Press.

Lochner, K., Kawachi, I., & Kennedy, B. P. (1999). Social capital: a guide to its measurement. *Health & Place, 5,* 259-270.

Lord, R., & Hall, R. (2003). Identity, leadership categorization, and leadership schema. In D. van Knippenberg & M.A. Hogg (Eds.), *Leadership and power: Identity processes in groups and organizations* (pp. 48-64). London: SAGE.

Lord, R. G., Brown, D. J., & Harvey, J. L. (2001). System constraints on leadership perceptions, behavior and influence: An example of connectionist level processes. In M. A. Hogg & R. S. Tindale (Eds.), *Blackwell handbook of social psychology: Group processes* (pp. 283-310). Oxford, England: Blackwell.

Maloney, W., Smith, G., & Stoker, G. (2000). Social capital and urban governance: adding a more contextualised "top-down" perspective. *Political studies, 48,* 802-820

Moscovici, S. (1974). Social influence I: Conformity and social control. In C. Nemeth (Ed.), *Social psychology: Classic and contemporary integrations* (pp. 179-216). Chicago, IL: Rand McNally.

Moscovici, S. (1976). *Social influence and social change*. London: Academic Press.

Muntaner, C., Lynch, J., & Smith, G.D. (2000). Social capital and the third way in public health. *Critical Public Health, 10,* 107-124

Nye, J. S. (1990). *Bound to lead: The changing nature of American power.* New York, NY: Basic Books.

Nye, J. S. (2004). *Soft power: The means to success in world politics*. New York, NY: Public Affairs.

Office for National Statistics, UK. (2001). *Social capital: A review of the literature.* Retrieved from http://www.ons.gov.uk/about-statistics/user-guidance/sc-guide/the-social-capital-project/index.html

Paicheler, G. (1988). *The psychology of social influence*. Cambridge, England: Cambridge university Press.

Papastamou, S. (1986). Psychologization and processes of minority and majority influence. *European Journal of Social Psychology, 16,* 165-180.

Pratto, F., Sidanius, J., & Levin, S. (2006). Social dominance theory and the dynamics of intergroup relations: taking stock and looking forward. *European Review of Social Psychology, 17,* 271-320.

Psaltis, C., & Duveen, G. (2006). Social relations and cognitive development: The influence of conversation types and representations of gender. *European Journal of Social Psychology, 36,* 407-430.

Putnam, R. D. (1993). The prosperous community: Social capital and public life. *The American Prospect, 13,* 35-42

Putnam, R.D. (1995). Bowling alone: America's declining social capital. *Journal of Democracy, 6,* 65-78.

Putnam, R.D. (2000). *Bowling alone: The collapse and revival of American community.* New York, NY: Simon & Schuster.

Sammut, G. (2011). Civic solidarity: the negotiation of identities in modern societies. *Papers on Social Representations, 20*(1), 4.1-4.24.

Sammut, G., & Bauer, M. (2011). Social influence: Modes and modalities. In D. Hook, B. Franks, & M. Bauer (Eds.), *The Social Psychology of Communication*. Hampshire: Palgrave Macmillan.

Schuller, T., Baron, S., & Field, J. (2000). Social Capital: A review and critique. In Baron, S., Field, J., & Schuller, T. (Eds.). *Social capital: Critical perspectives* (pp. 1-38). Oxford, England: Oxford University Press.

Shortt, S. E. D. (2004). Making sense of social capital, health and policy. *Health Policy, 70*, 11-22

Sidanius, J., Mitchell, M., Haley, H., & Navarrete, C.D. (2006). Support for harsh criminal sanctions and criminal justice beliefs: A social dominance perspective. *Social Justice Research, 19*, 433-449.

Thomsen, L., Green, E. G. T., & Sidanius, J. (2008). We will hunt them down: How social dominance orientation and right-wing authoritarianism fuel ethnic persecution of immigrants in fundamentally different ways. *Journal of Experimental Social Psychology, 44*, 1455-1464.

Woolcock, M. (1998). Social capital and economic development: toward a theoretical synthesis and policy framework. *Theory and Society, 27*, 151-208

Woolcock, M., & Narayan, D. (2000). Social capital: Implications for development theory, research, and policy. *The World Bank Research Observer, 15*, 225-249.

CHAPTER 16

CHANGING FIELDS, CHANGING HABITUSES

Symbolic Transformations in the Field of Public Service in Post-Soviet Ukraine

Anastasiya Ryabchuk

In March 2009 Kyiv city administration attempted to introduce official payments for many basic medical services, such as blood tests or vaccinations. This decision was widely discussed and criticized as unconstitutional (universal health care provision is guaranteed by the state free of charge to all Ukrainian citizens). But it also received support from many leading doctors and directors of hospitals who "spoke of the necessity of structural changes in the field and the impossibility and absurdity of free medicine" (Horetska, 2009). In fact, with transition to capitalism, many Ukrainian doctors began to speak in favor of privatization of health care, introduction of private medical insurance to lift the state's "burden" in this field, or of remuneration of doctors according to market principles. On November 27, 2007 the official newspaper of Kyiv city administration *Khreshchatyk* organized a round table "Free medicine does not exist," where doctors and administrators working in the field of health care said that "medicine should be managed like the economic field," "doctors should be paid according to the amount of services they provide" or "we should

Culture and Social Change: Transforming Society Through the Power of Ideas, pp. 275–295

tell people the truth that when we introduce private health insurance it will not be free, it has to be paid for." Head doctor of Kyiv maternity hospital No. 2 Tetiana Pykhnio confirmed that their hospital officially asks patients to make "charitable contributions" to receive "improved service and quality of care" (Horetska, 2009).

These doctors also encouraged thinking of health care in economic terms (as "services") as a remedy to the unsatisfactory state of Ukrainian health care and of the low economic status of doctors and nurses (who are forced to leave Ukraine to work in Western Europe where they are much better paid). Although these doctors do not directly challenge the right to universal health care for all Ukrainian citizens that is written out in the constitution, they demand the privatization of specific health care "services" and an opportunity to receive higher wages in a competitive environment of paid health care services, which indirectly challenges universal health care provision by the state and deepens existing social inequalities. Doctors are not the only ones—Ukrainian schoolteachers offer private lessons in afterschool hours (income earned from such tutoring often exceeds official salary), thus providing better education for children from wealthier families. University professors offer "consultations" to political parties or marketing agencies and sometimes cooperate with private firms selling research papers to students (a student may request a paper on a particular topic to be written for him or her for a specific deadline and professors do this work for money). Their contradictory demands are based on professionalism of public sector workers in a competitive "free market" environment on the one hand and service for the public good on the other. More generally, they indicate the ambiguity of the status of professional public sector workers in the countries of the former "Socialist block." By professional public sector workers I refer to skilled non-manual workers in the public sector, including lower rank civil servants, specialists in the fields of education, medical care and social protection, science and culture. They hold higher or specialist secondary education and come from the former Soviet stratum of "intelligentsia." They are employed by the state to fulfill its obligations towards its citizens (education, health care and social protection, as well as access to works of art and culture) and are paid from the state's budget.

Much has been said about the deteriorating state of public services in postsocialist countries in the 1990s. The structural changes (by which one usually means economic but also, more generally, objective material changes in other social institutions) in each of the Central and East European states can easily be tracked by analyzing both national and international statistics (the latter include reports by the UN, IMF, World Bank, etc.). At the other end of the spectrum there is also much research on individual or group psychological responses to societal transition (feelings of stress and dissatisfaction, coping strategies, "'anomie'" and difficulties in adaptation). However very little is said about the symbolic (discursive or ideological) transformations in the context of structural changes. In post-socialist societies symbolic transformations accompany structural ones, causing a great deal of social suffering for the people who struggle to affirm their social positions in a changing society but are unable to construct a satisfactory life narrative. The relationship between symbolic and structural changes refers to the classical sociological distinction between "culture" and "structure" (a Marxist distinction between "superstructure" and "base" or Foucault's distinction between "discursive" and "material" structures). How do people react to economic changes in their countries, how do they talk about them, make sense of them and adjust their behavior accordingly? In the case of Ukrainian health care workers, quoted above: why do they demand privatization of health care, introduction of paid services or personal insurance—something they could not even think of some twenty years ago, when all health care was provided by the state? In what way are the interests of this privileged strata of health care workers similar to or different from other workers in the field of public service who provide more ambivalent accounts or actively oppose privatization?

THEORETICAL BACKGROUND

This chapter deals with the process of symbolic transformations and identity construction of professional public sector workers in Ukraine during transition to capitalism. Burawoy and Verdery note that the so-called "transitologists" often forget that they are dealing with transitions: "When we speak of transition, we think of a process connecting the past to the future. What we discover, however, are theories of transition often committed to some pregiven future or rooted in an unyielding past" (Burawoy & Verdery, 1999, p. 4). In this chapter I propose to bring back into the picture the process of transition both "in things" and "in minds"—or, using Bourdieu's terminology, both in the field of public service, and in agents' systems of dispositions (habitus) within that field. I will use Bourdieu's conceptual apparatus as an instrument to understand postsocialist transitions, showing the relational nature of social reality and overcoming the dichotomies of structure-agency, macro-micro, past-present.

Using Bourdieu's terminology, one may say that the field of public service is a "field of struggles" and that these struggles are especially visible in a changing society. People occupying different positions in the field are differently predisposed towards the preservation or transformation of particular structures and practices. Post-Soviet change is therefore not only about the change in structures, but also about a change in habituses— in systems of durable dispositions that determine the way people perceive the world and act in it. In this paper I use a Bourdieusian approach to investigate symbolic transformations in post-Soviet societies. I present findings from my research on the social suffering of professional public sector workers (hereafter abbreviated as "pps workers") in Ukraine that I carried out for the MPhil degree at the University of Cambridge in 2005. My more specific question is: what new symbolic understandings arise in conditions of change and from whom, considering that people's habituses were suited to earlier ("soviet") structures. First I will present Bourdieu's key concepts in relation to post-Soviet transformations and then introduce the results of my case study, followed by discussion and analysis.

Navigating Through Symbolic Space

Social reality exists, so to speak, twice, in things and in minds, in fields and in habitus, outside and inside of agents. And when habitus encounters a social world of which it is product, it is like a "fish in the water": it does not feel the weight of the water, and it takes the world about itself for granted. (Bourdieu & Wacquant, 1992, p. 127)

The way we navigate through the social world depends on our positions (the point of reference—where we are looking from) and on our previous experiences (e.g., the process of socialization, through which we gain the necessary tools to make sense of it, learn certain patterns of behavior and thinking). Merleau-Ponty's comparison of the social world with a football field is especially relevant here: a football player is also like a "fish in the water"—knowing and feeling on a prerational level how to act, taking into account his position in the field and his previous experience of the game. The rules of the game in a social field usually remain stable over fairly long periods of time which allows social participants to reproduce certain practices and pass on their symbolical meaning from generation to generation. Pierre Bourdieu picks up Merleau-Ponty's comparison and introduces such terms as "field," "habitus" and "practice" into his studies.

However, despite such a general tendency to stability and reproduction of symbolic practices, which have often been the focus of Bourdieu's studies, change also occurs. A good example of such changes on both micro and macrosocial levels comes from post-Soviet East-European countries, where questions of social change are especially relevant: how does one system of symbols, cultural references and "things of value" push aside all the other ones and how do people accept (or resist) new rules of the game, reconstructing their identities and investing into new values as the situation changes?

I believe that these questions may very well be answered using Bourdieu's theory. First of all, it would be wrong to say that Bourdieu's studies deal only with reproduction and stability—most of his early work on Algeria ("Uprooting," "Work and Workers in Algeria," etc.) and the on Béarn province ("Le bal des célibataires") as well as his study of the academic field ("Homo Academicus") deal specifically with situations of change, and his theoretical questions address issues of both reproduction and transformation. Responding to the criticisms of Bourdieu's theory as "deterministic" and "failing to account for social change," I will show, on the contrary, that Bourdieu does include the possibility of change in his theory, and that it is relevant and applicable to conditions of social change in Eastern Europe.

Changing Habituses

Before proceeding further it is necessary to look at Bourdieu's concepts of field and habitus in more detail. Bourdieu's most cited definition of habitus sees it as "systems of durable dispositions, of structured structures that are predisposed to function as structuring structures." His tautology is deliberate since it helps resolve an important dichotomy in social sciences—of material determinism of the Marxist model on the one hand, and of the independence and rational action of individuals or social groups on the other.

> The notion of habitus accounts for the fact that social agents are neither particles of matter determined by external causes, nor little monads guided solely by internal reasons, executing a sort of perfectly rational internal program of action. Social agents are the product of history, of the history of the whole social field and of the accumulated experience of a path within the specific subfield. (Bourdieu & Wacquant, 1992, p. 136)

Because of his critical stance towards the currently dominant "rational choice" theories Bourdieu is often criticized for being "overly-deterministic" and failing to account for innovation and agency. The interviewer in "Introduction to reflexive sociology" asks in particular whether "the mediating concept of habitus really frees us from the "iron cage of structuralism" (p. 132) where "structures produce habitus, which determine practices, which reproduce structures" (p. 135). Bourdieu's answer is the following:

> Habitus is not the fate that some people read into it. Being the product of history, it is an open system of dispositions that is constantly subjected to experiences, and therefore constantly affected by them in a way that either reinforces or modifies its structures (p. 133)

People perceive the world based on their previous experiences, which causes a relative closure of the system (situations of "fit" between structures and habitus). But when there are radical changes in objective "material" structures (as in the case of the former Soviet Union) the "mental structures" of individuals are "out of place": "There are also cases of discrepancy between habitus and field in which conduct remains unintelligible unless you bring into the picture habitus and its specific inertia, its hysteresis,"—writes Bourdieu (Bourdieu & Wacquant, 1992, p. 130). We see this "hysteresis" in research of displaced migrants or of conflicts between generations—where there are radical disjunctions between subjective perceptions and objective reality. These "disjuctions" are especially visible in postsocialist societies, as witnessed by the following observation:

> We acknowledge that people's responses to a situation may often appear as holdovers precisely because they employ a language and symbols adapted from previous orders. This does not mean their vision of the world has been so "corrupted" by the socialist experience as to make them unfit for other ways of life; it means only that action employs symbols and words that are not created de novo but develop using the forms already known, even if with new senses and to new ends. (Burawoy & Verdery, 1999, p. 2)

This quote describes very well my own experience while conducting interviews with professional public sector workers in Ukraine: what I saw were applications of "Soviet" language and symbols to new "capitalist" ends, with simultaneous attempts to adapt to structural changes and to resist them. Whether old symbolic references are seen as "holdovers" or new ones are seen as dangerous innovations, there is a great ambiguity and difficulties in trying to harmonize the field and the habitus, which results in positional suffering of these workers.

Public Service as a "Field of Struggles"

Bourdieu determines a field as a configuration of objective relations between positions, occupied by individuals or institutions. According to Bourdieu, the notion of a field comes from a fundamental principle that "the real is relational," and that these relations are invisible structures of the field (rather than simple "interactions" between agents). A field is not static, but dynamic—similarly to a game, it is characterized by relationships of power and "struggles" over control of specific forms of capital, that are dominant in that field. Another similarity with a game is the "investment" that the social actors make in the field, believing that "the game is worth playing":

> The structure of the field is a state of the power relations among the agents or institutions engaged in the struggle, or, to put it another way, a state of the distribution of the specific capital which has been accumulated in the course of previous struggle and which orients subsequent strategies. This structre, which governs the strategies aimed at transforming it, is itself always at stake. The struggles which take place within the field are about the monopoly of the legitimate violence (specific authority) which is characteristic of the field in question, which means, ultimately, the conservation or subversion of the structure of the distribution of the specific capital. (Bourdieu, 1993, p. 73)

Every particular "struggle" in the field of public service builds upon an "accumulation of previous struggles" that have shaped actual state of the field, but also "orients subsequent strategies" and shapes the field's future state. We can see this tendency if we look at examples of recent struggles for or against changes in the Ukrainian public service. These changes happen partly as a result of the struggles of actors who occupy different positions within the field and are differently disposed towards the preservation or transformation of certain structures and practices. For example, one group campaigning for liberal transformations are top specialists (noted doctors, professors and scientists) who possess high levels of cultural capital but who only form a small percentage of public sector workers. They feel that, given more freedom, they will be able to "realize their potential" more fully and achieve both a higher social status in the public sector and a higher level of income (Symonchuk, 2003). The Soviet-inherited system of state bureaucracy, on the contrary, prefers to preserve the existing "rules of the game." These professionals are most likely to benefit from high levels of social capital (given the connections they have and positions they occupy as a part of the bureaucratic apparatus). Finally, the largest subcategory, on which I focus in this paper—the mass of professional public sector workers—define themselves by the "heroic image" of service for the public good, since disinterestedness in profit allows them to achieve social status and respect in society.

But while the changes in the Ukrainian public service come from the unresolved conflicts in the earlier state of the field, they in turn shape the positions that actors end up occupying and their subsequent dispositions towards social change. For example, the privatization of certain educational and health-care institutions has led to widening inequalities among teachers and doctors with similar qualifications but working in different sectors (private or public). Similarly, unequal regional development, especially along the rural-urban axis, means that workers in different communities have different opportunities to gain additional income or to change jobs. Therefore, the social suffering of some public sector workers can be explained through their marginal positions: in the public as opposed to the private sector, and in economically "depressed" regions as opposed to more successful ones.

RESEARCH FINDINGS: DISIDENTIFICATIONS AND IDENTITY CONSTRUCTION

In order to show how a Bourdieusian framework can help us better understand the processes of symbolic transformations I will use my own study of the social suffering of public sector workers in Ukraine as an empirical example. The main method applied in my research was in-depth semi-structured interviewing. I interviewed 16 professional public sector workers coming from three communities (one urban—K, one semiurban—B and one rural—S) and of a variety of socioeconomic backgrounds. I have focused on these workers as a distinct category, based on their occupation (skilled nonmanual work), qualifications (higher or specialist secondary education) and sector of the economy (public service). However, these distinctions do not resolve an important contradiction that I believe to be at the heart of the ambiguities about professional public sector workers' positioning in post-Soviet societies and a cause of their difficulties in self-identification during transition: where to focus in defining their status: on "professional" or "public sector worker?" The results of my study reveal positional suffering caused by the uncertainty of post-Soviet transformations and the role of pps workers in these processes.

"All They Think About is Money": Dis-identifications From The "New Middle Classes"

My respondents invested into a form of "cultural superiority," identifying themselves against the new ("entrepreneurial") middle classes who, as Katia, a museum worker from Kyiv put it, "may be wealthy, but in terms of culture are much lower than us." Nadia, a retired preschool teacher from Kyiv, stressed that "money does not bring happiness" and that she felt just as happy going to the forest, watching the sunset and reading books. She also mentioned that she taught the children "universal values, so that they grow kind and loving, hard-working, true patriots of their Motherland' and added: "I may be poor, but as the saying goes, poverty is not vice."

> Some people are in a hurry after material things. They want to have more and more. Cars, clothes, spending summer holidays at the Seychelles.... All these entrepreneurs, you know? All they think about is money! But does it bring happiness? (Nadia, K)

> All these new things: mobile phones, fashionable clothes—I don't need that. I know what's really important in life: true friendship, constant self-improvement. This is why I kept my job, even when it was difficult, back in the early nineties, when we weren't getting salaries for almost a year. Some of my colleagues quit, went to work in the private sector, as secretaries. But what kind of job is that? Answering phonecalls! My work is much more important! (Katia, K)

These two interviews show a rejection of the material values and a focus on "universal values," "true friendship," "constant self-improvement." My respondents, who were very poor economically and for whom many of the modern material comforts (such as a car or a mobile phone) and luxuries (fashionable clothes, summer holidays at the Seychelles) were unattainable, rejected these "material things" as criteria to evaluate one's position in society. Instead they looked for other criteria where they could be considered "higher up." Culture and values were therefore used as distinguishing factors, with such features as self-improvement (reading books), dedication ("I kept my job even when it was difficult"), friendship, kindness, and hard work. The economically successful new middle classes were described as being culturally inferior ("I don't need that. I know what's really important in life" or "But does it bring happiness?"), and their work as less important ("But what kind of job is that?"). A lifestyle that was unattainable for my respondents also became undesirable. Here we can refer back to Bourdieu's comment on the "lifestyle of necessity" where people "come to desire that, to which they are objectively destined" and "read the future that fits them, which is made for them and for which they are made" (Bourdieu & Wacquant, 1992, p. 130).

"They Just Drink Vodka All The Time": Dis-identifications From The "Working Classes"

The same criteria of "cultural superiority" and of the importance of one's work led my respondents to dis-identify themselves from the working-classes. They stressed that they deserve higher wages than the manual workers, describing the latter as dirty, uneducated and abusing alcohol:

> And you know how in the Soviet times some metallurgy worker or coal miner would be getting a salary five times higher than mine! And it still works like that! Oh, yes, its hard physical labour, but anyone can go down and dig some coal, and even unskilled workers, with no education, or even these alcoholics would get higher salaries! (Nina, B)

> We are doing important work, you know? Only imagine what would happen if all of a sudden all doctors stopped working. If they had stopped operating, going out to dying patients, prescribing medicine? That would be a disaster! ... This is why I think that doctors deserve high wages, much higher than some manual workers, they don't do much, they just drink vodka all the time. (Valentyn, K) These uneducated ones, dirty alcoholics, just because they were the "working class," yeah, this foundation of our "communist society," right? And me, I have to sit quietly and be happy with my miserable salary.... And I should tell you, I have a PhD, every other year I am attending courses to improve my qualification, I deserve more! (Mykola, B)

Materially my respondents were on the lowest positions in society and they felt that the efforts they have invested into education and "improving qualifications" did not pay off in terms of higher wages. However, they felt they need to refer to some group that would be even lower than themselves, if not materially, then culturally. In particular, they pointed out some "positive aspects of life": high levels of cultural capital and service for the public good ("Imagine what would happen if all the doctors stopped operating?"). Svitlana, B, told a story of her neighbor, who was an alcoholic and often came to ask neighbors for food, because she was constantly running out of money. She saw in this "begging" a "lack of dignity." She also mentioned that alcoholics stole pails and metal poles from her garden for recycling ("so they can then buy vodka"):

> And they steal vegetables from our gardens ... why do they do that? Don't they fear God? I would rather starve than steal, never-ever would I take what belongs to somebody else! We are working, making all these sacrifices ... (Svitlana, B)

Noteworthy here is Svitlana's accent on "sacrifices." Senett and Cobb (1977) in their study The hidden injuries of class also noted their respondents' focus on making sacrifices to distinguish themselves both from the upper classes "who just have an easy living" and from "those on the dole." Svitlana describes "sacrifice" through "preserving dignity" and "working hard" as opposed to "being lazy" and "stealing." She tried to make sense of her suffering by opposing herself to the "bad people": the "oligarchs" who "just stole our money" on the one hand, and the "alcoholics" who steal from her garden.

Skeggs' (1997) research on working-class women taking courses in social care also shows how women, for whom middle class lifestyles were unattainable, invested into a "caring self" and "respectability." They described the middle classes as "snobby," "the posh ones," "hoity-toity" or "stingy" and themselves as "kind" and "caring" (pp. 92-93). At the same time, by constructing a "caring self" they tried to be seen as different from the working classes, whom they described as "poor," "rough," "battering their kids" or "those without jobs" (p. 75). Dis-identifications of my respondents and investment into respectability as a form of cultural capital are strikingly similar. Skeggs concludes that "in every judgement of oneself a measurement is made against others" (p. 74). My respondents make negative judgements against others in order to affirm their own identities by investing in respectability, sacrifice, "universal values" and public service.

Discrepancy Between "Structure" and "Habitus"

Makeyev (1999, p. 217) claims in post-communist societies "former conventions, rules and modes of interaction are either partly deinstitutionalized already or not completely institutionalized yet." People "lose control not only of processes that are happening in society as a whole, but also of reproduction of many in individual and group identities" (p. 216). On the one hand, the accent on the quality of social guarantees, and the glorification of the image of teachers, doctors, scientists and artists created a "heroic" image of a dedicated worker serving the public good. On the other hand, the accumulation of problems in the educational and health care systems, corruption and the questionable quality of service and of scientific and cultural output led to pps workers being ridiculed as corrupt, undedicated and unprofessional. The dichotomy between the "heroic" and "ridiculous" representations of workers (Stenning, 2005) illustrates well the underinstitutionalized "transitory" stage, in which a set of former dispositions does not correspond to new realities.

Using Bourdieu's terminology, I describe this dichotomy as the discrepancy between "structures" and "habitus" (Bourdieu & Wacquant, 1992). Such discrepancy results in ambivalence, dis-identification and, consequently, the social suffering of my respondents. The inconsistency in the interviews of my respondents "shows [the] psychological misery of men and women who are unable to construct a satisfactory life narrative" (Reid, 2002, p. 349). A good example of such inconsistency in determining an individual's own position and role in society comes from Serhiy.

When I asked him whether he was giving private lessons to students, he interrupted my question and said:

> Of course! If parents pay for private lessons, then why not? Of course, I give their children private lessons. There's nothing wrong with that! It's not a bribe, I'm working for this money, I'm teaching. If schools were private, it would be the same thing: parents paying for their children to get a good education. (Serhiy, B)

However, later on in the interview he tells the story of a gifted but poor student, who was very good at maths but who "had no chance of entering university, because his parents had no money, so the best he could hope for was the local agrarian college." He describes how he tried unsuccessfully to encourage him to continue, but the student lost all interest in maths.

> This is wrong. I think the state has to make sure that all talented children, no matter what family they come from, have an equal chance of developing their potential.... Previously there were sports clubs, and summer camps and fun things to do, but now all these centres are only for those kids whose parents can pay, and poor parents get angry.... I say I really wish these places were free, really. But parents don't believe me. They think I get some profit.... But this is simply not true!

In the second example he tries to resist the "ridiculous" image of a teacher as corrupt and interested only in personal profit ("They think I get some profit.... But this is simply not true!"), and appeals to a "heroic" image of disinterestedness and service ("I tried to encourage him" and "I really wish these places were free, really!"). At the same time, the first extract suggests that he himself was contributing in a way to this image of the teacher thinking about personal gain and using the logic of the market to justify his actions.

In a similar way Sasha, a rural doctor, admitted that he took bribes from patients, but at the same time refused to present it as his own choice, preferring to see it as a necessity:

> R: Yes, I ask for payments from patients, but that's because I need to buy medicines myself, and also because I need to work extra hours without any extra pay, and I need to sustain my family too.... I think if the state can't do it, then hospitals should become private.
>
> I: Do you think this would resolve problems? R: Yes, some of them.... Although I don't know, actually, whether it's a good idea. Many people are poor.... I had this one elderly man who was like that. He fought in the war, and didn't have any legs. I just morally

> couldn't ask him for anything.... I feel embarrassed having to ask for a bribe. I'd rather not do it. I feel really bad, really. (Sasha, S)

Sasha concluded that "the state probably should keep a few free clinics" but that he "personally wouldn't mind working in a private one." Understanding the demand for their skills and their possession of high levels of symbolic capital made my respondents more disposed to refer to market principles and try to "adapt" to capitalist norms ("I personally wouldn't mind working in a private clinic," or "I work for this money. If schools were private this is how it would be"). However, an awareness of social injustice when encountering a 'gifted but poor student' or a "war veteran" returns them to the "heroic" image. They see in the adaptation to capitalist norms a possibility to improve their own positions. But at the same time they are not sure "whether it's a good idea" and whether the losses will not be greater than the gains (which can also be described as the difference between considerations of personal and public good). Their own marginal positions make them more aware of the structural causes of their situation, but these processes that remain beyond their personal control also increase their suffering.

Habitus as "a Set of Potentialities"

Preferring the tactic of "adaptation" or "resistance" as a response to suffering, and placing the accent on professional qualities or on disinterestedness and service are not random but also reflect structural processes and each respondent's position in the field. Bourdieu explains that "habitus reveals itself—remember that it consists of a system of dispositions, that is, of virtualities, potentialities, eventualities—only in reference to a definite situation." His research with de Saint Martin (1982) on bishops provides an explanation of why my own respondents at times stressed on their "cultural superiority" while at others identified themselves with the other poor. In their research Bourdieu and de Saint Martin showed that under certain conditions—a specific time period, a specific province—bishops "would have asked the worshippers in their parishes to kiss their ring in a quasi-feudal aristocratic tradition, while under other conditions they become 'red' bishops, ... radical clergymen in the defense of the downtrodden" (as cited in Bourdieu & Wacquant, 1992, p. 135). For my respondents the "conditions" were found on the one hand in their real opportunities to use their own symbolic capital to make additional income, and in their experiences of structural injustice on the other. A good example of these "specific conditions" comes from Halia, who lost her job in the local newspaper in the early 1990s and moved to work in the library:

> Half of the people were unemployed here in our village ... and then our newspaper also let many workers go, including me.... At the same time our librarian retired, and I just grabbed the job, seriously, just grabbed onto it with hands and feet.... You know, I was already reaching my fifties. I didn't have the energy to hustle, to look for something, like the young people, but I didn't want to sit at home either. I wanted to do something useful for the people. (Halia, S)

Noteworthy here is that her investment in the "heroic" image of the pps worker ("I wanted to do something useful for the people") is caused by a lack of alternatives ("Half of the people were unemployed," "I just grabbed the job" or "I didn't have the energy to hustle"). Later in the interview she admits that if she were younger, she would have left the village either to look for work in the regional centre, or if she were a man - in Moscow, at the construction site—"where all our men go now."

> I: But would you leave despite the importance of your work in the library?
>
> R: Yes, I think I would. But that's not even a question, because I can't. This village doesn't have a future. It's true that here I'm treated with respect, but also with pity. The library, in truth, is lousy.... New books haven't been delivered for twenty years. All the old ones have been torn apart, especially those on the school curriculum. And now it's not a proper library anymore. It has been moved to the school, and when the school closes down, they'll move it to the regional centre.

Her interview shows feelings of hopelessness ("this village doesn't have a future") and of investing into disinterestedness and public service because other options were closed to her. Similarly, Hennadiy, a rural schoolteacher, also invested in the "heroic image." He has been working at his school for 35 years and directs the local museum, founded by his grandfather:

> When Bolsheviks destroyed the count's palace and then the church, my grandpa ... quietly ... took everything that was valuable there—dishes, gold, statues ... and the icons and the chalices from the church.... He took it all, so it wouldn't disappear. Then, when things calmed down, he suggested opening a local museum at a party meeting. Our village is the only one in the region that has such a museum! And as long as I'm alive, I'll take good care of it. Although, when I die, everything will probably be stolen and sold off.... Even now, it's been moved to the school, and the school will be closed down, because there are too few students.

Because of their dedication, Hennadiy and Halia are among the most respected people in the village, and following Bourdieu, their investment in "disinterestedness" has helped them achieve a high social status they would not otherwise have, due to their low level of economic capital. At the same time, economic hardships and social change add to their heroic images a sense of hopelessness ("the school will be closed down"), strikingly similar to the doctor's confession in Albert Camus's novel *The Plague:* "I don't know if what I am doing makes any sense, if anyone needs this. But I am a doctor and I have to do my work."

My respondents in Kyiv often gave quite contrary answers. Tamara, a journalist, said that there is always demand for good specialists: "whether you're a teacher, or a doctor, or an engineer, if you are doing your work professionally, then you'll have money as well." She gave examples from her own experience working at literary competitions, or as an editor—apart from her main job where her salary was also very low.

> I: But not everyone has the same opportunities to make money outside of their job. For example, one of my other respondents, a librarian....
>
> R: No, don't say that. My friend is a librarian. At the University. So first of all she bought a photocopying machine to make some money, and she's also renting out the reading room when the library closes—for some private English lessons I think. So those who wanted to adapt adapted quite well. (Tamara, K)

Tamara's investment in the "adaptation discourse" is a result of the opportunities she has to use her own knowledge (in the field of literature) and skills (editing) for personal material gain. She believed in the presence of some "absolute space" (Watson, 2000, p. 200) where nothing apart from the individuals themselves prevents them from adapting and becoming empowered. But such logic fails to explain why Halia, who 20 years ago would have been in the same position as Tamara's friend, does not buy a photocopying machine or rent out her library's reading room for private lessons. Tamara's explanation of "wanting to adapt" is insufficient, as most inequalities are created not by personal choice but by structural factors, and it is in response to these factors that different dispositions are formed. What it shows, though, is the common denial of structural privilege by the more successful pps workers, who perceive their success in purely individualistic terms, in line with the neoliberal ideology. It also shows what is at stake in the field of public service and, more generally, in post-Soviet societies as such: a change in people's "attitude" towards liberal values of individualism as a necessary element of successful transition to capitalism.

ANALYSIS AND CONCLUSION: "PROFESSIONAL" OR PUBLIC "SECTOR WORKER?"

Sapiro (2006) argues that "intellectual professions" have always occupied a position between the state, entrepreneurship and industry. In countries with a more liberal tradition (United States or United Kingdom), the "bourgeois model" of independence and entrepreneurship became dominant, whereas in states with a more bureaucratic tradition (such as the French, the German, and the Habsburg empires) accent was placed on "intellectual service and public functions." In the case of the USSR the only legitimate model for nonmanual labor was in public service, where "the well-educated and highly skilled had to find meaning in serving society, not accumulating wealth" (Leven, 2005, p. 449). On the contrary, now we are witnessing an attempt to reverse the dominant models.

The dissemination of neoliberal ideology in postcommunist Ukraine led to the individualized "adaptation discourse" (Ryabchuk, 2009) and also to changes in the field of public service. The World Bank (2005) describes the Ukrainian public service sector as "too large," "overstaffed" and "unsustainable," arguing for the need to diminish the extensive network of public services. These changes are similar to the transition from the welfare state (with its extensive system of social protection) to more neoliberal models in several countries of Western Europe. For example in France, Bourdieu et al. (1999, pp. 182-183) show how neoliberal writers associate "efficiency and modernity with private enterprise, and archaism and inefficiency with the public sector": They identify "modernization" with the transfer into the private sector of the public services with the most profit potential and with eliminating or bringing into line subordinate staff in the public services, held responsible for every inefficiency and every "rigidity."

Crouch (2004) notes that pps workers are encouraged by neoliberal commentators to focus on their professional skills and "to seek no means of social improvement other than for themselves, and their children obediently to climb the career ladders established by the business elites" (p. 60). Their wider concerns are not articulated, instead the focus is on the "inefficiency" of public services, "increasingly taken to mean that they want these privatized," according to Crouch. Therefore, despite the fact that both social scientists and politicians have spoken a lot about the concerns of this social category, they have defined them as entirely at one with the market economy and adaptation to new realities. This is a good example of an attempt to change the habitus: within the framework of neoliberal ideology Ukrainian pps workers are also encouraged to position themselves as "professionals," among the dominant classes, while disidentifying themselves from public service and possible solidarity with the dominated classes. However, as my findings show, any change in habitus is a very slow and painful process and causes social suffering for the people concerned.

In conclusion I would like to say, that one should not disregard the relation between the symbolic and structural transformations in post-soviet societies. It is important to ask where do different social representations, identifications (and dis-identifications) come from and what changes they may cause as a result. Bourdieu's theory was found especially useful in my research of Ukrainian professional public service workers precisely for its ability to explain "symbolic transformations" in discourses and ideologies that shape these workers' identities without forgetting about concomitant changes in objective structures in the field of public service.

APPENDIX A: METHODOLOGY AND RESEARCH PROCESS

Methodology

Twelve semistructured interviews with professional public sector workers were conducted in December 2005 (with four more in April 2006) in three selected communities of different size and with different patterns of transition. The interviews took place either at homes of the respondents or at their places of work. Interviewees gave consent before the beginning of the interviews, they were asked permission to record the talk (all of the interviews were taped) and were advised that they do not have to answer the questions they may find uncomfortable, and can interrupt the interview at any time if they do not wish to continue. My knowledge of Ukrainian language was a significant advantage in carrying out and analyzing the results of the research.

I selected one rural, one urban and one small town community emblematic of the difficulties of the transition processes. The rural community (abbreviated as "S" in the findings section) is situated in the Sumy region, in North-Eastern Ukraine: a region that experienced highest levels of unemployment during the transition period (World Bank, 2005). It is emblematic of a community in decline: a sugar producing plant closed down in the early nineties and a collective farm that was growing sugar beets for the plant collapsed subsequently. Formerly a relatively large village of over 5,000 inhabitants with its own school, hospital, and even a local newspaper, it decreased in size to less than a thousand inhabitants. Many workers in the public sector lost their jobs (the hospital and the newspaper closed down) and teachers from the local school fear unemployment, since the number of students has fallen significantly and there are discussions of closing the school as well. At the moment the community still has a library, several social clubs and a local ethnographic museum, but budget allocations to these services have decreased and they were all moved to the local school into one "socioeducational complex" to save on staff and maintenance expenses.

The small town community, Baryshivka (abbreviated as "B"), is situated in central Ukraine, 60 miles south-east of Kyiv. It is a town of 13,000 inhabitants with two schools, a kindergarten, a hospital, police and fire stations, a local newspaper, a city council building with its own statistical bureau, and a railway station. Most of town's industry collapsed in the early 90s, although now some small-scale enterprises were created. Since the town is relatively close to Kyiv (less than two hours by train) almost a half of the working population commutes to Kyiv to work. Forced daily work migration and insecurity of employment (temporary, seasonal or low-skilled jobs) characterize this community. Professional public sector workers earn salaries that are much lower than even some of the unskilled workers who commute to Kyiv, and to keep up a decent lifestyle have to engage in petty commerce, work on the land or adopt other survival strategies. This community is emblematic of "hustling," where people try to keep up a decent standard of living.

And finally, Kyiv (abbreviated as "K")—the capital of Ukraine, has been experiencing economic growth and has the lowest unemployment rate of less than three per cent (World Bank 2005). At the same time, Kyiv is exemplary of widening inequalities as the gap between the richest and the poorest of its inhabitants is very visible. Public sector workers, financed from the state budget, earn significantly less than workers in the dynamic private sector. Many possibilities offered for "adaptation" to new conditions by employment in the private sector leads to social suffering of professional public sector workers who are caught between their dedication to work and external pressures to "adapt" in order to make higher incomes.

Prior contacts and preliminary knowledge of communities I went to enhanced my understanding of the socioeconomic spaces where respondents came from, and helped build a less-distanced, nonhierarchical and informal relationship between them and myself as an interviewer. I have selected respondents through personal contact using "snowballing" technique. A common concern with nonprobability sampling is that some voices and points of view may not be taken into account. However, random sampling was not practical in my case, because of time and resource constraints. Furthermore, even in the case of non-representative sampling or case-studies it is still possible to develop more general theoretical statements about regularities in social structure and processes (Becker, 1970). I addressed concerns with how far the data can be generalized through careful selection of respondents from different professions within the category of PPS workers, of different socioeconomic backgrounds and of a variety of lifestyles. (For a list of respondents' age, gender, profession and income see Appendix B.) I asked two filter questions before beginning the interviews: whether a person has been working in the public sector both before and after the fall of the Soviet Union (although I did interview those respondents who either retired or changed jobs in the last five years), and whether a person experienced any suffering or discomforts related to transformations.

Research Process

1. September 2005: I have located secondary sources of data and visited communities selected for research (in order to get a preliminary idea of the social spaces that the respondents come from and to make initial contact and arrangements for interviews to be carried out at a later stage).
2. October-November 2005: I have reviewed relevant literature and secondary data from studies of poverty and social suffering in post-communist societies, while identifying an "under researched" area in existing studies, which turned out to be a the causes social suffering of PPS workers in postcommunist Ukraine.
3. December 2005-January 2006: I have collected primary data in the form of semi-structured in-depth interviews.
4. January-March 2006: I have transcribed the interviews and analyzed the relationship between social suffering of "mass intelligentsia" and the changing social structure. At this stage original hypothesis was modified according to the actual findings of my research, and second stage of interviewing followed in April 2006 for respondent validation (Silverman, 2001, p. 233)
5. March-May 2005: I have put together and analyzed the findings of my research in relationship to more general social processes taking place in postcommunist Ukraine, such as changing social structure and widening inequalities, changes in the field of public service, adaptation and resistance to postcommunist transformations.

Appendix B: Information on the Respondents (All Names Have Been Changed)

Profession	*Gender*	*Age*	*Income*
Urban community			
1. Katia: Museum worker	F	46	560
2. Natalia: Accountant, former engineer and lecturer	F	44	1,600
3. Nadia: Retired pre-school teacher	F	77	480
4. Tamara: Journalist, editor	F	52	700
5. Olena: University professor (English language)	F	49	1,500
6. Valentyn: Doctor (paediatrics)	M	53	690
Small town community			
7. Serhiy: Secondary school teacher (Physics, Maths)	M	54	560
8. Svitlana: Secondary school teacher (Ukrainian language)	F	38	470
9. Liuba: Self-employed, former elementary school teacher	M	53	900
10. Nina: Retired nurse	F	74	440
11. Vera: Statistician	F	50	480
12. Mykola: Journalist of a local newspaper	M	43	550
Rural community			
13. Oksana: Secondary school teacher (Ukrainian literature)	F	58	520
14. Hennadiy: Secondary school teacher and museum worker	M	59	560
15. Halia: Librarian	F	54	420
16. Sasha: Doctor (general practitioner)	M	57	540

REFERENCES

Becker, H.S. (1970). *Sociological work: Method and substance.* Chicago, IL: Adline

Bourdieu, P. (1993). *Sociology in question.* London: SAGE.

Bourdieu, P. et al. (1999) *The weight of the world: social suffering in contemporary society.* Stanford, CA: Stanford University Press.

Bourdieu, P., & Wacquant, L. (1992). *An invitation to reflexive sociology.* Cambridge, England: Polity.

Bourdieu, P., & de Saint Martin, M. (1982). La sainte famille : l'episcopat francais dans le champ du pouvoir. In : Actes de la recherche en sciences sociales, No. 44-45, pp. 1-53.

Burawoy, M., & Verdery, K. (1999) *Uncertain transition: Ethnographies of change in a post-socialist world.* Lanham, MD: Rowman & Littlefield.

Crouch, C. (2004). *Post-Democracy.* Cambridge, England: Polity.

Horetska, T. (2009). *Likari pozytyvno stavliatsia do ideji zaprovadzhennia platnoji medycyny u Kyjevi* [Doctors in favour of paid medicine in Kyiv—In Ukrainian]. Retrieved from http://www.radioera.com.ua/eranews/?idArticle=15282

Leven, B. (2005). Corruption and reforms: A case of Poland's medical sector. *Communist and Post-Communist Studies, 38*(4), 447-455.

Makeyev, S. (1999) Procesy socialnoji strukturaciji v suchasnij Ukrajini [Social structural processes in Ukraine - in Ukrainian] In: Ukrajinske suspilstvo na porozi tretioho tysiacholittia, sociolohichnyj monitorynh 1994-1999, Kyiv, IS NASU, pp. 214-232.

Reid, D. (2002) Towards a social history of suffering: Dignity, misery and disrespect. *Social History,* 27(3), 343-358.

Ryabchuk, A. (2009) The implications of adaptation discourse for post-communist working classes. *Debatte, 1,* 55-64.

Sapiro, G. (2006). Les professions intellectuelles, entre l'Etat, l'entrepreneuriat et l'industrie. *Le mouvement social, 214,* 3-24.

Senett, R., & Cobb, J. (1977). *The hidden injuries of class.* Cambridge, England: Cambridge University Press.

Silverman, D. (2001). *Interpreting qualitative data.* London: SAGE.

Skeggs, B. (1997). *Formations of class and gender.* Thousand Oaks, CA: SAGE.

Stenning, A. (2005) Where is post-socialist working class? Working-class lives in the spaces of (post-) socialism. *Sociology, 39*(5), 983-999.

Symonchuk, E.V. (2003). Srednij klass: liudi i statusy [Middle class: people and statuses, in Russian]. Kyiv: IS NASU.

World Bank. (2005). *Ukraine jobs study: Fostering productivity and job creation.* (Report No. 32721-UA). Washington DC: World Bank.

Watson, P. (2000). Rethinking transition: Globalism, gender and class. *International Feminist Journal of Politics, 2*(2), 85-213.

CHAPTER 17

DEPENDENT INDEPENDENCE

A Mechanism for Conciliating Determinism and Freedom

Maaris Raudsepp

The chapter by Ryabchuk (this volume) describes post-Soviet societal and symbolic transformations through the experiences of social agents, using Bourdieusian theoretical lens. Rapid transition from state socialism to liberal capitalism has produced profound structural changes in the societal field, mainly the redistribution of various forms of capital and setting new rules of the game. Public sector workers have lost their symbolic capital and are compelled to redefine their position and reconstruct their professional identity. The author describes this transition at a stage where pre-existing and new structures coexist and interact: respondents use contradictory values (disinterested service for public good versus seeking profit according to market logic) and demonstrate ambivalent, divided habituses (highly paid professionals versus humble public servants). It is a fluid uncertain state where old and new symbolic resources are mixed: hegemonic Soviet values like self-sacrifice, sense of social justice and solidarity are positioned in the new context of liberal values of individualistic profit-seeking and the imperative to compete in the new societal field.

Culture and Social Change: Transforming Society Through the Power of Ideas, pp. 297–322

This phenomenon of hysteresis has caused a discrepancy between the inert former habitus and the rapidly changing field, which is experienced as positional suffering. Former highly valued humanistic pathos, rejection of material values ("poverty is not vice") is now confronted with objective relocation in the societal field (becoming "the poor as the new underclass" —Bauman, 1998). The author gives us a glimpse into the variety of psychological tactics of adaptation to radical change and the use of social knowledge in new identity formation. Public sector workers attempt to preserve the distinctiveness of their group and its self-esteem by defining themselves in terms of special mission and heroic victimhood.

It seems to me that analysis of this process within Bourdieu's framework is only partly adequate, focussing on the deterministic side of the social change: public sector workers are depicted as passive victims of macrosocial transformations who have fallen into a "social trap" (Bauman, 1997) and discouraged by a sense of hopelessness. In order to see the whole picture of social change where social agents are "dependently independent" (Valsiner, 1987) and describe more precisely the processes of symbolic transformation, I propose to expand the author's theoretical framework with notions from the theory of social representations and cultural psychology.

In the Ryabchuk's (this volume) description I see the effects and interrelations of three distinct processes: (1) on the unreflective level there is slow change of habitus as a deterministic response to structural changes in the societal field; (2) on the reflective level, social agents recognize changes in the collective representational field and reposition themselves within it, and (3) social agents realize their semiotic freedom by using symbolic resources for various forms of adaptation. Only the third process can produce variety of responses within the same habitus, which can be observed in Ryabchuk's respondents.

In the present chapter, each one of these levels will be explored in turn. I will first characterize each one of these processes in terms of cultural psychology. Second, I will add some observations concerning Soviet and post-Soviet transformations in the Estonian context. The two empirical illustrations concern trajectories of successive acculturation described in biographical interviews of elderly people and modes of post-Soviet adaptation among Russian speaking minority.

A SYSTEM THAT CHANGES: OBJECTIVE CONFIGURATION OF POSITIONS IN A FIELD

The meaning of any change can be determined only in relation to a wider context, in relation to some bounded whole and other elements in it.

There are various conceptual models for describing how multiplicity of positions form a symbolic space and how this space functions as an integrated whole.

According Bourdieu (1991, 1992) the social world is a multi-dimensional space, differentiated into relatively autonomous fields of practice. Individuals occupy certain positions in these fields on the basis of the amount of different types of capital they possess. Field as a "space of relations" acts as a "structuring structure," in that it guides activities of its agents through sets of enduring dispositions (habitus) which in turn generate intentions and actions that reproduce the field structure. There is a structural isomorphism between field and habitus, and a dialectical relation between macro- and internalized (embodied) structures, both of which are objective, "albeit located at different ontological levels and subject to different laws of functioning" (Lizardo, 2004, p. 394).

Habitus is conceptualized as an emergent property of the social system, thus fully deterministic and unavoidable—an agent "falls into habitus" (Bourdieu & Wacquant, 1992) and acquires system-specific "patterns of perceiving, feeling, thought and behaviour" without conscious effort.

> The habitus is necessity internalized and converted into a disposition that generates meaningful practices and meaning-giving perceptions, it is a general, transposable disposition which carries out a systematic, universal application—beyond the limits of what has been directly learnt—of the necessity inherent in the learning conditions. (Bourdieu, as cited in Lizardo, 2004, p. 392)

Each habitus-related position determines a certain viewpoint, a certain vision of the social world. "Worldview ... are views taken from a certain point, that is from a given position within social space ... the vision that any agent has of space depends on his position in that space" (Bourdieu, 1990, p. 130). This vision includes not only a "sense of one's place," but also a "sense of others' place" and a sense of distance between the positions (Bourdieu, 1991, p. 235). In other words, it reflects both a particular position and the whole. All positions and respective viewpoints are relational.

In Bourdieu's framework the sources of representational variability (i.e., coexistent interpretations of different kinds) are (1) different positioning in the field, (2) different trajectories that have lead to certain positions, (3) patterns of relations and interactions with other positions in the field. Although Bourdieu conceptualizes habitus as an open system that is modifiable through experiences, he stresses determinacy and stability of the habitus-field synchronic relation (Holton, 1997).

CHANGING FIELD OF REPRESENTATIONS

In social psychology a very similar holistic and systemic model was created in the theory of social representations. According to this theory, systemic and hierarchically organized fields of social representations (shared meanings) contain all the symbolic resources that can be used for communication in groups and societies. This field provides shared intersubjective content and common dimensions of meaning. Individuals and groups may differently position themselves in relation to these dimensions, in accordance with the representations they use for constructing social objects and interpreting reality. Certain positioning is linked to a specific set of social representations, which can be defined as meaning making and stabilizing systems that are revealed in beliefs, images, emotions, activities, lay theories, regulative ideas and other forms of collective thought and interaction (see Wagner et al., 1999). Social representations express the characteristics of (collective) subject, object and their relationship (meaning), and describe the "domesticated worlds" of certain groups (Wagner, 1998).

Doise (1994) analyzes social representations as implicit organizing principles ("structuring structures"). These abstract underlying principles (categories, dimensions, reference points) reflect the regulative influence of the social metasystem on cognitive functioning and they organize symbolic relations between social agents (Doise, 1994). According to these principles individuals or groups identify and differentiate themselves, choosing their relative positions within the representational field. Doise Clemence, & Lorenzi-Cioldi (1993, p. 4) note that: "More than consensual beliefs SR are ... organizing principles, varied in nature, which do not necessarily consist of shared beliefs, as they may result in different or even opposed positions taken by individuals in relation to common reference points." These organizing principles are usually not directly observable but are deduced from a pattern of responses: they may be described as dimensions in the semantic space that structure individual positioning, or as a set of implicit rules. This is a structuralist approach, which stresses the importance of underlying structures in the social and cognitive metasystems. These structures determine the symbolic space ("representational field"), which delimits the possible choices of symbolic positioning for members of a group. Diversity in the social field means that individuals position themselves differently, engaging with any phenomenon from a particular point of view relative to other agents (Clemence, 2001).

Sources of representational variability are (1) the heterogeneity of the symbolic field, and (2) the different positioning in the field (group identity, pattern of interactions). Representational field is the arena for "battle of ideas for hegemony." The resulting temporary configuration of representations depends not only on the balance of societal forces behind the processes of concerted action and interaction, but also on the tactics of introduction of new ideas—for example, using different communicative genres in mass communication (Moscovici, 1961/2008) or intentional transformation of symbolic systems (Sen & Wagner, 2009). Societal change is accompanied by more or less radical changes in collective representational field, which acts as symbolic legitimation of the new social structure. At the same time, older layers of representations are preserved in subordinate positions.

Comparing the notions of habitus and social representation, Wagner and Hayes (2005) point to the crucial differences: habitus is prereflective, nondiscursive and inarticulate system of dispositions, while social representations are discursive, always potentially verbalized and actively used in communication. Bourdieu (as cited in Lizardo, 2004): "cognitive structures which social agents implement in their practical knowledge of the social world—function below the level of consciousness and discourse." Habitus cannot be communicated, argued, debated or negotiated, but social representations are inherently communicative, they emerge and evolve in discourse and argument. In other words—while habitus represents prereflective level of basic habitual tendencies, social representations function predominantly on a reflective, semiotic level. Only after successful anchoring social representations may become habitual and form nonconscious tacit knowledge, that is, unreflected "background of intelligibility, forming taken-for-granted commonsense" (Daanen, 2009). Thus we can differentiate two levels of social guidance: the societal field guides its agents via inert and unreflective habitus, and more dynamic representational field guides social subjects with the help of explicit social suggestions.

SEMIOTIC FREEDOM: POSITIONING IN PERSONAL SYMBOLIC FIELDS

In addition to objective structural and representational fields there is still another level where various positioning is possible—personal symbolic field of each person. Ability to construct unique personal symbolic fields and change positions in them is specific to humans. As the result, there is lack of isomorphism between the collective and personal cultures. Each individual is unique while based on the same background of collective culture (Valsiner, 2008b, p. 280). The same idea is expressed by Lotman (2010, p.185) in describing the duality of human beings: on the one hand, they are isomorphic with the semiotic whole they belong to, and at the same time, they are individualized parts of this whole.

There are bidirectional relations between individual and the structures he is part of. On the one hand, an agent is influenced by the structure of fields and the configuration of forces in them (leading to the formation of a certain habitus), but on the other hand, he is relatively free to choose semiotic tools (available forms of culture) for regulating his activity. Semiotic cultural psychology (e.g., Valsiner, 1994, 1998, 2000) provides a theoretical perspective that considers dialectical relationships between sociocultural determinism and individual agency. Valsiner (1997, 2000) introduces the principle of bidirectionality of cultural transmission: alteration of processes of interiorization and exteriorization that mediate the field of social suggestions (collective culture) and individual psyche (personal culture). He says:

> In terms of the *boundaries that define the range of possibilities* of behaviour, any organism is fully *dependent* on both its own structure and the structure of the environment. At the same time, *within* the boundaries of the set of possibilities, an organism ... may have the opportunity of choice between different ways of behaving, or constructing new ways of acting. (Valsiner, 1997, pp. 174-75)

Field and habitus provide structural constraints for individual choices of activity. Essentially semiotic character of psychological functioning, using signs and symbols as cultural tools for creating meanings and using these meanings in the process of self-regulation is the basis of individual semiotic freedom. Semiotic level entails higher psychological functions which regulate our reactions after the initial habitual reaction has occurred. Bourdieu and Wacquant (1992) also differentiate habitual and reflective levels of behavior:

> The Stoics used to say that what depends upon us is not the first move but only the second one. It is difficult to control the first inclination of habitus, but reflexive analysis, which teaches that we are the ones who endow the situation with part of the potency it has over us, allows us to alter our perception of the situation and thereby our reaction to it. (p. 136)
>
> Agents become something like "subjects" only to the extent that they consciously master the relation they entertain with their dispositions. They can deliberately let them "act" or they can on the contrary inhibit them by virtue of consciousness. Or they can—put one disposition against another. (p. 137)

Semiotic character of human psychological functioning (i.e., reflexive behavior) has liberating potential: it enables freedom from the here-and now situation and from social suggestions. Vygotski (1999, p. 470) makes the point eloquently:

> The ability of humans to escape enslavement to whatever stimuli they happen to encounter ... through the active construction and use of symbols.... Human activity which has emerged in the process of cultural-historical development, is free activity—i.e. independent from immediate/actual need and from actual perceived situation, it is an activity that is directed into the future.

Semiotic mediation is the basis for personal freedom: with the help of self-(re)constructed semiotic tools (interpretation of the situation) a person can transcend contexts, "even to become another, become 'Homo multiplex' ... stag[ing] another social drama in the subjective sphere" (Vygotski, as cited Fogel, Lyra, & Valsiner, 1997, p. 161). Modulation of distance from the here-and-now situation—from maximal distancing to total immersion—constitutes a flexible resource for the personality (Valsiner, 1998). On the one hand, distancing (i.e., semiotic mediation) allows for reflection on oneself and the situation in new ways and retain personal autonomy. On the other hand, it can be inflexible and constraining, thus creating "semiotic imprisonment" (e.g., subduing oneself to any kind of fundamentalist beliefs).

Semiotic level of functioning brings about principled unpredictability of human higher-level activities. Lotman (2010) even claims that unpredictability (*nepredskazuemost*) is the main difference of humans as "semiotic organisms" from animals. Flexibility, plasticity, and indeterminacy are inherent to cultural-symbolic systems themselves (Fogel et al., 1997) and to human semiotic activity in the individual's relations with the cultural surrounding (Litvinovic, 1997).

Valsiner (1997, 1998) describes the phenomenon of dependent independence (or bounded indeterminacy) where a person, confronting a system of structural (external and internal) constraints, afforded by the social metasystem and habitus, is relatively free to construct his own meaning system, strategies of action, and belief orientation. He is dependently independent with the environment. External system of semiotic resources consists of general guiding principles (redundant cultural messages, bricolage of social suggestions) that channel (direct) and constrain (determine) the range of individual choices (variability) in particular situations. Sociocultural constraints provide general principles that organize individual cognition and behavior. Most general guiding ideas (e.g., democracy, freedom) are fuzzy and inherently contain contradictory positions and dialectical oppositions. Such fuzziness enables great flexibility in individual interpretation and positioning in relation to these guiding principles.

The power of semiotic freedom in personal culture may be realized in resisting external pressures. "Culture (as the system of semiotic operators) guarantees that any person would be ready to resist and counter-act social suggestions by the environment" (Valsiner, 2008b, p. 279). Similarly, Bauman (1976, p. 11) claims:

> The most dramatically distinctive feature of culture is the notorious ... human ability to decline to learn, to resist the conditioning pressure, to "make responses" to "stimuli" which are not preset in any imaginable material sense. Inventiveness, originality verging on waywardness characterize human beings at least as much as their ability to learn and their capacity for being conditioned.

An example of dialectical relation between societal control and semiotic freedom can be the strategy of silent resistance in Soviet mass media and literature. Strong external pressure was balanced by modes of creativity: explicit control was overcome by various "circumvention strategies" by writers and journalists—messages were communicated in disguised form (e.g., Lauk & Kreegipuu, 2010). Readers developed the skill to "read between the lines"—to catch the implicit message behind the explicit content.

Art is thus an exemplary sphere of semiotic freedom (see also Sayles, this volume). Lotman (2010, pp. 233, 236) stresses the role of art as the sphere of free meaning making: "art is the sphere of freedom compared to reality," "art leads a person into the realm of freedom, into the realm of mental experiments." Both human beings and art are inherently generators of unpredictability (*masterskaja nepredskazuemosti*). Lotman describes two mechanisms of semiotic activity: making familiar unfamiliar (analysis) and making unfamiliar familiar (synthesis). Defamiliarization (*ostranenie*—see Shklovski, 1925/1990) has been described as an artistic technique of forcing audience to see common things in an unfamiliar or strange way, in order to enhance perception of the familiar. Similar semiotic shift can be performed in everyday situations by any human being. "Semiotic behavior is always the result of a choice—transposing freedom from the sphere of ideas and theories into real life" (Lotman, 1992b, p. 321). Purposeful transformation of the representational field in post-revolutionary Russia was characterized by semiotization of behavior (Lotman, 2007)—for example, imitation of heroes and events of the French revolution. A historical example of such transposition is conscious semiotization of everyday behavior by a subgroup of Russian nobility in the 19th century (the Decembrists). Their aim was to enact high ideals (heroism, honor, freedom) in everyday behavior, to give high-minded meaning to their life. Semiotically marked behavior (e.g., imitation of exemplary personalities from history, cultivation of everyday civic virtues) as conscious choice was opposed to the routine habitual behavior (Lotman, 1992a). Human life may be purposefully organized according to the principles of artistic text, by borrowing various scripts and meaning contexts from the pool of cultural resources (see Mikita, 1999).

Semiotic self-regulation proceeds via different mechanisms: by transforming cultural forms into personal resources (Zittoun, 2007), by dialogical positioning, choosing positions in a symbolic field (Hermans, 2002; Raggatt, 2007), constructing meaning through dramatization, and creating an imaginary reality. Semiotic self-regulation becomes especially relevant in critical periods in one's life trajectory, which are strongly influenced by abrupt macrosocial changes (Zittoun, Duveen, Gillespie, Ivinson, & Psaltis, 2003).

Personal positioning may be understood as freedom and duty: translation of macrosocial influence (i.e., general meanings and social suggestions) into concrete situations, activities and tasks, with which an individual is engaged, and the coordination of macro- and microlevels. Taking a position means establishing some relationship with the representational whole and other elements within it. Even in occupying a fixed role position, a person has freedom to modify his inner personal position to express different modalities, styles or genres of representation (e.g., serious or humorous).

Subjective movement in the symbolic field, change of positions leads to the change of meanings, point of view (e.g., adopting the viewpoint of an actor or an observer). By adopting other positions and viewpoints a person develops his reflective abilities (Gillespie, 2006). Individual can modify his position in relation to sociocultural context along various dimensions, for example, between being "in" or "out" of the situation, playing different roles, realizing different modalities, relying on different representations, and so on. Zittoun, Gillespie, Cornish, and Aveling (2008) stress that heterogeneity (multivoicedness) of social knowledge can be used as a resource for personal distancing. One may also choose to be regulated by another representational field (e.g., artistic or playful or religious context). Semiotic freedom, in the Soviet reality of late socialism, is described by Yurchak (2005, p. 28):

> The performative shift of authoritarian discourse—that occurred in the 1950s and 1960s allowed Soviet people to develop a complex differentiating relationship to ideological meanings, norms and values. Depending on the context, they might respect a certain meaning, norm or value, be apathetic about another, continue actively subscribing to a third, creatively reinterpret a fourth, and so on. These dispositions were emergent, not static. The unanimous participation of Soviet citizens in the performative representation of speech acts and rituals of authoritarian discourse contributed to the general perception of that system's monolithic immutability, while at the same time enabling diverse and unpredictable meanings and styles of living to spring up everywhere within it. In a seemingly paradoxical twist, the immutable and predictable aspects of state socialism, and its creative and unpredictable possibilities, became mutually constitutive.

There is potentially limitless number of semiotic contexts, each of which with specific affordances (obstacles and opportunities) for the agent, providing tools for self-regulating and construction of meaning. Yet there are external and internal constraints to symbolic freedom: institutions constraining free meaning-making, limited access to cultural resources, the "scope" of semiotic horizon.

Habitus/mindset as a relatively stable system of dispositions, reflecting the conditions of its production, may also be used as a resource for adaptation and making sense of changing conditions. It is a mechanism that connects past with the future. In the changed environment it may be useful to preserve the old habitus in a latent form, ready for use in homologous conditions. We can speculate that remnants of Soviet habitus—resilience, flexibility, disguised resistance, idealism, heroism, self-sacrifice, collectivism, disposition of equality—may become a resource in appropriate conditions.

The situation of post-Soviet tranformations described by Ryabchuk (this volume) involves three levels of semiotic freedom: (1) making sense of the post-Soviet societal transformation as a whole, (2) making sense of one's changed position as a group member or one's changed position on personal level (identity shift), and (3) regulating distance from the here and now situation. Paradoxically the victims of the transformation tend to be reluctant to use the cultural elements of the socialist culture as resources for adaptation or resistance to changes (Eyal, Szelenyi, & Townsley, 1998). The strike described in Ryabchuk's chapter is a rare exception.

RESPONSES TO CHANGES: A MODEL OF PERSONAL RESPONSES TO STRUCTURAL CHANGE

External changes, novelty in the (cultural, political, social) environment, new rules of the game, perceived contradictions (between alternative and dominant representations, field and habitus, etc.) evoke inner activity. A changed situation requires a person to choose personal positions in the new whole, to realize his or her semiotic freedom. The process involves negotiations of the active person with the diverse collective-cultural suggestions and choice of personal response strategy, for example, buffering, neutralization, ignoring, transforming, or evaluation of social suggestions (Valsiner, 1998, pp. 393-394). On the one hand, there is more or less explicit social guidance, while on the other, there is a person's active construction of meanings, conforming or counteracting to (re)socialization efforts. Bounded indeterminacy is characteristic to this process: each social regulator creates the unity of both stability and flexibility. In other words, it creates at least two possibilities: to follow the regulation or to transgress it (Valsiner 2007); there is always a range of alternative responses within the given constraints. Dialectical opposition between obedience and disobedience or of adoption and rejection is described in Ryabchuk's chapter where "simultaneous attempts to adapt to structural changes and to resist them" were observed in public sector workers.

Meeting any semiotic challenge (new idea or practice, new norm, new ideology, alien culture) a person is caught by the emerging tension between opposing tendencies to accept or to reject the novelty. These dynamic oppositions define a continuum of possible responses. Let us describe some relatively stable positions on that continuum—denial, resistance, conformity and creative synthesis—to which both unreflective and reflective processes may lead.

Modes of Denial

Total denial—rejection of the novelty, which may be realized in exit, retreat, withdrawal, physical re-positioning (emigration), and maximal distancing. In Bourdieu's terms it means leaving the field, denial of the game, or choosing another field. On the representational field such distancing may take the form of absolute intolerance or erecting 'semantic barriers' in relation to the novelty—for example, the rhetorical tactics utilized by the French Communist Party to dismiss psychoanalysis, which entered society as a new idea in the 1950s (Gillespie, 2008).

Partial denial—remaining in the field but isolating oneself: "inner emigration," self-isolation, preserving old habitus in the changed field (e.g., Russian old believers' communities), survival of old representations and patterns of behavior. External field may change but a person preserves inner position on previous or alternative fields (e.g., vertical religious dimension), islands of previous mindset in the changed conditions (e.g., circles of prerevolutionary aristocracy in Soviet society (Chuikina, 2006). Ethiopian immigrants moving to Israel retain their core representations of the traditional society—diffuse (vs. differentiated) social roles, personal (vs. universal) criteria of fairness, ascribed (vs. achieved) status, loyalty to primary (vs. task oriented) groups, and so on. Such implicit system of societal representations prevents them from integrating into modern society and leave them in isolation (Levin-Rozalis, 2000). Berry's (2003) separation/isolation strategy in acculturation process seems to pertain to this category. This response may be collective or individual. Forcible individualization of response has been described by Bauman (1998, p. 189): "The post-modern society—interprets any extant and prospective social issue as a private concern ... de-socializing the ills of society." Public sector workers in Ryabchuk's (this volume) chapter seem to be subjected to such individualization of suffering. Hysteresis, inertia of mindset describes this response mode on the nonreflective level. On the reflective level a person may consciously try to preserve the old meaning complexes as an opposite process of changing them. Some analogy can be here seen with Sztompka's (2004) adaptation mode of retreatism (passivity, resignation) and ritualism.

2. Modes of Resistance

Active resistance may include activity directed at the changing of reality (dissident movements, voluntary associations, change of habits and rituals, individual protest actions like demonstrative violation of rules) (cf. rebellion strategy in response to cultural trauma in Sztompka, 2004). Castro and Batel (2008) describe resistance to novelty on individual, relational and institutional levels, using discursive arguments in public debate against new norms. Sayles (this volume) describes humor as a subversive form of social resistance.

On nonreflective level we can speak about "resistance or protest habitus," unconscious tendency to oppose any change or to exhibition of power in the form of rigid and strong external pressure. An example may be the notion of reactive identity (Vetik, Nimmerfeld, & Taru 2006)—a subjectivity formed in the process of constructing an "us-them" relationship in reaction to perceived assimilative pressure. It results in the solidification of old identities, strengthening of rigid identity boundaries. Personal unreflective resistance may be a response to excessive semiotic abundance ("semiotic over-determination") in the environment: automatic affective resistance can be expressed as ignoring omnipresent advertisements or rejecting monotonously repetitive social suggestions (cf. Valsiner, 2008a). Resistance may arise from the incompatibility of social suggestions with the existing habitus or identity. Jensen and Wagoner (2009, p. 226) describe resistance to transcendent representations if they do not resonate with the habitus: "The habitus ... becomes the fundamental unit of adoption or rejection when a new transcendent representation seeks acceptance in the immanent domain" (p. 222). Duveen (2001) defines resistance as "the point where an identity refuses to accept what is proposed by a communicational act, that is, it refuses to accept an attempt to influence" (p. 269). Unreflective resistance may acquire the status of a specific cultural form, like Estonian stubbornness/obstinacy (*eesti jonn*), which supports individual and collective resistance to any external pressure. Cultivation of resistance habitus may be a priority in socialization. The definition of "new Soviet man" included both conformist and resistance elements (Oushakine, 2004). Analyses of Soviet literature for children show prevalence of romantic ideals and behavior models exhibiting heroic resistance to oppression (O'Dell, 2010).

On reflective level resistance may be accompanied by argumentation—for example, criticism of liberal capitalism by Bourdieu (1998, 1999); Gandhi's project of nonviolent disobedience to colonial power (e.g., Sen & Wagner, 2009) and other examples of civic courage; courageous resistance as a special case of altruism (Shepela et al., 1999). On this level resistance needs semiotic scaffolding.

> The feeling of being in a trap is not enough, however, to raise those affected out of their predicament. At most, it can furnish the energy of disaffection needed for the change. But it must be guided and channelled, it must be given a name which relates individual suffering to the supra-individual roots of unhappiness. (Bauman, 1976, p. 110)

3. Modes of Social and Cultural Conformity

Examples of this strategy are the acceptance of the changed sociocultural reality, reinterpretation of one's own position and the positions of others; adoption of new hegemonic ideas (and "forgetting" previous ones), conversion, creating new I-position, redefinition of one's identity from a new point of view, obedience, stoic acceptance, humble submission. Similar kinds of response have been described as assimilation strategy in the acculturation process (Berry, 2003), or legitimizing identity—acceptance and rationalization of dominant institutions of the society (Castells, 1997).

In a nonreflective form it describes the situation where habitus coincides with the external structure, the world seems to be "normal," taken for granted, evoking passive "surfing on the waves," compliance and conformity. An example may be the phenomenon of "performative conformism" during late socialism—people performed speech acts and rituals as a "reproduction of social norms, positions, relations and institutions," reproducing themselves as a "normal" Soviet persons (Yurchak, 2005, p. 25).

When changes are smooth and slow, they do not provoke unreflective resistance: people begin to realize only gradually that something radical has changed in guiding principles. Gradual socialization of people into totalitarian regime in Nazi Germany is a historical example of this (e.g., Grunberger, 2005),

On the reflective level this mode of response may include calculated acceptance, opportunism. Goffman (1961, as cited in Jensen & Wagoner, 2009) describes conversion as an appearance of compliance with the norms (actually performing disguised passive rejection). But compliance may be also an active choice. "The person can, actively, take the role of "passive recipient" of cultural messages. This entails direct acceptance of / cultural messages/as givens, without modifications.... By active construction of the role of "passive recipient" the person temporarily aligns oneself with the "powerful others" (Valsiner, 1994, p. 255).

4. Creative Synthesis

Creative synthesis involves bringing together different influences (old and new social suggestions, treated as dialectical oppositions), through mutual dialogical modification, social inventiveness, transcending to a meta-level, finding a third way, constructing hybrid (higher order) identities, generating new ideas, breaking old meanings and stereotypes, arriving at new understanding, and transforming social rules and roles (see also "social constructiveness"—Wagoner, 2012, this volume). This response expresses individual creativity and unpredictability. A classical example is Sigmund Freud's ingenuity: when the Nazi powers insisted that he sign a statement saying he was not mistreated (as a condition for leaving Austria in 1938), he added sarcastically: *Ich kann die Gestapo jedermann auf das beste empfehlen* (I can heartily recommend the Gestapo to everyone). An example may also be creative "domestication" of official ideology as an everyday practice in late socialism: "Instead of resisting ideology wholesale, he effectively domesticated it, making it meaningful in his life" (Yurchak, 2003, p. 502), while reproducing the ideological system on the formal level, "many Soviet people—creatively reinterpreted the meanings of the ideological symbols, deideologizing static dogmas and rendering communist values meaningful on their own terms" (p. 504).

This response type has similarities with Castell's (1997) project identity, which seeks to redefine identity by transforming the overall social structure or with Berry's (2003) integration strategy in the process of acculturation, which tries to synthesize elements both from the host culture and culture of origin. Similarly Sztompka (2004) describes innovative adaptation strategies in response to cultural trauma—redefining the situation in positive terms, increasing one's social and cultural resourcefulness and attempting radical transformation of culture. These strategies are active and future oriented. Here again we can observe processes on two levels: unreflective realization of creative dispositions, and conscious effort to find new solutions. Different psychological techniques can be used for reaching creative synthesis:

- play: "Even in the universe par excellence of rules and regulations, playing with the rule is part and parcel of the rule of the game." (Bourdieu, 1990, p. 89)

- choosing different modalities, styles and genres of speech and action, for example, dramatization; using humour and irony, romanticizing or poeticizing the reality through elevated style, idealization of the actual together with the actualization of the ideal" (Valsiner, 2000, p. 58);
- positioning at the crossroads of between multiple symbolic worlds (cf. Gillespie, 2006, 2007), for example, creative potential of multicultural persons or persons with split (divided) habitus—situated in border spaces in society and during times of swift social change;
- defamiliarization: production of new meanings by making the familiar unfamiliar (Wagoner, 2008);
- expanding the relevant context temporally and spatially or actualization of another (imaginary) representational field. For example, in dialogical process of identity construction "in order to define our being in relation to the other perspective, we may evoke other voices and dialogues from other time and space contexts, thus expanding the ongoing dialogue temporally and spatially" (Märtsin, 2010, p. 78); for distancing from the harsh reality of war, a person may actualize an alternative context—Juri Lotman used to study French grammar while being a soldier during World War II (Lotman, 1995/2010); a young woman used fiction for turning routine work in home front fields into a poetic experience (Zittoun et al., 2008, p. 172).

Lotman (1992a) differentiates dualistic and ternary systems—in the first class of systems abrupt change destroys the old system entirely, in ternary systems abrupt change leads to partial preservation of the old and the synthesis of a new whole on the basis of old elements. Postsocialist social transformations tend to deny the past entirely. Still there are more creative possibilities.

> Instead of segmenting itself from the socialism, instead of identitying the future in terms of the negation of the past, transition culture might find a more creative reconciliation with it. We might anticipate then, a transition made not by negating socialism, but by establishing a more creative fusion with some of those elements that people miss, civility among them. (Kennedy, 2002, p. 275)

Different strategies may be used in different spheres of activity and situations. People may resist changes in one field and express complicity in another, there may be different levels of rigidity (flexibility) and various dynamics of positions. There may be dialogues (or lack of them) between "conformist self" and "resistant self" within the same person.

What are the processes that have lead to such heterogeneous pattern of adaptational modes? There is interplay between structural affordances (habitus, preexisting structures of meaning and practice), positioning on the representational field and using cultural elements as adaptation resources, and individual creativity (semiotic freedom). Cultural elements may act as scaffolding/contextual support for any strategy from conformism to resistance (e.g., providing exemplary cases of heroic resistance to illegitimate oppression). There may be more profound cultural logic behind the pattern of responses (e.g., avoiding interpersonal resistance in the Asian cultures).

Choice of modes of response stems from the interaction between unreflective and reflective levels, structural constraints and free choice. We can suppose that similar external patterns of response (e.g., resistance) are produced by different inner activities and mechanisms—for example, habitual unconscious dispositions and/or conscious deliberate choice between various alternatives, which depends on the available range of interpretative perspectives.

The overview of the theoretically possible choices gives us a wider context for understanding the realized and unrealized options of the "heroic victims" of post-Soviet transformations, depicted by Ryabchuk. In the next section, we will consider two additional empirical illustrations of this process, taken from studies currently being conducted in Estonia.

TWO EMPIRICAL ILLUSTRATIONS

Long Life Trajectories and Personal Adaptation Strategies

Traditionally acculturation has been conceptualized as a relatively short-term process that accompanies contacts between representatives of different cultures. Here acculturation has been studied diachronically, as a life-long process of adaptation to different sociopolitical regimes. Sociopolitical regime can be considered as a qualitatively distinct system of social suggestions. The aim of the study (Raudsepp, 2012) was to describe retrospectively such systems and their succession from the viewpoint of individual agents. How do people perceive relevant social suggestions of different regimes? What had they to learn and de-learn when a regime was replaced (semiotic means for displaying loyalty, hierarchy of social identities, legitimizing myths, etc.)? How did they maintain and reconstruct their identities in this process? Did they change conception of the self? How did they experience acculturation stress? What strategies were used for realization of personal freedom? What is the meaning of transitional de-structuration?

Empirical material consists of autobiographies and interviews with people who have experienced various political regimes and transitional periods during sociocultural changes. Estonian society has undergone several changes of sociocultural paradigms, processes of (re)adaptation and (re)culturation. Different paradigms have preserved as latent layers of culture, which should not be ignored in any analysis. Recent layers, carried by still living generations are: pre-war democracy and mild autocracy (the so called Estonian time), Fascist and Stalinist totalitarian regimes, mild Soviet regime, transitional anarchy, and liberal democracy. At present we are experiencing sociocultural heterogeneity: Estonia is both democratic, post-Soviet and globalizing. Different age cohorts carry different layers of meaning. Discrete sociopolitical systems are used for explaining and interpreting biographical events. Representatives of the oldest cohort have unique skills in adapting to arbitrarily changing structural forces and realizing their personal agency. They have experienced successive changes of (1) societal power fields (and respective habitus), (2) profound transformations of collective representational fields (new hierarchies of regulative ideas), (3) individual semiotic transformation of personal meaning fields. They have adapted to heterogeneous representational fields to which each consecutive social change adds specific elements and structures.

A generation is not homogeneous. Different choices in critical periods have differentiated this generation into distinct units that are charaterized by different trajectories through changing societal fields (Aarelaid, 2006; Corsten, 1999). Different modes of adaptation were partly determined by the logic of trajectory and positioning on sociocultural fields.

People who were born in the 1920s and met the same sociopolitical challenges in Estonia, could choose three general trajectories: denial (emigration), resistance or loyalty. Now there are two main interpretive frames for presenting their life stories: dominant nationalistic one and the former Soviet frame, used today as an act of passive resistance.

Among our respondents there were representatives of contrasting trajectories. An exemplary biography of actively resisting to Soviet regime, being victim of repressions, experiencing rehabilitation and finally public heroization has produced clear self-image of autonomous reckless fighter, "toughened up in Stalin's universities." A contrasting trajectory of conscious pro-Soviet choice, active participation in the Soviet transformations, and subsequent repositioning from the center to periphery of the symbolic field, from hero to antihero position in post-Soviet time, has produced a hybrid identity, aimed at reconciliation and compassion towards former victims. In both cases strong contextuality of life choices could be observed: there was a tendency to comply or resist to new social suggestions as an imitation of the choices of relevant others.

The following is a list of the various modes of symbolic coping that have been applied by our respondents:

1. Separation of old and new social suggestions (e.g., celebrating separate holidays by different members of the same family—socially disapproved Christmas for an old grandmother and approved New year's Eve for children, socialized in soviet institutions).
2. Self-distancing, isolation from the changed reality (e.g., private continuation of celebrating Soviet holidays, reluctance to express one's opinions in public).
3. Selective acceptance of novelty and selective denial of old representations and practices (e.g., separation of worlds of political necessity and individual freedom).
4. Creative integration of novelty and the familiar, synthesis of all regulative ideas into a meaningful symbolic system, metaposition in relation to closed ideologies (e.g., synthesis of nationalism and humanism, Estonian nationalism and Soviet mentality).

Transitional periods between different regimes are characterized by weakened structural determinism and higher level of individual agency. Transition periods are perceived as opening new opportunities and setting new barriers. Replacement of one sociopolitical system with another makes "visible" relevant structural determinants. Reflection arises when new social representations interfere with the old ones. Persons with long and varied life trajectories have habituated to ever-occurring political changes and modulation of psychological distance from varying social suggestions. Optimal social, cultural and biological capital has lead to wise and happy old age, although there is some disappointment in post-socialist reality (e.g., regretting the exclusion of many social groups and the disappearance of solidarity).

Structural Suffering and Semiotic Freedom of Estonian Russians

Approximately one third of the Estonian population is Russian-speaking non-Estonians who moved to Estonia during the Soviet period. They do not perceive themselves as immigrants as they were moving inside the territory of the former Soviet Union. Many of them tend to retain the Soviet identity long after the state has disappeared.

Brubaker (2000) introduces the term "accidental diasporas," which differ from ordinary migrants in three aspects: (1) accidental diasporas are formed due to the moving boundaries through people, not people over boundaries (2) they are formed abruptly, under the influence of dramatic and often traumatic reconfigurations of political spaces, and (3) they are formed without the participation and against the will of the diaspora members. Specificity of Estonian Russians as an accidental diaspora are sometimes overlooked. They provide a good example of the interaction between profoundly changed social field and inertia (hysteresis) of habitus.

This group found itself among the losers of transformation. Structural changes occurred on two levels: on the social field the group's position was changed (degraded into an ethnic minority status), and the group was recategorized (formerly legitimate Soviet co-citizens were officially relabelled as immigrants, deprived of automatic citizen rights in the new nation state). On the level of social representations the group began to be negatively marked, recategorized as occupants and oppressors. As a group they represented the unwanted Other (Petersoo, 2007) and experienced significant reduction of symbolic capital, as the Russian language was eliminated from the public sphere. Their very presence became unwelcome, they became strangers in their own home. Alienated from their habitus, many of them felt anxiety, ontological insecurity, and a sense of betrayal. Redefining one's identity (repositioning on the new social field) and change of the previous habitus was required.

After 20 years of the beginning of sociopolitical changes in Estonia local Russians have moved along different trajectories and have chosen various tactics of adaptation. By 2010 the distribution of citizenship choices is as follows: 50% of Russophones have naturalized into Estonian citizens, 25% of Russophones have opted for the citizenship of Russians Federation, 25% of local Russophones have remained stateless (aliens). These groups differ in their levels of integration into Estonian society, (re)definitions of identity, and acculturation strategies (Kruusvall, Vetik, & Berry, 2009).

What are the conditions for choosing one or another type of strategy? What are the conditions for realizing one's semiotic freedom, using cultural resources for symbolic coping? On one hand, there are structural constraints and affordances (social and cultural capital), channelling the particular choice, and on the other—availability of semiotic support for personal choices (e.g., resistance narratives). Various modes of adaptation to structural changes, described above, are realized in this particular context (citations are drawn from a recent focus group study (Raudsepp, 2010) among Estonian Russophones):

1. Exit, retreat, physical repositioning (emigration to Russia or other countries) ("*I do not like to live in Estonia, I do not feel comfortable here and I do not intend to stay here.*" Female, 22 yrs.).

2. "Inner emigration," self-isolation, preserving old habitus ("*My homeland is Soviet Union. Although it does not exist any more, I consider it still my homeland.*" Male, 25 yrs.). Specific mode of existence in Estonia is being "a person without definite citizenship" with a grey-colored alien's passport, it means being on a politically marginalized position.
3. Resistance to changes, protest, opposition. Vetik et al. (2006) describe the phenomenon of reactive identity—strengthening of rigid identity boundaries in response to strong external pressure. Russian citizenship may be a form of protest identity in Estonia. Reactive identity may take different forms, depending on the particular context. As a reaction to overwhelming pressure towards national identity, various kinds of "non-national" identities—either sub-national (local), ethno-cultural (e.g., Russian, ex-Soviet) or supra-national (e.g., European, Baltic) may become dominant. Vihalemm and Kalmus (2008, p. 23) maintain that "global orientation can be understood as pragmatic resistance, an opportunity for the minority to express contra-national identity". Excessive pressure to learn Estonian may lead to reactive refusal: "*I began to hate the Estonian language after they began to impose it forcefully. If I find that a language is necessary for me, I will learn it. If they enforce it, I will not learn it in principle*" (Female, 20 yrs.). Disguised resistance can be noticed among Russians who speak fluent Estonian and yet carry protest mentality—even the most integrated group shares dissatisfaction of the non-Estonians and perceives collective discrimination. Kennedy (2002) analyzes the position of Russian speakers in the context of transition and new ideology:

    In the old system, they argued, there was an inner freedom that ironic detachment could preserve. In the new system, freedom brought a new disposition that cannot be escaped. Ideology and everyday life resonate in ways that make inner freedom more difficult. Thus, although freedom might be associated with market and the future, and ideology with the place and the past, some of our subjects found a new kind of unfreedom in the present, and an intellectual quality lost in the past. (Kennedy, 2002, p. 188)

4. Social or cultural conformity, acceptance of the changed reality, redefinition of one's identity from a new point of view, conversion, assimilation, adopting dominant social representations (sometimes leading to "super-Estonization"). This is the path leading to Castells' (1997) legitimizing identity—acceptance and rationalization of dominant institutions of the society.

5. Creative synthesis, dialectical solution of the tension between system and agent, transcending to a metalevel, finding a third way is realized in hybrid identities, higher-order identities and the generation of new utopias. Interview studies (Hachaturyan, 2010) have shown that a socially active group of young Estonian Russians have disidentified themselves both from father or motherland and developed a strong supranational identity, defining themselves as Baltic Russians, Europeans or world citizens (*"We are outside the state, of this structure, we are a little bit above it"*). Ethnic identity has only instrumental meaning for them, language is perceived as a means of communication and thought, and not a rigid identity marker. Instead of monoethnicity, multiculturalism and multiple situation-specific identities are prioritized. Their mode of adaptation includes strong sense of mission and practical activities for the benefit of society.

CONCLUSION

Structures tend to change, sometimes very abruptly and extensively. Change of structures with human component proceeds in the interaction of structural determinism and individual creative freedom. There are three levels of interrelated changes: (1) objective and internalized structures—that is, social fields (with the emergent habitus), (2) "battle" of ideas and repositioning on representational fields, and (3) individual creativity in personal meaning fields, directed and constrained by the above mentioned two levels.

Rapid changes promote shifts on different levels: moving out of one's habitus ("comfort zone") while adapting to structural changes, and moving in the representational space in the process of realizing one's semiotic freedom.

> In Bourdieu ... there is the possibility—even the historical necessity—of a constant destabilization and a constant modification of common sense.... The world's meaning must be continually be reaffirmed and/or reconstructed as common sense precisely because it is a historical world constantly open to challenge and to struggle, because the possibility continues to exist that its meaning may slip away and be replaced with other meanings. (Holton, 1997)

There is positive and creative potential in a traumatogenic change—sociocultural trauma may be a "force of social becoming" (Sztompka, 2004, p. 194). Being out of balance may thus be a catalytic condition for the creation of novelty. Art is a cultural mechanism for modeling disequilibrium states and their overcoming.

Ryabchuk's chapter highlights a dramatic shift in radically changing social context of post-Soviet world. In the commentary I tried to complement this deterministic picture with the notion of semiotic freedom. Victims of social changes after repositioning on the societal field are still free to apply various semiotic adaptation modes, which may cure and compensate structural suffering.

We analyzed social change on two levels: unreflective level of habitus and reflective level of semiotic reconstruction. On the level of changing fields and changing habituses mainly deterministic processes occur. Interaction between individual sense-making and social knowledge (elements of representational field) produces unpredictability. Symbolic transformations of cultural elements are realized in the conditions of semiotic freedom, which leads to variable and unpredictable forms of individual adaptation to the changing reality. Together these two processes realize the bidirectionality of cultural transmission and enable the "deterministically indeterministic" course of human development in history and ontogeny (Valsiner, 1997, p. 238).

This is a never-ending circular process, whereby people are capable of creating novel meaningful situations (new ideas, semiotic means) and "to enter into those, to let themselves be guided by those, and distance oneself from those" (Valsiner, 1998, p. 388). Human beings create their problems through the use of cultural tools and they then try to use other tools to solve these problems. They are free to choose and create the semiotic regulators of thinking, feeling and action.

The power of ideas is revealed in two aspects: on the one hand, in catalyzing, planning and initiating social transformations, on the other in supporting social agents in their adaptation to the changes (i.e., symbolic resources used for overcoming collective trauma and structural suffering, and for uniting people into organized actions). Ideas are necessary for creating new utopias.

REFERENCES

Aarelaid, A. (2006). *Cultural trauma and life stories*. Helsinki: Kikimora.

Bauman, Z. (1976). *Socialism. The active utopia*. London: Allen & Unwin.

Bauman, Z. (1998). *Work, consumerism, and the new poor.* Buckingham, England: Open University Press.

Bauman, Z. (1997). Living without an alternative. *The Political Quarterly, 62*(1), 35-44.

Berry, J. (2003). Conceptual approaches to acculturation. In K. Chun, P. Balls-Organista, & G. Marin (Eds.), *Acculturation: Advances in theory, measurement and applications* (pp. 17-37). Washington, DC: APA Books.

Bourdieu, P.(1990). *In other words. Essays towards a reflexive sociology*. Cambridge, England: Polity Press.

Bourdieu, P. (1991). *Language and symbolic power*. Cambridge, England: Polity Press.

Bourdieu, P., & Wacquant, L. (1992). *An invitation to reflexive sociology*. Cambridge, England: Polity Press.

Bourdieu, P. (1998). *Acts of resistance: Against the new myths of our time*. Cambridge, England: Polity Press.

Bourdieu, P. (1999). *Acts of resistance: Against the tyranny of the market*. New York, NY: New Press.

Brubaker, R. (2000). Accidental diasporas and "homeland" nationalism in Central and Eastern Europe: Past and Present. – *Reihe Politikwissenschaft*. Political Science Series, 71. Vienna: Institute for Advanced Studies.

Castells, M. (1997). *The power of identity*. Oxford, England: Blackwell.

Castro, P., & Batel, S. (2008). Social representation, change and resistance: On the difficulties of generalizing new norms. *Culture and Psychology, 14*(4), 475-497.

Chuikina, S. - Чуйкина, С. (2006). Дворянская память: "бывшие" в советском городе (Ленинград, 1920-30-е годы). Санкт Петербург: Европейский университет в С.Петербурге.

Clemence, A. (2001). Social positioning and social representations. In. K. Deaux & G.Philogene (eds), *Representations of the social. Bridging theoretical traditions* (pp. 83-95). Oxford, England: Blackwell.

Corsten, M. (1999). The time of generations. *Time and Society, 8*(2), 249-272.

Daanen, P. (2009). Conscious and non-conscious representations in social representations theory: Social representations from the phenomenological point of view. *Culture and Psychology, 15*(3), 372-385.

Doise, W. (1994). Attitudes et representations sociales. In D. Jodelet (Ed.), *Les representations sociales* (pp. 220-238). Paris: PUF.

Doise, W., Clemence, A., & Lorenzi-Cioldi, F. (1993). *The quantitative analysis of social representations*. New York, NY: Harvester Wheatsheaf.

Duveen, G. (2001). Representations, identities, resistance. In K. Deaux & G. Philogene (Eds.), *Representations of the social. Bridging theoretical traditions* (pp. 257-270). Oxford, England: Blackwell.

Eyal, G., Szelenyi, I., & Townsley, E. (1998). *Making capitalism without capitalists: Class formation and elite struggles in post-communist Central Europe*. London: Verso.

Fogel, A., Lyra, M. C. D. P., & Valsiner, J. (1997). *Dynamics and indeterminism in developmental and social processes*. Mahwah, NJ: Lawrence Erlbaum.

Gillespie, A. (2006). *Becoming other: From social interaction to self-reflection*. Greenwich, CT: Information Age.

Gillespie, A. (2007). The social basis of self-reflection. In J. Valsiner & A. Rosa (Eds.) *The Cambridge handbook of sociocultural psychology* (pp. 678-691). Cambridge, England: Cambridge University Press.

Gillespie, A. (2008). Social representations, alternative representations and semantic barriers. *Journal for the Theory of Social Behaviour, 38*(4), 375-391.

Hachaturyan, A., & Хачатурян, А. (2010). Русскоязычная молодежная среда в период "второй волны" социокультурных изменений в Эстонии: Саморепрезентации участников добровольных объединений в биографических интервью [Russian-speaking youth during the "second wave" of sociocultural changes in Estonia: Self-presentations by members of voluntary associations in biographical interviews]. И.Белобровцева, Е.Душечкина, О.Коростелев, П.Лавринец, И.Лукшич, Л.Луцевич, Ф.Федоров. Русские в Прибалтике [In: I.Belobrovtseva et al. (Eds.), Russians in the Baltics.] (pp.189-200). Москва: Наука

Grunberger, R. (2005). *A social history of the Third Reich*. London: Phoenix.

Hachaturyan, A. (in press) The echo of fallen iron curtain—balancing between "own" and "other" culture: Self-representations among Estonian Russian-speaking youth in biographical interviews. To be published in *Cold War Traumas in the East European context* (working title).

Hermans, H. J. (2002). The dialogical self as a society of mind: Introduction. *Theory and Psychology, 12,* 147-160.

Holton, R. (1997). Bourdieu and common sense. *SubStance, 26*(3), 3-38.

Jensen, E., & Wagoner, B. (2009) A cyclical model of social change. *Culture and Psychology, 15*(2), 217-228.

Kennedy, M. D. (2002). *Cultural formations of postcommunism. Emancipation, transition, nation, and war.* Minneapolis: University of Minnesota Press.

Kruusvall, J., Vetik, R., & J.Berry. 2009 The strategies of inter-ethnic adaptation of Estonian Russians. *Studies of Transition States and Societies, 1*(1), 3-24.

Lauk, E., & Kreegipuu, T. (2010). Was it all pure propaganda? Journalistic practices of "silent resistance" in Soviet Estonian journalism. *Acta Historica Tallinensia, 15,* 167-190.

Levin-Rozalis, M. (2000). Social representations as emerging from social structure: The case of Ethiopian immigrants to Israel. *Papers on Social Representations, 9,* 1.1.-1.22.

Litvinovic, G. (1997).The semiotic argument for indeterminism in development. In A. Fogel, M. C. D. P. Lyra, & J. Valsiner (Ed.), *Dynamics and indeterminism in developmental and social processes.* Mahwah, NJ: Lawrence Erlbaum.

Lizardo, O. (2004). The cognitive origins of Bourdieu's Habitus. *Journal for the Theory of Social Behaviour, 34*(4), 375-401.

Lotman, J. M. (1992a). *Kultura i vzryv* [Culture and discontinuity]. Moskva: Gnozis.

Lotman, J. M. (1992b). Dekabrist v povsednevnoi zhizni [Decembrists in daily life] (pp. 296-336). *Izbrannye Stati I*. Tallin: Aleksandra.

Lotman, J. M. (2010) Ne-memuary (Non-memoirs). In M. Lotman (Ed.) *Jalutuskäigul Lotmaniga* (pp. 25-117). Tallinn: TLU Press. (Original work published 1995)

Lotman, J. M. (2010). *Nepredskazuemye mehaniszmy kultury* [Non-predictable mechanisms of culture]. Tallinn: TLU Press.

Mikita, V. (1999). Life as narrative: A bridge between psychology and semiotics. *Trames, 3*(53/48), 4, 215-226.

Moscovici, S. (2008). *Psychoanalysis: its image and its public.* Cambridge, England: Polity Press. (Original work published 1961)

Märtsin, M. (2010). Rupturing otherness: becoming Estonian in the context of contemporary Britain. *Integr. Psychol. Behav., 44,* 65-81.

O'Dell, F. A. (2010). *Socialisation through children's literature. The Soviet example.* Cambridge, England: Cambridge University Press.

Oushakine, S. A. (2004) The flexible and the pliant: Disturbed organisms of Soviet modernity. *Cultural Anthropology, 19*(3), 392-428.

Petersoo, P. (2007) Reconsidering otherness: Constructing Estonian identity. *Nations and Nationalism, 13*(1), 1-17.

Raggatt, P. T. F (2007). Forms of positioning in the dialogical self. A system of classification and the strange case of Dame Edna Everage. *Theory and Psychology, 17*(3), 355-382.

Raudsepp, M. (2012) Õnneliku vanaduse vormid: individuaalsed trajektoorid läbi kultuurimuutuste (in Estonian: Forms of happy old age individual trajectories through cultural changes). In A. Aarelaid (Ed.), *Teise laine kultuurimuutused Eestis* [In Estonian: Second wave of cultural changes in Estonia]. Tartu: Tartu University Press.

Raudsepp, M. (2010.) Ohutaju ja dialoogivalmidus (in Estonian: Sense of threat and readiness for dialogue among Estonians and non-Estonians). In R. Vetik (Ed.), *Integratsiooni monitooring 2010* [Monitoring of integration 2010. Report to Estonian Ministry of Culture]. Tallinn: RASI

Sen, R., & Wagner, W. (2009). Cultural mechanics of fundamentalism: Religion as ideology, divided identities and violence in post-Gandhi India. *Culture and Psychology, 15*(3), 299-326.

Shepela, S. T. et al. (1999) Courageous resistance. A special case of altruism. *Theory and Psychology, 9*(6), 787-805.

Shklovski, V. (1990). *Theory of prose.* Normal, IL: Illinois University Press. (Original work published 1925)

Sztompka, P. (2000). *Civilizational competence: A prerequisite for post-communist transition.* Retrieved from http://www.ces.uj.edu.pl/sztompka/competence.doc

Sztompka, P. (2004). The trauma of social change. A case of postcommunist societies. In J. C. Alexander, R. Eyerman, B. Giesen N. Smelser, & P. Sztompka (Ed.), *Cultural trauma and collective identity* (pp. 155-195). Berkeley, CA: University of California Press.

Valsiner, J. (1994). Culture and human development: A co-constructionist perspective. In L. P. van Geert, L. P. Mos, & W. J. Baker (Eds.), *Annals of Theoretical Psychology, 10,* 247-.298.

Valsiner, J. (1997). *Culture and the development of children's action: A theory of human development.* Chichester, England: Wiley.

Valsiner, J. (1998). *The guided mind. A sociogenetic approach to personality.* Cambridge, MA: Harvard University Press.

Valsiner, J. (2000). *Culture and human development.* London: SAGE.

Valsiner, J. (2007). *Culture in minds and societies: Foundations of cultural psychology.* New Delhi: SAGE.

Valsiner, J. (2008a). Ornamented worlds and textures of feeling. The power of abundance. *Critical Social Studies, 1,* 67-78.

Valsiner, J. (2008b). The social and the cultural. In T. Sugiman, K. J. Gergen, W. Wagner & Y. Yamada (Eds.), *Meaning in action. Meanings, narratives, and representations* (pp. 273-287) New York:, NY: Springer.

Vetik, R., Nimmerfeld, G., & Taru, M. (2006). Reactive identity versus the EU integration. *Journal of Common Market Studies, 44*(5), 1079-1102.

Vihalemm, T., & Kalmus, V. (2008). Mental structures in transition culture: Differentiating patterns of identities and values in Estonia. *East European Politics and Societies, 22*(4), 901-927.

Vygotski, L. S. (1999). Orudie i znak v razvitii rebenka. In *Pedagogicheskaja psihologia*. Moskva: Pedagogika.

Wagner, W. (1998). Social representations and beyond: Brute facts, symbolic coping and domesticated worlds. *Culture and Psychology, 4*, 297-330.

Wagner, W., Duveen, G., Farr, R., Jovchelovich, S., Lorenzi-Cioldi, F., Markova, I., & Rose, D. (1999). Theory and method of social representations. *Asian Journal of Social Psychology, 2*, 95-125.

Wagner, W., & Hayes, N. (2005). *Everyday discourse and common sense: The theory of social representations*. New York, NY: Palgrave.

Wagoner, B. (2008). Commentary: Making the familiar unfamiliar. *Culture and Psychology, 14*(4), 467-474.

Yurchak, A. (2003). Soviet hegemony of form: Everything was forever, until it was no more. *Comparative studies in Society and History, 45*(3), 480-510.

Yurchak, A. (2005). *Everything was forever, until it was no more. The last Soviet generation*. Princeton, NJ: Princeton University Press.

Zittoun, T. (2007). The role of symbolic resources in human lives. In J. Valsiner & A. Rosa (Eds.), *The Cambridge handbook of sociocultural psychology* (pp. 343- 361). Cambridge, England: Cambridge University Press.

Zittoun, T., Duveen, G., Gillespie, A., Ivinson, G., & Psaltis, C. (2003). The use of symbolic resources in developmental transitions. *Culture and Psychology, 9*(4), 415-448.

Zittoun, T., Gillespie, A., Cornish, F., & Aveling, E. L. (2008). Using social knowledge: A case study of a diarist's meaning making during WWII. In T. Sugiman, K. J. Gergen, W. Wagner, & Y. Yamada (Eds.), *Meaning in action: Meanings, narratives, and representations* (pp. 163-182). New York, NY: Springer.

CHAPTER 18

CONCLUSION

Cycles of Social Change

Eric Jensen and Brady Wagoner

The chapters of this volume show that social change is a complex, dynamic and ever-changing process. The chapters in Part I highlight the role of collective action and intergroup dynamics through case studies of crowds (Drury, Reicher, & Stott, this volume), minority groups' strategizing (Cornish, this volume), a simulated prison (Haslam & Reicher, this volume) and national development (Moghaddam, Warren, & Vance-Cheng, this volume). The chapters in Part II focus on a variety of communication forms, such as stories and metaphors (Cornejo, this volume; Ritchie, this volume), cultural diffusion (Kashima, this volume; Wagoner, this volume), scientific ideas, mass media and social media (Holliman, this volume; Jensen, this volume, Chapter 13). Finally, contributions in Part III introduce a host of other factors in the process of social change, including humor (Jensen, this volume, Chapter 12; Taylor-Sayles, this volume), social capital (Mendoza, this volume; Sammut, Andreouli, & Sartawi, this volume), the restructuring of social and professional fields (Ryabchuk, this volume) and 'semiotic freedom' (Raudsepp, this volume). These chapters have sought to capture the elusive subject of social change in their analytical lenses. The resulting snapshots of social change are inevitably fleeting and incomplete, yet together they point to general

Culture and Social Change: Transforming Society Through the Power of Ideas, pp. 323–338

characteristics that define social change in its many diverse and sometimes unpredictable manifestations.

In this concluding chapter, we aim to weave these diverse strands together in an integrative model of social change. Our starting point is an earlier publication (Jensen & Wagoner, 2009), in which we drew on insights from cultural psychology (on how ideas can be shared within a community) and sociology (on institutions and power). We used the development of the social representation of "public engagement with science" in the U.K. as an illustrative example to outline four phases of a "cyclical model of social change," which we characterized as being a continuous, long-term, contingent and culturally bound process. Here we develop this model in more general terms, incorporating insights from the preceding chapters.

Our starting point is a distinction put forward by Harré (1998) between what he called "transcendent" and "immanent" social representations. Here we will refer to them as "ideals" and "practices" respectively, in order to make the distinction clearer for a broader audience. "Ideals" are norms that are held at the level of discourse and ideas, while 'practices' are norms that are manifest in concrete social and professional practices, the bases of which practitioners themselves may not be able to reflexively articulate. Although these two dimensions of social and professional life overlap to a greater or lesser degree in particular contexts, they can be fruitfully conceptualized as interdependent levels existing in a dynamic and generative tension with one another (see also Raudsepp, this volume). Indeed, as we discuss below, there are distinctive processes that emerge from the interplay between these two dimensions, ensuring that social change is ongoing and yet society remains relatively stable most of the time.

To elaborate the distinction between ideals and practices and its utility for theorizing social change, we propose a general model of social change with four aspects or phases (see Figure 18.1). The word "phases" is helpful in that it highlights that we are discussing developmental processes, not static things; however, it is somewhat misleading because it might imply rigid phase boundaries and linear movement between the four phases. To avoid these unintended implications from the word "phases," we refer to them as "aspects" or simply "processes" in order to indicate a more holistic, fluid and dynamic account of social change. The four aspects of social change are summarized below:

1. *Communication processes*: Here we find a "struggle over ideas," where different social actors clash over normative ideals, for example, how to conceive of the public's understanding of science (Jensen & Wagoner, 2009) or how to represent new objects, practices or

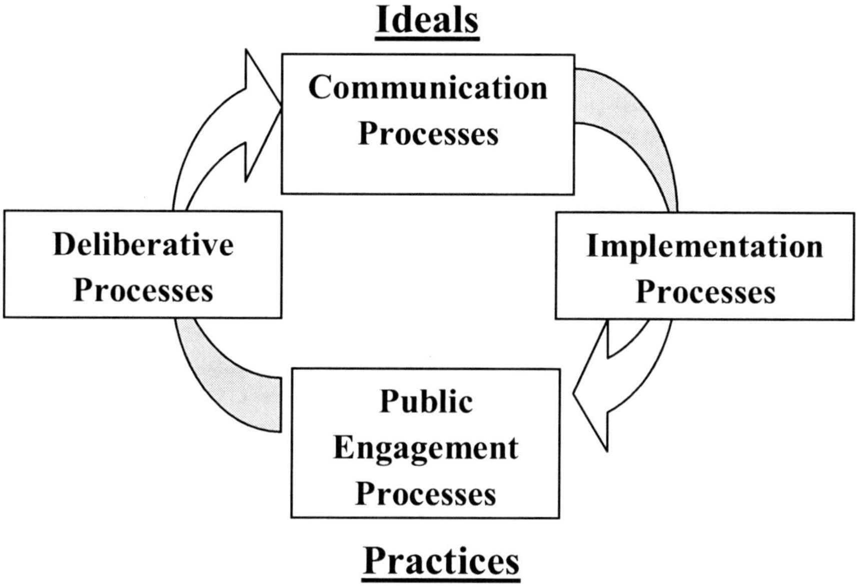

Figure 18. Four aspects of social change.

scientific developments and ideas, such as psychoanalysis (Moscovici, 2008). Through these processes, new ascendant ideas and norms emerge. There is a possible but not necessary relationship between the ascendance of a norm (e.g., scorn for cigarette smoking) and the codification of that norm in law (e.g. a cigarette smoking ban). That is, laws can come about for reasons other than the ascendance of a new norm (e.g. to protect the interests of wealthy political benefactors or cronies). At the same time, an ascendant norm may never find its way into law. Moreover, the ascendance of a norm is shaped by far more than the fraught construct of public opinion. Access to media (Holliman, this volume; Jensen, this volume, Chapter 12), economic and symbolic power (Jensen, this volume, chapter 13), cultural and social capital (Mendoza, this volume), rhetorical and artistic skill (Ritchie, this volume; Taylor-Sayles, this volume) and macroscopic changes in the broader socio-historical context (Ryabchuk, this volume) are but a few of the many factors influencing outcomes at the level of communication processes.

2. *Implementation processes*: Here ascendant ideas meet social and professional practices. Once a normative ideal is established it needs

to be implemented in concrete social practices, where it often meets resistance. For example, Castro and Batel (2008) outline a number of different strategies by which experts discursively accept the new norm of public participation in neighborhood redevelopment, while rejecting its implementation in the particular case they are involved in. Similar examples of different forms and levels of resistance to the implementation of ascendant norms can be seen throughout social and professional life.

3. *Public Engagement Processes*: Here social and professional practices and ascendant ideas come into contact with the behaviors, norms and preexisting ideas of affected publics and stakeholders. Conflict is most likely to arise in situations in which affected publics have entrenched economic or personal interests, values and habits, which are challenged by the new idea or norm. Whether valued resources are distributed in a manner commensurate with the new norm (i.e. rewarding adherence to the new norm) or the new norm connects effectively with the prior worldview of the affected publics are the most significant factors in the dialectic of acceptance/rejection operating in publics' engagement with new norms. For example, the transition to capitalism in post-Soviet societies shows that the introduction of new norms can fail when individuals retain dispositions formed to meet the demands of previous social conditions (Rausepp, this volume; Ryabchuk, this volume). Likewise, a new scientific development can be rejected by publics because it is seen to violate existing values and beliefs (Jensen, this volume).
4. *Deliberative processes*: If rejection processes become sufficiently widespread at either the implementation or public engagement level, a new norm can become subject to reflexive scrutiny. Some social actors may begin to articulate inconsistencies in practice, problems in the public or stakeholder reception of the norm or basic conceptual flaws that went unnoticed or were overridden in the norm's initial ascendance (e.g., see Ritchie, this volume). At this point, such actors may begin to formulate strategies for overcoming these problems, thereby returning the cycle to the same communication processes that inaugurated the norm for renewed debate and reframing. The example of the controversy over genetically modified (GM) crops in the U.K. illustrates this phase. A new norm of allowing GM was adopted by the government, implemented with general scientific and industrial acceptance but then rejected by publics whose latent concerns were amplified by tabloid news media (Jensen, 2009). The strength of the public backlash against GM sparked renewed deliberative and communication processes, this time with greater public involvement. The result was a new

norm for GM crops advocating 'further study' and delay, which was partially resisted by professional fields of practice in the biotechnology industry and the sciences but ultimately accepted as the status quo.

"Meta" factors in social change: This volume highlights a number of 'meta' factors that affect all of the social change processes described above. Factors such as power, voice, mass media, symbolic representation, identity, leadership, struggles over scarce resources and visual representations modulate who gets heard and has influence in each aspect of social change. Issues of access to influential institutions and resources, the capability to express oneself effectively and the negotiation of identities in particular social and cultural contexts modulate the development and embedding of new ideas and norms in society.

The description of our theory as positing a "cycle of social change" highlights the contingent tendency of social change to develop feedback loops and to recapitulate similar debates in different guises (e.g., Jensen & Weasel, 2006) when implementation and public engagement processes reveal problems, tensions and resistance. For example, new laws can subsequently be revoked if they are found to be impractical to implement (e.g., Prohibition) or they fail to gain widespread public acceptance (e.g., the Obama healthcare reforms in the United States). The model's definition of social change as "cyclical" also emphasizes that the beginning of any narrative account of a particular example of social change will necessarily have an arbitrary jumping off point, given that the present is always influenced by the past and preexisting structures in society. Therefore no "aspect" or "process" of social change can be considered an absolute beginning, nor should the processes defined above be understood as rigid steps in a linear process. Rather, these are heuristic distinctions, which are designed to offer analytic focus for a complex and dynamic phenomenon. The researcher can choose to approach a particular norm or development through the lens of one or more of these aspects, and we hope that bringing to light these dimensions of social change may spark further investigation into previously obscured factors. Below, we explicate each of the four aspects in turn, exploring the ways in which contributors to this volume help to clarify some of the processes involved in them.

COMMUNICATION PROCESSES

Communication processes are the sites of intellectual, rhetorical and discursive struggles over how something should be represented, that is, about how to characterize particular dimensions of our shared reality. A classic example of this is Moscovici's (2008) analysis of the "cultural battle" over the meaning of psychoanalysis in 1950s French society, described by Wagoner (this volume). Communication presupposes an intersubjective background of intelligibility based on a set of traditions and history of a social group. Kashima et al. (this volume) and Wagoner (this volume) argue that "new" ideas must be intersubjectively "grounded" within a social group's existing ideas and practices. In Moscovici's (2000, p. 37) words, "memory prevails over deduction, the past over the present, response over the stimuli and images over 'reality.'" If this is indeed the case, the new and old need to be conceptualized together as opposites in a generative tension (Wagoner, this volume), a dynamic that is aptly illustrated by both Ritchie (this volume) and Jensen (this volume, Chapter 12).

Ritchie (this volume) shows how Obama's political speeches (during his "change we can believe in" campaign) strategically drew on a stock of American stories and imagery—this strategy of communication is much more powerful in mobilizing people than a more argumentative form as one might find in an academic debate. Similarly, Jensen (this volume, Chapter 12) shows how media draw upon a cultural legacy of science fiction stories and imagery (i.e., *Frankenstein*), tapping into public feelings of uncertainty concerning new technologies, such as human cloning, which at the same time function to shape public debate on controversial issues. Both Ritchie (this volume) and Jensen's (this volume, Chapter 12) studies also illustrate how "metaphor transports us from the world of propositions to the world of dynamic meanings.... They are emotionally charged, socially shared, and have radical consequences in social bonds" (Cornejo, this volume, p. 123).

The mass media's importance in social change explains why it is so often brutally suppressed or co-opted by dictatorial governments. Suppression of subversive ideas, however, can sometimes be avoided by cloaking them in humor and irony. Jensen's (this volume, chapter 13) assessment of the entrenched conservative role of censorship in maintaining the status quo in both dictatorial regimes and democratic nations alike highlights the strength of resistance to new ideas that are inconsistent with the interests of the wealthy and the powerful. State-run mass media can also function as a powerful tool for framing social reality in a way that is favorable to those in power and thereby sustaining "pluralistic ignorance," whereby people remain ignorant of the fact that others share similar antiestablishment beliefs (Kashima Bratanova, & Peters, this volume). Of course, new media open up alternative avenues for dissident voices to contest dominant ideas, whether those ideas are promoted by authoritarian governments or by scientists seeking to form and maintain a consensus about anthropogenic climate change (Holliman, this volume).

Taylor-Sayles (this volume) further examines the role of censorship and the ways in which social actors seek to circumvent it through a focus on the world of art. She identifies art as a site of struggle over new ideas and norms, which often becomes the focus of censorship and accusations of obscenity when artists push beyond the boundaries of a given era's "common sense." She considers in detail how artists in recent decades have intervened in the public discourse about gender equality and heteronormativity through humorous and ironic art, which has challenged the viewer's assumptions about women and homosexuals, and thereby challenged the status quo. Art is a genre of communication, like the mass media, which responds to existing trends in society but also pushes the boundaries of what can be said. For example, Moghaddam et al. (2012) describe how Aleksandr Solzhenitsyn's *The Gulag Archipelago* (1972-75) broke the silence surrounding the brutal treatment of prisoners by the Soviet government. Through this literary/artistic intervention, a new intersubjective understanding of Soviet society and its previously unacknowledged foibles was formed. In sum, representation in art can be a powerful means of challenging existing social norms. It can impel us to reflect on the taken-for-granted "common sense" in a society, which otherwise goes unnoticed.

IMPLEMENTATION PROCESSES

The triumph of a new idea or norm through communication processes in the arena of public or expert debate and policy is only one dimension of social change. At some point, a new idea or norm must lead to changes in social and professional practice if social change is to occur and become embedded. It is in this process of implementation that normative ideals meet practice. Particularly in the case of policy implementation, institutions and organizations are mobilized to create practices that align with the ascendant ideals. For example, an ascendant concern about the public's lack of scientific knowledge resulted in implementation processes targeting multiple institutions. The institutions of formal education were called upon to focus greater efforts on STEM [scientific, technology, engineering and mathematics] subjects. Cultural institutions such as science museums and science centers were funded to promote greater scientific literacy amongst visiting publics. Furthermore, scientific institutions such as the American Society for the Advancement of Science (AAAS), the U.K.'s Royal Society and the British Science Association exhorted scientists to confront misinformation and promote science to broader audiences, among other institutional responses. Thus, a single ascendant norm diffuses into a multitude of institutional and organizational imperatives. Implementation, however, may be met with a variety of different responses by individuals and networks of practitioners tasked with putting such imperatives into action.

Strategic Responses to Change

In this volume, Raudsepp (this volume) outlines a number of possible reactions to inchoate social change developing around an ascendant normative ideal. In her case study of Estonia's post-Soviet transition to capitalism, she finds the dialectic of acceptance/rejection of the new norms and ideas taking four forms. First, some will engage in *denial* wherein people either physically withdraw from a field of practice that is affected by the changes being implemented (e.g., by choosing a new career, emigrating, etc.) or psychologically withdraw through self-isolation or ignoring the change processes under way. Secondly, others will engage in *resistance*: the active refusal to accept the social change being implemented. The third strategic response Raudsepp (this volume) identifies is *conformity*: that is, acceptance of the new norm and forgetting of the old. Finally, she describes *creative synthesis* as a response involving the hybridization of new and old ideas and norms.

Further elaboration of the dialectic of acceptance/rejection of new norms can be found in the work of Erving Goffman (1961), whose description of patterns of "resistance" could be applied to understanding the ways in which the dialectic of adoption/rejection of incipient social change plays out. He explored the responses of inmates and patients in totalizing institutions such as prisons or hospitals. Totalizing institutions exemplify both the power to impose norms from above, and the inevitability of resistance from below. Goffman (1961) enumerates four resistance strategies exercised by inmates when suffering "mortification of the self" or loss of face. He identifies (1) "situational withdrawal" wherein the inmates seek to mentally remove themselves from the identity-threatening situation through daydreaming and fantasy, (2) "establishing an intransigent line" through outright noncompliance, (3) "colonization" in which the inmates accommodate themselves to the humiliation by unrealistically comparing the institution positively with the outside world, and (4) "conversion" which involves inmates at least appearing to fully adopt the institutions' definition of reality. Paul Willis (1977) identified similarly patterned forms of unstructured, spontaneous resistance to the implementation of dominant values in his classic ethnography of a working class youth counter-culture in Britain.

While both "psychological denial" and "resistance" strategies are attended to in Goffman's (1961) study, one could make the case that inmates also demonstrate high levels of "conformity" to the norms of prison life. They effectively forget themselves and the world, as it exists outside of the prison. Zimbardo's famous mock prison experiment demonstrated how quickly inmates can come to accept the humiliation and monotony of being a prisoner (Haney, Banks, & Zimbardo, 1973). However, Zimbardo provides us with only part of the story: Reicher and Haslam's (this volume) replication and extension of his work demonstrates that "conformity" is not an inevitable strategy taken up by inmates. Conformity tends to occur when those in the system are not cognizant of alternatives and/or believe that they might have the opportunity to exit the marginalized group. "Resistance" or even "creative synthesis" can become the dominant strategy when (1) exiting the group is blocked, (2) alternative ways of organizing the system are conceived and/or (3) strong leadership is introduced into the inmates.

"Creative synthesis" is powerfully described by Bartlett (1923, 1928, 1932) in his analysis of "social constructiveness." According to Bartlett (1923), whenever new ideas and practices enter a society they are either assimilated into the old, displace the old, or constructively worked together into genuinely new pattern. The last of these possibilities, in which cultural elements from diverse sources are blended together, he calls "social constructiveness." This idea highlights that groups orient to the future through a "prospect" or "project" that they have for themselves. New ideas and practices can be welded together in such a way to contribute to the group's project for their own future development. For instance, the way in which psychoanalysis became incorporated into everyday thought and discourse through different social groups' use of the theory to advance their own interests is one example of social constructiveness (Moscovici, 2008; Wagoner, this volume). In the world of science, different empirical findings and theoretical contributions can be brought together in a new synthesis—Einstein's theory of relativity is an example par excellence drawing upon and integrating disparate ideas within theoretical physics. Likewise, Bartlett (1958) described his own work on remembering as a synthesis and development of his mentors' ideas. Finally, as already described above, art exemplifies bringing together diverse social influences into a genuinely new form with the aim of transforming social reality in a given direction (Moghaddam et al., this volume; Taylor-Sayles, this volume).

The Role of Institutions and Organizations

The implementation aspects of social change in our model include the adoption/resistance strategies described above, while maintaining an important role for the institutions and organizations sponsoring and interpreting a new ascendant idea. Our understanding of these latter dimensions of social change is guided by cultural sociologist Pierre Bourdieu, who has been an important influence in a number of chapters in this volume (especially in Part III). Bourdieu argues that fields of practice are governed by a structured logic. Through the selective allocation of resources, both symbolic and economic, the rules of the game in a particular field become real to the players within it. Bourdieu (1986, p. 471) notes, "the social order is progressively inscribed on people's minds" through the struggle for these resources. That is, the "objective limits" of the field become part of a "sense of one's place" in the field that is "acquired by experience" (p. 471) as a result of structural constraints which demand of individuals "a proleptic adjustment to the demands" of the field (Bourdieu, 1990, p. 66).

The common sense assumptions within a field of practice stem from "the fact of being caught up in and by the game [within a given field], of believing the game is ... worth playing and that the stakes created in and through the fact of playing are worth pursuing" (Bourdieu, 1998, pp. 76-77). The "unthought presuppositions that the game produces and endlessly reproduces" become the basis for action within the field (Bourdieu, 1990, p. 67).

> The economy of the field is the basis of "sensible" practices, linked intelligibly to the conditions of their enactment ... and therefore filled with sense and rationality for every individual who has the feel for the game. (Bourdieu, 1990, p. 66)

Over time, the "system of presuppositions inherent in membership in a field" (Bourdieu, 2005, p. 37) becomes embodied in the practitioner. The accumulated personal experience "turned into nature" is what Bourdieu labels *habitus*; this embodied phenomenon operates as a "generative principle of regulated improvisation" for practitioners (Bourdieu, 1977, p. 78). The habitus then becomes the fundamental unit of adoption or rejection when a new norm or idea enters the field. To be successful in reshaping practices within a field, new norms must be imposed through the reformation of systems of reward and punishment tied to the distribution of symbolic, cultural and/or economic capital within the field. The dialectic of adoption/rejection is moderated within implementation processes by such institutional and/or organizational restructuring of resource distribution to correspond with the newly ascendant norm or idea. This kind of structural change must be instituted for a new norm to be successfully embedded in long-term professional and social practices. However, structural change alone is insufficient to ensure the implementation of a new norm. New norms must contend with the common sense assumptions about the field, which are embodied in the *habitus*—or embodied cumulative personal history and disposition—of individuals. A new idea must be able to accommodate itself to the "universe of the tacit presuppositions that we accept as the natives of a certain society" or a certain field of practice (Bourdieu, 2005, p. 37). An idea or norm that is wildly out of step with existing common sense notions held by practitioners in a field is unlikely to be fully implemented, especially in the short-term. Of course, if the restructuring of resource distribution is fully and enduringly implemented, social change is still possible in the long-term as new beliefs and assumptions are developed over time. Thus, Bourdieu's theory of practice points to at least two main fulcrums shaping social change: (1) Restructuring the distribution of resources (i.e., "capital") within a field and (2) the level of coherence between the new norm or idea and preexisting "common sense" assumptions about the field inscribed on the *habitus* of practitioners. Moreover, we would add that rhetoric, framing and metaphor can be employed by savvy change agents to make the case that a new idea is in fact amenable to integration with existing "common sense" notions, but this requires a degree of prior knowledge about the field in order to actively manage the process.

PUBLIC ENGAGEMENT PROCESSES

Once a new norm becomes embedded in social and professional practices, the ascendant ideas emerging from the communication aspects of social change finally confront a broad spectrum of publics, who may not have fully participated in the original debate or discussion. The new norm encounters behaviors, norms and preexisting ideas and beliefs of affected publics and stakeholders, with a particularly high risk of conflict or active rejection when affected publics have entrenched economic or personal interests, values and habits at stake (Holliman, this volume; Jensen, this volume, Chapter 12).

Just as in the implementation aspect of social change, the degree to which valued resources are restructured to support the new norm (i.e., rewarding adherence to the new norm) and the norm's goodness of fit with "common sense" notions held by affected publics are the most significant factors in the dialectic of acceptance/rejection operating in publics' engagement with newly implemented norms. For example, introducing a new norm of recycling could be supported by rewarding publics for engaging in this activity and by reducing barriers in terms of the effort and time required to fully adopt the new norm. At the same time, recycling could be framed for publics in a way that fits with existing sensibilities such as "being frugal with scarce resources" (e.g., "a bottle saved is a bottle earned") in order to support norm adoption (see Ritchie, this volume).

Public reaction to new norms, ideas or technologies may be unpredictable and seem irrational to experts, policymakers or practitioners (e.g. see Jensen, this volume, Chapter 13). Yet, the "meta" aspects of social change—power, voice, mass media, symbolic representation, identity, leadership, struggles over scarce resources and visual representations—continue to exert strong influence on the ways in which the public engagement aspects of social change play out, as can be seen in the Jensen's (this volume, Chapter 12) discussion of the role of censorship in mass and social media and other cases discussed in this volume (e.g., Mendoza, this volume).

Public engagement processes are also influenced by the range of intermediary institutions in society that communicate new ideas to publics, including museums, zoos, universities and art galleries. Religion, music and other forms of creative expression all have a role to play in the construction of public opinion about a new idea (Taylor-Sayles, this volume), as well as the persuasive dimension of enticing publics into adopting a new norm such as recycling. Such intermediary institutions provide opportunities for public sentiment about a new norm or idea to "pool" and connect up with others facing similar issues or having similar concerns. When discussion of personal concerns with a new norm coalesces sufficiently, the overlapping deliberative aspects of social change may take hold as discourse broadens out beyond those immediately affected by the norm's implementation.

DELIBERATIVE PROCESSES

If rejection processes become sufficiently focused at either the implementation or public engagement level, a new norm can become subject to reflexive scrutiny. Some social actors may begin to articulate inconsistencies in practice, problems in the public or stakeholder reception of the norm or basic conceptual flaws that went unnoticed or were overridden in the norms initial ascendance. At this point, such actors may begin to formulate strategies for overcoming these problems, thereby returning the cycle to the same communication processes that spawned the norm for renewed debate and reframing. "Stretching social capital" may play an important role in this process (Mendoza, this volume), by articulating the "pooled" concerns of publics and marginalized groups to give them a voice in deliberative processes (Sammut, Andreouli, & Sartawi, this volume).

One way of conceptualizing an important dimension of such deliberative processes is through what social theorist Jürgen Habermas (1989) describes as the "public sphere" (cf. Eley, 1992). Drawing an ideal type from eighteenth century bourgeois café culture in Paris and London, Habermas defines the public sphere as a nexus where citizens without a direct stake in the issue could come together to discuss the issues of the day. The public sphere consists of an intermediary structure between the political system, on the one hand, and the private realm and functional systems involved in implementation processes, on the other.

Habermas constructs a normative understanding of the emancipatory potential of the public sphere, where reason and open deliberation result in the triumph of the better argument (cf. Baert, 2001). For Habermas (1989), this realm for critical-rational debate is based upon a "public of private people making use of their reason" (p. 51). In this model, the "streams of communication" that enter the public sphere are "filtered and synthesized in such a way that they coalesce into bundles of topically specified *public* opinions" (Habermas, 1996, p. 360). In his later work, Habermas (1987) makes it clear that he envisions these bundles of critical public opinion within the public sphere as the locus of resistance to overbearing state and economic rationality. Thus, the public sphere is viewed as the "main tool through which organized citizens can limit power and hold powerful actors accountable" (Young, 2000, p. 174).

We see the concept of the public sphere as a useful means of understanding deliberative processes. However, we would side more with feminist public sphere theorists such as Ryan (1992, p. 285) who advocate a "plural and decentered concept of the public" based on the principle that "notions of interest and identity need not be antithetical to public good." Indeed, Ryan emphasizes the inadequacy of a public realm dominated by bourgeois values, pointing out that those most disenfranchised and in need of a voice in the public sphere tend to express their views in a manner that is apprehended negatively within the formal bourgeois public sphere. For example, the crowds described by Drury et al. (this volume) and the grassroot groups' tactics described by Cornish (this volume) do not exactly fit the Habermasian ideal of rational debate. Indeed the protests of the disenfranchised are often perceived as "loud, coarse, and, yes, abrasive" (Ryan, 1992, p. 286). Young (2000, p. 178) concurs identifying the difficulty of engagement for the disenfranchised:

> The public sphere will properly be a site of struggle—often continuous struggle [because] ... it often takes considerable organizing, dramatic action, and rhetorical shrewdness for people whose concerns are excluded from that agenda to break through and gain access to public media that will ... disseminate their issues so that state institutions eventually deal with them.

As Mendoza (this volume) suggests, leadership from within such disenfranchised groups can help in getting their voices heard in the public sphere.

Bauman (1999) understands the public sphere in terms of the *agora* of Ancient Greece, which in its ideal form would allow for the coordination of citizens' public and private concerns. In sum, the *agora* model of the public sphere comprises a "territory of constant tension," "tug-of-war," and "dialogue, co-operation or compromise" (p. 87), where the "communal search for the common good" can take place under pluralistic conditions (p. 167). Certainly, the kinds of challenging art that Taylor-Sayles (this volume) discusses could be seen as part of this process of struggling for ever better norms and ideas within a noisy and chaotic modern day *agora*. We would see the inspiration for such spirited debates as typically stemming from the perceived failures and incongruences in ascendant norms encountered by practitioners and publics at the levels of implementation and public engagement.

The main point here is that deliberative processes involve reopening of prior debates and discussions and the introduction of new and alternative symbols and representations, which are taken forward into communication processes. Indeed, the line between deliberative and communication processes can become completely blurred as a new idea or norm begins to ascend and vie for dominance through art, media and other means. As such, it is important to keep in mind the constraints that operate across both deliberative and communicative processes. Among these constraints are disciplinary power exercised to maintain the status quo (i.e., as discussed in Foucault, 1977/1991) and the persistent pattern of exclusion from important debates of "those who do not or cannot speak in public, [and] who from inarticulateness, fear, habit, or oppression are [therefore] removed from participation in public life" (Gould, 1996, pp. 175-176). Such inequalities are fundamental to the development of social change in contemporary societies, but examples such as the Arab Spring indicate that even the most intractable forms of fear, oppression and exclusion from public life can be overcome.

CONCLUSION

In this chapter, we have proposed a cyclical model of social change, drawing on social theory, sociology, cultural psychology and empirical research to explicate the processes at work in this cycle. Clearly, explaining this model around four "aspects" or "processes" is reductive. There are many facets of each aspect we have identified, and it is likely that other aspects could be articulated. The four aspects of social change we have identified are intended to be generative rather than exhaustive, and we hope other analysts will identify further aspects or factors that modulate social change. The key point we wish to stress is that social change is not unidirectional or inevitable, even with the full backing of repressive and ideological state intervention (cf. Althusser, 1971). Partial adoption, resistance, conflict over resources and symbols, dynamism and contingency have always defined social and cultural change. In the era of globalization, and in light of the Arab Spring, it is clear that agonistic struggles to control the spread and hold of new ideas are only growing more intense and unpredictable.

NOTE

1. Geoff Eley (1992) notes that "public sphere" is not an adequate translation of the Öffentlichkeit referred to in Habermas's (1989) study. "An unwieldy aggregation of terms like publicness, publicity, public culture, and public opinion translates the term perhaps more accurately," connoting "something more like 'the quality or the condition of being public'" (p. 225).

REFERENCES

Althusser, L. (1971). Ideology and ideological state apparatuses (B. Brewster, Trans.) *Lenin and philosophy and other essays*. London: New Left Books.

Baert, P. (2001). Jürgen Habermas. In B. S. Turner & A. Elliott (Eds.), *Profiles in contemporary social theory* (pp. 84-93). London: SAGE.

Bartlett, F. C. (1923). *Psychology and primitive culture*. Cambridge, England: Cambridge University Press.

Bartlett, F. C. (1928). Social constructiveness (Pt. 1). *British Journal of Psychology, 18*, 388-391.

Bartlett, F. C. (1932). *Remembering: A study in experimental and social psychology*. Cambridge, England: Cambridge University Press.

Bartlett, F.C. (1958). *Thinking: An experimental and social study*. New York, NY, US: Basic Books.

Bauman, Z. (1999). *In search of politics*. Stanford, CA: Stanford University Press.

Bourdieu, P. (1977). *Outline of a theory of practice* (R. Nice, Trans.). Cambridge, England: Cambridge University Press.

Bourdieu, P. (1986). *Distinction: A social critique of the judgement of taste*. London: Routledge.

Bourdieu, P. (1990). *The logic of practice* (R. Nice, Trans.). Cambridge, England: Polity Press.

Bourdieu, P. (1998). *Practical reason: On the theory of action* (Gisele Sapiro (Chap. 1-2) & Randal Johnson (Chap. 4-5), Trans.). Cambridge, England: Polity.

Bourdieu, P. (2005). The political field, the social science field, and the journalistic field. In R. Benson & E. Neveu (Eds.), *Bourdieu and the journalistic field* (pp. 29-47). Cambridge, England: Polity.

Castro, P., & Batel, S. (2008). Social representation, change and resistance: On the difficulties of generalizing new norms. *Culture & Psychology, 14*(4), 475-497.

Eley, G. (1992). Places, publics, and political cultures: Placing Habermas in the nineteenth century. In C. Calhoun (Ed.), *Habermas and the public sphere* (pp. 289-339). Cambridge, MA: MIT Press.

Foucault, M. (1977/1991). *Discipline and punish*. London: Penguin. (Original work published 1977)

Goffman, E. (1961). *Asylums: Essays on the social situation of mental patients and other inmates*. Harmondsworth: Penguin.

Gould, C. C. (1996). Diversity and democracy: Representing differences. In S. Benhabib (Ed.), *Democracy and difference: Contesting the boundaries of the political* (pp. 171-186). Princeton, NJ: Princeton University Press.

Habermas, J. (1987). *The theory of communicative action: Lifeworld and System: A critique of functionalist reason* (Vol. 2). Cambridge, England: Polity Press.

Habermas, J. (1989). *The structural transformation of the public sphere* (T. Burger & F. Lawrence, Trans.). Cambridge, MA: MIT Press.

Habermas, J. (1996). *Between facts and norms*. Oxford, England: Oxford University Press.

Haney, C., Banks, W. C., & Zimbardo, P. G. (1973). Study of prisoners and guards in a simulated prison. *Naval Research Reviews, 9*, 1-17.

Harré, R. (1998). The epistemology of social representations. In U. Flick (Ed.), *The psychology of the social* (pp. 129-137). Cambridge, England: Cambridge University Press.

Jensen, E. (2009). Genetic futures and the media *The Encyclopaedia of Life Sciences*. Chichester, England: Wiley.

Jensen, E., & Wagoner, B. (2009). A cyclical model of social change. *Culture & Psychology, 15*(2), 217-228.

Jensen, E., & Weasel, L. H. (2006). Abortion rhetoric in American news coverage of human cloning. *New Genetics and Society, 25*(3), 305-324.

Moscovici, S. (2000). *Social representations.* Cambridge, England: Polity.

Moscovici, S. (2008). *Psychoanalysis: Its image and its public*. Cambridge, England: Polity Press.

Ryan, M. P. (1992). Gender and public access: Women's politics in nineteenth-century America. In C. Calhoun (Ed.), *Habermas and the public sphere* (pp. 259-288). Cambridge, MA: MIT Press.

Willis, P. (1977). *Learning to labour: How working class kids get working class jobs*. Farnborough: Saxon House.

Young, I. M. (2000). *Inclusion and democracy.* Oxford, England: Oxford University Press.

ABOUT THE AUTHORS

Eleni Andreouli is a doctoral candidate in social psychology at the London School of Economics and Political Science. Her PhD explores processes of national identity construction from the perspectives of different stakeholders within the British naturalisation context. Her research interests lie in the fields of social representations, identity, intergroup relations, citizenship, immigration and integration in multicultural societies. ADDRESS: Institute of Social Psychology, The London School of Economics and Political Science, Houghton Street, London, WC2A 2AE, U.K. E-mail: e.andreouli@lse.ac.uk

Boyka Bratanova is a researcher at the University of Melbourne. E-mail: bbratanova@nbu.bg

Rhea Vance-Cheng is on track to becoming the youngest student to graduate from the MA in conflict resolution program at Georgetown University. She completed the program for the exceptionally gifted at Mary Baldwin College and is particularly interested in the role of art in peace building. E-mail: rv75@georgetown.edu

Carlos Cornejo is a lecturer of psychology at the Pontifical Catholic University of Chile. E-mail: cca@uc.cl

Flora Cornish is a Reader in the School of Health at Glasgow Caledonian University and editor of the *Journal of Community & Applied Social Psychology*. Her research interests focus on community mobilization and public participation as means of bringing about health-enhancing social change.

She has a long-standing research engagement with sex worker led HIV prevention programs in India. E-mail: flora.cornish@gcal.ac.uk

John Drury is Senior Lecturer in Social Psychology at the University of Sussex. He specializes in research on crowd behavior, including crowd conflict dynamics, mass emergency and evacuation behavior, and variability in experiences of crowding/density. He has published over 50 papers and chapters in peer reviewed academic journals and books. He is currently involved in experimental research on the parameters of psychological crowding; ethnographic, analogue and questionnaire research on identity and health in protest crowds; and multimethod analysis of the interaction between crowd managers and crowd members in emergency event management.

Alex Haslam. Address: School of Psychology, University of Exeter, Exeter, EX4 4QG, UK. e-mail: A.Haslam@exeter.ac.uk

Richard Holliman is a Senior Lecturer in Science Communication at the Open University (OU), United Kingdom. In his research and teaching he explores the ways that (techno-) sciences are communicated via a range of media and genres, and how ideas about (upstream) public engagement with science and technology may be shifting and extending social practices. He recently led the production of a new postgraduate course in science communication as part of the OU's MSc in Science in Society. Examples of some of these course materials are available via iTunes U. In 2009 he co-published two edited collections that explore contemporary issues in science communication and public engagement. He has worked on two recent research projects: Invisible Witnesses (open.ac.uk/invisible-witnesses), which explored gendered representations of scientists, technologists, engineers and mathematicians on children's television in the United Kingdom; and Isotope, an interdisciplinary action research project where participants collaboratively produced (and now help to maintain) a community website for those interested in science communication (isotope.open.ac.uk). E-mail: r.m.holliman@open.ac.uk

Yoshi Kashima is a professor of psychology at the University of Melbourne. E-mail: ykashima@unimelb.edu.au

Martín Mendoza-Botelho is Assistant Professor of Political Science at Tulane University in the United States and specializes on issues of political economy and institutional strengthening in developing countries, with emphasis on Latin America. His academic experience includes work at the University of Michigan at Ann Arbor, the University of Cambridge;

the Catholic University of Bolivia and The George Washington University. Prior to his scholarly work he served at the Organization of American States (OAS) in Washington DC and the United Nations Children's Fund (UNICEF) among others. He has a growing number of publications and is also a reviewer for several academic journals. He received a national research award in Bolivia as part of the Program for Strategic Research (PIEB) and also several teaching awards at Tulane. He holds a PhD from the University of Cambridge, a Master's degree in Economic Development (MPhil) from the University of Glasgow and a Bachelor's degree (*Licenciatura*) in Economics from the Catholic University of Bolivia. E-mail: mmendoza@tulane.edu

Fathali M. Moghaddam is professor, department of psychology, and director, conflict resolution program, department of government, Georgetown University. His most recent book is titled *The New Global Insecurity* (2010). Address: Department of Psychology, White Gravenor Building (3rd floor), Georgetown University, Washington, DC., USA 20057. E-mail: moghaddf@georgetown.edu

Julian A. Oldmeadow received his PhD in psychology from La Trobe University in Melbourne, Australia, in 2005 and has since held positions at the University of Exeter, University of Cambridge, and University of York, where he is current a lecturer in social psychology. He has published research on a range of topics including small group processes, social influence, social identity and stereotype content, and responses to media images of terrorism. His current research interests focus on the formation and functions of stereotypes from a sociocultural perspective. He is a co-founder and editor of *Psychology & Society*. E-mail: julian.oldmeadow@psych.york.ac.uk

Kim Peters is a Kim Peters is a Research Fellow in the School of Psychology at the University of Exeter. E-mail: K.O.Peters@exeter.ac.uk

Maaris Raudsepp is a senior researcher at Tallinn University. E-mail: maaris.raudsepp@gmail.com

Stephen Reicher is Professor of Psychology at St Andrews University, United Kingdom. His research interests can be grouped into three areas. The first is an attempt to develop a model of crowd action that accounts for both social determination and social change. The second concerns the construction of social categories through language and action. The third concerns political rhetoric and mass mobilization—especially around the issue of national identity. He is the author of dozens of scholarly papers and book chapters on crowd behavior and leadership. He is a former editor of the British Journal of Social Psychology, and Fellow of the Royal Society of Scotland. Address: School of Psychology, University of St. Andrews, St. Andrews, Fife, KY16 9JU, United Kinddom. E-mail: sdr@st-andrews.ac.uk

David Ritchie is currently Professor of Communication at Portland State University, Portland, Oregon, L. He received his PhD in Communication Research from Stanford University. His primary research focus is metaphor use, story-telling, and humor in naturally-occurring discourse, with emphasis on urban communities and cultural institutions. Dr Ritchie was recently Visiting Researcher at the Open University, U.K. as part of the "Living with Uncertainty" project (Dr. Lynne Cameron, PI) funded by the Research Council of the United Kingdom. Dr. Ritchie is a member of the Metaphor Analysis Network, funded by the U.K.'s Economic and Social Research Council. Recent publications include *Context and Connection in Metaphor*, Palgrave-Macmillan (2006) and " 'Everybody Goes Down': Metaphors, Stories, and Simulations in Conversations' (2010), *Metaphor and Symbol, 25*, 123-143. His most recent conference presentation was titled "'To Maintain a Civil Society': Metaphors and Stories in Talk About Public Safety" (2010), presented at the 8th International Conference on Researching and Applying Metaphor (RaAM) in Amsterdam. Dr Ritchie can be contacted at: cgrd@pdx.edu; web page http://web.pdx.edu/~cgrd/

Anastasiya Ryabchuk received her PhD at the Ecole des Hautes Etudes en Sciences Sociales (EHESS) and is a Lecturer at the National University of Kyiv Mohyla Academy. E-mail: anastasia.riabchuk@libero.it

Gordon Sammut is Associate Lecturer in Social Psychology at the University of Malta and doctoral candidate in social psychology at the London School of Economics and Political Science. His work aims to develop a social-psychological conceptualization of the "point of view" that draws on the works of Asch in light of the theory of social representations. His main interests include psychosocial models in the social sciences, attitude measurement and public opinion, the epistemology of representations and phenomena, gestalt social psychology, and issues relating to opinion formation and argumentation. ADDRESS: Department of Psychology, University of Malta, Msida, MSD2080, Malta. E-mail: gordon.sammut@um.edu.mt

Mohammad Sartawi is a doctoral candidate in social psychology at the London School of Economics. His thesis is concerned with various versions of Islamic belief that circulate in Muslim communities in London. More specifically his interest lies in the relationship between faith and everyday practices in identity construction seen through his ethnographic engagement with British Muslims in some of London's mosques. His interests include social identity theory, social representations, phenomenological epistemologies, cultural studies, and social/ collective action. He is the coordinator of the LSE Social Representations Group and a member of the Social Psychological Research into Racism and Multiculturalism group. E-mail: M.M.Sartawi@lse.ac.uk

Lisa Taylor-Sayles is a professional artist whose art and research most often explore the intersections of art, gender and communication studies. She teaches in the Communication Studies and Art Departments at Clark College in Vancouver, WA. Sayles holds a MS in Communication Studies from Portland State University and an MFA in Visual Art from The Art Institute of Boston. E-mail: lisa_sayles@hotmail.com

Clifford Stott is Senior Lecturer in Social Psychology at the University of Liverpool, having previously held posts at Bath University and Abertay Dundee. With Steve Reicher and John Drury, he developed the Elaborated Social Identity model. His research work has concentrated on understanding the conditions for the peaceful versus conflictual behavior in football crowds. He is particularly concerned with the practical translation of theory. He has trained police forces all over the U.K. and Europe, and acted as a consultant on crowd policing to a number of governmental and international bodies.

Brady Wagoner completed his PhD in psychology at University of Cambridge and is now Associate Professor at the Aalborg University (Denmark). He has received a number of prestigious academic awards, including the Sigmund Koch Award, Gates Cambridge Scholarship and the Jefferson Prize. His books include *Symbolic Transformation: the mind in movement through culture and society* (Routledge, 2010), *Dialogicality in Focus: Challenges to theory, method and application* (Nova Science, 2011), and *Development as a social process: Selected writings of Gerard Duveen* (Routledge, in press). Additionally, he is on the editorial board of three international Journals (*Culture & Psychology, Frontiers of Quantitative Psychology and Measurement*, and *Integrative Psychological and Behavioral Science*) and is founding co-editor of the journal *Psychology & Society*. E-mail: wagoner@hum.aau.dk

Zach Warren is completing a PhD in psychology at Georgetown University. His MA is from Harvard University and his interests include juggling, running marathons, and researching in Afghanistan. E-mail: zw35@georgetown.edu